Donated to SAA by
Cara Duffy & Family
so that many more
can be uplifted and
inspired by this little-
known philanthropist,
whose efforts continue
to benefit the public
to the present day
from a century ago

Additional praise for *Ellen Browning Scripps:*
New Money and American Philanthropy

"McClain offers a riveting portrait of how one woman's pragmatic yet free-spirited generosity greatly enhanced the region by privileging social justice over personal gain."

—SETH MALLIOS, coauthor of *Cemeteries of San Diego*

"McClain brilliantly captures the uniquely American story of the remarkable Ellen Browning Scripps."

—HEATH FOX, executive director of the La Jolla Historical Society

"McClain has shed light on the lesser-known landscape of West Coast philanthropy in which Miss Scripps played such a significant role . . . McClain's proficiency and passion for her topic are *sans pareil*."

—ERIC T. HASKELL, professor of French studies and humanities and director of the Clark Humanities Museum at Scripps College

"This definitive and comprehensive examination of Ellen Browning Scripps and her wide-ranging contributions to women and the larger community is greatly welcomed by those of us who value the power of the written word, especially at this time in our history when the stories of women's accomplishments can serve as a beacon to girls and young women everywhere."

—ASHLEY GARDNER, former executive director of the Women's Museum of California

"Compelling. . . . Molly McClain has an extraordinary ability to bring this amazing lady alive as a role model for women of all ages and backgrounds."

—DOUG DAWSON, executive director of the Ellen Browning Scripps Foundation

"This book is well written, extraordinarily thorough and informative, and is a strong contribution to California, media, and women's history. This is a terrific story."

—KATHLEEN A. CAIRNS, author of *The Case of Rose Bird: Gender, Politics, and the California Courts*

ELLEN BROWNING SCRIPPS

ELLEN BROWNING SCRIPPS

New Money and American Philanthropy

MOLLY MCCLAIN

UNIVERSITY OF NEBRASKA PRESS   *Lincoln and London*

T 16909

Publication of this volume was assisted by a grant from
the Friends of the University of Nebraska Press.

♾

Library of Congress Control Number: 2017936202

Set in Janson by Rachel Gould.
Designed by N. Putens.

To my beloved sister, Cady

CONTENTS

ILLUSTRATIONS

14. Scripps Institution of Oceanography in La Jolla, designed by architect Irving J. Gill, ca. 1910

15. Annie Scripps, 1890

16. Ellen Browning Scripps in her library at South Molton Villa

Following page 102

17. Conservative businessman John D. Spreckels

18. IWW activists protest in downtown San Diego, 1912

19. Virginia Scripps with her half-sister Ellen

20. Virginia Scripps traveled the world

21. The Bishop's School faculty softball team, ca. 1915

22. Ellen Browning Scripps created a playground for the children of San Diego

23. Mayor Edwin M. Capps thanks Ellen Browning Scripps for her contributions to the city of San Diego

24. Ellen commissioned architect Irving J. Gill to rebuild South Molton Villa after a fire in 1915

25. South Molton Villa II (1915–16) is considered to be one of Irving J. Gill's masterworks

26. An aerial view of Ellen's La Jolla estate, ca. 1917

27. Scripps Memorial Hospital, designed by William Templeton Johnson

28. Ellen converted her Pierce-Arrow limousine into an ambulance and donated it to Scripps Memorial Hospital

29. Ellen Browning Scripps, 1919

30. At age ninety-one Ellen took her last long trip to Yosemite National Park

31. Architect Gordon B. Kaufmann designed Scripps College in the Mediterranean Revival style

32. The first class at Scripps College, class of 1931, in front of Toll Hall

PREFACE

California, 1903.

She was a plain woman. Soft-spoken, with only a trace of an English accent. Just over sixty-six years old, she attracted little interest among the travelers on the train that wound its way along the Pacific Coast from the seaside colony of La Jolla to its terminus in San Diego, California. Her clothes, though expensive, were several years out of date.

Then she smiled. Her face softened, and the lines around her eyes creased with pleasure at the sight of three small children seated on a horse-drawn wagon. When the train stopped at the station, she rose quickly, went to the door, and waved.

Startled, a fellow passenger nearly said aloud, "Oh, how beautiful she is!"[1]

The woman was Ellen Browning Scripps. In her youth, she had been an editor, a writer, and an active supporter of women's suffrage. She worked alongside hard-drinking journalists in Detroit newsrooms and campaigned for Susan B. Anthony. A shrewd businesswoman, she invested her money in the rapidly expanding Scripps chain of newspapers until she became a millionaire several times over. Like other nineteenth-century women, she endured the kind of discrimination one can only imagine today. She had earned her wrinkles and the right to wear an old-fashioned hat.

Life experiences, however, had not hardened Scripps but made her more compassionate. Recognizing that many people struggled to compete in an increasingly capitalist society, she worked to improve educational opportunities for ordinary men and women. In the faces of children she saw the potential for a new world governed by hope and guided by a sense of community. She trusted—and invested—in that.

ACKNOWLEDGMENTS

I am very grateful to Scripps College for permitting me to use the extensive Ellen Browning Scripps Collection. Judy Harvey Sahak, former director of the Ella Strong Denison Library, offered invaluable guidance and insight, while Dorran Boyle kindly assisted with various requests. Research materials and photographs also were made available at the following institutions: Altadena Historical Society; Beverly Hills Public Library; The Bishop's School; University of California, San Diego; The Huntington Library; La Jolla Historical Society; La Jolla Woman's Club; the Fogler Library at the University of Maine; the Bentley Historical Library at the University of Michigan; San Diego History Center; San Diego Public Library; Scripps Institution of Oceanography; and the Beinecke Library, Yale University. Special thanks to the staff of the Mahn Center for Archives & Special Collections at Ohio University Libraries for their assistance during my visit and for making much of the E. W. Scripps Collection available online.

This book could not have been written without the encouragement and support of many colleagues and friends. I am very grateful to Iris H. W. Engstrand for her encyclopedic knowledge of San Diego history and her steadfast friendship. John Trifiletti encouraged me to start what we both thought would be a short project. Several friends read drafts of the text and offered criticisms and corrections. My most sincere thanks to Cynthia L. Caywood, Colin Fisher, Mark A. Kishlansky, and Jerry Stratton for finding errors that escaped my eye. James B. Guthrie both read the manuscript and provided valuable insights into the life and career of architect Irving J. Gill. Derrick R. Cartwright, meanwhile, shared his research on artist Robert Henri. I also appreciate the helpful information provided by Mary Katherine Allman, Mary Boehm, Diane Kane, Carol Olten, Sandra Spalding, and Suzanne Weiner. My beloved dog, Twister, meanwhile, helped me to "sit" and "stay" long enough to complete this book.

The University of Nebraska Press provided an excellent home for this book. Thanks to editor Bridget Barry for her patience and good advice. Thanks also to the College of Arts & Sciences at the University of San Diego for several faculty research grants.

The dedication is my final, heartfelt acknowledgment.

INTRODUCTION

In 1926 the cover of *Time* magazine was graced with a portrait of a ninety-year-old philanthropist named Ellen Browning Scripps. Each week the magazine profiled men (and a few women) who were making the news: politicians, industrialists, actresses, and heavyweight champions. Franklin D. Roosevelt appeared on the front cover, as did Henry Ford, Ethel Barrymore, and Jack Dempsey. Scripps may have been one of the richest women in the country, but she was far from being a celebrity, much less a household name. In fact, *Time* introduced her to its readers as if it had discovered a new planet in the solar system or an unknown element for the periodic table. Who was this immensely rich woman? Why was she determined to give millions upon millions of dollars away?[1]

Born in London, Scripps grew up in rural poverty on the Illinois prairie. She went from rags to riches, living out that cherished American story in which people pull themselves up by their bootstraps with audacity, hard work, and a little luck. In the late nineteenth century this meant overcoming rigid class barriers, racism, sexism, and hostility to ethnic groups. She came of age at a time when farmers and factory workers invested in the dream of upward social mobility, believing that they could improve themselves by their own efforts. They made best sellers out of Horatio Alger's tales of good-hearted boys who escaped poverty and achieved middle-class status in great urban capitals like Boston and New York.

It helped that there were examples of self-made millionaires such as Andrew Carnegie who started life in the United States as an immigrant textile worker and became the richest man in the world. Other titans of industry rose from modest backgrounds: Cornelius Vanderbilt, who built his wealth in shipping and railroads; John D. Rockefeller, the founder of Standard Oil; Jay Gould, railroad developer and speculator; and J. P. Morgan, banker and financier. Often described as "robber barons," these men lived in a country that prized industry and ingenuity; encouraged the development of new technologies; and tolerated the existence of corruption, exploitation, and greed. Mark Twain humorously described the period as the Gilded Age, when glittering fortunes could be made through graft, speculation, and other dubious schemes.

Despite the lack of female role models, Ellen Browning Scripps made an astonishing amount of money without either manipulating the stock market or exploiting the masses. She and her brother Edward Willis "E.W." Scripps (1854–1926) created America's largest chain of newspapers, linking midwestern industrial cities with booming towns in the West. Scripps newspapers were cheap to produce, easy to read, and pitched to a working-class audience. Less well known today than the papers run by Joseph Pulitzer and William Randolph Hearst, Scripps newspapers transformed their owners into millionaires almost overnight. By the 1920s Ellen was worth an estimated $30 million (equal to $416 million in 2016 dollars), most of which she gave away.[2] In 1903 she established the Scripps Institution of Oceanography in La Jolla, California, the oldest and largest center for ocean and earth science research. She appeared on the cover of *Time* magazine after founding Scripps College in Claremont, California. She provided major financial support to The Bishop's School, the La Jolla Recreational Center, Scripps Memorial Hospital, the San Diego Zoo, the San Diego Natural History Museum, and Torrey Pines State Park. She also donated millions of dollars to organizations worldwide that promised to advance democratic principles and women's education.

Despite the myths that sustained ambition, no one really expected a poor farm girl to accumulate so much wealth, least of all Ellen herself. Ellen knew more about knitting stockings and milking cows than reading a balance sheet. She grew up in a rough-and-ready farmhouse in the small town of Rushville, Illinois, a railway stop at the edge of civilization, among other British immigrants who hoped to make their fortune in the United States. Known as the Prairie State, Illinois had been admitted to the Union less than two decades prior to Ellen's birth. Its only substantial city, Chicago, was still a ramshackle settlement with mud paths for streets and nearly as many cattle as people.

Ellen first strayed from the path of conventional behavior when she attended Knox College, one of the few educational institutions to admit women, even if it did not yet grant college degrees. She studied science and mathematics, graduating in 1859 with a certificate from the Female Collegiate Department. Afterward, she returned to Rushville to teach in the stereotypical one-room schoolhouse. Classroom attendance was sporadic, with long gaps timed to major farming chores. When the American Civil War broke out a few years later, she moved in with her sister and helped cook, clean, and wash clothes at the end of her school day. Her life was characterized by constant, ceaseless toil, to which she silently acquiesced.

Ellen made another unusual choice when she decided to give up her job as a schoolteacher and head to Detroit in 1865, at that time a burgeoning industrial center in the West. She joined her brother James E. Scripps (1835–1906) in publishing the *Detroit Evening News*, the start of the Scripps family fortune. Tall, with a nervous disposition and a short temper, James was determined to succeed where other newspaper owners had failed. He kept costs down with ruthless efficiency, going so far as to save every scrap of paper in the office so that it could be used again. He employed family members in order to keep wages low. George H. Scripps, a Civil War veteran, operated the business office; William A. Scripps ran the printing department; the teenaged Edward W. Scripps sold subscriptions; and Ellen worked the copy desk. They lived together with James's growing family in a modest Victorian house not far from the railway tracks along Michigan Avenue.

Between the ages of thirty and forty-five, Ellen worked long, hard, twelve-hour days at the *Detroit Evening News*, returning home to her brother James's house to care for his small children. She traded childcare for rent and invested the bulk of her income. There was no indoor plumbing, no electricity, and only one servant to do the scrubbing and cleaning. After the evening meal, she and James sat down with the cash box to count their nickels and pennies; they also prepared newspaper copy for the next day. At seven o'clock the next morning, they were back in the office again. There was no reprieve. Her younger brothers could escape from work, but Ellen shouldered both a woman's duties and those of a man.

It took a great deal of courage and determination for Ellen to deviate from the roles that Victorian women were expected to play. If she had followed the example of her female relatives, she would have married, had children, and led a domestic life as the wife of a farmer or a small-town tradesman. Instead, she attended college. After she began her career as a teacher, she could have chosen to marry if for no other reason than to supplement her substandard wage. But Ellen went to Detroit, where she and her brothers used their newspaper to wage war on capitalist elites. For the first time in her life, she had a purpose that absorbed her energy and utilized her considerable intelligence. She neither sought nor needed a male protector and, as a result, remained single for the rest of her life. Ellen felt herself to be an "anomaly," a woman who did not fit into any known classification scheme.[3]

Ellen's values, however, were characteristic of many women her own age. Like most Victorians, she glorified home and family, even if she did not have one of her own. She was devoted to her relatives—brothers and sisters, nieces and nephews, in-laws and cousins—and felt it her duty to care for and protect those in need. She admired moral courage, self-sacrifice, and cooperation, and she hero-worshiped men such as President Abraham Lincoln. An abolitionist, she was committed to ending the practice of slavery and aiding the helpless and downtrodden. Still, when she tried to practice the female virtues so admired in the Victorian era—patience, piety, and submission—her intelligence and good sense (not to mention good humor) usually got in the way. She was better with frugality and industry, at least in the early years.

It was her good fortune to invest in newspapers at a time when nineteenth-century Americans had become mesmerized by the printed word. Newspaper subscriptions increased exponentially during the Civil War as people hungered after news about troop movement, battles, and casualties. Once the habit was formed it was hard to break. Subscriptions kept rising during the 1870s and 1880s when publishers introduced "one-cent" or penny papers to booming western cities such as Chicago, Detroit, and St. Louis. In the 1890s a journalist remarked, "It was during the war that the American people contracted the newspaper habit, from which they have never recovered."[4] Cheap prices encouraged working-class readers to indulge their taste for sensational gossip, true crime, sports, adventure stories, and fashion. Advertisers quickly jumped on board. By 1900 news had become a commodity to be shaped, packaged, and marketed with an eye to profit. James Scripps had been there at the beginning, and Ellen had thrown in her lot with him. She took her salary in shares, made loans to bridge cash-flow gaps, and never withdrew her principal. A working woman, she understood both the value of property and the insecurity of wealth in the modern age.

Ellen made a staggering fortune through her investments in both the *Detroit Evening News*—one of the most profitable newspapers in the country—and the Scripps-Howard newspapers, now the E. W. Scripps Company. In the 1890s she encouraged E.W. to leave Detroit for new horizons in the West and loaned him the money to build the first economically efficient chain of newspapers in America. They lived together for several years at a ranch called Miramar on a chaparral-covered mesa in San Diego, California. The land, though cheap, had little to recommend it; even the Pacific Ocean was fifteen long, dusty miles away. From Miramar, E.W. directed the beginnings of what would become a great newspaper empire while Ellen began to wonder if she would ever be free from her family. Far from being the ideal Victorians, the Scrippses were divided into feuding camps that clashed over power, personality, and property. In her darkest hours, Ellen imagined living on a desert island "where no one shall . . . make me afraid; and where the air that I breathe will not be tainted, nor my ears polluted with the foul smell and sound of money."⁵

At the turn of the century, San Diego was not quite a desert island, even if it resembled one. While a small population of Anglos had settled along the border in the wake of the U.S.-Mexican War, California was still a newly acquired territory rather than a well-populated American state. The real estate market had crashed just before Ellen arrived, leaving behind cheap land, abandoned homesteads, and empty hotels. It took a lot of imagination and foresight to suppose that San Diego would one day be a cultured urban center, much less an earthly paradise of sun, sea, and sand. This is what Ellen would help it to become by financing schools, hospitals, parks, libraries, and museums.

Like many women born into the Victorian era, Ellen understood philanthropy as a form of social advocacy. Unable to vote, she exercised her power to define what was important to her community by investing money in institutions that would contribute toward the greater public good. This meant education for ordinary men and women without regard to their race, class, or religion. It also meant civic engagement. She believed that people, no matter what their views, should be free to speak their minds without fear of harassment from authorities. Their participation in political life could only further democracy. In this way, she set San Diego's public agenda for decades to come.

San Diego's development coincided with the antimodernist movement that swept through Europe and America in the late nineteenth century. Urban life—fast-paced, individualistic, and profit-driven—had been a source of anxiety for centuries, particularly among the landowning classes. By the 1880s, however, doubts about modernity had become widespread. Industrial advances, together with the rapid expansion of cities, caused people to think anew about the world they had built. They began to recognize that the triumph of modern culture had not produced greater freedom but, in the words of one historian, "a spreading sense of moral impotence and spiritual sterility—a feeling that life had become not only overcivilized but also curiously unreal."⁶

San Diego offered newcomers the opportunity to build a different kind of city, one with farms, not factories, geraniums, not smokestacks. Property owners drew on the aesthetic philosophy of John Ruskin and adopted new approaches to urban planning such as the Garden City and City Beautiful movements. Utopian novels as different as Edward Bellamy's *Looking Backward* (1888) and William Morris's *News from Nowhere* (1890) informed debates about the future of the city, as did dystopian accounts of the rise of an urban proletariat and the decline of American industry. It was here that Ellen reconsidered her future as a capitalist and experimented with a new way of life.

When she was sixty years old, Ellen made a new life for herself in La Jolla, a rustic arts colony overlooking the ocean. She built a modest bungalow, befriended her neighbors, and began experimenting with utopian ideas about personal expression and progressive social change. Through book clubs and other civic organizations, she and other La Jolla women delved into the great issues of the day: efforts to extend scientific knowledge, suffrage, the peace movement, and a variety of other progressive causes. During World War I they channeled their activist agenda into the war effort. Ellen wrote, "We are the women to whom the world looks; upon whom the world depends in these crucial times. Each and every one of us is part and parcel of the great whole."[7]

Unlike many of her wealthy contemporaries, Ellen became a capitalist with a conscience. She led crusades against the corruption and injustice of urban life, advocated social and political reforms, and championed the labor movement against big business. She joined the National Woman Suffrage Association in 1873, not long after it was founded, and considered herself to be a Republican before she had the right to vote. She would go on to support the American Civil Liberties Union (ACLU) and the League for Industrial Democracy, among other left-wing causes.

For all her millions, Ellen did not act the part of the wealthy woman. She kept few servants, lived frugally, and wore out her old clothes. She ate sparingly, slept under the stars on a roofless porch, and took public transportation around San Diego until she was eighty years old. She spent money only on items that would benefit the greater community.

She opened her extensive gardens and grounds to the public and made her car available for use by neighbors and friends. In the words of one journalist, she regarded her wealth as "a trust for the benefit of humanity" rather than a source of status for her family or herself.[8]

Although she was generous to members of the Scripps family, Ellen did not help any of them get rich. She disapproved of inherited wealth, taking the view that men and women ought to be responsible for their own welfare rather than enjoy lives of privilege based on the work of earlier generations. Having come from a modest background, she had no desire to further the growth of an American aristocracy. She wanted instead to help ordinary people improve themselves through access to science, art, literature, and education. In summing up her philanthropy, she wrote modestly, "I feel that I have been instrumental in the inception and development of . . . progressive educational factors for the people."[9] In fact, she supported "the people," defined broadly, in a generous way.

While Ellen's unwillingness to be recognized for her philanthropic work has prevented her from becoming as well known now as Carnegie, Rockefeller, and other male peers, she did not lack acclaim. The *New York Times* described her as "a pioneer in modern American journalism" who had perfected the art of philanthropy. *Success* magazine wrote that her influence helped to leaven "the selfish materialism that too often goes with the accumulation of wealth." The *Peoria Sunday Morning Star*, meanwhile, described her as "one of the really great women of America," one who was committed to giving money wisely "where it will do the most good—with the least harm."[10] Her lawyer, J. C. Harper, was so confident of her legacy that he collected every letter, memorandum, and scrap of paper that that he could find, storing them in the offices of the E. W. Scripps Company for posterity. More than fifty years later, her story can be told.

Ellen's letters and diaries—now in the archives of Scripps College—reveal a woman whose modern and democratic ideas about wealth speak to us today. She believed that education could improve the conditions of ordinary men and women and gave money to institutions that worked for social and political change. She felt that investments in the community—rather than gifts to her family—would lead to a better and more progressive future for children yet unborn. Finally, she drew friends and neighbors into her projects, encouraging them to think about philanthropy as a grass-roots effort rather than a shower of gold from above.

Ellen's story is particularly important in light of the concentrated wealth being produced in our "New Gilded Age."[11] Since the late 1970s, a growing number of entrepreneurs, financiers, and chief executives—many of them women—have become immensely rich. Fortunes exceeding $1 billion are often made in one generation and handed down to the next. How will these new capitalists spend their money? What forms will philanthropy take? Perhaps the life of Ellen Browning Scripps will inspire both billionaires and those still seeking the American Dream.

CHRONOLOGY

1902	Newspaper Enterprise Association founded
1906	Endows the Scripps Institution of Oceanography
1907	United Press founded
1909	Founds and endows The Bishop's School with Eliza Virginia Scripps
	Commissions artist Albert Valentien to illustrate California wildflowers
1911	Commissions artist William Leon Dawson to illustrate *Birds of California*
1914	Endows lecture series at Pomona College
1915	Donates money for Scripps Pier and an aquarium
	Founds the La Jolla Playground and Community House
	Finances the new La Jolla Woman's Club building
	Hires architect Irving J. Gill to rebuild South Molton Villa after a fire
1916	Donates land to YWCA camp at Asilomar in Pacific Grove, California
1917	Funds the YWCA's Hostess House at Camp Kearny
1918	Funds (later endows) Scripps Memorial Hospital
1919	Funds the Egypt Exploration Society and gives books and antiquities to the San Diego Museum Association
	Finances construction of new women's campus at Pomona College
1920–32	Funds the San Diego Society of Natural History
1921	Funds construction of the Athenaeum Music & Arts Library in La Jolla
	Develops Torrey Pines State Reserve
	Eliza Virginia Scripps dies

1922	Funds construction of the San Diego Zoo
1923	Finances the construction of Torrey Pines Lodge
	Founds Scripps Memorial Park in Rushville, Illinois
1924	Builds a lath house and public tea room on her La Jolla estate
1926	Founds and endows Scripps College
	Finances a new building for the San Diego YWCA
	E. W. Scripps dies
1929	Donates tower and chimes for St. James by-the-Sea Episcopal Church
1930	Donates athletic field at La Jolla High School
1931	Finances the construction of the Children's Pool
	Donates the Cottage-Retreat for Women Students (SDSU)
1932	Dies in La Jolla, California

CHAPTER I

A Lapsed Victorian

"I wonder how you are picturing Miss Scripps," Katharine Scripps wrote to her niece in 1927. "She has broken loose from all conventional lines in thought. She calls herself a socialist—a Soviet, a Bolshevik. She decries churches and churchgoing, and observance. She flames up in defense of many things that seem wrong to most people, and yet to see her you would see a very thin-boned, frailest woman, self-effacing almost to shyness, and you would have to know her from others to get any idea of what she is thinking—what doing. A very interesting, wonderful character, and a contradictory character, too."[1]

Ellen, or "Miss Scripps," was over ninety years old when her sister-in-law made these observations. She had never been a conventional woman, and, after suffering in silence for many years, she abandoned any such pretense. She shed the baggage of her Victorian upbringing, rejected her brothers' condescending and often patriarchal attitudes, and stepped free from the trappings of a bourgeois life. An old woman, she felt as rebellious as the child she had once been.

Ellen often recalled her youth while sitting in the sunroom of her La Jolla house, wrapped in blankets against the chill, and watching the swells off the Pacific coast. Sometimes she asked to hear old family letters written by her father and grandfather in the 1840s.[2] Other times she talked about her childhood and early career in Detroit. She told a friend that her first memory was of "a little red rocking chair" that she had loved. She recalled being called "a little liar" when she was three or four years old for claiming that she knew the location of a ring that she had dropped on the floor.[3] She talked about dressing and caring for her younger brothers—William, George, and John—and reminisced about "The Monthly Star," the newspaper that she and her older brother James had created as children.[4] She described her early years of poverty and claimed that she could still live on fifty cents a day: "I have seen the day when 50c looked like a fortune to me."[5]

She thought that things might have turned out differently if her family had not tried to force her into a straitjacket of piety and obedience. "As a child, I hated to be *forced* to anything," she said. "I hated the word 'must.' If my elders could have only understood me better, things might have been different."[6] But she would not be coerced. She attributed her rejection of organized religion to the fact that she had been forced to accept, uncritically, the central tenets of the Anglican faith. As an adult, she experimented with a number of Christian denominations, but she never felt comfortable in any one of them. In the end, she allowed that faith in nature—God's creation—was as close to religion as she was likely to get.

There was a streak of nonconformity, both religious and political, in the history of the Scripps family. Ellen's great-grandfather William Scripps consorted with London radicals who sought parliamentary reform and universal male suffrage. Their efforts would lead to the development of Chartism, possibly the first mass working-class labor movement in the early nineteenth century. Fearing government persecution, William Scripps abandoned his shoe manufacturing business and immigrated to the United States in 1791. He converted to Methodism during the Second Great Awakening, joining a new generation of converts that stressed the equality of all believers, the power of personal revelation, and the importance of social activism. He also became an abolitionist.[7]

Other members of the Scripps family fit comfortably into a Victorian frame. One can imagine them in starched collars and unflappable hoop skirts, hands folded, lips buttoned up, and children firmly under control. They followed "proper" codes of conduct, showed respect for the law, deferred to their social superiors, and worshipped at the altar of mammon. Over the course of the nineteenth century, they became entrenched members of the bourgeoisie. Ellen's grandfather William Armiger Scripps, Jr., was a sharp-witted businessman who edited the *London Daily Sun* and *True Britain*, newspapers published by the government to counter the prorevolutionary press. After making a small fortune in publishing and other entrepreneurial activities, he retired to a manor house on the Isle of Wight. He and his wife, Mary Dixie, raised seven children, among them James Mogg Scripps, the father of Ellen Scripps and her siblings.

Ellen's father was ill-suited to the fast-paced world of commercial London. A tall, lanky man with a shock of dark hair, James Mogg Scripps had inherited his father's intelligence but not his talent for making money. Instead, he made a modest living as a bookbinder. He and his family lived above the shop at No. 5 South Molton Street, a small slanting street of red brick and plaster buildings close to Oxford Circus. He could produce beautifully tooled calf and morocco bindings with decorative endpapers, but he could not compete with large workshops that had begun to use binding machines.[8]

James Mogg did have a gift for producing children, however. His first wife, Elizabeth Sabey Scripps, gave birth to two children before dying in childbirth at the age of twenty-six. Only one, Elizabeth Mary Scripps (1831–1914), survived to adulthood. His second wife, Ellen Mary Saunders, bore six children between 1833 and 1840, five of whom survived: James Edmund Scripps (1835–1906), Ellen Browning Scripps (1836–1932), William Armiger "Will" Scripps (1838–1914), George Henry Scripps (1839–1900), and John Mogg Scripps (1840–63). Ellen Mary died at the age of thirty-eight from breast cancer, leaving behind a lengthy testimonial about her conversion to an evangelical form of Anglicanism. Ellen bore the legacy of this conversion in her middle name, "Browning," after Rev. J. H. Browning of Hope Chapel, Bristol.[9]

Ellen was five years old when her mother died. She spent the next several years among well-mannered, church-going aunts who entreated her to repress her "naughty evil tempers" and to pray for the forgiveness of her sins.[10] She learned to sublimate her true nature and play the part of a pious, submissive, and dutiful child. Had she remained in England, she might never have abandoned this script. Instead, fortune would bring her to the shores of America, where she could hope to lead a more adventurous life.

The Illinois Prairie

In 1844, having failed at business, James Mogg decided to leave London for the United States. He set out with six children who ranged in age from three to thirteen for Rushville, Illinois, where his uncles John and George Scripps lived with their families. After a forty-four-day journey across the Atlantic, he and the children secured passage across the Great Lakes to Chicago. A pair of covered wagons took the family and their belongings across the prairie toward Ottawa, just southwest of Chicago. From there, they traveled south along the Illinois River, arriving in Rushville on June 29, 1844.

It must have been startling for Ellen to find herself on the flat grasslands of the Illinois prairie after growing up in London, an urban metropolis with a population of nearly two million. Instead of great thoroughfares like Oxford Street and Regent Street, she encountered muddy lanes and slow-moving creeks that wound their way through marshy bottomland. The prairie looked like a vast ocean of grass that shimmered in the breeze. In June and July the roadsides were lined with colorful wildflowers: wild bergamot or bee balm, purple and white prairie clover, black-eyed Susan, and pale purple coneflower.

Rushville, a rough but thriving market town, was the seat of Schuyler County with over one thousand residents. Steamboats had just begun to ply the Illinois River, and it was thought that Rushville, located between the Illinois and Mississippi Rivers, was in a position to become the metropolis of the West. Pork packing was the most significant local industry due to the town's location in the middle of vast clover and bluegrass pasturages. In fact, one of the first things that visitors noticed was the abundance of pigs on the outskirts of town.

James Mogg expected to work with his uncles in their tannery, but he soon found that he had no aptitude for this kind of manual labor. He feared that he had made "a grand mistake" in coming to Illinois, but he would not think of returning to London, even though his father urged him to do so. He wrote, "It was on the children's account that I came, believing that I could do nothing for them in England. They, no doubt, may do well here."[11]

Within a few months of his arrival, James Mogg married again. His third wife, Julia Osborn, was a schoolteacher who had moved from Ohio to Rushville four years earlier. Their family expanded quickly. Between 1847 and 1854, Julia gave birth to five children: Julia Anne "Annie" Scripps (1847–98), Thomas Osborn Scripps (1848–53), Frederick Tudor Scripps (1850–1936), Eliza Virginia "Virginia" or "Jenny" Scripps (1852–1921), and Edward Willis "E.W." Scripps (1854–1926).

In the end, James Mogg decided to settle on 160 acres of land that his father had purchased during a visit to Rushville in 1843. He built a small house and began to improve the land. Within a few years he was growing turnips, spring wheat, rye, corn, and cucumbers. Livestock consisted of twelve head of cattle, seventeen pigs, twenty-three geese and ducks, three or four dozen chickens, and four sheep. His cousin John Locke Scripps reportedly said, "You may go all over the States and find no prettier place than Cousin James's farm."[12]

Farm activities engaged the whole family. The boys awoke at four or five o'clock in the morning to feed the horses and cattle before returning to the house for breakfast; they then cut wood and worked in the stables. After the cows were milked, young Ellen hauled the milk down to the cellar. In the winter she learned how to turn livestock into ham, sausage meat, and lard. She and her half-sister Elizabeth harvested apples and collected nuts, baked bread, and knit their own stockings. Elizabeth explained, "We were expected to be busy every minute."[13]

Gifted with an inventive mind, James Mogg was not content with mere farming but turned his talents to a variety of get-rich-quick schemes. He tried coal mining, brick and tile making, tanning, ice quarrying, and lumber milling—with little success. Although he worked hard, he never seemed to be able to make ends meet. Ellen later described him as "a helpless bookish man" and something of a dreamer.[14]

The Scripps family lived close to the edge of financial ruin. Ellen ate cornmeal puddings for breakfast, lunch, and dinner until she could do nothing but push her plate away. With no hired help, Ellen became the one who took care of her stepmother's babies, aided her partially deaf older sister, and helped wash, cook, and clean.

Good eyesight and a strong voice made Ellen the designated reader when the family gathered around the hearth after supper. This became her favorite time of day. Her father had a large collection of books, with the result that Ellen and her ten siblings got a better education than most children who were raised on the prairie. E.W. remembered "a rather long row of little leather-bound volumes of Peter Parley's works" that they read as children.[15] There were also works of history, theology, and philosophy, including John Locke's *Essay on Human Understanding* (1690) and Thomas Paine's *Age of Reason* (1795), "a beautifully bound edition of Shakespeare, about a dozen volumes," and a collection of English poets such as Samuel Taylor Coleridge and William Wordsworth.

Many of the books in the Scripps collection were the products of the romantic era, a period of revolt against social and political norms. Writers encouraged people to reflect on the great moral questions of the day, from abolitionism to women's rights, and emphasized the importance of heroic action. Ellen was particularly drawn to heroes, ordinary people who took extraordinary action in the interest of all humanity.

Blue and Gray, Black and White

The "great man" in Ellen's life was her second cousin, John Locke Scripps, who also lived in Rushville. Physically slight, he had a thick head of black hair that distinguished him from other family members. She described him as "a sort of composite Jupiter and Apollo and Shakespeare and John Wesley, and fully combined their attributes—power, beauty, wisdom, sweetness, and spirituality."[16]

John Locke imparted his love of literature, as well as his support for the temperance and antislavery movements, to Ellen. A schoolmaster, he taught advanced subjects such as Latin, mathematics, and physics to students of both sexes and all ages.[17] He was a frequent visitor to the Scripps family home. Ellen recalled that he "took upon himself to give lessons to the younger members of the family in deportment, courtesy, language, and to reprimand kindly though severely all tendency to slang—which was very mild in those days."[18]

John Locke became involved in politics and journalism on the eve of the Civil War. He helped to establish the *Democratic Free Press* with William Boss and later became a partner in the *Chicago Tribune* with Joseph Medill. He used the papers to advance both his abolitionist agenda and Abraham Lincoln's career. In 1860 he wrote a biography of Lincoln that was subsequently used in the presidential campaign. Boss once said, "J. L. Scripps made Lincoln president."[19]

Ellen's admiration for her cousin John Locke led her to establish a domestic newspaper with her fourteen-year-old brother, James. She was just twelve years old but already the family correspondent in place of her overworked father. In 1848 she and James put together a hand-written periodical called "The Monthly Star" for family and friends. They modeled their work after the *Family Herald*, a popular London newspaper, and produced three sheets of news each week.[20]

James was a serious and hardworking, if somewhat timid, boy with a talent for mathematics and a strong interest in business. His letters to his grandfather gravitated toward the exact: he included seasonal temperatures, the price of pork, and the height of his siblings. Ellen, he wrote, was "13 years, 2 months old, 4 feet 10 1/8 inches high," while two-year-old Annie was "2 feet, 10 ½ inches high."[21] Later in life he took to carrying a collapsible yardstick in his vest pocket in order to measure whatever came his way.[22]

Ellen, meanwhile, was a quiet and imaginative girl with a mind of her own. When her stepmother did not need her assistance with infants and household chores, she read voraciously. E.W. recalled her as a neatly dressed young woman with a book in her hand. "She was either teaching me spelling, the primer, or reading to me stories, or talking to me, explaining things that were read about or things around me," her brother later wrote.[23]

When Ellen was ten or eleven years old, she lost nearly all her teeth due to the ignorance of a Rushville physician. He treated a childhood illness—probably constipation—with calomel, or dimercury dichloride, which was supposed to purge her body of impurities but instead caused her teeth to fall out. Since there were no dentists in Rushville, Ellen waited six weeks to get fitted with a set of dentures. Unable to eat solid food, she subsisted on rice and milk. She wore false teeth for the rest of her life, one reason why she rarely smiled in photographs.[24]

At age thirteen Ellen began attending the Rushville Seminary and High School with her brother James. Though they came from a farming family, they received exceptional educations intended to prepare them for college-level work. Their high school principal, Alonzo J. Sawyer, was a graduate of Knox College; he would go on to become professor of mathematics at the University of Chicago.[25] James recalled classes in algebra, geometry, natural philosophy, moral philosophy, rhetoric, Latin, and Greek. His ambition at the time was to attend college, "but my father felt unable to incur the expense, and besides needed my services at home. So in the spring of 1851, I bade adieu to the seminary for good."[26]

Ellen, however, was able to continue her education. In 1856 she matriculated at Knox College in Galesburg, Illinois, one of the few educational institutions to admit women, even if it did not yet grant college degrees. Her grandfather had left a legacy to finance three years of study, and her father decided that Ellen was the only one of his children who could be spared from the farm.

At college Ellen became a committed Republican, an abolitionist, and a supporter of the temperance movement. She joined the First Congregational Church of Galesburg and admired its minister, Rev. Edward Beecher. A close friend of martyred abolitionist Elijah P. Love-joy, Beecher had helped organize the first antislavery society in Illinois before leaving for Boston in 1844. After his return to Galesburg in 1855, Beecher's home became a stop on the Underground Railroad, which led southern blacks from slavery to freedom.

Ellen was deeply impressed by the scholarship and advocacy of the Beecher family. She read Harriet Beecher Stowe's *Uncle Tom's Cabin*

(1852), a best-selling antislavery novel.[27] She also heard stories of the writer's brothers, Henry Ward Beecher and Charles Beecher. In 1857 Knox College President Jonathan Blanchard warned students against attending a local Shakespeare recital by a popular speaker, Mrs. Macready, by telling them that "she *knew* altogether about one-fourteenth as much as Charles Beecher *forgot every night.*" Ellen remarked, "Quite complimentary to that gentleman, wasn't it?"[28]

While Knox College offered a liberal atmosphere, it was not without its flaws. Ellen noted that the president had a "peculiar spite of all womankind which shows itself in some way or other nearly every morning." Neither she nor her fellow students took it altogether seriously, often laughing at his odd remarks. One morning he read a verse of Scripture before the female seminarians that "according to *his* version or at least to his *reading* ran as follows: 'The God of Israel saith, Why you are the most disorderly beings I have ever known.'" She added, "Of course the house couldn't stand that and simultaneously burst into a laugh at the imminent risk of displeasing the worthy President."[29] The women of Knox College may have faced prejudice with a skeptical eye, but prejudice there was nevertheless.

Ellen was a talented student whom her friends remembered as both clever and kindhearted. Jessica W. Bechtel recalled Ellen as "a pleasant companion, *very witty*, willing always to help. . . . She was quiet and well liked, and very clever with her pen even in those early days."[30]

If, as Ellen entered adulthood, her views were conventional, her experiences were not. She was one of a small number of women who received a rigorous education, one that was equivalent to that received by men. She did not study what might be regarded as soft subjects, instead concentrating on experimental science and the intricacies of mathematics. Her literary abilities were mostly developed to entertain her brothers and sisters who were too young or exigent to receive similar training. She had an eye for details and a slightly mischievous temperament. Beneath the veneer of widely held ideas was an independence of mind and a self-confidence not often on display from a farm girl who entered college more familiar with pigs than with people.

After graduating in 1859, Ellen returned to Rushville. Once the prospective capital of the Midwest, it had become slow, sober, and seedy. Many of the old buildings had become dilapidated, causing it to look like one of the old mountain towns of New England. According to one visitor, it was the kind of place where "quiet, old-fashioned, but respectable and substantial people, who believe more in meeting houses and ministers than they do in modern enterprises, would naturally delight to live in."[31] At a marriageable age, Ellen began teaching school and attending local events, but she did not acquire a husband. "A school teacher's life is a sort of humdrum, monotonous existence," she told her brother George. She occasionally played chess with a neighbor, Mr. Morse, but noted with disappointment, "He does not know much about it and it does not amount to much."[32]

Ellen was twenty-five years old when the American Civil War broke out in 1861. She understood the conflict as a battle to preserve the Union against secession by southern slaveholding states and shared the desire of abolitionists to end the practice of slavery. Ellen later remembered it as a war fought "not for power or territory but for the great principles of the enfranchisement of man—the political, social, intellectual, and spiritual freedom of the world."[33]

During the war, Ellen helped to organize the Soldiers' Aid Society. In addition to gathering supplies, she and other women made socks, suspenders, and other items for use in military hospitals.[34] After 1862 the organization coordinated its efforts with that of the newly established U.S. Sanitary Commission (USSC), a civilian organization authorized by the federal government to provide sanitary and medical assistance to the Union forces. Ellen helped her neighbors to organize a county fair for the purpose of aiding sick and wounded soldiers. Schuyler County raised $2,000, according to an article in the *Citizen*, and, perhaps more important, provided a venue in which "party spirit" was laid aside for the good of the whole.[35]

The Civil War unleashed a spirit of patriotic volunteerism that Ellen had never encountered before. Through her work with the USSC, she came to realize that women had the potential to make a significant difference in public and political life. Thousands of women—rich and poor, from big cities and small towns—donated their money, time, and labor in support of a worthy cause. Many of these women had never before engaged in public service on a national scale, nor had they interested themselves in reform movements, the women's suffrage campaign, or abolitionism. Now, however, they saw what participation in a large national organization could do both for themselves and for their country. Ellen came to the conclusion that "organized service" was central to the good of the nation: "In union is not only strength, but wisdom and justice and efficiency and beneficence."[36]

Ten members of the Scripps family fought in the Civil War, including Ellen's brothers George and John. The former was wounded at Vicksburg, while the latter died in a skirmish in Blue Springs, Tennessee. After Ellen's brother-in-law died as a Union prisoner of war in the notorious Andersonville prison in Georgia, Ellen moved to Hamilton, Illinois, to care for her sister and her two small children. Elizabeth, nearly deaf, suffered from severe rheumatism and was temporarily unable to look after her children, aged two and four.

The Civil War ended on April 9, 1865, when Gen. Robert E. Lee surrendered his army at the Appomattox Court House. Less than a week later, President Lincoln was assassinated by John Wilkes Booth, a southern sympathizer. A national outpouring of grief followed; millions of people attended Lincoln's funeral procession and viewed his body and funeral train en route to Springfield, Illinois. His death on Good Friday led to inevitable comparisons with Christ, "reinforcing belief in the war's divine purpose, realized through the sacrifice of the one for the many," in the words of one historian.[37]

The news of President Lincoln's death caused deep distress among members of the Scripps family. E.W. recalled, "The grief and mourning . . . was as great in the case of Lincoln's death as it was in my own brother's being killed."[38] Ellen wept for both her president and her country. In years to come, she celebrated the anniversary of Lincoln's birth each February 12 by placing an American flag outside her house.

When Ellen looked back at the war years, she remembered "the wholesale decimation by slaughter, the lack of women's nursing, though not the dearth of women's tears, the terrible loss of life by wounds and disease."[39] She learned that while men may die, women have to endure. The generation of women who survived the 1860s found that they needed employment and a living wage, a political voice, and a role in providing welfare to those in need. Ellen would take these lessons into the future, making an independent life for herself as a journalist in Detroit while remaining committed to reform.

CHAPTER 2

The Evening News

The Civil War marked a turning point in the history of the nation. It disrupted ordinary patterns of living and caused deep personal tragedy; at the same time, it created opportunities for remarkable success. For Ellen, the war opened possibilities for personal and social transformation as people began to free themselves from old ways of thinking. From her disciplined education and wide reading she came to believe in social reform and progress, the development of human potential, and the achievement of "a broader and more inclusive ideal of true liberty."[1] In years to come, she would commit herself to the construction of "a permanent, progressive democracy" based on the brotherhood of humanity and the equal rights of men and women.[2]

After the war, Ellen saw no reason to remain in Illinois. Her youngest sibling, Edward or "E.W.," was twelve years old and no longer in need of a teacher and surrogate mother, though Ellen would continue to serve as his champion. In 1865, when her older brother James offered her the opportunity to live with him and his new family in Detroit, she took it, leaving behind her life on the prairie for a hard-working industrial city on the straits of Lake Erie.

Detroit boomed in the years after the Civil War, becoming one of the most important industrial centers in the Midwest. It produced steam engines, stoves, and railway cars and wheels, as well as chemicals, boots, shoes, and tobacco products. The Michigan Car Company, founded in 1864, made railroad cars for the Union Army; it later became the leading railroad car manufacturer in the country. The Detroit Safe Company established an enormous factory in 1865 to produce fireproof safes made from iron and steel, while the Detroit Stove Works made cast-iron parlor stoves such as the Acme Jewel. The city had a number of chemical and pharmaceutical companies, including Parke-Davis and Company, best known for inventing gelatin capsules to disguise the taste of medicine. Manufacturers processed grain, lumber, copper, and iron ore and produced white lead and zinc paints.[3]

Detroit's population expanded along with its industry, growing from 45,619 in 1860 to 116,340 in 1880.[4] Like many western cities, Detroit hosted a large number of transient working-class men who lived in boardinghouses and cheap hotels not far from the warehouses along the riverfront. Brothels, saloons, German beer halls, billiard rooms, and other businesses catering to young bachelors were located on the east side of the city. Fashionable residential neighborhoods, meanwhile, lay to the northwest of the central business district.[5]

When Ellen arrived in Detroit in December 1865, horse-drawn streetcars had begun to traverse the city. Streets were paved with cobblestones or cedar blocks, and gas lamps lined most of the principal streets.[6] A sewer system, built in 1836 and extended in 1859, meant that the River Savoyard was no longer used as an open drain.[7] Residences and business blocks increasingly were constructed of brick, rather than timber, in order to lessen the danger of fire. The celebrated Merrill Block contained stores, workshops, apartments, a bank, law offices, and a combination ballroom and concert hall.[8]

James Scripps worked in the offices of the *Advertiser and Tribune*, located on the corner of Jefferson and Woodward Avenues. He had arrived in 1859, having worked briefly as a commercial reporter on the *Chicago Press & Tribune*. He had intended to fight in the Union Army, joining the Detroit Light Guard and studying tactics at night, but the newspaper's owner convinced him to stay on as manager, arguing that plenty of men could be had for the army, while men who could organize papers were scarce. James bought an interest in the paper and shortly afterward engineered the consolidation of the *Advertiser* with the *Daily Tribune*.[9] In 1862 he married Harriet Josephine "Hattie" Messinger, the daughter of innkeepers from Vermont.

In the early nineteenth century, the vast majority of newspapers were broadsheets, often described as "blanket sheets" due to their cumbersome size. One New York paper measured 35 by 58 inches and included eleven columns of news and advertisements. The papers were serious, heavy, and old-fashioned, the kind that "the steady merchant of pure Knickerbocker descent had been accustomed to season his morning cup of coffee."[10]

In the 1830s the *New York Sun* and *Herald* experimented with a small tabloid format using four letter-size pages. Priced at one cent each, they became known as "penny" papers, appealing to working people who sought sensational stories rather than businessmen who required facts. The *Springfield Republican*, meanwhile, pioneered the use of short articles and a straightforward, easy-to-read prose style. James had great respect for its editor, Samuel Bowles, whom he credited with beginning the work of condensing journalism.[11]

James, ambitious to increase his wealth, saw small, cheap newspapers as the wave of the future. The Civil War had created a rapidly expanding market for news with the result that newspaper subscriptions doubled and tripled within a few years. Unable to convince his partners to abandon the old-fashioned broadsheet format for a smaller tabloid size, he considered starting a newspaper of his own.

Ellen was eager to help. Soon after her arrival, she began taking classes in telegraphy at the Bryant & Stratton Institute in Detroit. "For the life of me, I cannot see what use she is going to make of the art," James wrote, "but she got her mind set on it and there was no diverting her." She also read voraciously. "She has three or four books constantly on hand at one time," James noted, "and devours, I should say, on average, a book a day."[12]

James recognized that his sister had a brilliant mind, though he could not admit that she was smarter than he. He noted: "Find Ellen can read

Latin much faster than I can, having a better memory for meaning of words, but she is much less careful about understanding the grammatical construction than I am. Excels me in memory and quickness of perception but not in application and thorough investigation of a subject."[13] He gave her a job as a feature writer reviewing concerts, theater performances, and books.

Ellen was one of many nineteenth-century women who earned their living as writers or editors, though their work often went unrecognized, particularly if they used pen names or initials. In fact, the *Advertiser and Tribune* had published regular reports by Lois Bryan Adams, who had moved from Michigan to Washington, D.C. Her columns, written in the form of letters, described life in the nation's capital during the Civil War. Other contemporary journalists included Mary Clemmer Ames, who wrote for the *New York City Independent*, and suffragist Lucy Stone, editor of the *Woman's Journal*.

Ellen earned a reasonable income in Detroit. In addition to working at the paper, she also taught at a local school, possibly the Detroit Female Seminary. She drew a salary of $10 (about $150 in 2016 dollars) per week from the *Advertiser and Tribune*, investing most of it back into the paper.[14] By 1870 she owned $4,000 (about $75,000) worth of stock and received a 1 percent dividend. She spent some of that money on herself. Diary entries show the purchase of neckties, a dress, a corset, handkerchiefs, paper, envelopes, gloves, a "green ribbon," and a brooch.[15] She had few major living expenses, as she traded childcare for rent and food.

From the beginning, Ellen took a businesslike approach to her financial affairs. She did not give money to her younger brothers and sisters but instead loaned them sums at an interest rate of 4 or 5 percent. She kept track of her loans in her diary, writing on May 3, 1870, for example: "Lent father fifty-one dollars, making one hundred dollars borrowed up to date, for which he gave me his note." By the end of 1870 she had saved $1,000 (about $18,700), which she then invested.[16]

Of course, there was a downside to being competent and solvent, as Ellen found out in 1871. In January she was called home from Detroit to take care of her father during a severe illness. Her stepmother and siblings Annie, Virginia, Fred, George, and E.W. still lived on the farm, so there was no lack of people to care for James Mogg. But the family needed her nursing and housekeeping skills; they did not appreciate the fact that she was a working journalist in Detroit. With her usual good grace, Ellen accepted a daughter's duty, packed her bags, and returned home to Rushville, Illinois.

Returning Home

In Rushville, Ellen had relatively little work to do and a good deal of time to enjoy her brothers and sisters. Her two favorites, E.W. and Virginia ("Jenny"), were seventeen and nineteen years old, respectively. In 1865 the former had been a talkative, red-haired twelve-year-old who was constantly getting into scrapes. Ellen had served as his teacher and protector, since his mother, Julia, often tried to beat the devil out of him, quite literally, using a thick rattan cane or leather strap. He later wrote, "I do know that my mother, then, and during all of my boyhood, felt that I was naturally wicked and that I would probably go to hell when I died."[17] His teacher Mrs. Putnam felt much the same way and, according to his sister, did nothing but "scold, slap, whip, snap, and look mad all day."[18] Ellen, on the other hand, thought that E.W. was a prodigy and encouraged his education. "Ellen read Shakespeare to me before I could read it myself," he recalled.[19]

By the time Ellen returned to Rushville, E.W. had grown into a tall, gangly teenager with tufts of facial hair and a pronounced cast in his left eye. He looked somewhat disreputable and admitted that he often acted like a "country lout."[20] Uninterested in farming but eager to earn money, he figured out how to get the neighborhood boys to do his chores while he supervised the operation. His mother thought that he would end up in jail, but his brother George thought him to be "a wonder of a boy." E.W. said George told him and others that "there was no use bothering about me, that I was going to get along in the world, and that I could take care of myself [better] than anybody else in the family or out of it."[21]

Virginia, meanwhile, had become a handsome young woman with a gift for poetry and a strong dramatic streak. She delighted Ellen with

her constant chatter and self-important manner more suited to a plu-
tocrat than a ploughgirl. She also enjoyed going to parties. Suffering
from a hangover one Saturday morning, she protested that she could
not milk the cows, that "she should 'die in a fit' and she had 'such a
famous headache that she shouldn't live till night,' etc., etc." Ellen told
their brother, "You know her stereotypes. . . . Ma and Aunt Kate did
the work in the kitchen and everywhere else."[22] In 1872 Virginia left
home to attend a female collegiate seminary in Newberry, Indiana,
but she quickly grew weary of her studies. Ellen wrote, "She finds her
dignity of no avail there and she comes home with woeful tales of the
indignities she is subjected to."[23]

Ellen's brothers George and Fred worked the Rushville farm. George,
severely injured during the Civil War, was cautious, economical, and
somewhat gruff. A short man, he had taken up smoking, chewing tobacco,
and playing cards as a way of accentuating his masculinity. E.W., however,
described him as "diffident" and suggested that he had a taste for sexual
adventure. He thought him to be "reckless and careless of anything"
except money.[24] Still, George made a success of the farm, buying eighty
acres of land from his father, as well as several nearby farms, stocking
them with calves, colts, and old horses. By 1873 he had accumulated
land and stock worth $13,000 to $15,000 (about $265,000 to $306,000).[25]

Fred, meanwhile, tended to be both lazy and dishonest. Like his father,
he came up with any number of get-rich-quick schemes that he could
never see through. In 1872 Ellen described how he and some friends
supposedly went turkey hunting; instead, they stole several birds from
a nearby barn.[26] She later wrote, "Fred's abilities evidently don't lie in
the direction of farming."[27]

When E.W. left home for Detroit at age eighteen, Ellen wrote to her
cherished brother each week and asked for letters in return. She told him
that she missed him most when she was reading aloud to the family in
the evenings, as "I generally succeed in reading all my hearers (myself
included) into a blissful state of unconsciousness. Last night, current
matter having failed, I had recourse to the bookcase and lighted on 'Idylls
of the King' and read 'Enid' through at the close of which George was

discovered peacefully snoozing on the lounge, Ma in a composition of similar placidity in the arm chair, Jennie nodding to the fire, and Father dreaming, I suppose, of the good old times sixty years ago."[28]

Two significant events brought Ellen back to work in Detroit: the death of her father and the foundation of the *Detroit Evening News*. James Mogg passed away on May 12, 1873, after a long illness, leaving his daughter feeling bereft of purpose and unsure of the future. No longer needed in the role of caretaker, she felt time hanging "most woefully heavy on my hands." She wrote to E.W., "I feel like those souls who in the evening cry, 'Would God it were morning!' and when morning comes, 'Would God it were evening!' I never knew before how much meaning lay hidden in the little phrase so often and so tritely quoted, 'Othello's occupation's gone!'"[29]

For a month after her father's death, she lingered in Illinois with her sisters Annie and Virginia. She wrote, "The house is desolate enough and, though I'm afraid I don't add much to the cheerfulness of its aspect, I help fill it a little bodily." In the mid-Victorian era, women bore the burden of mourning by keeping vigil at home, wearing black, and undertaking few, if any, of their ordinary tasks. Ellen soon tired of such practices, writing, "I shall be so glad to plunge into work—work of any kind, it doesn't matter much what, so it keeps the mind employed."[30]

A Working Woman

Fortunately, Ellen was needed in Detroit. In 1873 a happy accident gave James the money he needed to establish a penny paper of his own, the *Detroit Evening News*. Ellen took a job as writer and copyeditor with an income of $15 to $20 (about $300 to $400) per week.[31]

The first issue of the *Evening News* appeared on Saturday, August 23, 1873. It sold ten thousand copies at two cents each, half the price of other Detroit papers. It had four pages, six columns, and eighteen-inch sheets, the smallest size sheets that the press could handle. The newspaper began to pay for itself within its first two years of publication. Its daily circulation soon exceeded that of long-established Detroit papers. By 1875 it was producing an ordinary run of seventeen thousand papers.[32]

Circulation boomed among Detroit's working classes in part due to the introduction of what was called personal journalism, articles that exposed scandals and mocked the pretensions of elites. The staff felt free to innovate, leading to the paper's reputation as a "sensational sheet." James exercised little control over the newsroom, stepping in only when there was a serious problem. As a result, talented men like Robert B. Ross, an ex-printer, ex-hobo, and ex-Confederate captain, were able to surprise even themselves by their "brilliance of mind and force."[33] He and the city editor, Michael J. Dee, were considered two of the most "wild and reckless" newspapermen who ever gathered together in one room.[34]

Ellen's editorial work was crucial to the early success of the *Evening News*. Her labors were varied but included proofreading, copyediting, and occasionally typesetting. She arrived in the office at 7:00 a.m. and often worked late into the evenings. Her brother E.W. recalled her long hours: "We worked until five or six o'clock; then, going home, Ellen assisted with the house work, sometimes cooking, sweeping, and doing other work. No sooner was the light supper over than Ellen and James would sit down to work, preparing copy for the next day." He estimated that they never worked fewer than sixteen hours a day, seven days a week, during the first year of the *Evening News*.[35]

Among Ellen's most important contributions to the *Evening News* was the Miscellany, a collection of short feature stories garnered from the telegraph line and other papers. The invention of duplex telegraphy, which connected two parties with one another in both directions, in 1872 had lessened the cost of utilizing the telegraph and extended its use in the newspaper business. Since Ellen never included a byline for her work, it is difficult to identify her contributions. Examples, however, include the following snippets: "Cats are dying of trichinosis in Richmond. This will be great catastrophe for the sausage makers" and "Portsmouth, N.H. produces annually, in addition to numerous temperance orders, 120,000 barrels of ale and 90,000 gallons of rum."[36] One newspaperman described them as four- to ten-line "pictures" painted by an artist who found wry humor in follies of human nature.[37]

Ellen also played an important financial role. Instead of drawing her salary, she invested it in the paper. She loaned James money and helped him with the books. In January 1877 he noted in his diary: "Ruling ledger and adjusting accounts with Ellen in evening."[38]

Ellen's brother George acquired a third interest in the paper in return for selling his farm in Rushville and handing the money over to James. He moved to Detroit and became the business manager. Thrifty and shrewd, he was known for his capacity to gruffly say "No!" to requests for money. He also had no qualms about firing on the spot any careless printer.[39] James, meanwhile, counted out and sold the papers to the newsboys and carriers, collecting nickels and pennies in a tin cash box.

The teenage E.W. sold subscriptions to the *Evening News* before becoming head of the circulation department and, later, editor. He hung around the newsroom, talked with reporters, and "chummed with the printers."[40] He never won the approval of his older brother James, however, largely because of his mischievous behavior. E.W., for example, incited reporters to "raise as much hell as possible."[41] He knew that his brothers thought him to be an arrogant knave, but his devil-may-care approach sold newspapers.[42]

The *Evening News* survived the 1870s—a period of economic depression—as a result of the Scrippses' ability to cut costs. By eliminating wide margins and narrowing the size of the columns, James saved paper while maintaining competitive advertising rates. Every piece of paper in the office was recycled, including envelopes that arrived in the mail. E.W. later explained, "We had to keep our expenses down—or go broke."[43] A family-owned and -operated business survived by overworking and underpaying its members. By bringing his brothers and sisters into the operation, James made it possible for his newspaper to endure growing pains that bankrupted other concerns. His frugality was surely a sign of good management, but it was exploitation that turned the profits.

Ellen, for her part, continued to play her role as the dutiful Victorian sister. She cared for James's growing family and moved with them into a new house on Lafayette Street. There were four children to look after: Ellen Warren (b. 1863), Anna Virginia (b. 1866), James Francis (b. 1870), and Grace Messinger (b. 1878). Her brothers also needed care.

In February 1879 she nursed her brother George through a bad attack of erysipelas, a skin infection causing fever and chills, returning to the office the following day.[44] She also looked after James, who suffered from severe headaches as a result of overwork and anxiety.

The newspaper's aggressive approach to local reporting led to a number of serious libel suits in which James was named as defendant. In order to avoid future criminal action for libel, James incorporated the *Evening News* on August 23, 1876, the third anniversary of the paper. He took thirty of fifty shares of $1,000 par value, while George received sixteen shares. Ellen got two shares, E.W. was offered one share, and cousin John Sweeney received one. James certainly owed Ellen more, given her work and financial investment in the paper, and E.W. knew that "he was owing me several times the cost of my share."[45]

Ellen was disappointed to have been so easily undervalued. It only got worse. James began to hire new editors—all male—to oversee the day-to-day business of the paper. He also came to rely on the telegraph news agencies such as the Associated Press to supply the kind of content that Ellen had provided in her Miscellany. Instead of being placed in a respected position in the office, she was shuffled off to the proofreaders' room. James occasionally asked for her advice, but only because "he is glad to be bolstered up and supported by anyone, no matter who," she wrote acidly.[46] In 1880 Ellen received a gold watch from James as both a birthday gift and a not-so-subtle reminder that her career as a journalist was coming to an end.[47]

In the 1880s Ellen turned her attention to E.W.'s career, hoping to carve out a place for herself in a world dominated by men. She encouraged James to place E.W. at the head of the newly acquired *Cleveland Penny Press* and made sure that he had a successful start by sending him news stories and features that she gleaned from a score of daily newspapers that came to the *Evening News* office on the exchange list of papers that shared their content. He recalled, "Every morning, the mail brought me one or two envelopes from Detroit, mailed the night before, containing copy that had been prepared by my sister. The amount of matter was simply enormous. It would often amount to two or three columns."[48] Printed under the headlines "Matters and Things," "Personal Paragraphs," and "Random Notes," it was among the most valuable copy that the paper printed in the early days. For years afterward, E.W. made sure that two or three members of his staff pored over other papers for tidbits of news.[49] The value of Ellen's copy later persuaded E.W. to establish the Newspaper Enterprise Association, the first syndicate to supply feature stories, illustrations, and cartoons to newspapers.

In 1880 E.W. headed to St. Louis, a booming city with a large number of blue-collar workers, to launch the *St. Louis Chronicle*. It was a difficult undertaking, as the paper competed against Joseph Pulitzer's *Post-Dispatch*, which had a circulation of eight thousand and a commitment to serving the interests of the working classes. At the same time, James was dealing with staff members who tried to break away and form their own paper in Buffalo, New York. He kept control over the venture—and gave the journalists a cut of the profits—but not without a great deal of frustration. His anger spilled over into letters written to both E.W. and George in which James accused them of meddling in his business and acting like "d——d fools."[50]

Ellen encouraged E.W. to lie low and wait for his opportunity to take an important place in the family business. She pointed out that James could only serve as nominal head of the Scripps papers, not as the real leader, because of "his habits of life, his extreme cautiousness, and his domestic relations." As the newspaper business expanded, there would be opportunities for E.W. to take a more influential position.[51] In the meantime, she counseled, "be content to take a subordinate position and to be snubbed—as age always likes to snub youth simply because it is youth—until, by sheer force of your own merits and capabilities you can rise superior to all and compel respect."[52]

Ellen also fussed over E.W.'s health, fearing that he suffered from chronic dyspepsia and a tendency toward depression. E.W. drank heavily, smoked cigars, and ate only enough to sustain his gangly six-foot frame. Suffering from constant colds and bronchial trouble, he feared that his health was broken. Ellen, who had little use for most doctors, told him to find a reputable, honest physician in New York or St. Louis: "If he says leave off smoking, do it. If he says live on milk, do it. If he says go to Europe, I am ready to go with you in a week's notice. But don't postpone any longer a cure that each month will make more difficult to effect."[53]

Although her own health was excellent, Ellen felt old and weary. "I've had to do a man's work long enough, and I'm tired of it," she told her younger brother, hoping that he would take some of the burden of responsibility off her shoulders.[54] To that end, she encouraged him to hire younger women on the Scripps papers. In 1880 she recommended her cousin Fanny Bagby for a position on the *Cleveland Press*. She also suggested that her sister Virginia be allowed to work on the *Evening News*: "I cannot think of anything else that she can do. There is no great demand in the world for maintained women—or, indeed, for any other kind."[55]

American and Abroad

Now in her forties, Ellen continued working in Detroit through 1881. When James took a five-month trip to Europe, E.W. stepped in as president of the incorporated *Evening News* and the newly founded Scripps Publishing Company, which directed the business interests outside Detroit. All the papers were doing poorly, particularly the *St. Louis Chronicle*. In the spring of that year, E.W. faced charges of criminal libel after the *Cleveland Press* published a demeaning remark about another editor.[56] Ellen was not particularly concerned, as rival newspapers often used such tactics. E.W., however, was shaken by the episode. He started taking opium in order to get a decent night's sleep.[57]

Fearing that her brother would become really sick if he kept working at this pace, she suggested that E.W. take a break from the family business. In fact, Ellen needed to get out of Detroit herself. In August 1881 she wrote, "I am back in the office again and this room is probably the hottest place this side of Hades which accounts for mental flatulence."[58] She planned to go to England in November in order to see relatives, but without her brother's company, she would travel no farther.

Finally, E.W. agreed to take a break from business, given the disappointments and "mortifications" of the past year: "I would like to run away from Cleveland, from all my old friends elsewhere, from everything that has anything to do with my present life or past, and start all over again somewhere else."[59] Instead, he accompanied his sister on a lengthy trip to Europe. For two years they traveled leisurely through Europe, North Africa, and the Near East. She rode a camel in Egypt and braved a bathhouse in Algiers. She also witnessed firsthand the agricultural crisis that would encourage mass migration from Italy to the United States in the 1880s.

In order to occupy her time, Ellen decided to write a series of travel letters for the *Detroit Evening News* and the *Cleveland Press*. Scripps family members often turned their travel experiences into newspaper copy. James had published descriptions of his 1864 voyage to England; in 1881 he chronicled his five-month trip to Europe, later published as *Five Months Abroad* (1882).[60] An aspiring gentleman, James positioned himself as a member of the cultural elite, taking note of antique treasures, visiting Gothic cathedrals, and giving advice about traveling via steamships and railways. As knowledge of art was a form of social currency in the nineteenth century, he emphasized how much he knew about the Renaissance masters and great museums such as the Uffizi, the National Gallery, and the Louvre.

Ellen, on the other hand, made an effort to make her travel writing interesting and accessible to working-class men and women. To that end, she focused on the daily lives and activities of ordinary people, paying particular attention to issues of class and race, wealth and poverty, education, the status of women, cities and industry, clothes, food, and religion. She rarely mentioned political figures and almost never discussed current events such as the rise of socialism, the Anglo-Egyptian War (1881), and the formation of the Triple Alliance among Germany, Austria, and Italy (1882). Instead, she focused on stories that gripped the imagination, such as a bullfight in Madrid. "It was positively the dangedest finest description of a bullfight ever written," recalled one journalist, ". . . so good that it had to be read to the staff before being sent into the composing room."[61] The hunger of the newspapers for copy was insatiable, and Ellen was by now an accomplished reporter. Her impressions would fill columns as they would imaginations.

Ellen returned from Europe in June 1883, expecting to pick up her old life on the *Evening News*; instead, she found herself without a job after her eighteen-month absence. James no longer needed her editorial skills, though he expected her to continue to reside in Detroit and care for his five young children. Annie remarked that her brother's family "quietly presume that you belong to them."[62]

E.W., meanwhile, was determined to make it as a newspaperman. When he and James inevitably clashed, he counted on Ellen to come to his aid. In 1883 she quietly refused to go along with a scheme that would remove E.W. from effective control of the *Cleveland Press*. Angered, James demanded that she sell him all of her various newspaper interests for a large sum. She flatly refused.[63]

Ellen provided more than advice and support to her younger brother; she also loaned him considerable sums of money. By the mid-1880s she was earning at least $5,000 (about $127,000) per year as a stockholder in the various Scripps papers and had enough reserves to loan her brother $3,000 to $10,000 (about $76,000 to $254,000) at any given time.[64] According to her brother, she was "a very clever accountant" who kept "exact records of transactions" and at no time "conducted herself so as to lead me to suppose that she did not intend to exact from me every penny that was due her."[65]

When James fell ill in 1887, E.W. sought to gain control over the Scripps newspapers. By this time there were four distinct corporations: the Evening News Association (the *Detroit Evening News*), the Scripps Publishing Company (the *Cleveland Press*), the Post Publishing Company (the *Cincinnati Post*), and the Evening Chronicle Publishing Company (the *St. Louis Chronicle*). E.W. overhauled the editorial staff of the *Evening News*, adding new men such as George Gough Booth, a Toronto-born businessman who had married James's eldest daughter.[66] E.W. established the Scripps-League Bureau in New York for the collection and transmission of news by wire and mail and generated additional advertising revenue. He also supported investigative journalism, sending one reporter on an expedition to Alaska and another to study electoral methods in the South. In 1889 he sent a delegation of Detroit workingmen to the Exposition Universelle in Paris, where they would see the newly constructed Eiffel Tower.[67]

Ellen, meanwhile, traveled with James and his family to Europe, where her brother recovered remarkably quickly. His interests turned to expenditure rather than accumulation, and he became obsessed with collecting art. In Paris he bought copies of Old Masters to donate to the newly established Detroit Institute of Arts. He got particularly carried away in Florence, a city filled with antiquarian shops and art dealers. News of his purchases soon spread throughout Tuscany, causing him to be beset by everyone who had a picture to sell or knew someone who did.[68]

Ellen did not share her brother's interest in art—or his need to make his name as a collector. In fact, she saw it as evidence of his desire to launch his family into Detroit society and wondered whether it was worth the cost. "I have no doubt that his end will be gained—his name will be perpetually before coming generations in connection with a valuable art collection for the public," she told E.W. "But, bah! What does it matter what becomes of a man after his death!"[69] She also recognized that social climbing would be difficult for a man who published a newspaper that frequently made fun of Detroit elites. In fact, James had a hard time persuading the board of the Detroit Institute of Arts to accept his gifts and faced "sneers and doubts" about their authenticity.[70]

Ellen's second trip to Europe seemed to wear her down, not the least because she was saddled with responsibility for her brother's children. She told E.W. that there was not much time for reading or studying with her nieces and nephews in tow: "I shan't be sorry to divide the care of them with their legitimate protectors."[71] She nursed her sister-in-law Hattie through a long illness in Rome before returning to England for a quiet vacation on her own.

At fifty-two years of age, Ellen felt that she had arrived at "an indifferent period of life, when nothing makes very much difference to me."[72] E.W. tried to give Ellen a sense of urgency about business, perhaps thinking that this would get her out of her travel-induced torpor: "I am afraid you are getting as moody and perhaps as eccentric as any of us. You are 'drifting,' life seems to be affecting you unwholesomely. I propose to advise you to come home and go to work like the rest of us, on something."[73]

She may have been drifting, but she did not tolerate male condescension. When E.W. suggested that she pursue the same kinds of activities as other unmarried women, she replied, "I am puzzled over your supposititious 'old maid line of conduct' that I am likely to pursue. To my own humiliation I must plead utter ignorance of what such line of conduct should or would be. I am an old—a *very* old—maid in years, but in everything else I'm—an anomaly. I don't know anything about what an old maid ought or is expected to be or to do."[74]

When Ellen returned to Detroit in 1889, she was greeted by what was now the all-too-typical spectacle of Scripps family warfare. E.W.'s unfettered control over the *Evening News*, in particular, his extravagant spending, had gradually alienated his older brother George, who had been one of his biggest supporters. James, meanwhile, was infuriated by the changes made since he had left, particularly the purchase of new presses and the rapid expansion in the size of the paper.

Ellen, as always, tried to mediate the dispute. She warned her younger brother that James remained in a physical condition that left him irritable and depressed. She told James, meanwhile, that E.W. was hurt by the fact that he was always treated as an immature boy rather than a thirty-six-year-old man: "You have never recognized him as an equal and have treated his successes and his mistakes as a man would treat those of a boy. What hurts him is not your opposition but the manner of it."[75]

James, however, wanted nothing more to do with his younger brother; in December 1889 he asked E.W. to step down from his position as the president of the Scripps Publishing Company and turn over the management of the *Cleveland Press* to James.[76] He also threatened to seize control of the *Cincinnati Post* by calling in a loan of $14,000 (about $356,000) made to E.W. some years earlier.[77] Ellen came to the rescue by loaning her younger brother the money to pay off his loan.[78] She also promised him that, in the affairs of the Scripps Publishing Company, she would give him her proxy.[79]

But the worst was yet to come. In early January 1890 the board of directors of the Evening News Association displaced E.W. and elected James as president in a secret meeting. At the same time, E.W. was fired as president of the Scripps Publishing Company, the company that published the *Cleveland Press*.[80]

Ellen, exhausted by the family feud, imagined moving to England, one of the few places where a single woman could live comfortably on her own. She particularly liked the spectacular coastline of Devon with its ancient rock formations, turf, and heather. Here she had found rest for the spirit and beauty for the mind.[81] Instead, she headed to California for what she imagined would be a short trip. Forty years later, it would still be her home.

CHAPTER 3

The Realm of Queen Calafia

In January 1890 Ellen traveled to California, the westernmost part of the United States. Inspired by the writings of a fifteenth-century novelist, the Spanish had named the region after a fictional Queen Calafia, who ruled over a land of griffins and gold. Unlike earlier settlers, Ellen did not intend to make a fortune in the gold rush or speculate in real estate. In fact, she felt detached from the business of life—making and spending money—and in need of a change. She decided to visit her sister Annie, who had found a home in the San Francisco Bay area, then head south to San Diego to visit a cousin who worked on the *San Diego Sun.*

Julia "Annie" Scripps left Illinois in search of a remedy—both spiritual and physical—for crippling rheumatoid arthritis. In 1887 she joined the Remedial Institute and School of Philosophy, also known as the New Order of Life, in Alameda. One of many utopian communities in the late nineteenth-century West, it offered "a life of brotherly love" guided by the pseudoscientific principles of its founder, Dr. Horace Bowen. Annie considered Alameda to be a "Paradise" where she was sure to be healed.[1]

Ellen traveled to California with her brother Fred, who had endured a recent illness, either malaria or rheumatic fever. They found Alameda to be a shabby town located on a flat marsh. There were scattered one-story houses, grass-grown streets, and a row of squalid beer gardens and breweries lining the bay.[2] Fred quickly decamped for the nearby

Byron Hot Springs while Ellen stayed with her sister. She attended several Theosophical lectures on karma and reincarnation and listened with considerable skepticism to Dr. Bowen explain his "new theology," which accounted for the origin of disease.[3]

Annie appeared little changed in three years, "perhaps a little thinner and her hair a trifle grayer," Ellen wrote. Her hands, however, were "entirely out of shape," and she could not use her right arm. Her swollen knees were drawn so close together that it took an hour to get her into and out of bed. Ellen noted, "She can read very little now; write less, and work none at all. Still, she feels 'well,' and is apparently happy."[4]

Seeing little reason to remain in northern California, Ellen and Fred traveled south to San Diego to visit their cousins Hans and Fanny Bagby. The latter worked as a journalist for several Scripps papers before joining the staff of the *San Diego Sun*. They arrived on February 15, 1890, took rooms at the one-hundred-room Horton House, and set about viewing the city.

Founded by the Spanish in 1769, the city had developed along the western end of the San Diego River valley in an area now known as Old Town. In the 1860s Alonzo Horton promoted development of New Town, or downtown, along the shores of a natural harbor, not far from the U.S.-Mexico border. By the late nineteenth century, San Diego had a small urban population of approximately sixteen thousand residents, most living by the coast or on one of the hills overlooking the bay. An economic boom in the 1880s had brought gas, electricity, telephone service, and a steady water supply from San Miguel and the Cuyamaca Mountains. The boom also encouraged the construction of new houses—everything from modest Victorian cottages to exuberant Queen Anne–style homes. San Diego was not a big city like Detroit, with museums and concert halls, but it did have a library, a high school, and a branch of the YMCA.

Transportation was adequate if not spectacular. Steamships regularly transported goods and passengers up and down the Pacific coast, while the California Southern Railroad, established in 1880, linked up with the transcontinental railroad at Barstow. Within the city, a streetcar system traveled between D Street and Old Town at the foot of Mission Valley. Ferry services between downtown and Coronado Island in San Diego Bay made possible the development of a spectacular Victorian hotel, the Hotel del Coronado, which could accommodate a thousand guests. This was one of the first places that Ellen and Fred visited, spending one Sunday morning wandering through the hotel and the grounds.

Ellen was not immediately charmed by San Diego. It poured rain the first few days, leaving her little to do besides meet the "prominent" citizens introduced by her cousin Fanny. Ellen's reputation as a journalist and publisher had preceded her, with the result that she found herself "more of a lioness than was agreeable to one of my pacific nature. I could have had, had I chosen it, entrée to the best circles of the city."[5] Those circles were not highly exalted, she soon found, as "a rude, rough pioneer element" was everywhere. People spoke in "a language of slang, short epithets, and 'wag,'" while their sense of self-worth was as inflated as the prices.[6]

In 1890 Southern California was still reeling from the effects of a regional economic depression caused by railroad overbuilding, bank failures, and the collapse of the real estate market. Ellen knew many families from her hometown that had moved to the region, invested in real estate, and lost thousands of dollars. A Methodist minister named Stevenson who had preached in Rushville, Illinois, continued to boost investment opportunities in Monrovia, an agricultural community located to the east of Pasadena: "He was one of the biggest boomers of the lot. Affects to regard Monrovia as a Paradise and is trying to inveigle his friends into this Garden of Eden."[7]

Although she was wary of boosters, Ellen did see opportunity in San Diego. There was plenty of land and water; in fact, the region was experiencing one of the wettest periods in its history. San Diego had an average annual rainfall of ten inches near the coast and over forty inches inland, providing plenty of water for irrigating crops.[8]

She also was captivated by San Diego's mild climate. The winter months were sunny and warm, while the summers were cool and dry; temperatures never fell below 32 degrees and rarely exceeded 90. In

March, she reported, "the sun is very hot, and vegetation is like ours of summer. People were bathing in the sea today. Open windows are a luxury. Green peas and other summer 'garden sauce' has become monotonous. The sky is as blue and cloudless as that of Southern Italy; the dust 10 inches deep."[9]

Fred, eager to move to San Diego, convinced his sister to purchase 160 acres of land in Mira Mesa, not far from a railroad flag stop, where he could start a citrus farm.[10] His health was improved remarkably in California, "a condition that could be only attributable to the climate," and Ellen was only too willing to help him get a new start.[11]

A Fresh Start

When she returned to Detroit, Ellen suggested that E.W. separate his financial interests from those of their brother James and move to the West: "It may seem a pity to your ambitions to check in its mid-career a business which promises magnificent growth and results. But, after all, what is it we are doing but amassing money and becoming monopolists?"[12] Together, they would escape, albeit briefly, from the world of newspapers. They could make a home for their elderly mother and sisters Virginia and Annie, offer employment to brothers Fred and Will, and provide a comfortable retirement to their brother George.

E.W. was ready for a change. In 1890 he had just finished reading Edward Bellamy's utopian novel *Looking Backward: 2000–1887*, which emphasized the vast inequalities between rich and poor. The protagonist, a young Boston gentleman, goes to sleep in 1887 and wakes up more than one hundred years later at a time when individuals have put aside their self-interest in order to work for the good of the whole. Tenements and smokestacks disappear to be replaced by tree-lined streets, parks, and public buildings of "a colossal size and architectural grandeur." Everyone feels himself or herself to be a member of an "industrial army" working for "one great business corporation," the state. The result, according to Bellamy, was the end of poverty and great wealth, "the solidarity of the race and the brotherhood of man."[13]

An ardent capitalist, E.W. was startled by Bellamy's critique of modern society. He wrote to Ellen, "I was surprised to find myself thoroughly absorbed and interested in it. When you read it, did you not feel that you were being attacked and justly attacked for your selfishness and your folly? Did you not feel your own hands dripping with the blood of your murdered victims? I did. I feel now that I am doing altogether wrong. I have not yet decided whether I can do entirely right but I am sure I can do a great deal better than I am and I am going to try."[14]

Ellen had long disapproved of the accumulation of vast wealth even by dedicated philanthropists. In his much-discussed article, "Wealth," industrialist Andrew Carnegie argued that great fortunes could be used in a responsible and thoughtful manner to reduce the stratification between rich and poor. Ellen noted tartly, "He has amassed $20,000,000. The question of benefitting mankind should have been considered and solved at a time and in a way that should have prevented his becoming a millionaire."[15]

Although the move to California helped to launch a newspaper empire that would make both Ellen and E.W. millionaires many times over, that had not been their intention. E.W. later wrote, "I did not wish to come to California for money. I wanted to get as far away from the detestable temper [the ability to make money] as possible."[16]

In November 1890 Ellen and E.W. purchased six hundred acres of land, formerly part of the ex–Mission San Diego de Alcalá, and began building a ranch house on a wide, flat-top ridge overlooking Mira Mesa.[17] It was named Miramar (in Spanish, "sea view") after Emperor Maximilian I's palace on the Adriatic Coast, later replicated at Chapultepec in Mexico City.[18] A villa with four one-story wings around a central courtyard, it had crenellated towers, Romanesque windows, and a promenade on the roof. By the time the house was completed in 1898, there were forty-nine rooms, most containing a fireplace, running water, and a telephone line. By the end of 1896, Ellen calculated that she personally had invested $28,624 (about $833,000 in 2016 dollars) in Miramar.[19]

Miramar was more than just a house; it was a utopian experiment in family living that E.W. hoped would rank among "the most famous of dwelling places." He imagined a domestic space that would provide companionship and care for the elderly and infirm, a source of income for his brothers Fred and William, and "isolation and privacy" for individual families, including his own.

E.W. had begun a new phase in his life, having married nineteen-year-old Nackie B. Holtsinger in 1885. By the early 1890s they had a picture-book house and farm at West Chester, Ohio, as well as four young children: James George (b. 1886), John Paul (b. 1888), Dorothy Blair (b. 1890), and Edward Wyllis McLean (b. 1891). Two additional children would be born during their years in California: Robert Paine (b. 1895) and Nackey Elizabeth (b. 1898).

San Diego changed E.W. for the better, or so he claimed. He shed his formal black suit and mustache, gained thirty pounds, grew a beard, and dressed in "last year's clothes" and a crumpled old hat. He and Nackie frequently traveled by horseback along canyons, across mesas, and up mountains. Days were spent hunting and shooting quail, inspecting the ranch's dams and cisterns, planting orchards, and wrangling with the irrigation district. He reflected that the family, too, was "greatly benefited by being here." His sons James and John "seem to have at last developed from children into boys," while his dog, Duke, was transformed: "From an aristocratic, exclusive, gentlemanly sort of dog, he has come down to being a common rough pug. . . . He no longer poses as a beautiful statue, but rolls around in the dust and dirt, basking in the sunshine."[20]

Ellen, too, was changed by life in California. She began to feel more independent, both financially and emotionally. In the past she had lived with other family members in either Detroit or Rushville, worked in the family business, taken care of small children, and nursed relatives through illnesses and pregnancies. She always felt that she held an "anomalous position" within the family; she was not financially dependent on her brothers, as she received dividends from most of the Scripps newspapers, but she was still an aging spinster without a home of her own.[21]

Now in her fifties, Ellen also spent time exploring the region, calling on neighbors, and making herself useful at home. She and her brothers often took a team of horses to the Mission San Diego de Alcalá, at that time a picturesque ruin, returning along chaparral hillsides and canyons with live oaks and sycamore trees. Other days, they drove to the seaside at Del

Mar, twenty-three miles north of the city, where the view from the beach was remarkable. They explored San Diego's backcountry, from the rocky heights of Grossmont to the scenic El Cajon Valley with its vineyards and olive trees. Ellen traveled south to Ensenada, Mexico, where she walked along the bay and collected seashells, and made frequent trips north to Altadena, where Will Scripps had established a ranch with orange groves.

In the evenings the Scripps invited guests to Miramar. They played music and card games, talked by the fireside, and ate a substantial dinner. Ellen had made friends with a neighboring English family, the Jessops, and a young woman named Katharine Peirce who owned a forty-acre ranch. She reconnected with her cousin Lida Scripps, whose poor health had brought her from Illinois to San Diego. She also met many of the enterprising women of early San Diego, including the city's first female doctor, Dr. Charlotte Baker; the botanist Mary Snyder; and the pioneering horticulturalist Katherine "Kate" Sessions, who was good friends with Miss Peirce.

By 1903 the ranch boasted groves of Torrey and Monterrey pines, as well as ornamental gardens with jacaranda and magnolia trees. Climbing vines twisted around the veranda of the house, and a mound of purple bougainvillea covered one side of the barn. Nackie raised roses, while E.W. developed a "remarkable collection of cacti" and planted over twenty-seven varieties of eucalyptus trees.[22]

E.W. also purchased a three-story Victorian house near downtown San Diego where his wife and family could stay during their visits to the city. Known as the Britt-Scripps house, it is located at the corner of Maple and Fourth Streets in Bankers Hill.

To Detroit and Back Again

Frequent trips back to Detroit made Ellen realize that she did not want to go back to her old existence. She described the "sad, unsatisfactory, unprofitable life" led by James and his sons-in-law, who sat around the dinner table "like dumb beasts" intent on eating as much as possible within a given time. "There is no recreation, no conversation, no friendly banter, or kindly intercourse," she noted. "It doesn't seem natural. I am sure it isn't wise."[23] Her stock in the highly profitable *Detroit Evening News* made it necessary for her to attend annual board meetings, and she may have continued to work for her brother James. Payroll records indicated that she was still employed as an editor through March 1894.[24]

The other Scripps newspapers, now controlled by E.W., continued to prosper. In 1894 E.W. formed a partnership with Milton A. McRae, a determined young man who rose through the ranks of the Ohio papers to become one of E.W.'s top lieutenants. E.W. referred to him as a "human steam engine," so assertive in his manner, so big and strong physically, that "it was impossible for him not to impress others with his own belief in the *Post* and in himself."[25] George Scripps was persuaded to join the partnership in 1895. The group managed the *Cincinnati Post*, the *Cleveland Press*, the *St. Louis Chronicle*, the *Toledo News-Bee*, and the *Kansas City Star.* They also acquired newspapers in Memphis, Oklahoma City, Evansville, Terre Haute, Columbus, Denver, Dallas, and Houston. In 1899 E.W. reported that business affairs in Cincinnati and other eastern cities were flourishing: "I think the *Press* and *Post* will continue to more than double their former profits, and for the past two or three months each of them have far exceeded the Detroit paper. Even the little *Kentucky Post* is turning out big profits."[26]

In the late 1890s E.W. began to acquire papers in California, including the *Los Angeles Record*, the *San Diego Sun*, and the *San Francisco News*. He considered them to be independent of the Scripps-McRae League and part of what he called Pacific coast penny papers, or the West Coast group. In the Pacific Northwest, the growing profitability of working-class newspapers led to the creation of the *Seattle Star*, the *Spokane Press*, the *Tacoma Times*, and the *Portland News*, all pitched to dock workers, miners, lumbermen, and cannery workers and all part of the West Coast group. By 1905 E.W. estimated that profits on "my little Western papers" were many times greater than those of his eastern ones, particularly when he factored in investments of capital and labor.[27]

Like other Scripps newspapers, the Pacific coast dailies championed the interest of working-class readers. The *Los Angeles Record* developed a reputation for its sympathetic coverage of strikes at a time when the public was generally hostile to industrial action. It also promoted the cause of organized labor. Editor B. H. Canfield claimed that the *Seattle Star* and other papers "really established union labor in the northwest."[28]

Ellen followed her brother into these newspaper ventures. E.W. explained that they stood together "on exactly equal footing, sometimes, as to shares and values in case of purchasing, and cost in case of founding, and [Ellen] has on the average been more successful than I have."[29] He did not always approve of her interest in turning a profit, but he readily agreed when she asked to invest in new papers. In 1898 he wrote, "There is no good of your making any more money but I suppose you are entitled to exercise those instincts which you have inherited in common with your brothers."[30]

One of the most successful undertakings would be the Newspaper Enterprise Association (NEA), which provided editorials, features, illustrations, and cartoons for the Scripps papers. Along with the Scripps-McRae Press Association, it had developed out of the need for news copy less expensive than that provided by the Associated Press (AP). A staff of writers working out of Cleveland now did what Ellen once had done for the *Detroit Evening News* and the *Cleveland Press*, that is, provide six to eight columns' worth of human-interest stories to newspapers across the country. Editor in chief Robert F. Paine recalled, "A bright woman's 'Miscellany' became a world influence, a delight in millions of homes."[31]

In 1907 E.W. broke the AP's monopoly on news by uniting three of the Scripps press associations under the name United Press (UP), later United Press International.[32] Every day the wire service provided twelve thousand words of copy by telegraph to subscribers across the United States. Roy W. Howard, who had started as a reporter on the *Cincinnati Post*, became vice president and general manager. He would later become codirector of the Scripps-Howard League of newspapers.

A businesswoman, Ellen read every financial statement and communicated frequently with editors, lawyers, and accountants. She and E.W. talked or wrote nearly every day; their letters are filled with details about newspaper revenues and distribution figures, acquisition plans, and personnel issues. She had a "particular hankering for business information," in the words of her brother, and could get testy if she was kept out of the loop in matters concerning her interests.[33] To that end, E.W. directed Lemuel T. Atwood, financial head of the Scripps-McRae newspapers, to send Ellen a "carefully prepared" semiannual financial report of her property and to be prepared to send any account books to her "at any moment on instant demand."[34] In 1905 he wrote, "She is capable of attending to her own business, and she knows it, and she does it."[35]

A Young Jewel

In addition to keeping track of her financial affairs, Ellen began to enjoy the pleasures of a prosperous old age. In 1894 she considered buying a cottage by the sea either in La Jolla or Del Mar. She loved her cozy tower room at Miramar but yearned for space of her own. At her brother's house she found herself caring for E.W.'s young children, whom she adored. She knew, however, that she no longer had the "freshness and vigor of mind" to continue this for long.[36]

E.W. dissuaded her from considering a move to Del Mar, as the village was almost deserted in the winter, and the three or four families who lived there were in an "almost deadly feud—one faction against the other." He also explained that its location along the coastal route between San Diego and Los Angeles was not ideal. He described it as the "great high road of tramps and criminals between north and south— especially those bad citizens fleeing to the wilds of Mexico."[37]

As a result, Ellen turned her attention to La Jolla. During the 1880s the village had been little more than a summer campground. San Diegans flocked to the area's beaches during the warm months, spending their time bathing in the sea, looking for seashells, fishing, and living in the sunshine and fresh air. They camped on the bluffs overlooking the cove until hotel-cottages became available on Prospect Street in 1887. An article in *The Land of Sunshine* touted it as "A Tented City by the Tide" and "the favorite summer camping ground of nearly all San Diegans."[38]

After 1894 tourists began to arrive in considerable numbers as a result of a railway line that hastened the long, dusty, fourteen-mile journey from San Diego through Pacific Beach to La Jolla. It now took only an hour to get from Union Station to the main intersection of Prospect Street and Fay Avenue.

Like Ellen, many visitors felt the urge to colonize this beautiful stretch of coast by buying lots in the La Jolla Park subdivision and building houses. Anna Held developed the Green Dragon Colony and invited artists and musicians to share a few rustic cottages on the cliffs above Goldfish Point. Dr. Joseph Rodes built a nearby bungalow that, after his death, became a rental property named Brockton Villa. Two redwood cottages, Red Rest and Red Roost, were built above the cove. By 1898 there were nearly one hundred homes in La Jolla.[39]

In 1895 Ellen's niece Florence "Floy" Scripps Kellogg rented the Green Dragon bungalow and invited her aunt to take tea. Floy was spending the winter in La Jolla while her two small daughters visited their grandfather at Miramar. Ellen wrote, "It is rather shanty-like outside, but very cozy within. There is a very large, deep fireplace with a crane and pot and trivet." It could be cold and damp in February, so heat and light came from the fireplace, a coal-oil stove, and an alcohol lamp. "It was all so nice," she wrote, that "I am thinking of having a cottage of my own."[40]

It had taken many years for Ellen to accept the fact that she could have her own house. There was nothing in her upbringing that could have helped her justify such an expense. A Victorian woman, she was supposed to live under her brothers' authority and to care for future generations of Scripps children. But she had never been conventional, and she felt even less so now that she was approaching the age of sixty. It wouldn't cost so much after all. La Jolla was a dusty old beach town, undiscovered despite its spectacular ocean views. She might quietly slip away and make a new home for herself among the driftwood and sea grass.

The following year Ellen began to build her first home, South Molton Villa, on the bluffs above the sea. She brought her unmarried sisters with her, liberating them from the obligations of a patriarchal home. In the process, she began to realize her own power. She was not a spinster, unvalued and unloved, but a seed of change in the slowly evolving landscape of San Diego.

CHAPTER 4

A Young Jewel

Ellen was sixty years old when she bought land in La Jolla and began building South Molton Villa, the first house that she had ever owned. Located on a bluff overlooking the Pacific Ocean, the land sold for $800 (about $23,000 in 2016 dollars), while the cottage cost $9,000 (about $262,000) to build.[1] It took her some time to realize that this was not just a communal living space for her and her unmarried sisters—or an "old maid's establishment," as she once called it—but a home of her own.[2] Building and maintaining the structure, decorating, painting, gardening, and landscaping gave Ellen a sense of stability. She started to be part of a community with the other residents of La Jolla, establishing friendships outside her extended family circle for the first time in many years.

La Jolla reminded many well-traveled tourists, including Ellen, of the French and Italian Riviera. The California coast, of course, was much wilder than the Côte d'Azur. Long-time resident Ellen Morrill Mills recalled that in the early 1880s the village "was just a beautiful expanse of grey-green sage brush and darker chaparral, with patches of brilliant wild flowers here and there, from the top of Mt. Soledad to the Cove."[3] Even after the town was laid out, the streets were little more than cow paths, muddy in the rainy season and dusty the rest of the time.[4] The seascape was dramatic, with caves hollowed out by the action of the waves and unstable sand dunes. An 1899 advertisement promised "weird and fantastic freaks of nature formed along the rock shore, which must be seen to be appreciated, such as Cathedral Rock, Alligator Head, Goldfish Point."[5]

Ellen began looking at property in February 1895, but she did not make a purchase until April 30, 1896, when she bought Lots 4 and 5 in Block 35 of La Jolla Park, a subdivision created by Frank Botsford.[6] She commissioned the architects Anton Reif and John Stannard to draw up plans for a large cottage on Prospect Street overlooking the ocean.[7] While in Chicago, she had viewed a number of "modern" houses in Rogers Park, referring to the Queen Anne and Italianate styles popular in the late Victorian period. She decided, however, that she preferred a simpler, "colonial style, if it can be suited . . . to the cottage size." Colonial Revival architecture had become particularly popular along the East Coast. She told E.W., "I like its simplicity and unpretentiousness while it can be made as ornate as one chooses."[8]

In 1897 her brother Will Scripps worked with the architects to design a two-story house.[9] The side of the house facing Prospect Street was rectangular, with a low-pitched hipped roof topped by a railed rooftop platform and two chimneys. A wide entry porch with classical columns covered the front door. The north façade, meanwhile, was built in a modified Queen Anne style. A round tower jutted out from the northeast corner, exposing dramatic views of the bluffs, cove, and sea.

Ellen's cottage was larger than many of the surrounding structures, but it was nothing like the "cottages" built in places like Bar Harbor, Maine. In 1895 she had visited Mount Desert Island, off the coast of Maine, where palatial residences commanded magnificent sea and mountain views. Joseph Pulitzer, owner of the *New York World*, had built a $300,000 cottage close by the water's edge, "and there are plenty of others almost as grand and as costly," she told her sister.[10]

Ellen named her new house South Molton Villa (sometimes spelled South Moulton Villa) after her family's home on South Molton Street, London, where she had been born. The name suggested family continuity, better times, and pride in her English origins. A poem in her guest book read:

In Old South Molton Street
In London, England, 6,000 miles away
Our Family, some sixty years ago
First saw the light of day . . .
To perpetuate the name, the place, and old associations, of past
    four generations . . .
For with due Reverence for Birthplace
Childhood-days, and Home and Recollection
The name shall ever stand, for the Villa-by-the-Sea,
In California Land
   'SOUTH MOLTON'[11]

In the early years, Ellen shared her house with two sisters, Annie and Virginia. Annie had moved from Miramar with her companion, Miss Kaley, and two nurses in August 1897, and she remained in La Jolla until her death in September 1898. Her rheumatism had become so bad that she was virtually crippled, though she occasionally felt well enough to take a horse and carriage around town. Ellen loved her dearly, describing her as "very gentle, patient, and quite a religious person" with an "intelligent face." Ellen also considered Annie to be the smartest member of the family, in her words, "the ablest of the lot."[12] Ellen read aloud to her in the evenings from works such as George Eliot's poem "O May I Join the Choir Invisible" (1867), and together they listened to phonograph records.[13]

Virginia lived at South Molton Villa during the winter, spring, and summer months, returning to Rushville, Illinois, each autumn to visit relatives and look after the family farm. Sixteen years younger than her sister Ellen, Virginia had developed from a wild girl into an energetic and intelligent woman who had become accustomed to a degree of independence. She never married, having been disappointed in an early love affair, but traveled a great deal and acquired a large number of friends. She had long wanted to come to California but turned down E.W.'s invitation to live at Miramar in 1892, reminding him, "I am not very much beloved (as Ellen is) by every one and I doubt if any of you will consider me anything of an acquisition to the community if not a positive incubus and a general nuisance." Unlike her elder sister, who could "adapt herself to any and all circumstances," Virginia needed more freedom than life at the family compound could offer, particularly given the fact that her brother had taken on the role of "mayor and monarch of all you survey and sole proprietor of house, etc., etc., with the whole family bowing down to you and worshiping you."[14]

Virginia had no such problems with Ellen, who, without condescension, offered a home in which Virginia could invest her time and energy. At South Molton Villa she cooked, cleaned house, worked in the garden, and hosted numerous guests. She also planned picnics, card parties, beach excursions, day trips to Los Peñasquitos, and longer journeys to rural areas like Lakeside, El Cajon, Alpine, Ramona, Julian, and Warner Springs. Ellen noted, "Jenny must live in the atmosphere of action and thinks it is the life for everyone else."[15]

A Woman's Town

If Ellen professed not to know what a rich spinster's life comprised, she slipped easily into its routine. With the help of her sister Virginia, Ellen gradually stepped out of her intimate family circle and began to acquire a large set of female acquaintances. The village had a growing population of summer and year-round residents, many of whom were unmarried women or widows. She remarked that in the early days "it was a woman's town."[16]

Among her friends were Eleanor Mills and her sister Olivia Mudgett, whom Ellen described as "the old-time 'bone and sinew' of the community."[17] Eleanor, a native of Maine, had moved to La Jolla in 1890 with her husband, Anson P. Mills, and her daughter, Ellen. She worked as a real estate agent while her husband, a former lawyer, served as a handyman, painting and fixing up rental cottages. They lived at Kennebec Lodge at the corner of Prospect Street and Fay Avenue, right across from the railway depot.[18] Olivia, meanwhile, lived in a Victorian house called Villa Waldo, built in 1894. The widow of a prominent shipbroker, she had graduated from Belfast Academy in Gorham, Maine, one of the oldest women's colleges in the United States, and lived for a time in New York City.

The sisters drew Ellen and Virginia into the center of La Jolla's social life. Olivia often had young people over for music and dancing; she and Eleanor also hosted socials at the Pavilion, a meeting place for both tourists and La Jolla families that was located near Coast Boulevard and Girard Avenue. On New Year's Day in 1898 the Mills family invited forty-eight people to a party at the Pavilion that included music, singing, and an old-fashioned Virginia reel.[19]

In the summer there were card parties, dances, suppers, and picnics almost every day. Holidays in particular drew crowds into La Jolla. On July 4, 1898, the railroad brought an estimated 1,600 people into town to see the fireworks and an "illuminated dive" in which daredevil Horace Poole covered his body with oil and set himself afire before jumping into the ocean from a springboard placed over the caves.[20] High school students came for "straw rides" and an occasional "Tally Ho," or horse-drawn coach ride, while tourists gathered abalone shells by the shore at low tide.[21] Fishing was popular, and people regularly caught white sea bass, barracuda, spotted bay bass, calico, halibut, mackerel, yellowtail, and rock cod. They also organized sports. In 1899 a group of young people held a concert and dance to raise money for a tennis court; they also laid out golf links on the cliffs above the cove. In 1902 Anson Mills reported, "Golf is all the rage now. A great many of the ladies are playing, getting ready for the ladies' tournament next Saturday."[22]

Ellen and Virginia joined the card club that met at the Pavilion on Saturday nights.[23] They also invited neighbors over to play whist, a popular trick-taking card game that originated in eighteenth-century England. In February 1899 Ellen noted in her diary, "Mr. Kennedy and Mr. Robinson spent the evening. Played whist. Candy and oranges."[24] A whist club met on Friday afternoons at the Reading Room, and its members also socialized at one another's houses.[25]

The Scrippses became members of a women's literary and current events club that in 1899 became the La Jolla Woman's Club. Members met every Wednesday afternoon between September and June, gathering first at the La Jolla Hotel, next at the library's first Reading Room, and later in the Sunday school room of the Presbyterian church or in one another's houses.[26]

At a time when few women had college educations, clubs provided a venue in which their members could advance their knowledge and intellectual skills. Ellen researched women's literature, in particular, California poets, and contributed to a discussion entitled "The Literary Aspects of Genesis." Virginia, meanwhile, gave a talk entitled "Some of the Interesting Women Writers of This Century."[27] Club members also discussed current events such as U.S. territorial expansion following the Spanish-American War and women's suffrage.[28] In October 1899 Irene Robertson gave a paper entitled "Municipal Housekeeping," while Eleanor Mills spoke on the subject of British imperialism in Africa, or "Cape to Cairo." The club subsequently talked about the troubles in South Africa that would lead to the Boer War.[29]

In 1902 the La Jolla Woman's Club became the first club in California to join the General Federation of Women's Clubs.[30] The following year, members hosted a meeting of the County Federation that brought five railroad cars full of women to La Jolla for lunch and a program of music and papers.[31]

An active member of the club was the poet Rose Hartwick Thorpe, whom Ellen had met on her first trip to San Diego in 1890. At age sixteen Rose wrote "Curfew Must Not Ring Tonight," about a young heroine who prevents the death of her lover at the hands of Oliver Cromwell during the English Civil War. This poem, first published in the *Detroit Commercial Advertiser*, gained the attention of Queen Victoria and achieved "universal popularity"; it was translated into nearly every world language and recognized as a classic.[32] Rose often visited the Scripps sisters. Ellen described her as a "very pleasant, unassuming lady" and noted that her daughter "displays great artistic skill."[33] In 1901 Rose and her husband moved to a La Jolla bungalow known as Curfew Cottage, where she wrote *The White Lady of La Jolla* (1904), immortalizing a local legend about the death of a newlywed in one of the caves.[34]

The British writer and suffragist Beatrice Harraden (1864–1936) was another local celebrity. She often spent time in La Jolla with her friends Agnes and John Kendall, who visited from Waverly Ranch in El Cajon. Small, dark-haired, and bespectacled, she was known for her best-selling novel *Ships That Pass in the Night* (1893), about a serious-minded intellectual woman who falls in love with a fellow patient at a tuberculosis sanitarium in Switzerland. Beatrice published fourteen novels, short stories, and children's books and coauthored a travel guide, *Two Health Seekers in Southern California* (1897). Her short story about a Shropshire inn, "At the Green Dragon" (1894), inspired Anna Held to name her La Jolla cottage the Green Dragon, and the two women became friends.[35] During an early visit to La Jolla, Beatrice met Ellen Scripps's cousin, the journalist Fanny Bagby Blades, and Ellen's sister Annie. Ellen reported that the novelist "had a great deal to say of her admiration of Mrs. Blades, also of Annie. Of course, we didn't talk 'shop,'" referring to their mutual interest in the publishing business.[36] They appear to have kept in touch, for the Scripps archives contain a signed photograph of Beatrice with the words "Miss Scripps—With kindest greetings from Beatrice Harraden."

The atmosphere of early La Jolla affected the young people in town, some of whom went on to be writers or to get advanced educations. Seventeen-year-old Ellen Mills became a writer, starting by serving as La Jolla correspondent for the *San Diego Tribune*. She later became a published poet and co-owner of the *La Jolla Journal*. Harriet Cleary, daughter of Dr. and Mrs. George and Mary Cleary, went to Stanford in 1898.[37] Hazel Marjorie Woodruff received her undergraduate degree at the University of California, Berkeley, in 1905. She went on to teach history at National City High School and later served as a faculty member at a school for boys in Honolulu.[38]

Gardens and Wildflowers

Once settled into her new house, Ellen began to buy up adjacent properties in order to develop a large garden. In March 1899 she called on Eleanor Mills with a check for $250 (about $7,400) "for the two lots adjoining mine on the north."[39] In 1903 she bought the remaining six lots in Block 35—the site of South Molton Villa—for $3,000 (about

$83,400). She now owned approximately 2.5 acres of land bounded by Prospect Street, Coast Boulevard, Cuvier Street, and Eads Avenue.[40]

Kate Sessions supplied the earliest plants. In March 1897 Ellen wrote in her diary: "Will and self spent the day at La Jolla. Building going on all right. Met Miss Sessions there and made some arrangements for planting."[41] At that time, Sessions had just begun her career, which turned her into San Diego's preeminent botanist, horticulturalist, and landscape gardener. She had begun to plant trees in Balboa Park and to introduce California native plants into local gardens.

Ellen often brought seedlings from Miramar; in early January 1898 she "gathered quantities of flowers and took to La Jolla—violets, pansies, roses, carnations, and double petunias."[42] She planted vegetables and melons, despite the fact that squirrels, gophers, and rabbits were "making general havoc in the garden."[43] She also picked up various plants on her trips through the backcountry of San Diego.[44] Her early garden included roses and lilies, a wild cherry tree, two Torrey pines, and a dracaena that was eaten by William Froehlich's cow.[45]

In 1899 Sessions redesigned the garden, adding lawns, hedges, shrubbery, and a grouping of fifteen stone pines (*Pinus pinea*) grown from seeds that Ellen had brought from Italy.[46] Anson Mills, who detailed the comings and goings of visitors to La Jolla, wrote in his diary at the end of November, "Miss Sessions was here today. She is arranging the grounds at the Scripps Place."[47] By 1906 the landscaped garden, with paths, hedges, parterres, specimen trees, and a croquet ground, was open to anyone who wanted to enjoy the scenery and the view.[48] A female visitor "passed and winded around through the numerous walks in [Ellen's] beautiful flower garden . . . overlooking the ocean. . . . It is a beautiful home, colonial style and extensively improved."[49]

While Ellen was not a close friend of Kate Sessions, she appreciated her horticultural expertise and scientific interests. She occasionally visited Sessions's home near Balboa Park in the company of her sister-in-law the former Miss Peirce, now Katharine Scripps. In November 1899 they drove downtown and "spent the evening at Miss Sessions', who has a large collection of butterflies, beetles, and other entomological specimens."[50]

She also saw the horticulturalist at the 1915–16 Exposition, describing her as one of Katharine's "ancient old cronies . . . fat and flourishing."[51]

Ellen had long appreciated the beauty and novelty of California's wildflowers. On one occasion, Mrs. U. S. Grant, Jr., and friends came out to stay in the Green Dragon. Ellen and her cousin Lida filled the cottage with flowers: "The chicories (wild cucumber) which grow thereabouts in abundance we used for draping the mantle, windows, etc., and we filled everything we could find with flowers—poppies, cyclamen, yellow violets, painted cup, etc., etc. They were really lovely and were greatly admired by the guests, who came in numbers during the day."[52]

Ellen considered collecting wildflowers after being introduced to the work of an English botanist living in Bordighera, a northern Italian coastal town not far from the French Riviera. In February 1889 she viewed "a collection of some 800 watercolor paintings of the flowers of the Riviera" done by Rev. Clarence Bicknell, who had recently published his work and founded a museum. His works depicted the flowers of Liguria, an area known for its mild climate and spectacular natural beauty, and included anemones, ranunculus, and rock roses. Ellen thought that the paintings were "beautifully done, forming an interesting and valuable collection."[53]

In 1909 Ellen commissioned the artist Albert Valentien to paint wildflowers of California with the intention of publishing the set when completed. She first met the artist when he designed copper doors for her fireplace. Later she went to his house on Georgia Street in San Diego to see his paintings.[54] Impressed, she commissioned a thousand sheets that included trees, grasses, and ferns. In May 1909 she wrote, "Mr. Valentien came over to tell me that he 'is the happiest man in San Diego.' Is very enthusiastic about the 'collection' of wildflowers he will make and very grateful for the order."[55] He visited several times over the course of the next few years to bring samples of dried wildflowers and to show her his growing portfolio.[56]

Improvements by Irving J. Gill

Ellen also made the acquaintance of Irving J. Gill, who at that time was a partner in the architectural firm Hebbard & Gill. His posthumous reputation as a pioneer of the modernist movement in architecture can be explained in part by the survival of the La Jolla structures commissioned by Ellen.

In 1899 Gill drew up plans for enlarging South Molton's kitchen and adding a modern, flat-roofed wing on the east side of the house, replacing a porch.[57] E.W. approved of his ideas, telling Ellen, "I think Gill is just old enough, just sensible enough, and with just enough ambition to fit into the job."[58] At Gill's suggestion, Ellen repainted the house, from yellow with white trim to poinsettia red with green trim. She noted in her diary, "Mr. Gill and Miss [Anna] Held here to lunch. The former gave certain points of advice about the building and repair, advises repainting the house."[59]

Gill returned in 1904 to make additional changes to South Molton Villa. According to Ellen, the young man "made several practical and artistic suggestions" that included rebuilding the chimney, preventing water from leaking into the cellar, remodeling the kitchen, adding a tile porch, and installing new cabinetry.[60] In December she viewed one of the structures that he was building at First Avenue and Robinson Street in San Diego, describing it as "cheap, concrete, and artistic."[61] She recommended it to her cousin Lida Scripps, who moved into the cottage in April 1905.[62]

Ellen had Gill draw up plans for a library to be located in a separate building west of the main house. Construction started in the spring of 1905 with the removal of shrubbery and the arrival of a railway car full of cobblestones from Pacific Beach.[63] A conservatory was built on the south side of the library and furnished with plants by Sessions.[64]

"Old La Jolla"

In 1905 La Jolla had yet to experience the kinds of "improvements" that would transform this sleepy summer colony into a year-round tourist destination. There were no graded streets, cement sidewalks, or gas or electric lights in the houses. Water trickled into the village through a two-inch pipe, providing barely enough for daily needs. Nathan Rannells, owner of a livery stable, recalled, "Many a night I have stayed up long after midnight to fill the tank and troughs for my horses."[65] There were only three bathtubs in town and no indoor plumbing or sewers. At the center of the village, a cobblestone trough with a bougainvillea-covered pergola provided water for horses and dogs.[66]

The general store, Chase and Ludington's, stood at the corner of Wall Street and Herschel Avenue, serving as both the post office and, for a time, the local saloon. At five o'clock in the evening, many of the 350 villagers gathered at the post office to pick up their mail and exchange gossip.[67] Horse-drawn wagons arrived in the village several times a week with meat and produce. Louis, a rancher and butcher, brought "good meat and cheap, no extra charge for choice cuts," while Charlie, "the small shriveled up old Chinaman," drove a one-horse vegetable wagon. Charles Dearborn's cow, meanwhile, provided the town's milk supply.[68]

One early resident described La Jolla as "a very friendly place, not at all like the small towns of the East."[69] People were neighborly, dropping in for visits rather than making formal calls. According to Ellen, "It didn't take a very big house, or a classical program, or an elaborate menu to entertain as evening guests the whole community—men, women and children. For our literary tastes were not hypocritical; nor were our appetites capricious, and we always had a 'feast of reason and a flow of soul,' even if it was of light weight."[70]

Years later, Ellen looked back on this period with nostalgia, despite the fact that she played an important role in the development process. She recalled her feelings about La Jolla in a 1919 speech given to the La Jolla Woman's Club:

How we loved her [La Jolla], in those far off days, unvexed by city turmoil, untroubled by national and international problems! How we loved the sunshine that flooded the homes, glorious sunsets that empurpled the seas and bejeweled the hills; the white surf that lapped her feet; her own little mountain that crowned and fortressed her. How we loved her shell-strewn beaches, her unstable sand dunes, her legend-haunted caves, her rock-bound pools teeming with life and color, her wave-carved Cathedral Rock, even her dusty roads and grass grown foot paths which lured us to unexplored wonders of sea and land.[71]

CHAPTER 5

A Cold Shower of Gold

By the turn of the century, Ellen was a wealthy woman in her own right. She owned a considerable amount of stock in the various Scripps companies, and she continued to invest in the newspapers that E.W. started in the West. In 1894 she held stock in the *Detroit Evening News*, the *Cleveland Press*, the *Cincinnati Post*, the *St. Louis Chronicle*, and the *Kentucky Post*. She also owned part of the family farm in Rushville and half of the ranch at Miramar. Her assets totaled $201,800 (about $5.74 million in 2016 dollars).[1]

She did not, however, have as much money as some of her male siblings. The incorporation of the *Evening News* in 1876 had provided her with only two shares of stock, while James, the founder of the paper, got thirty, and George took sixteen due to his ability to provide ready cash. Ellen never mentioned this as a grievance, but she must have chafed at it, for her work on the paper was every bit as valuable as that of her younger brother. E.W. later recalled: "George H. Scripps got more than his share, considering his ability and the work done, of the wealth won by the joint family effort in building up the Scripps institution, while Ellen for many years, I can see now, got less than her share."[2]

George H. Scripps

George, three years younger than his sister Ellen, had never married. He had returned home injured after the Civil War and spent nearly a decade on the family farm in Rushville before moving to Detroit. Hardened by his years in uniform, he drank heavily, smoked cigars, chewed tobacco, gambled, and outraged his church-going brother James by his liaisons with less-than-respectable women. One particularly scandalous episode forced him to leave Detroit for Europe in 1878. As he grew older, his taste for sexual adventure became less tolerable to family members, particularly those who had to live with him. His sister Annie went so far as to tell him that he was a "nasty bad man" whom she could not trust with her female friends.[3]

George may not have been respectable or easy to live with, but he was rich. He held shares in the *Detroit Evening News*, the *Cleveland Press*, the *Cincinnati Post*, the *Kentucky Post*, and the *St. Louis Chronicle*.[4] He also owned a considerable amount of Detroit real estate and some shares in Colorado gold mines. According to family members, he lived like a miser, rarely spending any of his fortune. George's role in the family was that of "the money getter and the money saver."[5]

Ellen occasionally took her brother to task for his unwillingness to spend money, even on his own family. In 1888 she criticized him for "rolling in wealth" while other members of the family were "drudging in poverty." She suggested that he help their brother Will in business or loan him money so that he could start a business of his own. She told George, "What use is money anyway, except for what it brings and why shouldn't it be better to spend our money on those who are of our own flesh and blood."[6]

George, however, decided to distribute his money after his death rather than during his life. And the end did not seem far away. By the 1890s he was seriously ill with what doctors described as a "catarrh of the stomach . . . a result of a worn out constitution."[7] He was lame in one leg and suffered from mild depression. One morning he greeted E.W. by saying, "What is the good of living any longer anyhow?"[8]

Many family members thought that George would die without making a will, particularly given his tendency to drag his feet when it came to making important decisions.[9] If he resided in the state of Ohio, his property would be divided among those siblings who shared the same parents: James, Ellen, and Will. If he died as a resident of Michigan, his estate might be shared among all of his brothers and sisters, including Elizabeth, Fred, Virginia, and E.W.[10] It did not occur to anyone that George might settle his estate in such a way as to deprive James of control of the Scripps Publishing Company, particularly given the terms of the quadripartite agreement signed in 1887. This arrangement had ensured that the major stockholders would not sell their stock to "outsiders." Only Ellen declined to participate in what she considered a legally dubious scheme.

In the early 1890s E.W. made a concerted effort to draw George—and his money—out of James's camp and into his own so that he could retain control of the *Cleveland Press,* a paper that he had founded as a young man.[11] E.W. feared that John Sweeney, James's protégé, or Edgar B. Whitcomb, who had married James's daughter Anna in 1891, would be placed in control of the newspaper. Neither of them thought of it as anything other than a "money making machine." E.W., on the other hand, had a personal investment in the paper. Through his hard work he had transformed it from a small local paper into one that he considered "the superior of the [*Detroit Evening*] *News* in every point save its receipts."[12]

Ellen supported her brother in his efforts to maintain, even gain, control of the Scripps newspapers. From her point of view, E.W. wanted to invest in the business, while James and George only sought immediate profits. George thought it was all very well for E.W. to build up the business for future generations. "He is not living for the present. James and I are. We want our money now." She added sharply, "James wants to build churches, endow hospitals, establish art museums, beautify his home. And George, I suppose, wants enough to furnish him in decent clothing at least, which his present means don't seem to do." She admitted that her attitude toward James was antagonistic but claimed that, as a stockholder, she had every right to act according to her own best interests.[13]

She also helped to convince George that their younger brother would be a better business partner than James. The *Cleveland Press*, the *St. Louis Chronicle*, and the *Cincinnati Post* were growing rapidly in both advertising and circulation due to E.W.'s policy of building up, not "squeezing," the papers.[14] At the same time, many of the family's other investments—a wholesale grocery store, a planing mill, and a lumber firm—had become money-losing headaches.[15] She and George spent five months in California with E.W. and his family at Miramar, taking horseback rides through the canyons and picnicking at Del Mar. George was soon on his younger brother's side.

George paid dearly for his alliance with E.W. Soon after his return to Detroit in April 1892, he found that he had been kicked out of his old office at the *Evening News*, a room that he considered his sanctuary or "den." He was moved to an upper-floor office in the Lafayette Street building at a time when his lameness made it difficult for him to get up stairs. The reasons given added insult to injury, according to Ellen, "namely that some of his friends were objectionable persons, and his habits—of smoking, playing cards, chess, etc., in his office—were a bad example and precedent to the employees." At the same time, he discovered that his bedroom at James's house had been moved from a large, sunny room overlooking the garden to an uninviting little room overlooking the barn, stable yard, and rubbish enclosure. He could get no air at night without leaving his door open, leaving him exposed to the view of servants going up and down the back stairs.[16]

George considered both moves to be calculated affronts, particularly given his disability. He left James's house, never to return, taking up residence first with his brother Will and later with his niece Floy and her husband, William Kellogg, in Detroit. According to Ellen, her brother felt that this had been "a deliberate attempt to mortify him, and to define his position to both children and servants as an inferior, and outside the family pale."[17] George attributed the insults to both James and his son-in-law George Booth, who was increasingly active in the family business.

Ellen regretted the hostilities between her brothers but knew that she could do little to change them. She wrote, "I feel now like one of those old worn-out dilapidated horses that is driven blindfolded and trembling with fear into the arena, hearing the clash and clang of weapons but knowing nothing of what it means though instinctively guessing what it portends—a neutral thing, the victim alike of friend and foe. I am essentially being made a scapegoat for other people's mistakes."[18]

James made one attempt to restore his old alliance with George. In August 1892 he explained to him how dangerous it was to side with E.W., who was "unboundedly ambitious. . . . He is not satisfied to stand on his own bottom but wants to build his fortunes on ours." He regretted that George and Ellen were blinded to the situation and predicted that in a few years E.W. "will be all the dominant power and the great capitalist of the concern."[19]

George, however, refused to return to James's side. Instead, he turned over his proxy to his younger brother and in 1894 joined E.W. and his new partner, Milton A. McRae, in the Scripps-McRae League. The three men pooled their stock and put it in the hands of E.W. as trustee. In this way, E.W. became the controlling stockholder of the *Cleveland Press* and the *St. Louis Chronicle*, as he already was that of the *Cincinnati Post*. He did not intend to interfere with James's management of the *Evening News*, but he hoped to promote a *"rapprochement of the two divisions of the concern."*[20] George, meanwhile, gained an office and position of responsibility in the firm "far beyond anything he has ever before had."[21]

While he was in San Diego, George also made a last will and testament, disinheriting James and his children and leaving the bulk of his estate to E.W. and Ellen. According to his sister Virginia, George "declared he would so leave his property that J.E.'s sons-in-law should never have a cent of it."[22]

In the years before his death, George communicated with James only indirectly. He did not even go into his brother's house to attend the party marking the twenty-fifth anniversary of the *Evening News* but instead waited in a rented carriage at the edge of the estate. McRae begged him to come in, "but George was in his most stubborn mood, angrily refused and emphasized it by bursting out with the remark that he 'would be damned if he would ever come into that house again.'"[23]

George's final illness began in late September 1899. He suffered from constant pain, became depressed, and often exhibited anger during business meetings. With the encouragement of his siblings, he went to a sanitarium in Asheville, North Carolina, to recover in the high altitude of the Appalachian Mountains. His condition, however, did not improve. In mid-October E.W. telegraphed his sister that George's recovery was impossible.[24] He asked her to come east, as his niece Floy had done, to attend to him, adding, "There is only one reason why I might wish you at Asheville. It is a delicate matter, this of acting for George. If he recovers, he will declare all efforts to have been useless and all expense wasted. If he does not recover, there will be plenty of people to attribute wrong motives to anyone who does anything."[25]

Ellen left San Diego on November 5, 1899, for North Carolina. When she arrived, she found George in bed, weak and thin and pale, troubled with nausea, taking only beef extract for nourishment. He was glad to see his sister, and they spoke every afternoon. As the weeks passed, however, his mental state deteriorated, and he showed "great mental disturbance and forgetfulness" more than ever before.[26]

In January 1900 George was moved from North Carolina to San Diego aboard a private railway car, the *Oceanic*.[27] He spent his final days at Miramar, where he continued to suffer from pleurisy and stomach distention. He ate very little and only rarely sat outside in a tent or was wheeled through the garden in a chair. The doctor finally brought back a blood analysis showing cancer.[28] Ellen sat up with him during the last two nights of his life, watching him suffer with pain that could only be eased with opiates. He died on Friday, April 13, 1900, at the age of sixty.[29] After a funeral at Miramar, his remains were sent to Los Angeles for cremation and then to Rushville to be buried in the family plot on Easter Sunday.[30]

Lawsuits

George died with an estate valued at $1.7 million (about $49.5 million). It included a one-third partnership in the News and Tribune Printing Company and two-fifths interest in the Scripps-McRae League, in addition to real estate, mining interests, and industrial stocks. As promised, he left James nothing. Instead, he bequeathed his sixteen shares of capital stock of the Evening News Association of Detroit to E.W. and his twenty-three shares of capital stock of the *Cleveland Press*, along with a smaller number of shares of the *Cincinnati Post*, to Ellen. He gave his niece Floy his interest in the *St. Louis Chronicle* and his sister Virginia eight hundred shares of capital stock of the *Cincinnati Post*.

Neither Will nor Fred inherited any newspaper stock. Instead, George left the former one-half of his interest in all real estate held jointly between himself and James in Detroit and Wayne County, Michigan. He also appointed Will one of his executors, along with E.W. To Fred he left $10,000 (about $291,000) and 566 shares of capital stock of the Edison Illuminating Company of Detroit; he also wiped out Fred's debts to him.

James was astonished to learn that his brother's death deprived him of a controlling stake in the *Evening News*, "his own little ewe lamb," and he was furious to realize that George's shares would go to E.W., with whom James had a long-running feud. In fact, he went so far as to call the will and testament a "legacy of hate."[31]

James decided to contest the will, thinking that, at the very least, he could force E.W. to sell him George's stock in the *News*. In May 1900 Ellen reported an "unpleasant conference" with family members and lawyers in Detroit.[32] She warned James that if it were left up to her, she would fight to the bitter end, until "every penny of the estate had been swallowed by the courts and lawyers." She pointed out the danger of creating a never-ending family feud that could only lead to "'a legacy of dishonor and disunion.'"[33]

The attempts to break George's will produced eleven separate lawsuits over the course of a decade. One involved the question of George's residence—Detroit or Cleveland—as the probate of the will and the administration of the estate would be different under the laws of Michigan and Ohio. Another charged that George had been unduly influenced in the creation of his will; "James E. Scripps has practically declared, under oath, that George H. was crazy, and that I was a scoundrel," summarized E.W.[34]

The fight over the Scripps estate attracted the attention of rival newspapers, relaying the scandal from Detroit to San Diego. In 1900 the *San Diego Union* produced an article alleging that E.W. had influenced his brother in the disposition of his estate.[35] This was one of the few times that Ellen wished she did not live in "a little village like La Jolla where one person's business is everyone's business."[36]

The worst part for Ellen was being accused of helping E.W. gain control of George's estate. James wrote to her soon after their brother's death, "I will not go into the way poor George was deluded, imposed upon, and enthralled to secure the control of his property. . . . But you seem blind to the fact that the Scripps-McRae League aspires to dominate all the property of the family." He compared E.W. to the railroad developer and speculator Jason "Jay" Gould, a robber baron who "built his fortune by the ruin of everyone else with whom he was associated." He could not believe that she would be party to "so wicked a crime," adding, "You are really the key to the whole matter. Without your support he could go no further in his schemes."[37]

She was also subjected to a verbal tirade from her brother Will, who in 1900 was both ill and emotionally unstable.[38] She told E.W., "I was utterly unprepared for the onslaught that he began as soon as we entered the house; and sat literally benumbed into silence."[39] Fortunately, Will's wife, Katharine, had no interest in pursuing a divisive quarrel. She encouraged her husband to come to terms with E.W. and accept the fact that he had inherited a half-million dollars' worth of Detroit real estate rather than even more valuable newspaper stock.[40]

Elizabeth Scripps Sharp was more difficult to pacify, having been left out of her brother's will entirely. At seventy years of age, she was practically blind and deaf and required constant medical care.[41] Concerned about her welfare, Ellen and E.W. offered her a generous annuity. Elizabeth refused, however, as she and her daughter, Mary Billemeyer, had been encouraged to believe that they could get much more money if George's will was broken.[42] Ellen was appalled, writing, "I feel hot with humiliation that any one of my blood should be so lax in morals as to deliberately rob a dead man."[43] When she made her own will in 1903, she specified that if George's wishes were set aside, "and my brother James and my sister Elizabeth inherit a portion of his estate, then I revoke all bequests to them, or to such of them as inherit."[44]

As the contest over George's estate dragged on, the Scripps brothers and their lawyers began to approach a settlement. Jacob Chandler Harper, general counsel for the Scripps newspapers, represented the executors, while Elliot G. Stevenson worked for James. In 1903 they came to a tentative agreement by which E.W. would sell to James the sixteen shares of *Evening News* stock that E.W. had inherited in exchange for all of James's holdings in papers controlled by the Scripps-McRae League and pay him an additional $200,000 (about $5.6 million) in cash.[45]

Litigation filed by James's protégé Sweeney, occasioned by the quadripartite agreement, kept the family quarrel alive for many more years. The Scrippses revisited business decisions that dated back to the 1880s, stirring up accusations of unethical practices, faulty bookkeeping, and irregular methods of business.[46] E.W. went so far as to write, "James E. was the first to invent some new method of helping himself out of a common till."[47] James, meanwhile, thought that E.W. had deceived and defrauded him, having learned of the secret deal made with Sweeney in 1887. Ellen began to work through her brothers' correspondence in order to provide background for the lawyers. She read hundreds of letters, appending a brief summary to each.

By the end of 1905 James was an aging, tired man ready to end the fight. He traveled to California that winter to spend time with Will's family in Altadena and to visit Ellen in La Jolla. He spent his seventy-first birthday at South Molton Villa, surrounded by family members, including E.W. and his wife. Ellen told her younger brother, "It has made me very happy to see how thoroughly James has entered into this life. I had thought he would be restless and critical. Instead of which it seems to have opened up a new phase of life to him. I have been surprised to see how appreciative he is of everything, how content and happy he has been."[48]

In May 1906 Ellen went to Detroit to be with James during his final hours. She wrote that he was now in a condition more "lethargic than comatose. He lies as if asleep most of the time but is easily aroused to take food and medicine and respond to any question with a nod or shake of the head. Last night when I came in he was sleeping apparently as naturally and unconsciously as a little child. Once or twice today he has recognized me, and kissed me. But he does not talk or even try to speak."[49] He died so softly and quietly that only the experienced eye and touch of the nurse detected it. Ellen quoted observers at the death of Saint Bernard of Clairvaux: "We thought him dying when he slept, and sleeping when he died."[50]

George's estate was finally settled in 1910 after the Michigan Supreme Court rendered the opinion that the quadripartite agreement was illegal.[51] Many of his assets had already been distributed to beneficiaries who had pledged to return the monies if the case was lost. His personal effects went to Ellen. In early 1911 she received a package that contained, among other things, a pair of opera glasses, some old copper coins, a small bottle of gold ore, a gold nugget, several rings and watches, a cribbage box, and an empty coin purse.[52]

For years, Ellen had wanted George to do something with his money, writing, "If he could only be brought to realize the opportunities and resources to be made available by the judicious expenditure of his capital a new life would open up to him—capabilities and interests far reaching and universal instead of limited and selfish—such as he has never experienced before in his investments."[53]

As her brother had never given any of his money to charitable organizations, Ellen decided to do it herself, starting with the Marine Biological Association, now the Scripps Institution of Oceanography. This also would be her first plunge into philanthropy, and, perhaps for that reason, she copied down the poem by Lily A. Long, "The Diver," that first appeared in *Harper's Magazine* in May 1906, altering some of the lines:

I have plunged into life, oh God,
As a diver into the sea
Knowing and fearing naught
Save thine old command to me

To grope, and search for the truth,
Hidden wherever it be.
So I search, for I trust in Thy word
Thou Lord of the Truth and of me![54]

Like the diver in the poem, she used philanthropy to cleanse herself—
and the Scripps name—of the scandal that had tarnished them for a
decade. She also ensured that on her death her fortune would end up
going to organizations dedicated to the good of society, not in the hands
of family members.

CHAPTER 6

Down to the Sea

Ellen began her career as a philanthropist with a decision to fund a group of marine biologists working out of the boathouse of the Hotel del Coronado. The Marine Biological Association, the brainchild of Professor William E. Ritter of the University of California, Berkeley, became the Scripps Institution for Biological Research (later the Scripps Institution of Oceanography) after Ellen decided to provide a significant endowment. She asked that their first permanent building be named after her brother George. Apart from her fascination with the natural world and her love of the Pacific Ocean, she felt that the legacy would counteract the negativity caused by the very public family quarrel over George's estate. She wrote, "It is not by trying to wipe out old sores and injuries but by substituting useful and worthy ambitions and objects to be attained that reformation must be wrought."[1]

In the nineteenth and early twentieth centuries, the ocean challenged contemporaries already keen to comprehend and control vast spaces such as the Arctic, the African jungle, the heavens, and the interior of the earth itself. Matthew Fontaine Maury, author of the pioneering *Physical Geography of the Sea* (1855), compared the study of the sea to astronomy: "There were in the depths untold wonders and inexplicable mysteries."[2] Jules Verne, in *Twenty Thousand Leagues under the Sea* (1870), imagined the ocean as an untamed frontier, "a vast reservoir of nature," containing thousands of species discoverable using the tools of Linnaean science.[3]

After 1870 millions of Europeans and Americans—tourists, business travelers, and emigrants—gained direct experience of the open sea. The rapidly expanding industrial economy made it possible for middle-class people to spend leisure time at the beach sea bathing, collecting and displaying seashells, and yachting. It also produced technologies such as the steamship that popularized ocean travel. The construction of the first Atlantic submarine telegraph cable in 1866, meanwhile, was a communications breakthrough touted as the eighth wonder of the world.[4]

Like her contemporaries, Ellen spent a good deal of time on the shore. She waded through tide pools, encouraged by the popular writer Charles Kingsley, who saw the examination of nature as a wholesome, morally uplifting activity. His *Glaucus; or, The Wonders of the Shore* (1855) described natural history as a way to feed the imagination, develop a methodical and scientific habit of mind, and marvel at the "fantastic variety" of God's creation.[5] In La Jolla she enjoyed the sight of seals "disporting on rocks" and admired the "beautiful phosphorescence in the ocean at night." She wrote in July 1901, "Spent the evening on the beach watching . . . the waves full of a soft liquid fire."[6]

She also visited aquariums, newly popular tourist destinations that revealed the astonishing variety of sea life being discovered by deep-sea dredges. The world's first public aquarium opened at the London Zoo (1853) with more than three hundred different types of marine life, including fish and species of invertebrates. Many other public aquariums and marine research stations followed over the next forty years.[7] In 1882 Ellen visited the Brighton Aquarium, prominently located in an English seaside resort, which had the largest display tank in the world at that time. She described it as larger but less interesting than the one that she had seen in Berlin, though she enjoyed feeding the sea lions. She also viewed the aquarium in London.[8]

Soon after moving to La Jolla, Virginia developed a large collection of sea mosses, shells, and live organisms. She decorated her bedroom with abalone shells, large strands of kelp, and a "sea moss 'frieze'" made from pressed and dried mosses between dark wood moldings. She draped a fishing net over her mantel, anchored by shells and sand dollars, and created a tableau of lobster shells and barnacles within the fireplace.[9] In January 1902 Ellen wrote that her sister "brought up a number of the sea animals which are interesting to watch in movement and structure—abalone, sea urchins, sea slugs, pea rabbits, sea anemone, starfish, serpent star, keyhole limpets, blue slugs, etc." After finding "more live treasures" at the beach, Virginia bought an aquarium in Pacific Beach.[10] She described her activities in a poem:

> Lulled to sleep have I been each night
> By the ocean's deep roar in its might
> As it surged and beat on the rocky shore
> That's but a stone's throw from the door
>
> Each morn have I waked to gaze with delight
> On old ocean aglow with rosy sun light
> Many days have I spent on the seashore
> Gathering sea mosses and shells galore[11]

In 1895 Ellen met Mary Snyder, one of the leading botanists in the United States and an authority on marine algae.[12] Ellen admired her collection of over sixty different varieties of sea mosses, "all of which she has mounted beautifully, classified, and given their scientific names."[13] Ellen and Virginia often visited the home Snyder shared with her husband, a retired German professor, in Pacific Beach. In 1898 the former wrote, "Jenny and self drove to Pacific Beach. Spent an hour with the Schneiders [Snyders] looking at Mrs. S.'s collection of algae."[14] Later that year, the naturalist came to lunch "and gave names to Jenny's collection of sea mosses."[15]

Mapping the Deep

In the early twentieth century, oceanography was a relatively new field galvanized by advances in dredging technology. In the 1870s the HMS *Challenger* expedition surveyed nearly 70,000 nautical miles, cataloged over

4,000 previously unknown species, and set records for sounding (down to 26,850 feet) and dredging (from over 18,000 feet).[16] The expedition's findings, published in fifty volumes, laid the groundwork for marine science and deep-sea exploration. Inspired by the work of their British counterparts, American scientists pioneered the next generation of dredging technology. They also began to develop research laboratories, including the Marine Biological Laboratory at Woods Hole (1888), Hopkins Marine Laboratory (1892), and the Puget Sound Biological Station (1903).[17]

Dr. William Ritter, the founder of what became the Scripps Institution of Oceanography, viewed the study of marine life as a window into the origins of life itself. A Harvard-trained zoologist, he believed that the study of organisms in their natural environment could help scientists understand "the vast scale on which things are done in the ocean, and the literally infinite complexity of cause and law there in operation."[18] That study also might help to substantiate Charles Darwin's controversial theory of evolution.

Ritter first visited San Diego in 1891 with his new bride, Mary Bennett Ritter, a young medical doctor. He recently had been appointed head of the Zoology Department at the University of California, Berkeley, and was completing his PhD dissertation on the retrograde eyes of the blind goby, a fish found under the rocks below Point Loma.[19] He and his wife met and befriended an important future supporter, Dr. Fred Baker, a well-known local surgeon and expert on mollusks who lived at Roseville on Point Loma with his wife, Dr. Charlotte Baker.

An ambitious man, Ritter dreamed of establishing a world-class facility on the Pacific coast. Between 1892 and 1902 Ritter and his colleagues set up temporary research sites at Pacific Grove near Monterey, Avalon Bay on Santa Catalina Island, and San Pedro harbor in Los Angeles. However, they had been unable to persuade a donor to take responsibility for a permanent biological laboratory.

In 1903 Ritter returned to San Diego on the advice of his friend Baker, who thought that "the splendid bay at San Diego should not be overlooked. . . . [F]or such work as you are planning, I feel sure San Diego offers the greatest chances of any point on the coast."[20]

Baker also promised that funds for a research laboratory could be raised from the wealthy residents of San Diego, in particular, the Scripps family. Baker played poker with E.W. and knew that he might be interested in funding a scientific endeavor, particularly since he had just inherited a considerable amount of newspaper stock from his brother George. Baker told Ritter, "He takes no interest in biology, but has come to the rescue generously. If you could interest him and his sister, Miss Ellen Scripps, they might put your whole project on its feet. . . . They are reputed to be worth several millions."[21]

Baker's recommendation was sufficient enough to get both Ellen and E.W. to invest in the project. The Scrippses had known the Baker family from their early years in Rushville. They also relied on the Bakers' professional services. Dr. Fred Baker was an eye, ear, nose, and throat specialist occasionally used by Scripps family members. Dr. Charlotte Baker was a general practitioner whom Ellen first consulted in 1893 with a bruised rib following a road trip to Julian.[22] They also knew the couple as musicians who played the violin at concerts at the Pavilion and the Green Dragon colony.[23]

In early 1903 E.W. sent Baker a check for $500 (about $13,900 in 2016 dollars), adding that his sister could be relied on to contribute $100 "and more if necessary."[24] The money would be used to establish a biological laboratory in the Hotel del Coronado's boathouse at Glorietta Bight.[25] Manuel Cabral, one of the best Portuguese fishermen in San Diego, would do the deep-sea dredging work using a rented schooner. Ritter and his staff planned to camp alongside tourists in the midst of Tent City, a popular vacation retreat located along a ten-mile isthmus known as the Silver Strand.

Investing in Science

Ellen first met Ritter on March 27, 1903, when she attended his public lecture in downtown San Diego. She and her companions were clearly inspired by his talk, because a few days later, "all but self went to Pacific Beach this afternoon, got plenty of sea pansies and bubble shells."[26] A week later, she ordered Richard Lydekker's *New Natural History* (1890), a six-volume set containing 72 colored plates and 1,600 engravings of mammals, birds, reptiles, fishes, and invertebrates.[27]

During the summer of 1903 Ellen spent time with Ritter and his colleagues at Coronado. In mid-July the scientist called at South Molton Villa and spent an hour, "greatly interested in Jenny's specimens," some of which had been collected in Hawaii the previous year. Shortly afterward, Ellen made two trips to the biological laboratory with Virginia and E.W.[28] The latter made a significant impression on Ritter, who later recalled "this unique person cruising around in the laboratory among the workers, to see for himself what was going on." He speculated that this was the newspaper magnate's first sight of anything like a scientific laboratory, because he went from table to table, inspecting whatever was visible.[29]

In August 1903 E.W. and Ellen hosted Ritter and his colleagues to Sunday dinner at Miramar. They were joined by Fred Baker and his collecting companion H. P. Wood, secretary of the Chamber of Commerce, who turned the discussion to the possibility of creating a permanent biological station in San Diego. After that conversation, a letter of intent was drawn up for the purpose of forming a marine research association. E.W. reminded Baker that he did not want to be "personally prominent" on the board of the new institution: "The real active members of the society should be gentlemen and ladies who are interested in biology, and who have leisure time to fill out such as I have not got."[30]

Ellen and Virginia later stopped in Berkeley following a trip to Mount Shasta, intending to see their neighbor Anna Held's sister. Unable to locate her, they spent the afternoon at the university, where they met Ritter and his colleague Charles A. Kofoid, "both of whom interested themselves very kindly in me," wrote Ellen. She noted that Ritter "insisted on our going home with him and seeing his wife who is ill in bed but who received us kindly."[31]

Ritter took the opportunity to impress on Ellen the importance of funding a permanent biological station in San Diego. He recalled, "I took them home with me, after showing them the university, got Miss Ellen into my study alone and succeeded surely in working up her interest still further, and also in giving her more insight into our plans and needs."[32] He hoped to create an "organized unit of biological research" in which salaried staff members made a coordinated effort to investigate marine life and share their findings. He modeled his idea on the practices of astronomical observatories, where scientists worked as a team, and on the activities of the Liverpool Marine Biological Committee, with its laboratory on the Isle of Man.[33] He found Miss Scripps to be receptive to the idea, if not yet sure of the part she would play: "There is no doubt about the genuineness of her interest and the intelligence of it too. . . . I do not believe the idea of making the whole enterprise hers, so that it might be named after her, has seriously entered into her thoughts as yet."[34]

The San Diego Marine Biological Association, founded at the end of September 1903, drew up a mission statement that included a plan "to carry on a biological and hydrographic survey of the waters of the Pacific Ocean adjacent to the coast of Southern California; to build and maintain a public aquarium and museum; and to prosecute such other kindred undertakings as the Board of Trustees may from time to time deem it wise to enter upon."[35] E.W. had insisted that a public aquarium be part of the long-term plan. Trustees included Homer Peters, president; Ellen Browning Scripps, vice president; Julius Wangenheim, treasurer; Dr. Fred Baker, secretary; and W. E. Ritter, scientific director. E. W. Scripps and James MacMullen of the *San Diego Union* served as additional board members. E.W. and Ellen each agreed to provide $1,500 (about $41,700) per year, as did Peters. E.W. also offered the use of his yacht, the *Loma*, for dredging.[36]

As early as 1903 Ellen and E.W. had discussed the idea of moving the biological laboratory to La Jolla. The latter asked about the ownership of the pavilion, located just south of Rocky Point, used for dances and other public entertainments. Ellen wrote that he had a "view to [the] Biological Station using it for workroom."[37]

Ritter also thought that a move to La Jolla would be beneficial. The Coronado boathouse was not steady enough for microscopic work with high magnifying lenses; it also lacked running seawater. La Jolla, meanwhile, offered many advantages, particularly if they could secure a location above the cove. The abyssal depth of the sea could be reached at a short distance from the shore, and there was clean ocean water and rocky shores for collecting. Ritter later wrote, "Rocky shores, mud-flats, kelp-beds, tide-pools, open ocean and almost land-locked bays" made it an ideal base for biological research.[38]

In early 1905 the Marine Biological Association secured a temporary lease of land in La Jolla Park, just above Alligator Point (the site of the La Jolla Cove Bridge Club), and began to plan a new laboratory. The architectural firm of Hebbard & Gill designed a small wooden building, sixty feet long and twenty-four feet wide, with an aquarium-museum. Fund-raising began that spring when Dr. Fred Baker led a "stirring discussion" at a meeting of the La Jolla Improvement Association. He and Rev. J. L. Pearson of Union Church collected over $1,200 (about $33,300) from La Jolla residents. Another substantial donation came from Harvard-based biologist Alexander Agassiz, who visited San Diego in March 1905 and provided books and scientific equipment worth $1,000 to $2,000 (about $27,800 to $55,600).[39] Virginia Scripps gave $300 (about $8,300) for the purchase of glass tanks and display cases, while biologist Mary Snyder donated her collection of mounted specimens of local seaweed.[40]

As soon as "the little green laboratory at the cove" was completed, Ritter and his colleagues began conducting surveys of the coast and giving weekly lectures to the La Jolla community. The staff included Kofoid, who concentrated on single-cell creatures known as protozoa, and Harry B. Torrey, who studied jellies and sea anemones. Sixteen students and several visiting professors also worked in the laboratory over the summer.

In July 1905 Ellen attended Ritter's "biological lecture," delivered at the pavilion, and Kofoid's talk on ocean "phosphorescence," a phenomenon caused by plankton that emitted a brilliant blue-green light at night.[41] Later in the year, she brought Virginia and twenty friends to the laboratory's open day to view an exhibit of "sea specimens" and hear a talk by Dr. Ritter.[42] She also visited the lab on her own, as she was interested in Kofoid's "microscopic work—especially of the animalcule forming phosphorescence for the ocean."[43] When the scientists and their students were invited to Miramar on a holiday weekend in 1906, she went along as chaperone for the ladies.[44] She also enjoyed some lighthearted entertainment presented to the public as a "Celebration at the Biological Station. Special Attractions!" and including "starfish stunts under the direction of Dr. Jennings," a fish-eating contest, the "latest summer styles" in plankton nets, and "the muzzling of the great eel, Pussy, for the protection of visitors."[45]

At the end of 1905 Ellen talked with both E.W. and Ritter about creating an endowment for the Marine Biological Institution.[46] By this time, many of the difficulties surrounding George's estate had been resolved, even if lawsuits were ongoing. E.W., as trustee, planned to make a partial distribution of the estate in 1906 and to present Ellen with stock and cash worth $38,500 (about $1.05 million).[47] She felt that this would be a good time to remember her late brother and his love of the seashore through a large gift.

She decided to provide an endowment of $50,000 (about $1.36 million) to the institution, announcing her decision on January 30, 1906, during a lunchtime meeting at South Molton Villa. President Benjamin Ide Wheeler of the University of California, Berkeley, traveled to La Jolla for the occasion, together with Judge James W. McKinley, chairman of the regents' committee. According to Ellen, both seemed "greatly pleased with La Jolla and with prospects of Laboratory and Association," though they could not commit to provide the institution with any further funds from the university's budget.[48] They did, however, contribute resources toward the publication of scientific work and the loan of some apparatus and books.

William E. Ritter

Ellen was particularly glad to support a man whose worldview she both understood and appreciated. Ritter had progressive views about both science and society, stressing the value of cooperation over competition. According to one naturalist, "He believed that organisms are best understood in the context of their physical environment and best studied by specialists working together. These views were a departure from those of many of his contemporaries, who preferred to reduce the natural world to isolated, quantifiable, laboratory examinations of individual organisms."[49] Moreover, Ritter was convinced, as he wrote, "of both the fundamental unity and the fundamental diversity of all nature . . . that the whole of nature is a system."[50]

Ritter argued that Darwin had been misunderstood by many of his followers, in particular Herbert Spencer, who coined the concept "survival of the fittest" and applied the theory of evolution to human culture and societies. In his writings, Ritter emphasized that natural selection was only one, and possibly not the most important, means by which species changed over time. He wrote, "The *fact* of transformation of species rather than any particular hypothesis as to *how* the transformation is caused, was Darwin's central interest."[51] He also pointed out that the "*struggle-survival doctrine*" had been used to justify "much cruel, destructive practice particularly in the industrial world, and now that biology herself has found the doctrine to be so largely erroneous, it would seem the bounden duty of biology to rectify as far as may be the harm that has been done."[52]

Ellen approved of Ritter's ideas, particularly his "theory of life," a belief that all organic beings, including humans, are subject to the principle of evolution.[53] In 1924 she told E.W., "I was very much interested in your conversation with Mr. Ritter" on the subject of the latter's forthcoming book, *The Natural History of Our Conduct* (1927). In it, Ritter argued that man was part of nature, not the product of supernatural forces, and might be studied as such. Ellen wrote that "the gist of it so coincides with my own ideas, subconsciously and unreasoningly arrived at: that the whole system of the universe must be comprised in one word, *Life*. Of its origins, or methods, or purpose, people can only form theories. But that there is no such distinction as the words spiritual and material imply seems to me unquestionable."[54]

For Ellen, the study of the ocean promised to mediate the truths found in both science and religion. In 1899 she quoted Aubrey L. Moore, one of the first Christian Darwinists, writing, "Christianity . . . teaches still that

God is the eternally existent One . . . the Eternal energy of the natural world and the immanent reason of the universe."[55] She read Emerson's "The Progress of Culture," in which he suggested, "Science corrects the old creeds; sweeps away, with every new perception, our infantile catechisms; and necessitates a faith commensurate with the grander orbits and universal laws which it discloses."[56] She also copied down a poem from William Herbert Carruth's "Each in His Own Tongue":

> Like tides on a crescent sea beach
> When the moon is new and thin
> Into our hearts high yearnings
> Come welling and surging in—
> Come from the mystic ocean,
> Whose rim no fool has trod,—
> Some of us call it Longing
> And others call it God![57]

E.W. likewise approved of Ritter's research agenda, though he was far more interested in "this damned human animal" than in any marine organisms.[58] Ritter speculated that at the outset "it was the novelty of the undertaking at La Jolla that appealed to him. Here was a small group of earnest university men trying to start an enterprise for making scientific investigations on the life of the Pacific Ocean and the Ocean itself. This was the sort of thing that he had never come in contact with before, and that in itself was calculated to appeal to his curiosity."[59] As E.W. grew more familiar with the work of the laboratory, he recognized that the term "biological" needed to include "men as well as fishes and the myriads of other things that live in the sea."[60] Over the course of his long friendship with Ritter, he challenged the scientist to explain the contributions that marine biology could make to the study of the human community and encouraged him to take up philosophical issues in his work.[61]

E.W. also wanted to engage Ellen in an intellectual and charitable endeavor at the end of her life. Around 1907 he told the scientist: "Ritter, I want you to get my sister Ellen so deeply interested in this project that she will forget her age. She is seventy-one and our family drop off at seventy-one or seventy-two years, and I know Ellen is thinking about it. I want her to become so absorbed in something that the next two or three years will pass before she realizes it. So I am going to urge her to build this laboratory in memory of our brother George." Then he added, "She was so poor in her younger days that she has never been able to feel rich. Now I want her to give away all her surplus money instead of leaving it for me to attend to. . . . I want her to make her benefactions during her own life."[62]

Ellen, for her part, did not plan on dying anytime soon. In fact, she felt strong enough to plan a trip to Japan with the Ritters in 1906 and changed her mind only because she felt the need to look after her siblings Elizabeth and Will, both of whom were failing in health. She told Mary Ritter, "I couldn't make people understand why I had to abandon the trip and so I did not try. Their 'obtuseness' surprised me. But perhaps it is only because of a different mental structure. It wasn't a case of 'ought' with me at all—simply a case of 'must.'"[63] Instead, Virginia traveled to Japan, sending back gifts such as Japanese trays, a China crepe silk dress, and several colored photographs enlarged from Kodak views.[64]

Over the next few years, Ellen made several important contributions to the biological laboratory. In 1906, after the *Loma* foundered on the rocks of Point Loma, she decided to give her endowment of $50,000 (about $1.4 million) to the Marine Biological Association as a lump sum. She told Kofoid, "The fund may be drawn upon for any proper and necessary expenditure for the association, such as purchase of land, erection of building, purchase of boat, laboratory or equipment, or running expenses of the laboratory."[65] This gift enabled Ritter to buy and equip a new boat, the *Alexander Agassiz*, launched August 21, 1907.[66] It also allowed him to plan for the construction of a new laboratory. Initially, he had hoped to build it in La Jolla Park, but he faced a number of obstacles, including the possibility that sewage might contaminate La Jolla Cove.

La Jolla Shores

In 1907 the Marine Biological Association purchased 170 acres of land located on "the barren cliffs beyond La Jolla," now known as La Jolla

Shores.[67] E.W. and Ellen had strongly recommended the purchase of this city-owned land, Pueblo Lot 1298, as it would provide room for future growth and isolation from "the inevitable growth and rush" of La Jolla. They argued, "The advantages for the future (if only in the ownership of so large a tract of land of rapidly increasing value) are beyond computation."[68] As part of the deal, Ellen promised to provide $10,000 (about $260,000) to build a road from La Jolla through the tract to the Torrey Pines near Del Mar (then the Biological Grade, now La Jolla Shores Drive). This would become the main route north from San Diego to Los Angeles.[69]

The construction of a new laboratory proved to be controversial largely because of the expense associated with hiring architect Irving J. Gill. "He is one of those kind of men," E.W. warned, ". . . who could make a very fine design that would be only useful providing there was plenty of money on hand to meet any cost."[70] In fact, Gill's initial estimate was remarkably high, $48,000 (about $1.25 million), and only later dropped to $15,000 (about $390,000).[71] Nevertheless, Wangenheim, the treasurer of the board, supported the architect and guaranteed to pay any cost that went over the estimated amount. Ellen, meanwhile, told Ritter not to worry about her brother's strongly worded opposition to such a great outlay of money, presented in a disquisition entitled "Biological Station Begins to Be a Disappointment" (1909).[72] She asked, "Ed has written you a letter hasn't he?" Then, with a twinkle in her eyes, she said, "You know Ed and I do not *always* agree."[73] E.W. later admitted, "I have a great predilection for temporary construction; on the other hand, I believe that my sister much prefers substantial and permanent work."[74]

In July 1910 Gill completed the George H. Scripps Laboratory, a simple, two-story structure made of reinforced concrete that could withstand both fire and earthquakes. It stood on a beach terrace at the foot of a steep hill leading up to a higher mesa on land covered with grass and low shrubs. The spare and uniquely modern structure had a flat roof with two iron-framed skylights and many large external windows. Inside were individual workrooms, a large aquarium room, a shop, a storage room, janitor's quarters, a library, an apparatus room, and a lecture hall.

Internal doors were made of dark, varnished wood with a single large inset panel. The building was equipped with gas, freshwater, and electrical lights. To the west of the structure was a sixteen-foot cylindrical concrete tank that could supply twenty thousand gallons of saltwater.[75]

In order to ensure the success of the laboratory, Ellen encouraged Ritter to make a permanent home in San Diego. She wrote in April 1909, "I congratulate you on the progress you have made with your book, but shall feel more like mutual congratulation when it is once finally in press; and you are free to give your time as well as your interest to the work here." His description of his work and that of his colleagues stimulated her interest and caused her to exclaim: "I could—if lots of obstacles were not in the way—feel like paraphrasing the remark . . . 'almost thou persuadest me to be a'—biologist!"[76]

To that end, Ellen announced her intention to contribute another $250,000 (about $6.7 million) to the biological association. She donated $150,000 (about $4.03 million) on the following conditions: first, that the work of the station be carried on according to Ritter's biological ideas; second, that Ritter serve as scientific director; and third, that all property of the Marine Biological Association be conveyed to the regents of the University of California. In addition, she ensured that a fund of $100,000 (about $2.7 million) "for certain family and newspaper purposes" would be added to the biological endowment on the death of E.W. and his heirs.[77] She also continued her annual contribution of $9,000 (about $242,000).

E.W., meanwhile, contributed $1,500 (about $40,300) per year and lectured Ritter on the importance of thrift and common sense. He admitted, "I have been so schooled and trained in business that I have acquired the vulgar habits of my vulgar class; and, as a consequence, I am more provoked by any sort of a business mistake, bookkeeping or otherwise, than I could be exhilarated by the feeling that I had helped to discover ten thousand new kinds of bugs."[78]

At one point E.W. imagined a planned community called Ellentown located on forty acres adjoining the campus. The settlers would be like his sister, "retired professional, literary, and other quiet people who

TIME

The Weekly News-Magazine

MISS ELLEN SCRIPPS
. . . *another Oxford rises*
(See Page 20)

VOL. VII, No. 8   FEBRUARY 22, 1926

1. Ellen Browning Scripps appeared on the cover of *Time* magazine after founding Scripps College in 1926. Ellen Browning Scripps Collection, Ella Strong Denison Library, Scripps College.

2. Ellen's father sketched the Scripps family home in Rushville, Illinois, in 1846. Ellen Browning Scripps Collection, Ella Strong Denison Library, Scripps College.

3. Ellen's brother James E. Scripps founded the *Detroit Evening News*. Photo ca. 1870. E. W. Scripps Collection, Mahn Center for Archives & Special Collections, Ohio University Libraries.

4. Ellen Browning Scripps worked as a journalist and an editor in Detroit
ca. 1875. Ellen Browning Scripps Collection, Ella Strong Denison Library,
Scripps College.

5. E. W. Scripps was instrumental in founding the *Cleveland Press*, followed by dozens of other newspapers in the Midwest and West. Photo ca. 1880. E. W. Scripps Collection, Mahn Center for Archives & Special Collections, Ohio University Libraries.

6. In her fifties, Ellen Browning Scripps imagined making a new life for herself in California. Ellen Browning Scripps Collection, Ella Strong Denison Library, Scripps College.

7. E. W. Scripps's wife, Nackie, with their children, 1896. E. W. Scripps Collection, Mahn Center for Archives & Special Collections, Ohio University Libraries.

8. E. W. Scripps ran his newspaper empire from his home, Miramar, in San Diego. Photo ca. 1914. E. W. Scripps Collection, Mahn Center for Archives & Special Collections, Ohio University Libraries.

9. In the 1890s La Jolla was the favorite summer camping ground of San Diegans. Photo ca. 1897. San Diego History Center #80:8104-130.

10. Ellen Browning Scripps built her home, South Molton Villa, on a bluff overlooking the Pacific Ocean. San Diego History Center #22287.

11. George H. Scripps stands with the wild and occasionally reckless E. W. Scripps and fellow journalist Robert B. Ross in 1875. E. W. Scripps Collection, Mahn Center for Archives & Special Collections, Ohio University Libraries.

12. Members of the Scripps family gathered at Miramar just before George H. Scripps's death in 1900. *From left*: Virginia, Ellen, Fred, E.W. with son Robert Paine, Thomas Osborne Scripps, Nackie, Katharine, William A. Scripps, Harriet, James E. Scripps, and Elizabeth Scripps Sharp. E. W. Scripps Collection, Mahn Center for Archives & Special Collections, Ohio University Libraries.

13. Virginia Scripps decorated her bedroom with sea mosses, shells, and strands of kelp gathered from the beach at La Jolla. She later donated her collection to the Scripps Institution of Oceanography. Collection of the La Jolla Historical Society.

14. (*above*) Scripps Institution of Oceanography, La Jolla, designed by architect Irving J. Gill. Photo ca. 1910. San Diego History Center #79:101.

15. (*right*) Annie Scripps came to California seeking a remedy from severe rheumatoid arthritis, having spent time among Christian Scientists in the Midwest. Photo 1890. E. W. Scripps Collection, Mahn Center for Archives & Special Collections, Ohio University Libraries.

16. Ellen Browning Scripps invited her neighbors to talk about books and ideas in her library at South Molton Villa. Ellen Browning Scripps Collection, Ella Strong Denison Library, Scripps College.

naturally seek association with scientific men." Given the problems created in La Jolla by newcomers with significant wealth, he decided that there should be no "fine or even moderately costly homes . . . such as will cause the inhabitants of humbler homes to feel any sort of inferiority in the matter of financial status." He imagined advertising it as "An Odd Place: A New Town Where High Thinking and Modest Living Is to Be the Rule."[79]

In July 1912 the biological association became a department within the University of California, Berkeley. It was renamed the Scripps Institution for Biological Research of the University of California and would have included the names of both George H. and Ellen Browning Scripps if the latter had agreed.[80] This arrangement put the organization on solid financial footing and made it possible for the Scripps family, among others, to make further contributions. The trustees, meanwhile, worked on getting a $15,000 appropriation from the California State Legislature in 1913.[81]

Assured that her investment was safe, Ellen gave $60,000 to be used for the physical development of the institution and operating costs. She made possible the construction of twelve cottages for permanent and summer staff and their families, a commons with a dining hall that seated forty, a new director's residence, a Ford Model T and a garage, as well as service and storage buildings. A saltwater circulatory system was installed with an electric pump that could deliver 2,100 gallons an hour to the laboratories and aquarium. In addition, workers built a sea wall in front of the laboratory in order to prevent the embankment from erosion.

In 1915 Ellen donated another $100,000 (about $2.4 million), making possible the construction of a pier and an aquarium. Built of reinforced concrete pilings and a plank deck, the pier provided a landing place for boats and a source of saltwater for the aquariums. It was replaced in 1988 with an all-concrete structure, the Ellen Browning Scripps Memorial Pier. At the same time, a public aquarium containing nineteen cement tanks was erected north of the laboratory building. At first, Ritter and Kofoid were averse to such a "material and showy" project, thinking it would drain money from research work, but they acceded after Ellen provided sufficient financial support.[82] It was later replaced by the Thomas Wayland Vaughan Aquarium-Museum (1951) and the Stephen Birch Aquarium-Museum (1992).[83]

Ellen's gifts also provided for a new library-museum building (1916) designed by San Diego architects Wheeler & Halley, which freed up space on the second floor of the laboratory. Located just east of the original Scripps building, it was used for public lectures and displays. In 1918–19 it had 6,700 bound volumes and a large number of pamphlets and journals.[84]

Ellen particularly enjoyed seeing the ocean from the pier. In October 1916 she described the "wonderful phosphorescence entertainments the sea is giving us" so late in the year. Ritter had invited her to the pier to see a "brilliant display with the fish of all kinds, porpoises, sharks (there is a whole school of the latter), carrying on their 'stunts' just underneath the surface of the water." Walking to the end of the structure, she viewed "the wonderful automatic apparatus for measuring the tides, recording the change of temperature, etc."[85]

Inspired by the ocean, she purchased three "submarine paintings" depicting tropical fish and coral landscapes by Zarh Howlison Pritchard, who sketched them underwater while wearing a diving suit. The artist exhibited his works at the La Jolla Woman's Club and gave a talk "with lantern slides of the paintings made under the sea." Ellen noted that he came "as a friend of Professor Ritter's, who is much interested in pictures."[86] She donated the works to the Scripps Institution in 1917.

Later Ellen also funded the publication of a book on marine life by Myrtle Elizabeth Johnson of National City and Harry James Snook entitled *Seashore Animals of the Pacific Coast* (1927). She agreed to loan the authors the $6,000 that they needed to publish it with Macmillan.[87]

Ellen and Ritter never talked about money, as her age and gender made her less approachable than her brother.[88] She told E.W., "Evidently he relies on me if he fails to convince you of the necessity of the expenditure to carry out the objects he is seeking—'woman's mind very much more impressionable than man's,' in his experience. The length and depth of a woman's purse doesn't seem to signify."[89]

For his part, Ritter considered Ellen to be a deeply intelligent woman, every bit as smart as her brother. He once spoke of her "perspicacity" to E.W., who also admired his sister, though he had a low opinion of women's intellect in general.[90] The latter relayed this to Ellen when the biological station was in need of building funds: "This is not the first time that Ritter has told me that he found you more intelligent than myself and possessed of more perspicacity. Whenever I turn him down on any of his projects, he makes this wonderful discovery of your great superiority over me."[91]

As much as Ellen appreciated science, the ocean remained a source of beauty and mystery to her, part of the "sea of consciousness in which we float and live."[92] She continued to write with feeling about her experiences on the shore. In 1918 she described coming in from an hour on the beach: "It was high tide at 7:30 [a.m.], and the waves seemed mountains high breaking over the rocks. But the great beauty lay in the geysers when the rushing surf was forced up through narrow clefts in the rocks to a height of 60 or 70 feet, each one forming a beautiful rainbow at its apex with the sun in the background. The tidal rush seemed to me more stupendous than I had ever witnessed before."[93]

CHAPTER 7

Old Age, New Age

At the same time that Ellen worked to establish the Scripps Institution of Oceanography, she also began to search for purpose in her own life. She had never been particularly speculative, having worked too hard to have time to question the nature and meaning of existence. She had no use for mysticism, and she was impatient with the claims of Spiritualists, many of whom she had encountered through her sister Annie. When she was in her sixties, however, she began exploring both New Thought and Theosophy in an effort to gain both self-knowledge and a sense of the changing times in which she lived.

After 1860 many mainstream Christian denominations began to lose ground to esoteric religion, or alternative spirituality. Historians describe this as part of a "crisis of intellectual faith" that stemmed from the publication of Charles Darwin's *Origin of Species* (1859).[1] People slowly began to realize that the supernatural revelations of the Bible did not accord with empirical discoveries made in the fields of biology, geology, history, and paleontology. They also started to challenge crude and harsh statements of religious dogma voiced by nineteenth-century evangelicals. Doctrines such as original sin, reprobation, vicarious atonement, and eternal punishment seemed particularly unattractive themes in a humanitarian age. Instead of abandoning faith entirely, many people turned to unorthodox forms of spirituality such as New Thought, Theosophy, and

Christian Science for answers. White middle-class women in particular were drawn to alternative religions that offered them a unique role in elevating the Anglo-Saxon race, advancing civilization, and inaugurating a new millennium of peace and harmony.[2]

Ellen had long since abandoned the hellfire-and-brimstone Methodism of her childhood and started to explore other faiths. After leaving the Presbyterian Church in 1879, she became interested in Unitarianism and attended services in Detroit. On moving to California, however, she only occasionally went to church. She spent most Sunday mornings reading or walking on the beach while other family members attended services in La Jolla at the First Church of Christ, which held Episcopal services in the morning and Congregational-Presbyterian ones in the afternoon. She once wrote that listening to a symphony orchestra "was better than a year's Sunday sermons."[3]

Like many Victorians, however, she remained deeply influenced by the Christian ideals of humility, self-sacrifice, and renunciation of desire, particularly as they applied to women. Ellen admitted that she knew all too well how to surrender her own will, "I suppose because I am a woman, and woman's first lesson and only is submission."[4] Having spent her early life "constantly employed in some altruistic endeavor," she continued to contribute to the comfort of others, even at the expense of her own needs and wishes.[5] Her sister-in-law Katharine described her as a "remarkable person—such simplicity—such humility, such self-effacement seems hardly possible."[6] Mary Ritter, meanwhile, thought that her husband's patron had a self-sacrificing streak that "amounted almost to self-immolation." She found it particularly strange that Ellen refused to dress the part of a wealthy woman, saying, "'No one needs less to eat or to wear than I.'"[7]

Ellen had difficulty accepting the bounty that the universe seemed determined to offer, particularly as money kept coming in. She could be extremely frugal when it came to spending on herself, if generous to others. Mary Ritter noted that Ellen rarely bought new clothes: "The hat she wore when I first saw her was of several vintages past and she wore the same hat at least two or three years longer."[8] She implicitly compared Ellen to Phoebe Apperson Hearst, whose husband had made a fortune in the legendary Comstock Lode. Unlike Ellen, Hearst used fine clothes and jewelry as a way to signify her social elevation from a Missouri farm girl to a San Francisco philanthropist.

Of course, Ellen had no need to acquire fancy clothes to live in La Jolla. Between 1905 and 1915 the village was "badly torn up and very dirty" as a result of street improvements and new construction, making it impractical to wear anything but the simplest outfits.[9] She owned several tailored black suits that she had purchased in the 1890s but wore them so seldom that she did not feel they needed to be replaced. Moreover, having traveled through Europe and viewed the trappings of aristocracy, she had no use for pretentious middle-class San Diegans who thought that they could score a social coup by wearing expensive clothes.

Ellen was troubled not by thrift but by the residual belief that the pursuit of wealth was at odds with her identity as a Christian woman. Like many middle-class Victorians, she saw "success" and "womanhood" as antithetical. Men—the motors of economic productivity—were supposed to be driven by competition and the desire for success; women, on the other hand, were meant to use their altruistic hearts to ameliorate the inequalities rampant in industrial society. It is for this reason, perhaps, that she turned to the New Thought movement, which, among other things, helped women to legitimize their desire for wealth and personal expression.[10]

Women's Wisdom

The New Thought movement, popular from the 1870s through the 1920s, emphasized the individual's power to shape his or her own reality via affirmations, meditation, and prayer.[11] Practitioners believed in the existence of God as an impersonal universal mind or creative intelligence with no particular incarnations. They rejected original sin and believed that salvation consisted in the realization of oneness with a universal spirit. For women in particular New Thought offered freedom from the kind of misogyny found in Christian scriptures. Without sin, there was no need for women to bear the shame of Eve. This was particularly appealing to Ellen, who once told a friend, "I don't believe anybody is born bad."[12]

Several members of the Scripps family were interested in New Thought, including Ellen's sister Annie, who experimented with a variety of spiritual self-help techniques in order to deal with the symptoms of rheumatoid arthritis. In the early 1880s she spent time in a sanitarium in Quincy, Illinois, run by Dr. Maria Augusta Fairchild, a prominent figure in the hydropathic movement and the author of *How to Be Well* (1879).[13] On Fairchild's recommendation, Annie went to live with a Christian Scientist practitioner, Dr. Silas Sawyer of Milwaukee, Wisconsin, who had studied with the denomination's founder, Mary Baker Eddy.[14] After two months of treatment Annie felt that she had made considerable improvement. She told her sister, "Ellen, you know this is not 'mind cure.' Save as we acknowledge that there is but one mind, God, Spirit, Principal, call it what you will which controls *all*. That nothing is not save what He created, that being good. God. He could create no evil, hence evil does not exist as a reality and sickness is an error is destroyed by Truth."[15] Fairchild later introduced her to Dr. Bowen and his Remedial Institute and School of Philosophy in Alameda, California. Annie wrote, "I have so baffled all her efforts, and she is determined that I shall yet be physically whole!"[16]

Annie's spiritual journey brought her into contact with radicals and reformers at the cutting edge of social change. She wrote, "The sort of people that I have been thrown with for the last ten years have be[en] reformers, radicals, and progressives, and I can plainly see how I have simply gone on with the thought that governs the class. I am in it, and have no desire to leave it."[17]

In 1899, following her sister's death, Ellen took nearly one hundred pages of notes on a course of lectures presented by Abigail "Abbey" Perkins Cheney, wife of the poet John Vance Cheney and an advocate of New Thought.[18] Cheney's lecture emphasized the creative powers of the individual mind. Like the Transcendentalists, she argued that one could not rely on the evidence of the senses but instead had to seek a spiritual reality through the use of mental discipline. Ellen jotted down: "Our work is to *dominate self*. Concentrate your thought in love; *be love*. 'I am love.' . . . Mechanical at first, it will cease to be repetition.

Thoughts become tissue. They build the body."[19] She noted techniques of meditation, including breathing practice, "concentration on some ideal thought," and relaxation. "It was by relaxation—sitting in the stillness—that psalmist and the prophet received the truth," the speaker explained.[20]

Cheney also spoke to women's realization of their power and potential. "Woman has been discovered during the last 50 years," she said; "rather, she has discovered herself. Found she was a reasoning being, and decided to put her powers to the test; to use these powers in professional business and art, life, and work."[21] She told her audience, "We must awaken people to the consciousness of their own power" and prevent them from clinging to traditional beliefs, neglected opportunities, and sorrow. "Cease to think of grief," she advised, and "make yourself positive for good."[22]

Ellen also began to explore Theosophy, one of the major metaphysical movements of the late nineteenth century along with New Thought, Christian Science, and Spiritualism. Founded in New York in 1875, the Theosophical Society aimed to unite all seekers under a single "brotherhood of humanity" dedicated to the exploration of religious concepts drawn from both Asian religious traditions (such as karma and reincarnation) and Western Christianity. It also sought to investigate psychic phenomena. According to one scholar, Theosophy "appealed to a segment of white, middle-class, intellectual women who sought greater control over their lives, usefulness in the world, and spiritual power as women."[23]

Helena Petrovna Blavatsky, a founding member of the New York Theosophical Society, provided the core texts for the movement, *Isis Unveiled* (1877) and *The Secret Doctrine* (1888). The latter, read by Ellen in 1909, aimed to rescue ancient truths that formed the basis of all religions, the accumulated Wisdom of the Ages, which had been passed down from one early race to another.[24] The two-volume, 842-page work had a profound impact on contemporary readers and would later influence the Indian independence movement and the twentieth century's New Age movement.

Theosophy was particularly prominent in San Diego, where Katherine Tingley (1847–1929), head of the Theosophical Society of America, founded the Point Loma Universal Brotherhood and Theosophical Society, popularly known as Lomaland. Established in 1897, it consisted of the Temple of Peace, a residential facility, and the Raja Yoga Academy. The community grew from 95 men and women in 1900 to 357 in 1910.[25] Among the better-known residents were Albert G. Spalding, the sporting goods magnate; plein air painter Maurice Braun; Clark Thurston, president of the American Screw Company; and August Neresheimer, a New York diamond broker. Lomaland's eclectic architecture—blending South Asian, Greek, Egyptian, and Victorian features—contributed to its popularity as a tourist destination. Visitors viewed Greek and Shakespearian dramas performed at the first open-air Greek theater in the United States. They also attended theatrical performances, concerts, and Theosophical lectures at the Isis Theater, formerly the Fisher Opera House, in downtown San Diego.

In March 1901 Ellen attended a lecture on Theosophy given by Constance, Countess Wachtmeister, a disciple and intimate friend of Blavatsky, remarking, "Seemed to me rather superficial."[26] Nevertheless, she was sufficiently interested in the subject to hear Col. Henry S. Olcott lecture on "the rise and spread of Theosophy" following a meeting of the Federation of Women's Clubs.[27] Together with Madame Blavatsky, Olcott had helped to found the Theosophical Society in 1875. Later that year, Ellen sat up until midnight talking about the subject with her friend Agnes Thompson.[28]

In 1904 Ellen joined a Theosophical reading group led by biologist Mary Snyder, a recent widow who later served as president of the La Jolla Woman's Club. The group consisted of a dozen members, most of them La Jolla women.[29] Ellen occasionally hosted the Theosophical reading group when they had visiting speakers. In May 1904 Mrs. Prince spoke to fifteen women in the parlor at South Molton Villa, illustrating her lecture with a "series of charts to explain certain facts and doctrines by symbols."[30]

Between 1904 and 1908 they read a series of works by Annie Besant, a well-known British socialist, women's rights activist, and supporter of Irish and Indian self-rule. In the 1890s Besant became a leading member of the Theosophical movement, representing it at the World's

Columbian Exposition and speaking to audiences around the world. In 1893 she visited British India and, fascinated by what she saw as the Hindu religion's advanced spirituality, translated a number of Sanskrit texts into English, most notably the Bhagavad Gita in 1905. She went on to write numerous books and pamphlets and give lectures that introduced Eastern religious ideas to Western audiences. Ellen and her circle read *Reincarnation* (1892), *Man and His Bodies* (1896), *Building of the Cosmos and Other Lectures* (1894), *Ancient Wisdom* (1897), *A Study in Consciousness* (1904), and *Thought-Forms* (1905).[31] In 1908 Besant served as president of the Theosophical Society and a decade later became the first female president of the Indian National Congress.

Besant's Theosophical writings offered solutions to the Victorian crisis of faith. A secularist and a radical, she rejected supernatural explanations of human existence and promoted evolutionary theory. She believed, like Blavatsky, that God had revealed himself over time in a gradual process that would shortly bring the dawn of a new age in which the human race would become increasingly spiritual in nature.[32] She also emphasized women's duty of service to humanity: "What are we here for, save to help each other, to love each other, to uplift each other?" she wrote.[33]

In 1906 Ellen and her circle read Alfred Percy Sinnett's *Esoteric Buddhism* (1883), said to have been derived from his communications with Ascended Master Koot Hoomi (or Kuthumi), a spiritually enlightened being who drew on the experience of his past lives to help humanity.[34] They also discussed karma, reincarnation, the building of the cosmos, and astral projection, among other subjects.[35]

Ellen occasionally enjoyed a little dry humor at the expense of the Theosophists. In a letter to Mary Ritter, who was on her way to Japan, she wrote, "This is wishing you a continuation of perfect sailing for the rest of your trip; and a glorious time on *terra firma*. . . . I shall try to follow at your heels when you land again. If only I were spiritualized enough to go on a little journey in my astral body!"[36]

Virginia, meanwhile, took the faith more seriously. Years later, when Ellen made her first visit to the Point Loma Theosophical Society, she told her sister that she must have made "a profound impression on the community at some time of your visit (or visitations) there" because the guide received Ellen's party with great enthusiasm: "I think he would have liked to summon Madame Tingley to do some kow-towing could we have waited."[37]

Contact with Theosophists gave Virginia the idea that the color purple had personal significance. Theosophists associated it with the moon, the source of female cosmic power, while the Indian chakras (or "wheels" in Sanskrit) identified it with the crown of the head, suggesting spiritual connection, knowledge and understanding, and higher realms. Despite the fact that San Diego newspapers mocked Tingley as the "Purple Mother" with a dog named "The Purple Inspiration," Virginia identified herself with the color by wearing purple or violet dresses and naming her cottages the Iris and the Wisteria.[38] On one occasion, she told a young woman wearing a lavender dress, "'You go home now and take that dress off, and never wear it again.'" The girl later explained, "It was her color. No one could wear lavender but Miss Virginia Scripps."[39]

Ellen and Virginia also showed interest in Indian culture and religion as reinterpreted by Theosophists. They attended a slide lecture on India given by Rev. R. B. Taylor of the First Presbyterian Church and later met Mrs. Arthur Smith, founder of New York's Vedanta Society, "who has written and lectured on various subjects connected particularly with Indian architecture, art, music, religion, etc."[40] On a trip to Mount Shasta in 1903, Ellen and Virginia encountered the Hindu master Swami Ram and heard him speak on "the religion and spirituality of the Hindoos" at the Shasta Mountain Home resort.[41] They also heard Benjamin Fay Mills, an evangelist who had been converted to socialism by George Herron, lecture on the Bhagavad Gita.[42]

In 1906 Virginia traveled through India as part of an around-the-world trip before meeting up with the Ritters in Japan.[43] She brought home a small ivory elephant and a model of the Taj Mahal, a white marble mausoleum thought to be one of the finest examples of Mughal architecture.[44] She made another voyage in 1921, traveling from Calcutta (Kolkata) to Colombo in Sri Lanka.[45]

Theosophy encouraged Ellen to think about the possibility of "life waves," predestined periods of time during which people evolved into a new state of consciousness. Theosophists identified seven stages of evolving life, from the lowest elemental kingdom to the highest, humanity, and argued that the turn of the twentieth century marked the end of one great cycle and the beginning of the next. Ellen recognized seven-year intervals as important turning points in her life. She wrote, "I find on 'looking backward' and taking measurements that my life has run and broken and renewed in periods of about 7 years—strictly speaking from 6 to 8 years—when some vital change has taken place."[46] She moved from England to America when she was eight years old, started high school at thirteen, and attended college at twenty. She began teaching in 1864 and moved to Detroit seven years later. Subsequent intervals included her first trip to Europe, her move to California, and the construction of her first house.

Still, Ellen could never quite come to terms with the idea of an afterlife. She was dubious about the idea that the essence, or soul, confers personal identity and survives the death of the body. She once asked her friend Mary Eyre, "Do you believe in the afterlife? About this immortality, do you believe in the continuance of personality?" The latter responded with her belief that the spirit of energy within people "must have been derived from somewhere and would continue." She noted that Ellen "would be interested, and listen, but I don't believe she ever reached a conclusion in her own mind on which she could really lean." Ellen thought that there was only "a possibility of continuance," whether reincarnation or continued life in a spiritual realm.[47]

As a result, Ellen never became particularly interested in Spiritualism, a popular movement often associated with Theosophy due to Blavatsky's role as a medium. Ellen went to her first séance in 1908 with Virginia, noting, "Some queer and inexplicable things took place."[48] The following year she attended a séance at the Spiritualist Temple located on Seventh Avenue and B Street in San Diego. She described the session, led by John Slater, as "a remarkable performance as showing his psychic power." He seemed to know details about people who had died years before, "unknown and unrecorded" by posterity.[49] She remained unconvinced, however, and thereafter attended only occasionally. In 1919 she wrote to Virginia that she had been invited to "a 'psychic' or spiritual séance at Mrs. Bell's and did not get home till past 11—the natural man filled up with hot chocolate, sandwiches, and cake to the extent of sleepiness and forgetfulness of the spiritual food that had been primarily bestowed."[50]

Science and Health

Ellen preferred systems of belief that recognized the power of the mind to alter reality, such as Christian Science. She explained to E.W., "Of course, I'm not a 'red' believer in Christian Science but neither do I believe it to be all 'rot.'"[51] She particularly appreciated its basic principle: the power of positive thinking. Mary Baker Eddy, the founder of the movement, encouraged people to believe that the mental or spiritual world was the true reality, while physical and/or emotional conditions were secondary creations of the mind. Healers then could use the creative powers of their minds to persuade patients that "harmony is the fact, and that sickness is a temporal dream. Realize the presence of health and the fact of harmonious being, until the body corresponds with the normal conditions of health and harmony."[52] While negative thoughts might produce negative situations, spiritual thoughts could materialize into positive reality.

Spiritual healing was a reasonable alternative to Victorian medicine from Ellen's point of view. Doctors often failed to cure illnesses; in fact, some of their remedies proved worse than the disease. In 1890 a wrenched knee caused her to spend time in a sanitarium in Hamilton, Illinois. She told her brother that after a "two-week siege of boils . . . I am more out of conceit with 'doctors' than ever before, and I have never had much faith in the fraternity." Afterward she decided, "I am taking no 'quack's' advice that doesn't correspond with my own common sense."[53]

The Church of Christ, Scientist, attracted many people in early twentieth-century San Diego, so much so that its congregation quickly outgrew its first building at Third Avenue and Ash Street, designed by Irving J. Gill. In 1909–10 the architect completed a harmonious, reinforced-concrete structure that still stands at the corner of Second Avenue and Laurel Street in Bankers Hill.

Many Scripps women followed the teachings of Christian Science, including Will's wife, Katharine, and E.W.'s wife, Nackie. The former attended meetings of the Christian Science Association and unsuccessfully tried to convince E.W. to turn over his property on Fay Street in La Jolla to the church. When bad health forced her to use the services of doctors, she repented "her want of faith in Christian Science."[54] Nackie also found value in the religion. In 1906 Ellen wrote, "I hope she won't lose faith in the truth of Christian Science teachings if she does in the efficacy of its treatments. That is where we are liable to make a serious error—in making a system responsible for its accidents and apparent exceptions."[55]

Positive thinking helped Ellen make it through periods of family crisis, the death of loved ones, and the inevitable pains of growing old. In 1898, shortly after her sister Annie's passing, Ellen jotted down a quote from an inspirational speaker, the agnostic Robert G. "Bob" Ingersoll: "'The most perfect philosophy is to enjoy today without regrets for the past, or fears for the future.'"[56]

Ellen also took an interest in the new science of psychology, which developed in the late nineteenth and early twentieth centuries. She began by borrowing books from the La Jolla Library and subscribing to *Metaphysical Magazine*, a publication devoted to "the scientific examination of the laws of being; to a study of the operations and phenomena of the human mind; and to a systematic inquiry into the faculties and functions, the nature and attributes, of the soul—the *ego* of mankind."[57] In 1908 she heard a paper by Miss Sherman on the work of Charles S. Myers, cofounder of the British Psychological Society.[58] She kept up with modern psychological theories, according to her friend Mary Eyre, who went on to teach psychology at Pomona College. The latter wrote that Ellen was particularly interested in the "basis of behavior," telling her, "It seems to me that people ought to understand each other."[59]

As she explored alternative religions and modern psychology, Ellen became less and less convinced by Christian claims to ultimate Truth. She studied different religions, for example, giving a lecture on Quakers before members of the La Jolla Woman's Club in 1908. She found their doctrine to be "simple and direct" but had serious doubts about the inner light, or the belief in "something Divine, 'Something of God,' in the human soul," as a prominent Quaker historian and theologian put it.[60] She asked a friend, "How do you know that the 'still small voice' is the voice of God directing you? How do you know it isn't your own idea within yourself?"[61]

Nor did she have much patience with the pomp and ceremony of the Episcopal Church. Ellen thought "they were like children with a dramatic instinct," adding, "I don't know how they can fool themselves."[62] Because of her sister's faith, however, she tolerated the "great doings at the church across the way," referring to St. James by-the-Sea, even when she saw priests "white robed and carrying golden crosiers and other priestly emblems."[63]

Ellen's attitude toward traditional religion did not prevent her from providing financial support to La Jolla's churches. She donated small sums yearly to each church in the village. She thought that organized religion played an important social role in the community, even if she found little solace there. In 1921 she answered a questionnaire sent to her by the pioneering psychologist G. Stanley Hall, telling him that she remained as irreligious as ever: "If I have any religious belief it is crude, primitive, and non-essential," she wrote. "I find nothing in the church to satisfy me. My creed would be substantially socialistic—the brotherhood of man—in theory, if not in practice."[64]

Ellen's exploration of alternative religious practices brought her into contact with reformers, in particular, progressives and socialists. According to one historian, "Radicals were at the forefront of some of the most popular new religious movements of the nineteenth century, including Spiritualism, New Thought, and Theosophy."[65] The goals of the Theosophists, for example, included the formation of a Universal Brotherhood of Humanity "without distinction of race, colour, or creed."[66] Women involved in the Spiritualist movement also supported women's suffrage, the rights of labor, prison reform, and American Indian rights.[67] Proponents of New Thought, meanwhile, rejected Social

Darwinist theories of competition and organized settlement houses, day nurseries, and homeless shelters in cities like Boston, New York, and San Francisco. One prominent member of the Socialist Party wrote, "All the great men and women of the world have believed in what we call New Thought."[68]

For women in particular, nontraditional religions formed a training ground for reform activities. Margaret Fuller, for example, drew on Transcendentalist spirituality to argue for women's empowerment, allowing "the divine energy" to pervade nature and bring about "a ravishing harmony of the spheres."[69] Emma Curtis Hopkins, an advocate of New Thought, identified the Holy Ghost as feminine and imagined the coming of a third age in which "The Ministry of the Holy Mother" would achieve transcendence.[70] Hopkins saw activism as a sacred vocation in which women would transform religious and political institutions.

Ellen drew on these religious ideas to express her vision of women's role in creating a new society. She believed that every woman, having the "heart-wide sympathy that encompasses the human race," would necessarily reach out "and take into her heart and life every neglected child; every untaught man and every unblessed woman—be they where and what they may." The result would be the creation of a democracy that would be "spiritual, rather than material, a permanent, progressive democracy that shall be based, not on nationalism, but on the Brotherhood of Man."[71]

Ellen imagined a future in which the great issues of the day would be settled "not for the glory of some political party, not to safeguard fortunes in iron or steel or sugar or lumber, but absolutely according to the dictates of the mother's heart that is woman's great weapon; the world's great triumph."[72] She asked members of the La Jolla Woman's Club:

> Do you think if women knew their power and willed to use it that the pitiful cry of little children could be heard from the factories and sweatshops of our cities? . . . Can you conceive that if women had the power, and the will to use it, babies should be dying like flies from disease and starvation in this United States? . . . Do you believe

that if women had the power—and the will to use it—such a state of things as this could be, that in the City of New York . . . within the past 3 years, 5,000 innocent girls have been lured to the haunts of vice, left without redemption to go the downward path to hell? . . . If women had the power and the will to use it, do you think the gallows tree would still rear its loathsome form, that our crowded jails and penitentiaries, and hospitals and asylums should be the hotbeds of vice, and the menace of the community that they are?[73]

Ellen's exploration of alternative religions gave her a powerful new identity as an agent of social change. By breaking away from conventional thinking about religion, she was able to embrace her role as an educated woman with both money and political influence. She no longer apologized for her success but embraced it, using it to advance social and political causes such as universal suffrage, Prohibition, the labor movement, free speech, and world peace. She also encouraged girls and women to prepare for a new era of liberty in which they would think and act for themselves.

CHAPTER 8

A Feminist Speaks Out

Over the next two decades, Ellen dived into causes ranging from free speech to suffrage and Prohibition. Unwilling to cede San Diego's development to conservative interests, she supported progressive ideas that promised to heal the divide between labor and capital. Like others, she hoped that it would become a thoroughly "modern" city capable of never-ending improvement, expansion, and growth.

Between 1870 and 1920 urban populations increased rapidly as industrial development lured people out of rural areas and attracted emigrants from Europe and Asia. Cities could not keep pace with demands for housing, clean water, garbage collection, and sewage disposal, with the result that living conditions for the poor deteriorated rapidly. During times of economic crisis, the working classes expressed their fury by striking against industrial employers. According to one historian, the era saw "a series of massive nationwide strikes that ended up as pitched battles between labor and capital—factories and freight cars torched and smoldering; angry workers squaring off against heavily armed police, militias, the National Guard, and the U.S. Army; a crackle of gunfire; men, women, and children dead."[1] Sympathetic to labor, the Scripps newspapers reported on dozens of strikes between the 1870s and the 1910s, including the Great Railroad Strike (1877), the Pullman Strike (1894), and the Great Anthracite Coal Strike (1902).

E. W. Scripps thought that the result would be class warfare, a struggle for survival that would determine the future of the human race. Although he eschewed socialism as an irrational doctrine, he believed in the theory propounded by Karl Marx and Friedrich Engels in *The Communist Manifesto* (1848). Society was approaching the end of a historical process in which the proletariat would overthrow the capitalists or, at the very least, "compel the governing classes to give us a better government—that is to say, a fairer one, with more equal treatment of all classes and individuals."[2] Of course, he imagined a political system governed by males alone.

Ellen believed that women's leadership could resolve many of the problems facing industrial society. Her reading of New Thought texts led her to view women as pure, civilized beings with the capacity to save a nation divided by class conflict and to inaugurate a new era of spiritual peace and harmony, in her words, "a permanent, progressive democracy that shall be based, not on nationalism, but on the brotherhood of man."[3] Cooperation, not competition, guided human behavior and advanced evolution, in her view. Altruism, she reminded her brother, remained "a primal necessity of our nature; that we simply must do it, in spite of its apparent ineffectiveness; and whatever good it may do in reforming the people is purely an incidental thing in one's consideration."[4]

Ellen's beliefs put her in the company of female progressives and socialists who fought against economic injustice and worked for women's rights. They included Frances Willard, leader of the Woman's Christian Temperance Union (WCTU); suffragists Susan B. Anthony, Elizabeth Cady Stanton, and Lucretia Mott; the Women's Educational and Industrial Union; and clubwomen throughout America. Core beliefs included female solidarity, women's advancement through wage labor, temperance, and an end to men's abuse of power.[5]

Ellen defined herself as a progressive woman with socialist sympathies. Founded in 1901, the Socialist Party of America included a broad spectrum of activists, from union members and intellectuals, to Marxists and populists, heirs to the Puritans and emigrants from Russia, Spiritualists, Theosophists, and advocates of New Thought and Free Religion.

Socialists agreed that the capitalist economy needed to be replaced with a "cooperative commonwealth," but they divided over the methods to be used.[6] Gradually, the party split between those who wanted to work through the electoral process and left-wing reformers who demanded revolutionary change. Women in the movement also were separated into an older group of activists with domestic responsibilities and a younger generation, born after 1870, who committed themselves to party service.[7]

Ellen, at seventy-two years of age, favored the kind of Christian socialism advocated by Eugene V. Debs, a founding member of the Industrial Workers of the World (IWW) and a five-time Socialist Party candidate for president. A progressive champion for women's rights, he supported suffrage long before he converted to socialism. According to one historian, Debs "could be counted on, regardless of his designated topic, for a sentimental exhortation of women's virtue and an appeal for political equality."[8] He also was deeply Christian, describing Jesus as "the world's supreme revolutionary leader."[9]

In September 1908 Ellen joined a crowd of ten thousand people to hear Debs at a campaign stop in San Diego. She wrote, "Was impressed with the man's sincerity, gentle manner, and philosophical treatment of the subject of socialism." She was less impressed by the other speakers: "Of course, who preceded him, H. Austin Adams, was vituperous and ranting, A. M. Symons indulging in much sensational clap trap, and Mr. Simpson (who introduced Debs) hypocritical and fulsome."[10]

Inspired by Debs's advocacy of the working classes, Ellen and Nina Waddell shortly afterward organized the Every Man's Club in La Jolla, where men could socialize without alcohol.[11] The events of 1910–12, however, suggested to Ellen the need for a permanent place where both working classes and elites could gather together and form a community.

City Politics

At the turn of the century, San Diego was a "one-man town" dominated by Old Guard Republican businessman John D. Spreckels, an ally of E. H. Harriman, president of the Southern Pacific Railroad.[12] This was the great age of "machine politics," in which a party organization headed by a single individual, "the boss," commanded enough votes to maintain political and administrative control of a region. San Diego was "a part of California's system of 'government *of* the machine, *by* the bosses, *for* the public utility corporations.'"[13]

Spreckels began investing in San Diego in the 1890s, having acquired a fortune from his father, Claus Spreckels, the "Sugar King" of Hawaii. He established a coal wharf at the foot of Broadway and gradually gained control of the Coronado Beach Company, the Hotel del Coronado, Tent City, and the San Diego–Coronado ferry system. In 1892 he bought the city's horse-drawn railway system and converted it to electricity. The San Diego electric railway made possible the development of suburban neighborhoods such as Point Loma, Pacific Beach, La Jolla, Mission Hills, Hillcrest, University Heights, North Park, Normal Heights, Golden Hill, and Logan Heights.[14]

After the San Francisco earthquake (1906), Spreckels relocated his family to San Diego, building a mansion on Glorietta Bay in Coronado and buying up downtown real estate. He financed the construction of the Union Building (1908–14), Spreckels Theater and office building (1913), and Hotel San Diego (1914). He also organized the Southern California Mountain Water Company, which built the Morena and the Upper and Lower Otay dams, the Dulzura conduit, and the pipelines that brought water to the city. According to his rival, Col. Ed Fletcher, "Spreckels owned nearly everything of value in San Diego, including the morning Union, evening Tribune and a ten-million-dollar electric railway."[15]

Spreckels also dominated local politics, using his newspapers, the *Union* and the *Evening Tribune*, to support his interests. For example, the papers destroyed the nascent political career of William E. Smythe, a Democrat who crusaded for the irrigation of the Imperial Valley and a competitor in land and water development efforts. When Smythe ran for Congress in 1902, the *San Diego Union* belittled him for his short residence in the city, his stand on free trade, his "ponderous diction," and his "long-winded flights of political oratory."[16]

Spreckels worked with local "boss," Charles S. Hardy, who was said to have created "the most powerful political organization in the city's history," known as "The Push."[17] A butcher, meat distributor, and owner of the Bay City Market, Hardy maneuvered among the three key players in San Diego: Spreckels and his corporations, the saloonkeepers of the Stingaree (the vice district), and the Southern Pacific Railroad Company. According to E.W., who spoke with Hardy at some length, "He gives the 'Stingaree' some privileges and rights that are extralegal. He gives to the Spreckels' interests all that they must have and cannot get along without" while offering the Southern Pacific "the minimum of what that corporation exacts as the price of their acquiescence to his rule."[18] Although he ran a prosperous business, Hardy did not mix with "the so-called respectable classes." He was viewed by elites as "a man of a lower moral and social class," according to E.W., and was used accordingly.[19]

Hardy's rival was businessman George W. Marston, who represented, in E.W.'s words, "the respectable, moral, church-going, element of the city."[20] Marston exercised power not through saloons but through reform movements and "dry" organizations like the YMCA. The owner of Marston's Department Store, he was a progressive Republican activist who in 1908 worked with the Lincoln-Roosevelt League to curb the influence of the Southern Pacific and reform California politics.[21] He also believed that San Diego could develop as a commercial and manufacturing center without sacrificing either its environment or its visual aesthetics. "I believe in the 'city beautiful,'" he wrote, referring to a reform movement that promoted moral and civic virtue through architectural harmony, open spaces like parks and playgrounds, sanitary improvements, and modern transport systems.[22]

E. W. Scripps, meanwhile, crusaded against corporate corruption and "bossism" through his chain of newspapers, the Scripps-McRae League. The *San Diego Sun*, co-owned by William H. Porterfield, championed the common man and exposed corruption at the highest levels of city government. As a result, it was read by more people than "all of the other daily newspapers put together," E.W. claimed. Boss Hardy held no grudge, for he apparently told E.W., "You and your paper, *The Sun*, have been honest in whatever you have said, and whatever *The Sun* has said has been grounded not only on conviction, but generally on ascertained facts."[23]

Spreckels, meanwhile, railed against Scripps and the *San Diego Sun* during a speech given at the Hotel del Coronado:

A scurrilous, unscrupulous, and hypocritical newspaper, whose life depends upon stirring up discontent, arousing suspicion, and pandering to the envy and jealousy of the man in the street . . . is one of a numerous string of similar sheets owned by a multi-millionaire who has publically admitted that he made his millions by hounding other millionaires and by posing as the champion of the poor, downtrodden working man! . . . He has gone on piling up his millions by hypocritically pretending that if it were not for the watchful eye of his *San Diego Sun*, the people would be like poor, dumb sheep, devoured by those hungry wolves—the Spreckels interests, the gas company, the banks, the big merchants and manufacturers, and everybody else who is trying to build up San Diego.[24]

E.W. remained a skeptic on the issue of political reform. In 1908 he declined to support the Lincoln-Roosevelt League, telling Judge William A. Sloane, "*The Sun* will not come to your support as an organization simply because you represent some different theory or system than that represented by the present ruling 'machine.' *The Sun* will only voice the opinions and sentiments and desires of the great mass of the people: the common people."[25] He later wrote, "I had little use for the Lincoln-Roosevelt crowd . . . men who had all of the evil propensities of oppressive capitalism and lacked only the power to participate in and profit by the present Republican machine."[26]

Nor did E.W. believe that California's adoption of the Initiative and Referendum (1911), allowing citizens to place new legislation on a popular ballot, would succeed in breaking the monopoly of political power within the state. He told William E. Ritter, "The Initiative and Referendum is supposed by many of these people to be a perfect 'cure-all' in politics. I remember Boss Hardy once telling me that in just such a matter as this that under excitement the people as a whole could be stampeded and gotten to do things that no political machine or boss would even dare to do."[27]

Ellen shared her brother's political views, if not his doubts about the possibilities of reform. She endorsed the Anti-Saloon League's efforts to clean up the electoral process by closing down the bars and taverns where political bosses did much of their work. A longtime supporter of the WCTU, she encouraged the prohibition of alcohol and donated money to reformers who worked to make San Diego "dry."[28]

Ellen also supported the campaign for women's suffrage. In a speech before the La Jolla Woman's Club, she denounced antisuffragists who claimed that women were "too ignorant to vote, or too indifferent." She ridiculed the notion that wives and mothers "would neglect their homes and become cranks and brawlers from the housetops" should they get the vote. Nor did she think that "the sanctity of the home would be invaded and the purity of woman assailed by her entrance into the foul atmosphere of politics." Rather, she thought that women could make a positive contribution by cleaning "those Augean Stables" of political life, shunting aside party greed, personal ambition, and the sacrifice of principles to expediency.[29]

In Ellen's view, women were just beginning to understand their special role in the political process. "Sometimes," she wrote, "I think we do not appreciate the power which lies in our hands; and which—because we are women—must be a power for good." With the vote, women could "regenerate society" and bring an end to myriad abuses such as child labor, urban poverty, lynching, crowded penitentiaries and hospitals, and prostitution. "And the point and pith and weight of this power," she emphasized, "lies in the franchise. Woman's moral influence, her sympathy with the oppressed, her protestations against injustice and iniquity" had done little in the past to remedy such evils. The vote, however, offered an instrument "by which she can do effective work."[30]

In 1911 California women gained the right to vote after a hard-fought campaign led by the California Equal Suffrage Association, the Political Equality League, and the Votes for Women Club, among other organizations. Suffragists held mass rallies and spoke before congregations, unions, factory workers, and women's clubs. They used advertising and produced products such as pennants and posters, playing cards, shopping bags, and postcards. Campaign leaders distributed over ninety thousand Votes for Women buttons in Southern California alone.[31] The result was a narrow victory for Proposition 4—a legislatively referred constitutional amendment—in a special election held on October 10. Ellen noted in her diary, "Election returns show majority of about 3,000 for equal suffrage."[32] California joined Wyoming, Colorado, Utah, Idaho, and Washington as the sixth state to grant women the right to vote.

Meanwhile, in London, suffragists continued to wage a civil-disobedience campaign under the banner of Votes for Women. In 1911 they held demonstrations with as many as forty thousand women on the streets, threatened to force their way into the House of Commons, and smashed windows at the National Liberal Club and Whitehall Palace. Emmeline Pankhurst, founder of the Women's Social and Political Union, an all-women suffrage organization, was arrested along with many other women, some of whom were force-fed when they attempted hunger strikes.

Ellen had been involved in the suffrage movement since the days of Susan B. Anthony and Elizabeth Cady Stanton. She had joined the National Woman Suffrage Association in 1873 and supported the movement through her editorial work on the *Detroit Evening News*. When suffrage came on the ballot in California, Ellen made use of the E. W. Scripps papers in Los Angeles, San Francisco, Fresno, Berkeley, Oakland, and San Diego. Her brother later wrote, "I put all of the California Scripps papers at her service in this respect and so, in an indirect way perhaps, I believe she is responsible for the success of the movement in this state."[33]

After 1912 Ellen encouraged women to make use of their vote. She emphasized the achievements made by female voters in Wyoming, Colorado, Utah, Idaho, and Washington, concluding that most of the humanitarian improvements made in equal suffrage states had been largely the result of women's votes. She recommended "not to vote for party, but for principles, not for the man who stands the best chance of winning, but for the man who stands for the principles that we believe are the right ones, even though we believe that man will be defeated at the polls. The man may be defeated; the principles are eternal."[34]

The political climate in San Diego became increasingly reactionary after 1910 as citizens reacted to the Baja California Revolution of 1911—part of the larger Mexican Revolution—and the bombing of the *Los Angeles Times* building by members of the American labor movement. These two events paved the way in 1912 for San Diego's "free speech" fight, which pitted union supporters against vigilante groups.[35]

Revolutionaries in Baja California sought to overturn Mexico's existing social order, seize control of foreign capital, and redistribute land and factories to the workers. Led by Ricardo Flores Magón and the Los Angeles–based Partido Liberal Mexicano (PLM), the Baja California Revolution brought hundreds of would-be revolutionaries, IWW supporters or "Wobblies," adventurers, and soldiers of fortune to the border. In May 1911 a makeshift army seized Tijuana, hoisted a red flag with the slogan "Tierra y Libertad," and called on the people to "take the land." The garrison held the city for over a month before falling to Mexican federal forces.[36]

At the same time, Irish American trade unionists John J. and James B. McNamara went on trial for the bombing of the *Los Angeles Times* building in October 1910. Described as "the crime of the century," the explosion started a fire that killed twenty-one newspaper employees and injured one hundred more. The McNamara brothers pleaded not guilty to the charges and gained the support of the American Federation of Labor (AFL), defense attorney Clarence Darrow, and muckraking journalist Lincoln Steffens. The editor of the *Los Angeles Record*, a prolabor Scripps newspaper, went "all out" in their defense.[37]

E. W. Scripps considered both events to be evidence of "revolutionary warfare between the classes." In 1911 he invited both Darrow and Steffens to Miramar to discuss the case. There he showed them a disquisition that he had written, "Belligerent Rights in Class Warfare," suggesting that both labor activists and their employers acted outside statute law by engaging in acts of war and employing siege tactics. In the case of the nonunionized *Los Angeles Times*, employees might be considered as

17. Conservative businessman John D. Spreckels dominated San Diego politics in the early twentieth century. San Diego History Center #91:18564-1771.

18. In 1912 San Diego's crackdown on free speech and public assembly inspired IWW activists to protest in downtown's Soapbox Row. San Diego History Center #79:976.

19. Virginia Scripps (*right*) never married but lived with her half-sister Ellen. Ellen Browning Scripps Collection, Ella Strong Denison Library, Scripps College.

20. (*left*) The opinionated and often eccentric Virginia Scripps traveled the world. Collection of the La Jolla Historical Society.

21. (*above*) The Bishop's School encouraged women to participate in athletics and sponsored a faculty softball team. Photo ca. 1915. Courtesy of The Bishop's School.

22. Ellen Browning Scripps relocated houses on a residential block to create a playground for the children of San Diego. The Bishop's School can be seen in the background. Collection of the La Jolla Historical Society.

23. Mayor Edwin M. Capps thanked Ellen Browning Scripps for her contribution of the playground and community house to the city of San Diego. San Diego History Center UT #1390.

24. Ellen commissioned architect Irving J. Gill, a pioneer of the modernist movement in architecture, to rebuild South Molton Villa after a fire in 1915. San Diego History Center #80:7818.

25. South Molton Villa II (1915–16) is considered to be one of Irving J. Gill's masterworks. Collection of the La Jolla Historical Society.

26. An aerial view of Ellen's La Jolla estate, ca. 1917, showing the La Jolla Woman's Club (*center left*) and the Community Center (*center right*). Collection of the La Jolla Historical Society.

27. Scripps Memorial Hospital, designed by William Templeton Johnson, was located close to Ellen's estate on Prospect Street. Photo 1924. San Diego History Center #2597-28.

28. Ellen converted her Pierce-Arrow limousine into an ambulance and donated it to Scripps Memorial Hospital. She stands (*left*) with Ada Gillispie; her chauffeur, Fred Higgins; and an unidentified man. Collection of the La Jolla Historical Society.

29. Ellen Browning Scripps, 1919, as she entered the last and most expansive phase of her philanthropy. Ellen Browning Scripps Collection, Ella Strong Denison Library, Scripps College.

30. At age ninety-one Ellen took her last long trip to Yosemite National Park. She stands in the door of her Rolls Royce near her chauffeur, Fred Higgins; Katharine Peirce Scripps (*right*); and Hilda Gardner (*far right*). 1927. Collection of the La Jolla Historical Society.

31. Architect Gordon B. Kaufmann designed Scripps College in the Mediter-
ranean Revival style. On the left is Eleanor Joy Toll Hall (1927) and on right
Grace Scripps Clark Hall (1928). Scripps Photo Archives, Ella Strong Denison
Library, Scripps College.

32. The first class at Scripps College, class of 1931, in front of Toll Hall. Scripps Photo Archives, Ella Strong Denison Library, Scripps College.

"soldiers enlisted under a capitalist employer whose main purpose in life was warfare against the unions." Must James McNamara, who set the explosive, be condemned as a murderer? Or could he be considered a martyr or patriot? Perhaps "the real disturbers of the peace" were the "very selfish and very few who oppressively and unfairly take to themselves the greater share and far too great a share of the joint product of labor and capital and management"? Recognizing the dangers inherent in his argument, he explained that his paper was intended to provoke debate rather than to represent his true convictions.[38]

E.W. also sent a copy to Ellen, asking for her candid and confidential views on the subject. He wrote, "If McNamara caused the Times explosion, is he entitled to such condemnation as should fall upon an ordinary murderer?" Further, "would you as a woman refuse personal friendship and acquaintance of McNamara simply because he caused the Times explosion providing you knew he did?"[39]

While Ellen's reply does not survive, she did write a speech on the subject. She sympathized with the trade unionists even after they admitted their guilt. "I have been trying to look at this problem . . . from its various angles," she explained, and she found that she could not condemn the McNamaras, particularly after one of the brothers was sentenced to life in prison. "When it comes to the matter of brutal heartlessness," she wrote, "I think, with Lincoln Steffens, I would rather be Jim McNamara in the penitentiary than Judge Bordwell on the bench or the prosecuting attorney in his office seat." She asked, "If it was not murder what was it? If these men are not vicious and brutal, what are they? Why was the deed done? What does it mean? And that brings an entirely new set of principles and arguments and methods into the problem—the great problem of our day and country—the warfare between capital and labor."[40]

The Scrippses, however, represented a minority view. Most San Diego elites followed the lead of sugar-magnate John D. Spreckels, whose newspapers, the *San Diego Union* and the *Evening Tribune*, excoriated the McNamaras as criminals.

Fearful of violence in San Diego, city leaders cracked down on free speech and freedom of assembly. On January 8, 1912, the city council passed Ordinance 4623, which forbade public speaking in the city's commercial center, in particular, Soapbox Row. This area around Fifth Avenue and E Street had attracted large crowds, particularly in the summer of 1911, when a group of revolutionaries captured in Tijuana were released into San Diego. They joined labor unionists, socialists, street speakers, and working-class Anglos, blacks, Mexicans, and Chinese who lived in the Stingaree.[41]

The Scripps-owned *San Diego Sun* opposed the city council's action and predicted, "This ordinance will start a fight that will last for a long time and will be bitter all the time."[42] Trade unionists, socialists, church groups, and other activists also rejected the measure. The Federated Trades of San Diego endorsed a free speech fight and stated, "The right of free speech, of a free press and of public assemblage, are fundamental requisites in a free society."[43] In a letter to the mayor, the general secretary of the IWW warned: "This fight will be continued until free speech is established in San Diego if it takes 20,000 members and twenty years to do so."[44]

Shortly thereafter, protesters founded the California Free Speech League and encouraged people to head to San Diego and speak in the streets. Arrested by the police and thrown into jail, they kept coming. One pamphlet exhorted its readers, "Insist that the Constitution is the fundamental law of this land and go to prison; there you are fed out of a trough like swine, sleep on a bare cement floor without a rag to cover you!"[45]

Over the next several months, hundreds were arrested, inspiring a song printed in the *Industrial Worker* on May 1, 1912, entitled "We're Bound for San Diego":

> In that town called San Diego when the workers try to talk,
> The cops will smash them with a say and tell 'em "take a walk,"
> They throw them in a bull pen and they feed them rotten beans,
> And they call that "law and order" in that city, so it seems.[46]

On April 1 the *Sun* reported that protesters planned to gather in support of the 280 men who had been arrested for street speaking in San Diego, many of them "manhandled by the city's police."[47] "Singing the 'Marseillaise,' as it was sung in France more than 100 years ago, 10,000 of San Francisco's unemployed will start for San Diego within a week to take part in a 'free speech' fight being waged there by Industrial Workers of the World," the newspaper reported. It also published a letter to the editor that asked "how long the authorities are going to sit with folded arms while acts are being perpetrated in the streets of San Diego which would hardly be tolerated today in Russia." He went on to describe the testimony of a female reporter for the *Sun:* "I witnessed five big strapping city policemen beating, pounding, and kicking one little defenseless man . . . and when he got to his feet he was knocked down again until he moaned and hollered, 'My God, men, have mercy!'"[48]

Reactionary groups in San Diego, known as "vigilantes," took this as a challenge. Sanctioned by Spreckels and other prominent local businessmen, the vigilantes sought out protesters, attacked them with knives and clubs, forced them to kiss the flag and sing "The Star Spangled Banner," and drove them to the edge of the city.[49] A *Sun* reporter wrote that a posse of forty men carrying heavy clubs and armed with rifles and revolvers was patrolling the county line to prevent the influx of labor agitators. They intercepted a Santa Fe freight train, pulled off seventy-two IWW supporters, searched them, forced them to "run the gauntlet," and imprisoned them overnight in a cattle corral.[50] Vigilantes also abducted Abraham R. Sauer, the editor and publisher of the muckraking *Weekly Herald.*[51]

The editorial page of Spreckels's *San Diego Union* supported the vigilantes, proclaiming, "And this is what these agitators (all of them) may expect from now on." The *San Diego Tribune*, meanwhile, advocated taking the men out of the jails and shooting or hanging them: "Hanging is none too good for them and they would be much better dead; for they are absolutely useless in the human economy; they are waste material of creation and should be drained off in the sewer of oblivion there to rot in cold obstruction like any other excrement."[52]

The violence peaked following anarchist Emma Goldman's arrival from Los Angeles after having delivered a funeral oration for Joseph Mikolasek, an IWW man killed by San Diego police. On May 14, 1912, the day of the presidential primary elections, an angry crowd greeted her at the Santa Fe train station, promising to "strip her naked" and "tear out her guts." Her manager and lover, Ben Reitman, called the *Sun* to explain that she made it safely to the U. S. Grant Hotel only to learn that her lecture at Germania Hall had been canceled. He continued, "The fact that she cannot speak, however, is astounding. Honestly, would you think this was the twentieth century?" Goldman told a reporter that she had not come to take part in the free speech fight but "to find out what the actual situation is," not believing the reports that had appeared in New York papers. She said, "I was surprised at the crowd that gathered around me coming from the station, and the things they said about me. Some cried for a rope to hang me, and others called for some one to shoot me. They called me many names."[53]

Soon afterward, vigilantes kidnapped Reitman, drove him outside the city, beat him senseless, covered him with tar and sagebrush, and burned the letters I.W.W. on his buttocks. He declared that the police had aided in or connived at his abduction. The *Sun* interviewed a witness who explained, "'He was tarred and feathered,' said this man, '[b]ut not otherwise mistreated.'"[54]

Ellen, appalled by what had happened, spoke about the incident before the La Jolla Woman's Club.[55] She described the "disgraceful conditions that have prevailed in San Diego since the authorities undertook to suppress street speaking," telling fellow clubwomen,

> I think women would have managed the Industrial Workers of the World better, and less to the discredit of the city. Why, Los Angeles managed better. There last Monday for 4 blocks of the city marched 4 abreast men and women in the funeral procession of the man who was killed in San Diego by a policeman—in discharge of his duty! They carried in the midst the banner of the Industrial Workers of the World, with the great red flag of the anarchists, singing as they went the *Marseillaise*. There was not only no police interference but every assistance was rendered, even to keeping the traffic blocked while the procession of a thousand men and women was passing. Emma

Goldman delivered unmolested and un-hooted the funeral oration and banners carried bore such legends as these: "Our silence in the grave will be more powerful than the force you strangle today."

She continued, "The defenders of liberty are jailed and murdered, the vigilantes still go free," all in support of an ordinance that suppressed basic rights. She concluded by calling on women to take up the challenge of political power: "There is no wrong committed anywhere—legally or morally—that does not concern every one of us. . . . The time may not have come yet when we can work effectively in public policies; but it will surely come, and we ought to be ready."[56]

The *San Diego Sun*, one of the few newspapers to carry news of the IWW demonstrations, earned the hostility of the vigilantes and their backers, who, according to Scripps newspaperman Robert F. Paine, "included pretty near everybody." When a stream of Socialist Party leaders and union labor officials from Los Angeles began to arrive at Miramar in late May, E.W. himself was targeted by vigilantes. His son Jim heard the repeated threat, *"We ought to go out and get old Scripps!"* causing him to bring his father a pump shotgun and a box of shells. A crowd of men reached Miramar one evening but were turned back by a guard at the ranch gate, disappointing E.W., who had hoped for a chance "to defend my castle with arms."[57]

The End of an Era

Deeply upset by San Diego's free speech fight, E.W. began to withdraw from local politics. In 1914, following the death of his son John Paul, he left Miramar and headed to Washington, D.C. "The family all left yesterday morning," Ellen noted, "and for the first time in 22 years the household is completely broken up, and the house closed."[58]

Ellen remained hopeful about the possibilities for good political leadership. She wrote to her brother, "Now I am waiting—hopefully—for your letter from Washington. I am hoping that you will not be disappointed in the men you meet; that you will find them not altogether politicians or diplomats or time servers or grafters." She was sure that the nation's capital contained "men with high ideals and lofty aims who have good common sense, and who work 'for the joy of working.'" She particularly hoped that he would meet President Woodrow S. Wilson, whom she had supported in 1912, adding, "I don't want to hear about him, unless you find him a man 'worth while.'"[59]

In Washington, E.W. spoke with San Diego's newly elected congressman, William "Bill" Kettner, explaining that he could not lend him the support of the Scripps papers. He wrote to Ellen, "I told him that I liked him well enough personally to help him, if it were not that he was the representative, or perhaps the only choice, of Spreckels, the Chamber of Commerce, and that whole crowd out of which was organized the vigilantes committee." Kettner protested that he had not been involved in the violence. "I told him that made no difference," E.W. wrote. "He had never even expressed himself against the vigilantes."[60]

E.W. did not abandon the *San Diego Sun*, however. Although he did not intend to interfere in the management of the paper, he could not help reminding its editors of their responsibilities to the city of San Diego. In February 1913 he told editor Clarence A. McGrew that Scripps papers "should always be devoted to the service of the 95%, namely the working man and the poor and unfortunate." He asked him, "Under present local political conditions can the Sun serve the unpropertied class of San Diego politics in any other way than by giving the socialists every opportunity to present their claims and to expose what they consider to be the faults of their political opponents?"[61] In years to come, the *Sun* consolidated its reputation as "the only paper in San Diego which has any principles at all," according to progressive activist Dr. Charlotte Baker, "the only one which ever stands squarely for anything which is morally right, the only one from which we can hope anything except bitter opposition."[62]

Aware that "the capitalist class" controlled most of the press, E.W. continued his efforts to provide for alternate versions of the news. He claimed that his telegraph service, the United Press (UP), had prevented the Associated Press (AP) from monopolizing the wire stories. In his words, the AP was "the greatest aid that the big business interests could have had in the prosecution of their oppressive schemes." The UP, meanwhile, was "free and independent of corrupting capitalism."[63]

E.W. also supported labor issues with an advertisement-free newspaper, the *Chicago Day Book*. While all of the Scripps papers, including the *Detroit Evening News*, pitched their articles to the working classes, they were hampered by antiunion advertisers. Scripps described them as "the proverbial tail wagging the dog," suppressing articles, demanding special treatment, and influencing editorial policy. Scripps wanted papers that were "the servant of the common people and not of the money class and especially not of the advertising public." The *Chicago Day Book*, which had supported the McNamaras during their trial, became a favorite of organized labor in Chicago.[64]

Ellen approved of the *Day Book* and in 1914 met with editor Negley D. Cochran to consider an investment in "another adless newspaper."[65] E.W. had not intended to bother her with the details of the transaction but decided in the end to communicate with her directly rather than go through her lawyer. "Harper is thick-headed, of course," he wrote. "He is wonderfully friendly to the adless paper, but he can only see as through a glass darkly the figure that is to my eyes so clear and distinct." Ellen, on the other hand, had always been a source of excellent business advice. E.W. wrote to his sister, "Old as you are and female as you are, I am sure that your vision is clearer and your imagination more vivid in such matters than that of any man that I know of, to whom the subject could be presented." In fact, he thought that her intelligence—in a man— would be "enough to lift him head and shoulders above his fellows."[66]

Ellen remained deeply affected by the events of 1912. Like her brother, she became increasingly concerned about the protection of constitutional rights, including freedom of speech, freedom of the press, public assembly, and religious tolerance. She also recognized the need to provide progressive political activists, including socialists, a place to speak and be heard.[67] To that end, she ensured that La Jolla had spaces where people could express their opinions without fear of censorship by civil authorities.

CHAPTER 9

Sweet Virginia

In early La Jolla, Ellen was known as one half of the couple referred to as "the Scripps sisters." She and Virginia lived together at South Molton Villa, belonged to the same clubs, shared many friends, traveled together, and gave joint parties. They enjoyed a comfortable, companionable relationship, despite the fact that they were as different as two people could be.

A handsome woman, Virginia, or "Jenny," remained vital and energetic into her fifties and sixties. She wore her full head of white hair coiled up in braids and kept her figure trim and athletic by constant exercise and gardening. She had an expressive face and "a loose-jointed walk, leaning forward and rushing over the ground."[1] She could be assertive, demanding, forthright, and occasionally downright rude, qualities that led contemporaries to describe her as "eccentric." She was also kindhearted, good-humored, hardworking, and generous. Her sister's chauffeur recalled, "If she took a fancy to you, there wasn't anything she wouldn't do for you."[2] She made friends easily and inspired admiration for her courage and adventurous spirit, particularly among modern young women unburdened by the baggage of a Victorian upbringing.

Ellen, meanwhile, became increasingly frail as she aged. Always thin, she grew smaller still, masking her bird-like legs and arms under full skirts and long sweaters. Her face, considered very plain in her youth, was softened by fine lines and gently drooping skin along her jaw. She wore her hair as she had always worn it, pulled tightly into a donut-shaped bun on the top of her head. A contemporary described her as "quiet, reserved and unassuming, but a real power, nevertheless."[3] Ellen drew strength from her outgoing and opinionated sister. She relied on her judgment, appreciated her outspoken nature, and enjoyed the life and energy that she brought into the house.

"Two Peas in a Pod"

Ellen considered Virginia to be much like her brother E.W. in terms of energy, determination, and the ability to disregard the opinion of others. In fact, she often described them as "two peas in a pod." Her brother opined, "That might be because Virginia's maleness in quantity equaled mine, or my femaleness in quantity equaled hers."[4] Ultimately, he came to the conclusion that his sister would have been happier if she had been able to achieve her ambitions, that is, if she had been born male. As a woman, she could only expend her energies in emotional "explosions," while he, a man, had the ability to "expend my energies largely by pushing hard and pulling hard."[5]

Although Virginia had worked on various Scripps papers, she had been dissuaded from a literary career by her older brother James. She told Ellen, "J.E. always snubbed me" when she proposed such a thing, adding, "It was his cruel remarks that crushed in me all desire I ever had (which was not much) to write for publication." She preferred to express herself in private letters, "where the spelling is overlooked as a heritage descending from father to daughter."[6]

Virginia's unhappy relationship with her older brother put her squarely on E.W.'s side of the Scripps family feud. In 1900 she sent several letters to James, reminding him why their brother George had cut him out of his will. "I told him just what I told him 6 years ago," she explained to Ellen, "that George H. was hurt to the quick by his conduct in removing him from the *News* office. If you could have heard then the mean things James said of George H. you would never have forgiven him." She continued to describe her letter: "I say most emphatically that George

H. was most certainly in the full possession of his mind and there was no undue influence used. He had himself and George Booth to blame for George H.'s actions and no one else."[7]

Virginia's inheritance from George included stock in the *Cincinnati Post* and the Scripps-McRae newspapers. This substantial sum of money allowed her considerable freedom to travel, dispense patronage, buy land, and live independently of her sister for part of each year. Nevertheless, she remained a fixture in the La Jolla social scene and a frequent visitor to Miramar.

Cleaning Up

Virginia channeled her energies in a variety of different ways, most notably, by cleaning up La Jolla. She maneuvered through the dusty streets with a little wheelbarrow and shovel, picking up debris, including horse droppings, which she used to fertilize her lawn. Scandalized, one female tourist told a neighbor, "I think it a real disgrace for this place to employ a woman to clean its streets." She was told, "Don't worry. That woman is a very wealthy lady, and doesn't have to do any work except for the pleasure she derives doing it."[8]

Virginia's nephew recalled, "Every morning she walked around town picking up papers. If she saw anyone drop a piece of paper in the street, she ran after them shouting and waving her pocketbook or a stick. She really jumped men for spitting tobacco juice."[9] On one occasion, she decided to sweep out the local grocery. A resident recalled, "I was in the grocery store one morning and she came in and she asked the proprietor for a broom and he brought her the broom and wondered what she wanted the broom for and she said, 'Well, this store is terribly dirty—I'm going to sweep this place out—I'll just show you how you ought to keep a grocery store.'"[10]

Mabel Clark, vacationing with her parents in La Jolla after college, described Virginia as "the character of the place." She wrote, "She is a woman of 58, eats her breakfast at 8, and digs out on the street improving things all day unless she dresses up in a handsome purple gown or embroidered silk and looks stunning with her white hair and elegant clothes. She says she can work on the streets and yet be a lady." Clark thought that since Virginia's sister had a housekeeper, "this outdoor work is her way of letting off steam."[11]

Young girls in particular looked up to her. The ten-year-old Jean Bartlett used to hurry after school to help Virginia with her cleanup efforts. "I would pick up orange peels and papers right beside her," she remembered. "I really admired her—in an odd sort of way. She was so darned zany but she did get things done. She was a woman of action and I liked that."[12]

Philanthropy

Virginia owned two summer cottages, Wisteria Cottage and Iris Cottage, both built in the Arts and Crafts style. She was very generous with these properties, often loaning them out free of charge to family members, friends, and La Jolla residents who suffered incapacitating illnesses. One resident remembered her as "a wonderful woman. . . . [S]he used to bring people who were ill to her home to recover."[13]

Ellen looked after the cottages during her sister's trips to Rushville, but not without some degree of irritation. In 1913 she wrote, "How many more people are you going to loan the Iris to this winter?"[14] By her count, three different parties expected to borrow it in January. Later she asked, "Who is to pay for gas and electric bills in the Iris and Wisteria when empty?"[15]

Virginia's good works included taking food to families in the village and inviting neighbors to her Tuesday afternoon "open house" at South Molton Villa. Clark wrote, "We enjoy her bringing us around some batter for buck-wheat cakes before breakfast occasionally, but we dread her blunt, critical speech. She has been very nice to us girls and to mother, bringing us flowers and inviting us over for her 'Tuesday afternoons.'"[16] Every Tuesday, Virginia and Ellen held an open house, serving tea and sandwiches to visitors.

A churchwoman, Virginia focused her philanthropy on Episcopal institutions. At the end of 1905 she opened Wisteria Cottage to her fellow worshipers who had left the First Church of Christ, a Union church. Sunday services began on January 11, 1906, and continued through 1908. Ellen described this as "Jenny's church" and noted that the congregation often numbered as many as fifty people.[17] Wisteria Cottage was later used as a meeting place for the Altar Guild.[18]

Virginia, together with Ellen, provided the land and financed the construction of St. James by-the-Sea, an Episcopal church located directly across the street from Wisteria Cottage. Architect Irving J. Gill designed a modest structure inspired by Mission San Diego de Alcalá.[19] Dedicated on March 8, 1908, it was "crowded far beyond capacity" with La Jollans keen to view the new church and participate in the service.[20] Virginia donated two immense clamshells from the South Sea Islands, their edges rimmed with silver, for use as a baptismal font. The font was presented to the church by the children of the Sunday school.[21]

According to one resident, Virginia considered St. James to be "her own private church just the way the old families in France and England used to have their private chapels." She bossed around the resident clergyman, sometimes rebuking him right in the middle of the service. "If he said something she disagreed with or talked too long, she was known on one occasion to stand up and say, 'You'd better stop talking now, don't you see everybody is going to sleep?'"[22]

On another occasion, Virginia yelled at some carpenters who were hammering and pounding during a Sunday school rehearsal of a Christmas carol. When they ignored her, she broke into a tirade: "You god-damned fools, what do you mean by making such a noise? Don't you know you are desecrating the House of the Lord?"[23]

Travels with Virginia

"If I have any money get-at-able from [the] George H. estate later on I wish to travel, travel, travel. I am wild to be on the go."[24] Virginia was never happier than while traveling. Her projected and actual inheritance allowed her to see the world without being dependent on the generosity of relatives. Ellen had financed her first trip to Spain and Portugal in 1888–89.[25]

From La Jolla, Virginia sailed to Ensenada and the Coronado Islands.

She visited Tijuana, traveled into Mexico, and made several trips to the Grand Canyon, Yosemite, and other natural wonders of the West. She sometimes traveled with friends such as the widowed Louise M. Pebbles, one of La Jolla's "indestructibles"—little old ladies "who were buzzing around town as busily as if they were in their teens."[26] A resident of Chicago, Pebbles built a summer cottage called the Virginia, named after her granddaughter, and covered it with fifteen varieties of roses, calla lilies, geraniums, and other flowering plants.[27] She and her daughter, Mrs. Frank "Millie" Moore, joined Virginia on an excursion to Alaska in the summer of 1902, a voyage that Virginia repeated in 1913.[28] Another La Jolla friend, Olivia Mudgett, frequently joined her on trips to Miramar.[29]

In April 1902 Virginia went with her sister and sister-in-law to Honolulu to visit the Right Reverend Henry B. Restarick, the former rector of St. Paul's Church in San Diego, who had been created the first Episcopal American bishop of the Hawaiian Islands. After a week in Honolulu, they traveled to Waialua on Oahu's North Shore with its wide, coral-strewn beaches and coconut groves. From Honolulu, they sailed thirty-two hours to reach the Big Island. From the tropical atmosphere of Hilo, they traveled by horseback across lava beds to reach the Kilauea volcano, noting that the fissures in the crust "emit heat enough to set fire to wood placed within them, to pop corn, heat water, etc." They saw abandoned coffee plantations half-concealed behind hedges of wild roses, raspberry vines, and ferns.[30]

In 1906 Virginia visited Europe, Palestine, India, and the Philippines before joining William and Mary Ritter on their trip to Japan. Ellen wrote to her great-niece about a letter written to her from Japan: "I had another long, longer, longest letter from Aunt Jenny. She was having fine times riding about in jim rickshaws, going to Emperor's garden parties, buying new gowns which were 'dreams,' sleeping on floors in Japanese houses, and sitting on her toes as she ate her dinner. She did not say if she ate with chop sticks, but I don't believe she would have the patience for that when she got good and hungry—as she generally does about dinner time."[31]

The architect Irving J. Gill so enjoyed Virginia's company that he told Ellen he would be glad to join Virginia on a winter trip should she need a companion. Ellen wrote, "He begged me to tell you that he would be all ready at a moment's notice to serve in that capacity."[32] Sadly for Gill, this never transpired.

In 1915 the world came to San Diego in the form of the Panama-California Exposition. Ellen and Virginia had visited several world's fairs together, including the World's Columbian Exposition in Chicago (1892) and the Louisiana Purchase Exhibition in St. Louis (1904), where Virginia chose to celebrate her fifty-second birthday. In St. Louis they took an evening gondola ride on the Grand Basin, viewed a reenactment of the Anglo-Boer War, and visited the Neo-Classical Palace of Fine Art, among other activities.[33] Virginia was just as keen on San Diego's exposition, which, though modest, managed to successfully compete with San Francisco's Panama-Pacific International Exposition held in the same year.

At midnight on December 31, 1914, Virginia and Ellen attended the grand opening of the Panama-California Exposition accompanied by their niece Grace Scripps Clark and other family members.[34] They returned many times over the course of 1915 and 1916 to enjoy Spanish Colonial Revival architecture, beautifully landscaped grounds, and exhibitions of art that celebrated the ancient Maya, Inca, and Aztec civilizations. In January 1916 Virginia took several friends to hear a concert by Ernestine Schumann-Heink and Ellen Beach Yaw, recording artists for the Victor Talking Machine Company who had become international celebrities. Later in the summer, Ellen and Virginia picnicked with friends and family in the Pepper Grove.[35] The former remarked, "I shall be sorry when the grounds close to the public—if they do close—for everything grows more beautiful, it seems, each day."[36] She was cheered by plans to preserve the exposition buildings and make them the nucleus of a "great educational and recreational center in Balboa Park."[37]

Virginia spent a great deal of time in the company of family members. Of her many nieces, she held Florence "Floy" Scripps Kellogg, daughter of Will Scripps, in particular esteem. Floy was married to

Frederick "F.W." Kellogg, founder and president of the Clover Leaf Newspaper League, a group of midwestern papers that had been spun off from the Scripps-McRae League. After making numerous visits to San Diego, she moved with her husband from Kansas City to Altadena, California, in 1915. Like Virginia, Floy was "a 'gadder' par excellence" who loved socializing and organizing entertainments.[38] She was also a poet who, in her later years, published several volumes of poetry. In 1935 she and her husband bought the largely defunct La Jolla Beach & Yacht Club and turned it into the La Jolla Beach & Tennis Club, which still operates today.

Virginia enjoyed the company of talkative, intelligent women. In 1917 she met Margaret W. Vandercook, a New York writer who summered in La Jolla. Ellen wrote, "The Vandercooks have become a part of the family. Virginia has taken to them very decidedly, and is lavish in her attentions. . . . Mrs. Vandercook is a woman full of life, fervor and enthusiasm, interested in all things from the highest abstract to the lowest concrete quality—likes to go everywhere, to see and hear everything and to discuss all and any questions with discerning people."[39]

Virginia also befriended summer visitors to La Jolla, some of whom returned, hoping to find her at home. Ellen noted in her diary that a Mr. and Mrs. Mead from Pasadena had called at South Molton Villa while on a trip to San Diego: "Were here a year ago, and knew 'Miss Virginia' very well."[40] A Mrs. Slater, meanwhile, asked Ellen to tell her sister that "La Jolla did not seem just right without you."[41] After her 1904 visit to La Jolla, Helen Gardner wrote to her cousin, "I miss E[liza] Virginia ever so much. We have been together for 3 months and I can't get used to being without her."[42]

Not everyone appreciated Virginia's insistence on being neighborly. Marjorie and Robert Henri, for example, spent the summer of 1914 trying to avoid the youngest Scripps sister and her friends. Having come from New York on the strength of an invitation from artist Alice Klauber, they anticipated an avant-garde cultural scene. They appreciated the accommodations provided to them by Mary Richmond, who had commissioned architect Irving J. Gill to design a very modern concrete bungalow.[43] But they found the village to be "awfully dry and colorless and half asleep." After attending a few tea parties, Marjorie Henri realized that there were "women, women everywhere and none of them young or pretty. All look middle aged and passé, skinny and dried." She described La Jolla in a letter to her mother-in-law: "[It is] absolutely a woman's town. They own everything and run everything and talk politics incessantly. Just talk and empty phrases—things they've read. Twang, twang, twang. They are endless, and such Boosters—you wouldn't believe it, but it's Boost-Boost-California-California-Climate, etc."[44] Virginia Scripps was the worst of the lot. Marjorie and her husband encountered her for the first time on a train going into San Diego. The sixty-two-year-old, "spry as a chicken," proceeded to nab an unsuspecting young man and talk at him for forty-five minutes, despite his efforts to retreat behind a newspaper.[45]

Never known for leaving visitors to their own devices, Virginia called on the couple. Robert Henri made it clear that it was not convenient for him to entertain guests and refused to allow her to enter. Virginia was irate. Marjorie recalled, "She couldn't understand that she, Miss Virginia Squibbs [*sic*], owner and maker of La Jolla shouldn't be admitted. She told it to the whole town, and most of the people were glad that for once in her life she got it."[46]

Ellen and Virginia

Ellen tolerated her sister's eccentricities, including her ability to swear and drink whiskey neat. Driving through the San Joaquin Valley, Virginia pulled over to question a motorcyclist, "Where the hell are we?"[47] She routinely carried a small flask filled with liquor. Ellen recalled their sharing "a little bottle of brandy" during a grueling trip through the Grand Canyon in the 1890s; she told Harper that they "drained every drop and washed it out to get the last."[48] In 1914 she told Virginia, "You'd better lay in a stock of whiskey in case California goes dry—as we fervently hope it will!" She repeated the advice in 1916: "You'd better lay in a stock of the 'Old Crow' before going to Detroit. You know Michigan is a 'dry' state—or will be by Jan 1/17."[49]

Ellen could also swear, though she only rarely took a drink. She often suffered from "a sore mouth" due to ill-fitting false teeth. Once when asked how she was feeling, she replied that it was "just one damned thing after another," then laughed.[50]

Observers often contrasted Virginia with her quieter older sister. Ethel Calloway told a story of buying a dressy black hat with a coral bow to wear on a visit to the Scripps sisters. Virginia, answering the door, exclaimed, "Ethel, *where* on earth did you get that hat?" Ellen, meanwhile, welcomed her in the house and said, "Ethel, I think it's *such* a pretty hat." Ethel later wrote, "That, I'll never forget if I live to be a hundred. That's just typical of the two—Miss Virginia was outspoken, and Miss Scripps was so kind and darling."[51]

Virginia had a lust for life that manifested itself in her ability to shop and spend money. She had a good eye for fashion and a taste for buying very expensive clothes. In 1918 she spent $150 (about $2,360 in 2016 dollars) on a bright purple suit at Ballard & Brocket, an upscale women's clothing store in San Diego.[52] She also shopped for her sister, who found it difficult to select "smart" outfits to wear to parties. In 1916 Ellen wore one of Virginia's gifts to The Bishop's School's annual reception, "and people thought it nice." Margaret Gilman, head of The Bishop's School, told her, "What a beautiful gown, so pretty and so becoming," and added, "I wish Miss Virginia would send you one every day!"[53] Virginia only occasionally forgot that Ellen did not have her stylish figure, sending along what Ellen called a "Venus-shaped article."[54]

Virginia was also a hearty eater who loved to read descriptive accounts of food. In her letters, Ellen described the menu offered at dinner parties and receptions, "which I know you like to hear about." Lunch at the clubhouse included "hot clam chowder with crackers; hot macaroni and cheese; with various kinds of appetizing sandwiches; and fig jam; fruit salad with wafers, ice cream and cake; coffee interspersed and finally a table full of baskets of oranges and apples."[55] A pretheater supper at Katharine Scripps's house turned into a "veritable dinner—ham and tongue, escalloped potatoes, cauliflower, hot biscuits, tomato salad, and all the accessories of entrees and desserts."[56]

When Virginia was away, Ellen ate very simply. She told her sister, "I'm afraid you are living so luxuriously that it will seem like prison fare when you get back. Except when someone is here, I have got things down to a pretty plain table: no meats, no desserts, toast and coffee for breakfast, toast and tea for supper, and two or three vegetables for dinner—that is all!"[57]

Virginia played an important role in Ellen's life, heading off unwanted visitors and filling social space with conversation. She kept track of family news, local gossip, real estate transactions, and public entertainments; organized excursions; and dealt with tradesmen, builders, and gardeners. She also identified philanthropic projects that deserved her sister's attention. In fact, many of the investments that Ellen made in La Jolla can be attributed to the influence of the other "Miss Scripps."

CHAPTER 10

Educating Girls

Between 1907 and 1915 Ellen began a flurry of "building" in La Jolla, financing the construction of public spaces such as a library, a playground, a school, a women's club, a church, and a research center. She was not simply trying to improve the appearance of the village—or to increase property values—but to create the kinds of institutions that would encourage democratic principles, promote social progress, and contribute to what she described as "the evolution and uplift of the human race."[1]

Ellen's first significant project was The Bishop's School, a college preparatory school for girls established by the Right Reverend Joseph Horsfall Johnson, bishop of the Los Angeles Diocese of the Episcopal Church. His jurisdiction extended over all eight counties of Southern California, including San Diego. While Ellen had little interest in parochial education, she believed that the bishop could create a progressive institution that would help women to develop their intellectual capacities and gain a sense of purpose and self-worth. For someone who had shed her religious upbringing, she did a good deal for the Episcopal Church.

The Bishop's School was founded at a time of expanding educational opportunities for women. Between 1870 and 1900 the number of women enrolled in U.S. colleges and universities multiplied eightfold, from eleven thousand to eighty-five thousand. Women's colleges such as Vassar (1861), Wellesley (1875), Smith (1875), and Bryn Mawr (1885) became national institutions. Seminaries such as Mount Holyoke, Mills, and Rockford were rechartered as colleges in the 1880s. Women attended private coeducational institutions such as Boston College, Cornell, Oberlin, Swarthmore, and the University of Chicago. They also enrolled at large state universities in California, Indiana, Iowa, Kansas, Michigan, Missouri, and Wisconsin. Although elite men's colleges such as Harvard, Yale, Princeton, and Columbia did not admit women, reformers continued to press for access. Their efforts resulted in the creation of Barnard (1889) and Radcliffe (1894) as affiliated women's colleges.[2]

At the turn of the century, educational reformers established independent girls' schools that would prepare women for college. The Bryn Mawr School in Baltimore, established in 1885, offered one of the earliest and most innovative programs. Students studied English, history, geometry, algebra, laboratory sciences, German or Greek, and music. Other college preparatory institutions for women included the Brearley School in New York (1884), the Marlborough School in Los Angeles (1889), and the National Cathedral School in Washington, DC (1900).

Bishop Johnson was an energetic and enthusiastic supporter of education. He established one of the first diocesan summer schools in 1902 in Santa Monica and considered creating a college affiliated with the Episcopal Church. However, he finally came to the conclusion that the establishment of good preparatory schools was "the greatest contribution that the Diocese of Los Angeles could make."[3]

In 1907 he began laying plans for a girls' preparatory school in Sierra Madre, not far from Pasadena. He tapped Anna Frances O'Hare Bentham and Rev. Charles Edward Bentham to head the new school. At the time, Charles Bentham was rector of the Church of the Ascension in Sierra Madre. A Harvard graduate, he had attended Berkeley Divinity School and was ordained priest in 1901. Anna Bentham had been educated at the Boston Normal School and the Massachusetts Institute of Technology. When Bishop Johnson offered her the position of headmistress, she was head of the English Department at the Marlborough School.[4]

Not long after their appointment, the Benthams met the Scripps sisters while vacationing in La Jolla. Ellen had recently donated property on which Irving J. Gill would build the mission church of St. James by-the-Sea. Taking note of the Benthams' close relationship with the bishop, Ellen suggested that they review the plans and meet with the architect.[5]

In January 1908 Bishop Johnson approached Ellen and Virginia about the possibility of moving his proposed school to San Diego. Ellen wrote, "Bishop Johnson spent the afternoon here. Greatly admired the church. Had some conversation with him in regard to a plan that he has for establishing two schools under the direction of the church."[6] He imagined two separate campuses: a day school in San Diego and a boarding school in La Jolla.

Ellen supported the idea of a girls' school in La Jolla and promised to contribute the sum of $10,000 (about $266,000 in 2016 dollars).[7] She liked the bishop, an affable and engaging man, and trusted his good intentions. She later told one educator, "I have a high appreciation of Bishop Johnson's character and a great sympathy with his work and aspirations—as a man, not as a clergyman. My instincts and interests are educational—not religious (I feel as though I might be sailing under false colors if I did not explain this to you)."[8]

In order to generate revenue to pay for the construction of two campuses, the bishop started classes in a cottage behind a two-story house on Fifth Street in Bankers Hill, not far from downtown San Diego. On January 4, 1909, the first students, ranging in age from eight to fourteen, gathered for classes. Ellen noted in her diary that the Benthams "feel encouraged with the school prospects, having already 10 pupils."[9]

Ellen recommended that Gill be chosen to design The Bishop's School, encompassing a day school located at First Avenue and Redwood Street in San Diego and a boarding school in La Jolla.[10] In August 1909 Ellen met Bishop Johnson at the architect's downtown office to discuss plans for the new buildings in La Jolla. She wrote in her diary, "By appointment with Bishop Johnson at Mr. Gill's in relation to school. He promises him $25,000 for school at La Jolla." In October she wrote, "Bishop Johnson here all the morning looking around at lots and buildings. Also brought out plans of new school building."[11]

Gill's first structure on the La Jolla campus, Scripps Hall (1910), was a white concrete building with long arcades. An article in the *Craftsman* praised it as fireproof, sanitary, and "so free from superfluous ornament that it furnishes a new standard for architectural simplicity." The white walls captured the colors of the sunset and glowed "like opals." Inside, plain rooms allowed each girl "to express her individuality" by choosing the decorations.[12] Doors were made of a single panel of wood, and there were no moldings, cornices, or baseboards to collect and hold dirt. The architect's concern with health and sanitation reflected the contemporary belief that disease and poor health were caused by dampness, dust, germs, and air pollution. Gill's realization that buildings could solve social problems put him at the forefront of the modernist movement in architecture.[13]

Ellen became personally interested in The Bishop's School, contributing more money than she had planned. She explained to her attorney, "The execution of the building itself has not exceeded the cost originally contemplated but you know how things 'grow,' how one thing leads to and necessitates another—the improvement of the grounds, the artistic bills of finish, the furnishing, etc., etc." She believed that the school was "destined to be a grand institution" and therefore worth the investment. She wrote, "I feel more than assured that I have embarked on an undertaking that is almost limitless in its scope and power for good."[14]

Virginia also felt responsible for the future of the institution. She donated $20,000 (about $537,000) and several parcels of land in 1909. She later turned over most of her La Jolla properties to the school in order to create a scholarship endowment.[15] She worked on the grounds and maintained the tennis, croquet, and basketball courts outside school. Feeling that "trees were dirty," she refused to allow them to enhance the beauty of the stark white buildings.[16] A headmistress recalled hearing Virginia swear at Kate Sessions, who was trying to put in some native California shrubs that Virginia found unsuitable.[17]

Virginia tempered her strict oversight with entertainments for both teachers and students. Having purchased a new phonograph, she invited the teachers and students, as well as "a number of other musical folk," to hear recordings of Ruggero Leoncavallo's opera *Pagliacci*.[18] In 1912 she took instructors on a holiday trip to Miramar; the following year, she hosted a party of eighteen girls to a moving picture show and afterward to an "ice cream restaurant."[19] She attended numerous events at the school—luncheons and dinners, theatricals, concerts, and basketball games—often bringing guests and friends.

Virginia's eccentricities (which included rearranging the school's drawing room furniture) endeared her to students, who in 1914 selected her as the senior class mascot. They also included her as a character in a skit, "a 'take off' of the 'wise and reverend designers' of the school."[20] Ellen often gave her sister credit for the success of the institution. After Bishop Johnson's inspection in October 1914, she wrote, "I need not tell you (as the bishop will do, I trust, more thoroughly) how splendid he thinks the work you have done. . . . (He gave no credit to me, either!)"[21]

College Bound

From the start, The Bishop's School sought to prepare girls for college. The headmistress ensured that no student enrolled in the college preparatory program would be graduated "unless she has satisfactorily completed such subjects as are required for admission to the best Eastern colleges." Students also had the option of taking a degree in English or music, subjects that did not qualify them for college admission. Many girls, however, chose the more challenging preparatory course. In doing so, they emulated their teachers, young women with degrees from Vassar, Smith, Cornell, Wellesley, and the University of California.[22]

Headmistress Anna Bentham served as a role model for many students during her relatively short tenure. Tall, with auburn hair and a pale complexion, she projected a theatrical grandeur. Students recalled how she swept into a room in a white satin dress with a train, causing conversation to cease. When she attended athletic events, crowds stood up and applauded. Ellen recalled "her gracious majesty of bearing and white satin and smile moving regally about the audience."[23] However, Ellen did not entirely approve of her influence. "What's the use of expecting the school girls to wear simple head gear," she wrote, "when Mrs. Bentham leads off in those flaunting white ostrich plumes?"[24]

Tragically, Anna Bentham and her husband died within three weeks of each other. Anna suffered from severe diabetes and passed away in January 1915 at age thirty-eight, shortly after her husband's death from heart disease at age forty. An obituary in the *Los Angeles Daily Times* described her as one of the "foremost of women educators and leaders in Southern California."[25]

In 1915 Bishop Johnson decided to integrate the day school and the boarding school. Teachers would no longer have to travel between one campus and the other. The Bankers Hill property was leased to a former principal from Minneapolis who ran the San Diego Bishop's School for two years before financial losses caused it to close.[26]

The La Jolla campus, meanwhile, expanded to include three structures designed by Gill: Scripps Hall (1910), Bentham Hall (1912), and Gilman Hall (1916–17). Ellen toured the newest building "from cellar to roof (which came out in a 'sleeping porch')." She said that it was "large enough to accommodate 40 or 50 girls. The rooms are beautiful and every one with a fine outlook."[27]

Margaret Gilman became principal of The Bishop's School in 1915. She was the daughter of Arthur and Stella Scott Gilman, pioneers in women's higher education.[28] They helped found Radcliffe College and in 1886 founded the Gilman School for Girls in Cambridge, Massachusetts (later the Cambridge School of Weston). Margaret spent her early career at Radcliffe, where she served as head of house. She later became principal of the Lincoln School in Providence, Rhode Island, a Quaker preparatory school for girls. Bishop Johnson credited her for bringing that institution "to its present eminence and high standing."[29] Although she did not have her predecessor's flair for drama, she was earnest and well-meaning. Ellen found her to be somewhat trying, telling her sister, "I think you could 'meet her needs' better than I can. She seems to crave affection, understanding, appreciation, and a confidential friend, more than in me lies to bestow."[30] But Ellen admitted that Gilman made a significant impact on campus life: "The more I see of her the more I esteem her in her official position."[31]

Gilman kept academics foremost in the minds of students. After going to chapel early in the morning, girls spent the next five hours in the classroom. They attended two mandatory study halls, from 4:30 to 6:00 p.m. and from 8:00 to 9:00 p.m. Seniors took advanced classes in both geometry and arithmetic. They also developed a portfolio of their work for display at commencement. By 1916 Bishop's students were sufficiently well prepared to pass rigorous college entrance exams. In October 1917 Gilman told a meeting of the board of trustees "what last year's graduating class are doing: 1 at Vassar, 1 at Barnard, 1 at Occidental, 2 at Berkeley, 1 at Mills, and 1 at Syracuse, 1 in business (that is, Mary), 1 in society, and 1 a question mark."[32]

The school also emphasized sports, in particular, tennis and basketball. Students divided into two teams, Harvard and Yale, and competed with one another and, on occasion, girls from San Diego High School. In 1917 the teams changed their names to Army and Navy to recognize the United States' participation in World War I. In November 1917 Ellen reported: "The girls' basketball league of The Bishop's School— the Army and the Navy opposing forces had their contesting game in the afternoon, the army winning by one point—a very exciting game, I am told." On another occasion, she described girls engaged in "'high jumping' over a fixed rod four feet high."[33] Students later adopted the team names Purple and Gold to honor Ellen's alma mater, Knox College.

Educational reformers paid particular attention to physical activity as a way to prevent the kind of ill health that had plagued nineteenth-century women. Other solutions included fresh air, balanced meals, adequate ventilation, experimental water cures, and calisthenics. At Bishop's, boarders took cold baths, intended to stimulate intellectual activity. On warm nights they slept outdoors above the arcade of Scripps Hall. In addition to team sports, students attended calisthenics classes and competed in swimming contests at Del Mar.[34]

Female faculty and students also participated in community service activities. Many women during the Progressive Era believed in their capacity for advanced education and in their need for independence and an equal voice in the public world. They rejected the idea that women and men were the same, however, arguing that women's compassionate natures made them particularly suited to helping less fortunate members of society. Some followed the example set by Jane Addams and her Hull House settlement in Chicago and founded institutions such as San Diego's Neighborhood House. Others volunteered at hospitals, organized charity rummage sales, sponsored Girl Scout troops, and raised money through women's clubs. At The Bishop's School, students dressed dolls for patients at the Children's Hospital and packed supplies for the Mesa Grande Reservation and other missions in California and Alaska. During World War I, they rolled bandages for the Red Cross, raised vegetables, and donated money for military vehicles. A new class, Surgical Dressings, was even introduced into the curriculum.[35]

Students also applied their education to real-world problems. Helen Marston, class of 1912, attended Wellesley College but returned home to San Diego each summer to work at Neighborhood House, where she helped impoverished Mexican families. She later founded a local branch of the Women's International League for Peace and Freedom.[36] Katherine Haskell, class of 1921, graduated from Mills College and did postgraduate work at the University of Chicago and Purdue. She became a leader in the field of childhood education with her textbook, *The Nursery School: A Human Relationships Laboratory* (1950), and enjoyed a long career as a professor at Oregon State University.[37]

The Bishop's School combined an innovative approach to women's education with an emphasis on Christian character. The school motto, "Simplicitas, Sinceritas, Serenitas," expressed a desire to help students attain "strength and poise in their physical, mental and spiritual lives."[38] At the same time, the school was intended to be the foundation for a women's college in San Diego. According to a 1910 article, Bishop Johnson said that "if the city continues to grow, and The Bishop's School for Girls now being inaugurated keeps pace with the progressiveness of the city, that it will terminate in a women's college equal to any in the country."[39]

Bishop Johnson

Bishop Johnson continued to take an active role in the life of the school. During Bentham's illness, the bishop often came to campus. On one occasion, he stirred up the faculty and staff "from principal to cook-and-sauce man." He went so far as to call one staff member to account after "finding half a dozen donuts in the garbage pail."[40] He presided over meetings of the board of trustees, raised money for new buildings, created scholarship funds, and worried about budget deficits. Ellen told her sister that the bishop took up such tasks "with the understanding of a man . . . exercising a sort of paternal interest over the school."[41]

The bishop's wife, Isabel Greene Davis Johnson, also contributed to the welfare of the school by giving money for a chapel in memory of her mother. The job went to Carleton Monroe Winslow, who had just completed his work as architect in residence for the 1915 Panama-California Exposition in San Diego. Winslow designed a modest nave with choir stalls, exposed timber beams, and old Mexican pavement tiles on the floor.[42] St. Mary's Chapel, dedicated in February 1917, became the spiritual center of life on campus. In 1938 Winslow added transepts and a baptistery, while friends of the school donated money for stained-glass windows.

Ellen described Bishop's School events in letters to her sister, who spent part of the year in Rushville. Ellen once wrote, "How I [wish] that in these special functions you were here and I were 'there'—anywhere, anywhere out of the world of society!"[43] She maintained that socializing was difficult for her while at the same time participating in a whirlwind of activity. In June 1918 she wrote: "Mr. [Wheeler] Bailey has engaged us for dinner at his house Monday evening; Tuesday is the play at the club house; Wednesday is the Bishop's reception; Thursday evening a birthday party for the Bishop at Mr. Bedford-Jones's; and Friday the commencement exercises and I am in it for it all."[44]

Ellen encouraged the school to invite members of the La Jolla community to events. In 1916 she described the bishop's reception, which included dinner, dancing, and festivities in the auditorium, "which was hung with Japanese lanterns and the revelers made a very pretty and festive sight. The entertainment struck me as unusually gay, elaborately 'dressy' and *chic* generally, with far less dignity but much more *abandon* and joyousness than on previous similar occasions." She noticed, however, a very marked innovation—there seemed to be none of the old time "bone and sinew" of the community. You will understand what I mean when I say none of the "Millses and Mudgetts" were in evidence. In fact, I saw no one distinctively of other than the Episcopal Church there except the Browns and the Birchbys. The "community of La Jolla" was conspicuous by its absence. I don't know whether this was intentional but if so I think it was a mistake. The Bishop's School should be just as much a part of our community of La Jolla as any other public institution.[45]

In 1918 Marguerite Barton succeeded Gilman as headmistress. Bishop Johnson described her as "a very remarkable woman with great intellectual ability and fine culture."[46] She had graduated from Radcliffe College magna cum laude in 1898 with a major in English. In 1915 she completed a master's degree in English literature and in 1918 was elected to Phi Beta Kappa. She had taught English at the Cambridge School for Girls before moving to La Jolla. Gilman, who had decided to return to her native Boston, did everything she could to ease her successor's transition. Ellen wrote that "Miss Gilman . . . realizes what her own mistakes have been—through ignorance of her situation, and intends to do everything possible to help her successor, and for the benefit of the school itself. She is working hard to get everything into shape and matters so recorded and classified as to make Miss Barton's an easy initiation into the work."[47]

Barton did a great deal in her short tenure at Bishop's. She reorganized the school into three units—academic, domestic, and business—headed by members of the faculty. The result was "an entirely changed organization in character and conduct," according to several teachers. Unfortunately, she died in January 1921 after undergoing surgery for a gastric ulcer. Ellen noted, "Miss Barton had left the school in such admirable condition that the loss will be felt chiefly as a personal one." She added, "The school goes on just as though nothing had happened, the teachers all agreeing that that was the only right way of proceeding, but they all feel it very keenly. I think she had endeared herself very strongly to all the inmates of the building and to the community so far as it knew her."[48]

In 1920 and 1921 Virginia accompanied teacher Caroline Macadam and a group of Bishop's School students on an around-the-world tour, from Japan and China through India and the Middle East. Ellen told her sister about remarks made by an acquaintance who met the party while traveling: "Speaking of the girls, he calls them 'typically American' and 'exceptionally good looking.' But adds that he wouldn't change jobs with Miss Macadam for a thousand dollars in gold a month. His health would be shattered long before he could conduct that party of girls around this globe. He also says that every moment of the time spent with Miss Scripps he had thoroughly enjoyed!"[49]

A new headmistress, Caroline S. Cummins, took charge of Bishop's in 1921. Like her predecessor, she had been educated at one of the early women's colleges, Vassar, graduating magna cum laude in 1910. She took her master's degree in classics and taught at the Cambridge School for Girls. She came to The Bishop's School in 1920 to teach Latin and English in the lower school and to help with administrative tasks. However, Barton's death led the bishop to choose her as headmistress. At thirty-three years old, she was the youngest faculty member and the most recent arrival. However, she was also the daughter of a country doctor and had the reputation as "cool and clear in decision in times of emergency." Ellen felt confident in Cummins's abilities. She described her as "young (33) and pretty, and very modest about her attainments. . . . She says she would have preferred to have held the position of vice principal under a superior, but she will 'fill the bill.'"[50]

Cummins encouraged academic excellence during her thirty-three-year tenure. One student recalled, "Our preparation for college was so superior that many of us found college work much easier for that training."[51] The headmistress kept a weekly record of each student's grades in every subject, supervised the curriculum, made out the schedules, and edited the *Alumnae News*. She invited a wide variety of speakers and performers to campus, including Jane Addams, naturalist John Burroughs, author-adventurer Richard Halliburton, historian William

James Durant, poet Louis Untermeyer, and pianist Ignacy Jan Paderewski. She also emphasized the school's connection to women's colleges. Two stained-glass windows in St. Mary's Chapel represent seals of the "Big Seven" women's colleges, as well as Elmira College, which had given Ellen an honorary degree.[52]

Bishop Johnson spent a great deal of time in La Jolla in the early 1920s. Ellen noted that he made "frequent visits here. The Bishop's School is taking up much of his time and thought and work."[53] He "felt very proud of his La Jolla school" and enjoyed showing it off to educators visiting from the East Coast.[54] It compared favorably to the Harvard School, a boys' preparatory school in Los Angeles that he had purchased for the Episcopal Church in 1912.

Ellen offered the bishop the use of her bungalow and limousine when he came to La Jolla. Ordinarily, he stayed at the school, where he had his own bedroom and bathroom. However, this proved increasingly inconvenient, Ellen told her sister, as "he doesn't like being the only man among 100 women and other men enjoy meeting him in an establishment of 'his own.' He will have his breakfasts here, but I shall ask him to other meals for I also am a 'lone woman.'" They had long conversations over pancakes and maple syrup, for Johnson rose early and made breakfast his principal meal. On one occasion, he entertained her houseguests: "Bishop Johnson was in his happiest and most jovial mood at the breakfast table yesterday, which infected the rest of the party."[55]

Ellen supported the school for the rest of her life. She provided an endowment of $100,000 (about $2.7 million) and in 1924 gave $50,000 (about $693,000) for a new gymnasium with an auditorium and a swimming pool.[56] She also left a substantial bequest. At the end of her life, she told a friend that "one of the greatest delights of her life had been teaching." She believed that schools should be "an open door to knowledge" and that educational methods should reflect the "experimental age" in which Ellen lived.[57] The Bishop's School remains committed to her educational ideals.

CHAPTER II

The Playground and Community House

By 1914 La Jolla had changed from a modest seaside village to a year-round vacation destination with hotels, shops, and restaurants. Hundreds of new residents built bungalows on the cliffs overlooking the ocean and up the slopes of Mount Soledad. Two large hotels—the Cabrillo Hotel (1908) and the Colonial Inn (1911)—welcomed guests, while the Crescent Café, the Brown Bear, and Hamilton's Cafeteria served lunches and dinners. Businesses included laundries, bakeries, barbers, three grocers, two drugstores, a bank, a shopping emporium, a movie theater, several real estate offices, curio stores, and an auto repair shop. The community also had a weekly newspaper, the *La Jolla Journal*, founded in 1913.[1]

Economic development brought a substantial number of working-class people to La Jolla. Some were longtime residents, like the Rannells, who operated a livery stable and dairy; the Kennedys, who built many of the early cottages; and the Daynes, who were gardeners.[2] Others arrived after 1900 to work as carpenters, plumbers, painters, grocers, cooks, waiters, telephone operators, auto mechanics, gardeners, clerks, and maids. In 1913 nearly half of the La Jolla residents listed in the San Diego city and county directory were employed in some kind of trade. Jethro Mitchell Swain, who came in 1910, eked out a living as a farmer, peddling honey, eggs, and berries to local residents, while his wife, Alice, worked as a seamstress and laundress for The Bishop's School.[3] Eleanor Bennett, meanwhile, went to work as a maid and governess for the family of George M. Booker, owner of the La Jolla Merchandise Company, shortly after her arrival in San Diego in 1905. She explained, "I wished to make some money, I wished to be near the beach."[4]

La Jolla also had a growing population of black residents, many of whom lived between Eads Avenue and Cuvier Street. Thomas Debose, a former slave, came to La Jolla in 1892 from Champaign, Illinois, with five children. Described as "hard-working and thrifty," he raised and trained horses and bought real estate. His second wife, Henrietta Vanhorn, worked for the Brown family as a housekeeper and cook before opening up her own hand laundry business.[5] Henry Estill came to La Jolla in 1894 as a cook for Dr. Samuel T. Gillispie and his wife, Ada, founders of the La Jolla Sanitarium. Others worked as waiters and dishwashers, laborers, restaurant owners, laundresses, barbers, and hairdressers.[6]

In 1914 Ellen decided to do something for the ordinary people of San Diego. Until then, her contributions had benefited mainly well-to-do La Jollans: the Scripps Institution, St. James by-the-Sea Episcopal Church, and The Bishop's School. Now her progressive sympathies demanded that she turn her attention to "those handicapped in life's game by poverty."[7] The result was a playground and recreation center that served the working population of La Jolla, in particular, its children. By altering the physical environment of the city's youngest and most malleable residents, she hoped to change the moral environment of the modern city.[8]

The Playground Movement

In the decades before 1900, industrialization and rapid urbanization changed the face of childhood in America, creating multiple generations raised in tenements, in factories, and on the streets. Since few states required children to attend school, many parents sent their sons and daughters to labor in mines, factories, agriculture, canneries, and home industries and as newsboys, messengers, and bootblacks. By the turn of the century, 20 percent of all children aged ten to fourteen worked for wages.[9] Hull House founder Jane Addams noted, "Never before in civilization have such numbers of young girls been suddenly released from the protection of the home and permitted to walk unattended upon city streets and to work under alien roofs. . . . Never before have such numbers of young boys earned money independently of the family life, and felt themselves free to spend it as they choose in the midst of vice deliberately disguised as pleasure."[10]

Efforts to abolish child labor and establish minimum age laws met with little success. For over fifty years, reformers and labor unions urged state lawmakers to establish minimum ages for factory work, but few complied. In 1909 President Theodore Roosevelt convened the "White House Conference on the Care of Dependent Children," following an aggressive campaign for federal child labor law reform led by the National Child Labor Committee, the National Consumers' League, the American Association for Labor Legislation, and the General Federation of Women's Clubs, among other organizations. This led to the creation of the U.S. Children's Bureau (1912) and, indirectly, the Keating-Owen Child Labor Act (1916). Not until 1938, however, did the Fair Labor Standards Act ban child labor under the age of fourteen.[11]

Unable to keep children out of the factories, reformers focused on providing education and recreation outside working hours. The conditions of modern industry were thought to be particularly hazardous to the moral and intellectual development of young people. Harvard-educated philanthropist Joseph Lee wrote, "Shut up in a store or factory; sorting ribbons, adding up figures, mechanically tending a machine; repeating the same movement for hours, weeks, years; subject to the uninspiring security of a wholly ordered routine . . . what opportunity is given the boy to develop the power and genius that nature placed in him? Man is an outdoor animal."[12]

In 1906 Lee and educator Luther Gulick founded the Playground Association of America (later the Playground and Recreation Association of America) in the hopes that scientifically directed "play" could enhance the skills of working men and women, make them better citizens, improve their health, and enhance the quality of their lives. At first they focused their efforts on metropolitan areas like Boston, New York, and Chicago. Later they began to advocate for playgrounds in rural America through the publication of a monthly magazine, the *Playground*.[13]

According to the movement's founders, "play" shaped the moral nature of children and supplied necessary social training and discipline. Lee believed that children learned their "most abiding lessons" on the playground: "The boy without a playground is father to the man without a job; and the boy with a bad playground is apt to be father to a man with a job that had better been left undone."[14] For girls, games offered the opportunity for social development. A photograph in the *Playground* showed young women playing field hockey with the caption, "In playing team games suited to their strength, girls learn how to co-operate. A girl is deprived of a part of her birthright if she does not have the opportunity for team play."[15]

Reformers also advocated the creation of recreational facilities for "grown people" that would take the place of the saloon.[16] Working-class men most frequently socialized in bars and taverns, despite attempts by reformers to draw them out into the fresh air of public parks or into parish halls and libraries. In addition to alcohol, saloons offered attractive facilities, including "papers to read, games of all sorts, toilet rooms, free lunch, a place to smoke, and plenty of genial company with whom it is easy to get acquainted."[17] The problem, of course, was that the men could end up spending their salaries there, drawing their families into a downward spiral of poverty.

In the mid-nineteenth century, the YMCA was founded as an alcohol-free alternative to the bar or club, providing recreational facilities such as gymnasiums, smoking rooms, billiard tables, and libraries. Aiming to improve "the spiritual, mental, social and physical condition of young men," the YMCA and later the YWCA operated on the theory that "recreation alone can stifle the lust for vice," as Jane Addams once wrote.[18] The only drawback was the association's origin as an evangelical Protestant institution.

By 1900 it was thought that playgrounds could be equipped with a community house or recreation center to provide many of the same benefits of the YMCA on a nonsectarian basis. In addition to providing exercise facilities and meeting rooms for adults, community centers promised to help promote neighborliness among longtime residents and new immigrants, wealthy citizens and poor ones. They also provided places where "the newly arrived citizens may more quickly come into contact with American life and learn American traditions," thereby promoting civic participation.[19]

Working-Class San Diego

In the early twentieth century, the city of San Diego had a growing population of working-class people living in "slum conditions" along the downtown waterfront and in areas such as Little Italy, Chinatown, Barrio Logan, and Logan Heights. They included Portuguese and Italian fishermen who worked in the burgeoning tuna industry, Mexican laborers, blacks, and whites living in shacks, cottages, old houses, and cheap lodging houses.[20]

San Diego reformers Edith Shatto King and Frederick A. King documented the problems faced by public health officials as the city's population grew exponentially, from 17,700 in 1900 to an estimated 80,000 in 1914. The results, published in the *Pathfinder Social Survey of San Diego* (1914), revealed that the city was not the paradise advertised by real estate speculators. Sewage dumped directly into the bay caused outbreaks of typhoid; in fact, one city official told the Kings, the "harbor is nothing but a cesspool." Many poor families crowded together in "unsanitary shacks," routinely discarding their garbage in vacant lots or canyons. Tuberculosis remained one of the leading causes of death. Infant mortality rates, meanwhile, were high; in 1913, 85 babies died before one year of age, while 135 died before the age of five.[21]

Child labor, education, and recreation became issues, as many young people dropped out of overcrowded public schools between the ages of twelve and fourteen. Work permits allowed them to supplement their family's income by laboring in factories and stores or on the streets as newsboys. Some received vocational training and English-language instruction at institutions such as the Free Industrial School, the YMCA, and the YWCA. Others spent their leisure time on the streets or at dance halls, penny arcades, theaters, nickelodeons, pool halls, and bowling alleys.[22]

Unsupervised free time after school or work often led to juvenile delinquency. Boys often joined gangs that hung around the city waterfront or camped in canyons, "reveling in indecent stories, cigarette smoking, and crap shooting."[23] San Diego newspapers regularly reported the arrests of "young hoodlums" who damaged school property, robbed lunch wagons, and insulted women on the streetcars.[24]

In 1908 Lee F. Hammer, field secretary of the Playground Association, spoke before members of San Diego's Ladies' Civic Committee, urging the construction of playgrounds as preventatives of crime.[25] Not long afterward, a San Diego chapter of the Playground Association was formed to lobby the city for improvements.

The publication of architect John Nolen's 109-page study, "San Diego: A Comprehensive Plan for Its Improvement" (1908), encouraged the creation of public playgrounds.[26] Nolen, hired to create a development plan for the growing city, proposed a civic center plaza and a waterfront esplanade. He also recommended the development of small open spaces to be used as public gardens and playgrounds. He wrote, "Playgrounds especially designed for children of various ages and conveniently located near their homes and in connection with the schools must be provided sooner or later." He added, "The time to provide them is now before real estate values are prohibitive and before land of suitable character is monopolized for private purposes. The possession of play areas is a necessity of city life, and by obtaining them now San Diego can avoid the heavy penalty of procrastination which New York and other cities have had to pay."[27] A 1909 editorial in the *San Diego Union* repeated Nolen's advice and urged San Diego to follow the lead of "some of the most progressive cities in the world" by developing public playgrounds.[28]

The city's first play area, Rose Park Playground, opened in September 1910 on property donated by the board of education and private parties. Located at Eleventh Avenue and Island Street, it included well-lighted baseball diamonds and a gymnasium.[29] Authors of the *Social Survey* noted,

"The grounds were well equipped with play apparatus and supervised by men and women directors. They are open every afternoon and evening with a daily attendance of about 160. Boys' and girls' clubs meet regularly here, with the organization of boy scouts and camp fire girls as special features."[30]

The success of this venture encouraged the city to create a board of playground commissioners in February 1913. The newly appointed superintendent of playgrounds, Frank S. Marsh, explained that their aims were, "first, to keep the children off the streets; second, to give them wholesome play without compulsion; third, to develop a law-abiding spirit to offset the widespread gang movement, which cannot be adjusted by police methods."[31]

In 1914 the city opened two additional playgrounds: the two-acre University Heights Playground on Idaho between Polk and Lincoln Streets, and the Golden Hill Playground, located on the south side of Balboa Park at Twenty-Sixth and A Streets. The latter facility occupied ten acres and included children's equipment, athletic fields, a swimming pool, a gymnasium with bathing facilities, and a recreation center built to accommodate several hundred children and adults.[32] On July 11, 1914, Ellen attended the grand opening of the Golden Hill Playground and witnessed a program that included music, speeches, folk dances, a pageant by the Girl Scouts, exercises by the Boy Scouts, and a short play by the Camp Fire Girls. Young men played baseball games on the new diamond, while girls and boys exhibited their skills at volleyball, basketball, tennis, and croquet.[33]

The La Jolla Playground and Community House

Ellen became interested in developing a playground that could serve all the children of San Diego. She often met underprivileged children who came to La Jolla on excursions organized by the Free Industrial School, a philanthropic association founded in 1894 by clubwoman Hettie Carey.[34] Members of the La Jolla Woman's Club regularly devoted their last meeting of the club year to entertaining the children, providing lunch and seaside amusements. In June 1904 Ellen wrote in her diary, "Woman's Club lunched the Industrial School at the Pavilion. Some

150 fed bread and butter, lemonade, cake, and ice cream, with a ride in the merry-go-round for all."[35]

Ellen was particularly interested in helping orphaned children, "the little homeless, motherless, joyless waifs of the community." Having visited children's homes in Detroit and other eastern cities, she recalled the dead eyes of their silent occupants. She wrote, "I wanted to restore to some of them something of a child's natural heritage, pure air and sunshine in abundance, with an environment of freedom for life and limb." At one point, she considered turning South Molton Villa into a home for these "innocent victims of a machine-made system." She found, however, that "one can't always do what one would and there were seemingly insurmountable obstacles in the way of my will."[36]

Instead, she decided to build a playground on three lots located across the street from her house. Ellen's friends and neighbors sold her additional lots in Block 33 on the understanding that she would move their bungalows to other plots of land.[37] In 1911 she had workers relocate Nina Waddell's cottage—the Golden Rod—to a lot on Draper Street, and the following year, Irving J. Gill and his nephew Lewis Gill came out to see about enlarging Florence Arnold's cottages.[38]

Having acquired nearly the entire block, Ellen met with members of the board of playground commissioners in early 1914 to talk about turning over the land to the city for construction of a playground.[39] In April she wrote in her diary: "Play Ground conversations. Mr. Bard and Mr. Marsh, Superintendent of Playgrounds, drive out in morning bringing plans of laying out and equipment of different playgrounds. Went to Block 33 and took measurements preparatory to beginning work."[40] According to the *San Diego Union*, the commissioners prepared twenty different plans and outlines before one was finally decided upon.[41]

Ellen also began buying land south of the playground site adjacent to The Bishop's School. She explained to her lawyer that she wanted to relocate her newly acquired cottages there and to close Kline Street between Cuvier and Draper "without protest, thus enlarging the facilities of the playground."[42] Over the summer, workmen moved ten cottages to nearby plots of land and destroyed several others.[43] She noted in her diary, "Mr. Gill comes out and brings plan for arrangement of cottages in Block 19. Will redraw them to suit my ideas."[44] Together, they planned a bungalow courtyard with plenty of open space that she referred to as a "pleasure ground."[45]

Across the street, the La Jolla Woman's Club was under construction. A longtime member and former past president of the club, Ellen financed the new clubhouse, donated the six lots at the corner of Draper and Silverado Streets, and commissioned architect Irving J. Gill to create a spare, elegant, and functional structure in what would become the modernist idiom.[46] The clubhouse was partially surrounded by a covered passageway, or arcade, made of reinforced concrete. Front and side rooms opened to gardens and lawns that could serve as outdoor tearooms, study spaces, and promenades. Inside there was a large assembly room equipped with a stage, dressing rooms, committee rooms, a lunchroom, living space for a caretaker, and a kitchen.[47] When the club first met in its new home in October 1914, Ellen read a heartfelt speech in which she imagined the clubhouse as a temporal structure that would house "the true spirit of democracy, human justice, and perfect comradeship. And out of which shall go forth that spirit of love and service which meets no barriers, knows no boundaries."[48]

Flush with revenue from the Scripps newspapers, Ellen began spending money in an unprecedented manner. She donated $5,000 (about $122,000 in 2016 dollars) toward the paving of Torrey Pines Road, $5,000 for the restoration of the Mission San Diego de Alcalá, and another $5,000 for a new YMCA building. In June 1914 she told E.W., "I am spending a lot of money. There is nothing like 'getting the habit.'"[49] Shortly afterward she wrote, "I am crowded with 'affairs'—Club, Play Ground, house moving, land buying, assessment paying, etc., etc." She quoted Rudyard Kipling's 1895 poem, "If—": "For once, I think I am filling every 'unforgiving minute with sixty seconds' worth of distance run.'"[50]

The construction of the playground and community house began in August 1914. Irving J. Gill designed the community house in the same architectural style as the La Jolla Woman's Club and The Bishop's School, using the Aiken system of "tilt-slab" concrete construction.

Visitors would enter the large assembly room and clubrooms from an arcaded porch facing Prospect Street. On the south side of the building, Gill planned boys' and girls' locker rooms that were partially open to the sky, a unique idea intended to achieve "the maximum of ventilation and sanitation." The basement, meanwhile, contained a kitchen, manual training areas for boys and girls, storerooms, and a first-aid room "as white and businesslike as a doctor's office."[51]

The architect also designed a shallow wading pool for children, walled with concrete and surrounded by sandboxes and a vine-shaded pergola. According to one writer, this became the center of activity during the summer months when the older children were on the beach, "benches on the outer edge are utilized by the mothers, who sit with their sewing and mending while the laughing children splash happily in the sun-flecked water or romp in the white sand."[52]

The playground was divided into boys' and girls' sections, each with its own equipment, such as "traveling rings, steel slides, pole slides, vaulting horses, flying rings and horizontal bars." In addition, there were swings, see-saws, croquet grounds, a volleyball court, three tennis courts, and a baseball diamond. For special occasions, the tennis net posts could be removed and the entire space used for dancing, pageants, or outdoor celebrations. The grounds, lit at night by 1,000-watt lamps, were surrounded by concrete posts and heavy mesh wire.[53]

Completed in 1915, the community house was praised as exceptionally well provided with the most modern amenities. The auditorium had a small stage with ten changes of scenery, footlights, overhead lights, spotlights, and a moving picture machine. The boys' club room contained a pool table and indoor games, while the girls' club overlooked a broad expanse of green lawn. An adult clubroom, located to the west of the auditorium, was also used as a library and reading room. There was even a five-room bungalow built at the southwestern corner of the grounds for the new director, Joseph Hallinan. Hallinan had viewed modern recreation centers in Chicago and on the East Coast; he told the *San Diego Union* that "for completeness there is nothing like it."[54]

Ellen financed the $180,000 (about $4.4 million) playground and community house with the understanding that this would be a place where ordinary people could meet and speak their minds without fear of harassment from civil authorities. Until then, the only public gathering places in La Jolla were the La Jolla Woman's Club and various parish halls. The Pavilion had been torn down before 1909. The deed—drawn up with the help of E.W.—specified that the building and playgrounds must be maintained by the city "as a meeting place for public gatherings for the discussion of all questions of interest to the public . . . and no speaker shall be denied the privileges of the premises or buildings thereon, on account of any opinions that he or she may hold or give utterance to, provided only that while using the said premises he or she shall not contravene the laws of the State of California or of the United States."[55]

Ellen's lawyer, J. C. Harper, explained the context in an article for the *Rushville Press*: "Having in mind the disgraceful suppression of 'free speech' in San Diego a few years ago, Miss Scripps specified in her deed of gift that the place should be open to every one to express their ideas no matter what their views, providing they did not violate the laws of the United States or of California while using the premises."[56] In a later memorandum, he described his employer as "a profound believer in public discussions, free speech and free press."[57]

The deed specified that no alcohol be sold, served, or consumed on the premises; it also required the city to maintain buildings and equipment and hire competent directors and other employees. If any of these conditions were breached, the deed would be null and void, "and the said property herein described shall revert to the said Ellen Browning Scripps, her heirs and assigns forever."[58]

Ellen did not flinch over the high price of the playground and community house, even after her lawyer told her that the plan produced "a very unpleasant impression upon my mind." He wrote, "It calls not for a Community House but for an expensive clubhouse. A building costing so much, with such elaborate and expensive furnishings, cannot be a playhouse for the children of common folks, but it means from its very nature an exclusive and aristocratic clubhouse. Just as an expensive church edifice, with rich furnishings and elaborate service, is necessarily exclusive and is never the gathering place of the poor people of a community so I believe you will find it with such an elaborate clubhouse. This I am sure will be a sore disappointment to you."[59]

Ellen, however, believed that the ordinary people of San Diego deserved facilities of "the most durable and up-to-date character."[60] She told her lawyer, "I can understand your surprise and disapproval of the apparent extravagant outlay in the Play Ground enterprise. And, no doubt, you are correct in the assumption that the Commissioners have taken advantage of the opportunity to carry the scheme to an ideal perfection impossible to realize in municipal appropriations for such enterprises. But I think you are wrong in your conclusions that the promoters have lost sight of the main and only object of the design—the benefit of the people." She explained, "Concrete buildings are always expensive even with the greatest simplicity. I'm somewhat prepared for this by my experience in the Biological, Bishop's School, and Club buildings, none of which were kept within the initial estimate." She recognized that Golden Hill Playground's community house cost only $40,000 (about $1 million) but explained that it was "a wooden structure, entirely inadequate in size and apportionments to its needs, and can only be considered a temporary building."[61]

Welcoming Leisure

The playground and community house opened to the public on July 3, 1915. The *San Diego Union* reported, "La Jolla aroused itself from its usual complacency yesterday, and, amid enthusiasm, one of the most complete community houses and playgrounds in America was dedicated and turned over to the city, to be maintained for the children of San Diego."[62]

The ceremony opened with an invocation by Rev. H. Gough Birchby of The Bishop's School, followed by a report from the playground commissioner. Ellen then offered a brief speech before presenting the deed of the playground to Mayor Edwin M. Capps. She began:

> I would like to say, Mr. Mayor, by way of preface to the formal surrender of the property to the city how sincerely glad I am to have been

able to do something "worthwhile" for the home of my adoption—The country to whom I owe more than I can tell, and for whom I have a feeling of devotion second only, I think, to that of a "native daughter." And, in passing to you, Mr. Mayor, as representative of the City of San Diego, the deed of gift to this Playground I do it in the faith that amounts to assurance that, as it was conceived and founded, in a single-hearted desire to serve the people—so it will be carried on in the same spirit, and to the fulfillment of its ultimate possibilities.[63]

Mayor Capps thanked her on behalf of San Diego's parents and children, adding, "We would need fewer reform schools, fewer penitentiaries, if there were more public playgrounds in the world—playgrounds such as Miss Ellen Scripps has just presented to the city for the use of the people. The alley, the secluded stairway, the street, make for vice, but the playgrounds lead to wholesomeness, both in mind and body."[64]

The formal opening of the playground was followed by a folk dance by eight- and nine-year-old girls and an exhibition match in which the La Jolla basketball team defeated the visiting YMCA players. Inside the community house, motion pictures showed scenes of the workers building the San Diego & Arizona Railroad, which terminated in El Centro. In the evening, visitors danced and watched movies in the auditorium.[65] Ellen noted in her diary, "Formal opening of Play Ground with afternoon and evening performances. . . . Dances in the evening on the tennis courts."[66]

Reverend Howard B. Bard, a pastor of the First Unitarian Church of San Diego for several years, later wrote to Harper:

I wish you might have been at the "opening." It was a grand day, and I think one of the happiest Miss Scripps ever experienced. It surely is the most complete ground and house of its kind ever produced. That the people of La Jolla are wise to its privileges is attested by the crowds present every day. They kept the staff of directors busy about *fourteen* hours a day, so far. Its possibilities are wonderful, and Mr. Hallinan, the head director, is surely a great find. He is a man of vision and sees the possibilities of the whole plant.[67]

Over the course of the next two years, Ellen attended numerous activities at the community house. In November she sponsored a series of lectures by Dr. Jerome Hall Raymond, a lecturer for the University of California and former professor at the University of Chicago. She described his first talk, "Athens and the Revival of Hellenism in Greece," as "remarkably good."[68] That year she also attended lectures by Professor Ritter and Frank B. Linderman, author of *Indian Why Stories* (1915).[69] The eighty-year-old Ellen even joined a women's gymnastic class, telling her sister, "I think there is scarcely an afternoon or evening that hasn't something 'doing' as far as we can see into the future."[70]

Ellen remained highly satisfied with the work of the playground and community house. In March 1917 she gave a speech before members of the La Jolla Woman's Club in which she described playgrounds as "a mighty asset of the country's progress." She stated, "Today the nation is waking up—or has waked up—to a realization of the fact that the play hour of the child, as the leisure hour of the adult, is a vital—perhaps the most vital—part of the whole." She believed that "if we are to conserve the health, the morals, and the fine spirit of enthusiasm so vital to the welfare of our people, the greatest opportunity for good now lying within the field of social service is found in the Play Ground or its broader outgrowth—the Recreational Center." She concluded, "Play makes people happy, puts music into their souls, teaches people the art of working together, makes for international understanding. When play does these things it is the kind of thing that has a great place in the national life and is worthy of international promotion. And it may be that someday the world's battles will not be fought with cannon and shells, with overhead zeppelins and submarines, but on the athletic field. And I think we would all echo Shakespeare's cry, 'May God hasten the Day!'"[71]

The La Jolla playground was used by neighborhood children, black and white, rich and poor. In the 1920s the lack of segregation caused some tourists to complain; in many parts of the country, blacks were prohibited from using parks and beaches occupied by whites. One realtor went so far as to ask Ellen to build separate recreational facilities for "the colored children" along Draper Street.[72] She refused. Having fought for civil rights her entire life, she would not consider such a discriminatory idea. The playground and community house had been built to educate and inform citizens of every race, color, and creed. Her neighbors, particularly the old-timers, agreed. Her vision of La Jolla as a socially progressive community survived decades of social and political change and remains vital today.

CHAPTER 12

South Molton Villa

The light was draining from the summer sky over La Jolla when a pass-erby noticed smoke coming out of the vestry of St. James by-the-Sea. Around 8:30 p.m. on Saturday, August 7, 1915, residents gathered to watch as La Jolla's volunteer fire department doused a blaze that might have enveloped the entire church.

More than an hour later, as the firefighters returned home, Virginia Scripps saw smoke coming from the northeast bedroom of Iris Cottage, located not far from the church. She quickly roused Ellen and raised the alarm through the neighborhood. At the same time, a neighbor noticed a dark plume of smoke drifting from the cellar door at the rear of South Molton Villa. Someone smelled kerosene. Within minutes, "the big house" was also enveloped in flames.

Unable to contain the fire in Iris Cottage, volunteers turned their attention to Ellen's residence. Hampered by old and faulty equipment, they could not control the blaze, which spread from the basement to the attic. At 11:15 p.m. San Diego firefighters arrived on the scene and managed to save the building from complete destruction. Some furniture and pictures had been saved and the library spared, but many letters and personal papers that Ellen described as "invaluable" had disappeared.[1]

In the early hours of Sunday morning, as Virginia made coffee for the firefighters in the kitchen of Wisteria Cottage, Ellen considered their loss. She wrote in her diary, "Evening: an incendiary fire completely demolishes Iris Cottage; also entirely destroys my house, although much of the furniture was saved, and damaged the Episcopal Church to the extent of $500. No clue to the perpetrator."[2] The work of nearly two decades had been destroyed.

The Scripps Estate

Many changes had taken place on the Scripps estate in the years between 1907 and 1915, the most significant being the unification of Ellen's and Virginia's properties. Originally separated by a curving lane called Daisy Row, their properties in Blocks 35 and 55 were brought together by the creation of a new Daisy Row that linked to Eads Avenue at Prospect Street. In late 1907 the city council approved the closing of the old lane; early the following year construction began on a landscape garden that would connect South Molton Villa with Wisteria and Iris Cottages.

Virginia had purchased Wisteria Cottage, formerly owned by the Seaman family, in 1905.[3] Its first residents were E. W. Scripps, his wife and children, a maid, a governess, and a Japanese cook named Joe.[4] In 1908 Virginia renovated the cottage following plans made by Irving J. Gill. The architect added an open porch, a basement, a west entrance, and semienclosed loggias to the one-and-a-half-story wooden bungalow, along with a cobblestone foundation. He also designed a pergola linking the front porch to the street.[5]

Iris Cottage, located on the ocean side of Wisteria Cottage, had been moved from a previous location in early 1908, about the same time that construction began on St. James by-the-Sea. Virginia used it as a guest cottage, in conjunction with Wisteria Cottage, for family members and friends.

Ellen, meanwhile, hired Gill to make extensive alterations to South Molton Villa.[6] Between 1908 and 1911 he extended the sun parlor, located on the north side of the house, so that windows on three sides of the rectangular room provided views up and down the coast.[7] The sun parlor was furnished with rustic twig furniture made in the Appalachian Mountains.[8] The architect and his nephew Louis Gill also worked on the circular sunroom located in the northeast turret, replacing windows to prevent leaks. Still, the house remained far from watertight; storms caused rainwater to come through the windows, walls, and ceilings in such quantities that Ellen often had to work with mops and buckets to keep the place from being flooded.[9]

In addition, the architect made changes to Ellen's library, enclosing the octagonal conservatory that faced Prospect Street and adding a new room. An early photograph of the library showed Craftsman furniture, a round table with an Empire-style base, busts on pedestals, and Oriental rugs. Electric lights shaped like flowers hung from the rafters.[10] In 1912 Gill added another bookshelf-lined "fireproof" room with a glass skylight. A wooden table covered by a fine Persian carpet stood at the center.[11]

In 1908 Ellen decided to build a cottage, the Bungalow, on the site of the old croquet lawn. Gill designed a modest two-room wooden structure that would provide additional living space for visitors. A guest standing on Prospect Street would see South Molton Villa flanked by the library on the left and the bungalow on the right, both linked to the main house by pergolas. A driveway, located farther east on Prospect Street, curved around the back of the bungalow and provided access to the basement of South Molton Villa.[12]

The Scripps sisters renovated their properties at the same time that the railway changed its route through La Jolla. Since 1894 steam-driven trains from San Diego and Pacific Beach had headed north into La Jolla along Cuvier Street, turning east on Prospect Street and stopping first at the corner of Draper Avenue and second at the depot on Fay and Prospect. In 1908 railway engineers altered and extended the route, despite substantial opposition from residents. The newly created Los Angeles and San Diego Beach Railway brought a gasoline-powered engine east along Silverado Street before making a loop along Ivanhoe and heading west down Prospect Street. The cars, nicknamed Red Devils or Submarines, now stopped in front of the newly constructed Cabrillo Hotel (1908) before continuing their journey south along Fay Avenue to Silverado.

When railway workers began grading and scraping Prospect Street for the new line in March 1908, Ellen had to reconfigure the southern boundary of her property, changing the height of cobblestone walls and widening the sidewalks.[13] She planted mesembryanthemum, or ice plant, which provided a profusion of brilliantly colored flowers from spring to fall. In 1916 she described the "wonderful array of blossoms," writing, "The walls and terraces are one growing, gorgeous mass. I never saw anything like it."[14]

Kate Sessions created the landscape design for the new garden, which extended from Cuvier Street to the new Daisy Row. In September 1908 Ellen noted in her diary, "Miss Sessions came out in afternoon. Looked over the place with me taking notes and memoranda. Sent in my map of grounds. She is to put place in shape and give advice and suggestions as to future planting."[15] Sessions terraced the sloping hillside on the north side of the house and added a cement walk, lined with rosebushes, leading to the house from the west. Specimen trees included magnolias, palms, and Norfolk Island pines.[16]

The grounds around Wisteria Cottage, meanwhile, included a vegetable plot and a wildflower garden, which Ellen looked after while her sister traveled. She wrote in 1916, "I wish you could see your wildflower bed. It is a flaming glory. The godetias of every hue, white, cream, scarlet, crimson, mottled and striped, growing a foot or more high, have taken possession and are vying with the yellow poppies as to show while the under course still retains all the blue, white, purple, and pink dainty small ones."[17] Meanwhile, Virginia's vegetable garden produced "potatoes, onions, something that looks like cabbage, and tomato vines in healthy condition, but not yet bearing fruit."[18]

Minor changes to the boundaries of the Scripps estate took place between 1912 and 1916 with the grading of Cuvier Street and Coast Boulevard. The former became narrower in order to overcome the difficulty of terracing sidewalks, while the latter was widened.[19] The city also built a sea wall along the edge of the cliffs in order to prevent drainage from eroding the cliffs below Ellen's property.[20]

The Fire

At the time of the fire, Ellen was approaching her seventy-ninth birthday. Having funded a number of philanthropic projects for the people of

La Jolla, she was startled to realize that someone could hold a grudge against her. Perhaps her status as a wealthy woman had alienated a member of the working class, or her refusal to provide money had angered a desperate petitioner. A restaurant owner or shopkeeper might have been furious over her very public stand on "the liquor question" in La Jolla. One acquaintance even suggested that her brother E.W. might be at fault: "The class of fellows who blew up *The Los Angeles Times* is responsible for all deeds of this kind. . . . Is not that brother of yours something of a socialist? Well, that kind of teaching encourages crimes of union labor kind."[21]

In a letter to the *La Jolla Journal*, Ellen thanked her neighbors for their support during and after the fire and addressed the issue of class warfare. She admitted that the cause of the fire might well be "the industrial unrest so prevalent throughout the country, that has created—with too much justice—a spirit of antagonism towards wealth." She wrote, "I should like my friends in this class to know that I am, heart and hand, in sympathy with the oppressed; that my life and money are at their service. But I alone can be the judge as to the best way to serve them. I have been a workingwoman—and a hard one—all my woman's life, and I have learned the value of property."[22]

Ellen also discussed the issue of Prohibition, writing, "If I have given freely of my strength and means and prayers to secure prohibition for our state it has been in no way for my own benefit, but because I believe the sale and manufacture of intoxicating liquors to be a prime cause of the unhappiness and poverty of the industrial classes and because I believe that every working man would be honestly glad of the removal of his temptation." She concluded by stating her belief that the fires were "the act of an unbalanced, hence irresponsible being" who remained a danger to the community. "I will do what I can to aid in his apprehension, and restraint—not punishment!"[23]

In the end, Ellen discovered that her housekeeper, Mrs. E. D. Bartholow, had been the intended target, not her sister or herself. Police identified the "La Jolla firebug" as a forty-nine-year-old Australian laborer named William Peck who had done housecleaning and other odd jobs on the Scripps estate. He confessed that he had been drinking ("I was full of booze—I had been full of booze for days") and that he set the fires in order to exact revenge on the housekeeper, who had discharged him earlier that year. He was found guilty and sentenced to twelve years in the state penitentiary at San Quentin.[24]

After the fire, letters poured in from friends, relatives, and acquaintances throughout the country, expressing their condolences for Ellen's loss and thanking her for the many things she had done for the San Diego community. Some expressed their hope that her "wonderful library" had been spared; others recalled the happy times they had spent in her home.[25] Nearly all expressed their relief that the Scripps sisters were safe and unharmed. One wrote, "Of all the people on earth, you are the last one whom anyone in La Jolla should have distressed."[26]

South Molton Villa II

A week after the fire, Ellen spoke with Irving J. Gill about the possibility of rebuilding her house. Over the course of the next two weeks Gill drew up plans for a new fireproof concrete structure in the same modern architectural language as The Bishop's School, the La Jolla Woman's Club, and the community house.

At this point in his career, Gill had established his architectural identity as a modernist. His nephew noted, "He would not design a building otherwise."[27] He had begun shifting his practice to Los Angeles, where he found many clients who appreciated his aesthetic. In October 1915 he took Ellen and her lawyer, J. C. Harper, to see some of his recent work in that city, including the Laughlin house (1907–8), the Banning house (1911–13), and the Dodge house (1914–16), at that time under construction in West Hollywood.[28]

Gill's reinforced concrete structures were expensive to build, particularly when compared to wood-framed ones. Ellen justified the expense, writing, "Concrete buildings are always expensive even with the greatest simplicity." She considered Gill to be a "scrupulously careful, highly intelligent" architect who took a "personal interest in the matters of the highest kind," even if he rarely stayed within his initial estimates.[29]

Moreover, she had little interest in the fantasy Spanish architecture made popular by San Diego's Panama-California Exposition (1915). Designed by New York architect Bertram Goodhue, structures like the Foreign Arts Building (later the House of Hospitality) influenced the development of heavily ornamented Spanish Colonial Revival structures throughout the region. Examples in La Jolla include Casa de la Paz (1922), the San Carlos Electric Railroad Station (1924), Casa de Mañana (1924), Darlington House (1925), the exuberant pink La Valencia Hotel (1926), and La Cañada (1929), among others.

E.W., on the other hand, was less than enthusiastic about the modernist architect. He explained to her lawyer, "Ellen, whose aesthetic and artistic tastes are excellent as mine are the reverse, puts a high value on Gill, and it is not for you or me to pass judgment on matters of taste." He continued, "With us, Gill is a necessary evil. We want Ellen to have all the advantages of that taste of Gill's which she values, while she shall suffer as little as possible on account of his un-businesslike and wasteful methods."[30] Having built Miramar quickly and on the cheap, E.W. considered himself to be an authority on building practices.

E.W. and Harper monitored the construction of the new South Molton Villa and insisted that the project be completed quickly, no matter what the cost. E.W. wrote, "Every day that Ellen is out of her home will be an unhappy day. Every day that she spends in her re-established home will be a happy day for her." He added, "All her life, Ellen has been spending her time, her labor, and her money on anybody and everybody but herself. Now we have the opportunity, I think that we should spare ourselves no effort or inconvenience of any kind—or that I should spare no money expense on her behalf."[31]

Ellen intended to create not a showplace but a structure that could be used by the community of La Jolla after her death. E.W. suggested a home for girls of "good character" where they would receive special training and education, returning to one of Ellen's earlier ideas.[32] By this time, however, she may have imagined the creation of an art gallery, research library, and public garden like Henry E. Huntington would create in San Marino in 1919.[33] She owned many first editions and rare books, in addition to some valuable pieces of art. In the end, she left the decision as to her home's future use in the hands of her brother and his heirs.

Gill became personally invested in the look of the La Jolla house, getting down on his hands and knees to rub color into the damp unfinished concrete floors with his nephew Louis. Ellen noted, "The two Gills have been busy all day (albeit Sunday) in shirtsleeves and overalls . . . 'surfacing' the cement floors. . . . [T]o me it is 'a thing of beauty and a joy forever.'"[34] When finished, the floors had the appearance of old leather.

The new South Molton Villa, built between November 1915 and June 1916, has been described as one of the architect's "masterworks."[35] The three-story concrete structure had a large arched front porch. Gill retained the pergolas that led to the library and the bungalow on either side of the main house. In the main hall, a set of stairs led to the second floor. A visitor could walk through the hall and the drawing room into a rectangular sunroom with windows on three sides. According to Harper, "It commanded a view not only of the sea but a long stretch of the shore line both up and down the coast."[36] Ellen's office was located on the southwest side of the house, close to the library. On the opposite side of the house were the dining room, kitchen, breakfast area, and an enclosed wing facing Wisteria Cottage. Katharine Scripps wrote admiringly, "The house is elegant and beautifully simple."[37]

An unusual feature of the house was an elevator that led from the basement to the second-story bedrooms and solarium. Young relatives liked to ride up and down in it, but Ellen often forgot it was there. She told her niece Grace, "Another funny thing is that in my capacity for absent-mindedness, I find myself continually forgetting the existence of an elevator, and find myself walking up stairs and downstairs with 'impunity.'"[38]

Upstairs there were four bedrooms, three bathrooms, and porches and balconies that provided light and air. Three additional bedrooms were located in the aboveground basement alongside the laundry and boiler room.

Although some furniture from her old house had been spared, Ellen purchased additional pieces from the Frevert and Bledsoe Furniture

Company. She decorated the sunroom—her favorite space—with wicker tables and chairs. The drawing room and dining room, meanwhile, had formal pieces in black walnut. Photographs of the drawing room from 1916 show soft gray walls without moldings or baseboards, a Gill trademark. There were French doors curtained with lace, a large Persian carpet with a desk and footstool at its center, Empire-style armchairs covered in red velvet, matching tables flanking the fireplace, several small landscape paintings, and Arts and Crafts vases. The dining room, meanwhile, had two inset china cabinets, a black walnut sideboard and dining table, and a fireplace with several landscape paintings over the mantle.[39]

Ellen's bedroom, located on the southwest side of the house, contained twin beds, a vanity table, a dresser, and two plein air paintings. In her sitting room she had several overstuffed chairs, a bookcase, a small library table, and a desk, as well as a child-size chair.[40] She rarely slept in her bedroom, preferring an old wire-woven cot that she placed on the west porch "for the sake of the stars."[41]

Ellen and Virginia moved into the new house in early July 1916 and held their first family dinner party on July 20, inviting E.W. and Nackie; Fred and Emma; Katharine Peirce Scripps; Grace Scripps Clark; Agnes, John, and Nesta Thompson; and Hilda Gardner.[42] Agnes dedicated two poems to the house, "The Phoenix of La Jolla," and its owner. The former read:

Fair stands it, strong and beautiful
On consecrated ground by love and service blest.
Long may it like the Phoenix of the past
Out from the ashes wing,
Shed forth a richer life and still maintain
Its heritage of love and rich benevolence
That in the new, the old is not forgotten.[43]

The Automobile

Having built a very modern house, Ellen acquiesced to her brother's desire to give her the most advanced piece of technology available at the time: an automobile. For several years she had resisted buying a car, claiming that it was an unnecessary expense. In 1916, however, E.W. persuaded her to accept a Pierce-Arrow limousine along with a garage and a chauffeur. In his words, "She thought the time might come when she would have to surrender some of her peculiar independence to confirm to customs and especially to conditions of advancing age."[44]

In the early years Ellen had kept a horse and buggy to take her to Miramar; otherwise, she relied on the railway to take her downtown. She stabled her horse, Prince, with dairyman Charles Dearborn for $17.50 a month (about $510).[45] When the horse passed on, she did not replace him; instead, she took public transportation or got rides from her brothers or other friends or relatives. In 1914 an autobus company began competing with the railroad. Ellen wrote, "I like the autobus very much. In the first place, it picks me up and sets me down with all my packages at my own threshold. Then one gets all the fresh air without the dust and smoke and smell of soot or gasoline, to be had for a bigger price on the railroad."[46]

The first automobiles began to appear in La Jolla around 1908, although a number of San Diegans, including E.W., owned a car as early as 1903. In that year Ellen wrote in her diary, "Ed and Jim drove over in automobile. . . . From La Jolla to Miramar in one hour and five minutes."[47] She went on her first auto trip with Virginia in 1907, taking two of her brother's cars—a Packard and a Pierce-Arrow—in the event that one broke down.[48] By 1918 many people had purchased private cars. Ellen counted "100 automobiles (more or less) parked along Prospect and Draper Streets" on La Jolla's White Elephant Carnival Day.[49]

Ellen began building a garage and a chauffeur's house for her new car, a Pierce-Arrow, in 1916. In the early twentieth century, automobiles required regular maintenance by full-time staff members; they could not simply be parked on the street and repaired at a local garage. She decided to locate the buildings, along with a lath house, on the site of Iris Cottage, destroyed in the fire. Although Virginia had considered rebuilding the cottage, she decided to sell the lots to her sister and to buy instead two properties located across Daisy Lane from Wisteria Cottage.

W. P. Williams of Escondido built the concrete structures in the same style as South Molton Villa. The garage opened onto Coast Boulevard, while the chauffeur's cottage was tucked into the hillside just above it.[50]

Frederick "Fred" J. Higgins served as the chauffeur, having worked for Ellen's brother Fred over the previous twelve and a half years. The British-born driver brought with him a wife, two sons, and a dog, Queenie.[51] He recalled his employer being "very economical" with a stubborn streak: "If she once said 'No,' you might just as well give up! But she normally reconsidered later on." Still, "she never treated anybody like a servant, ever."[52]

In 1917 Virginia built another garage for Higgins's Ford, which he had been parking in the alley below Wisteria Cottage.[53] It had single-wall construction with wood siding, a high-pitched roof, and a cobblestone foundation. It is known today as the La Jolla Historical Society's Carriage House.

Ellen loved her new car, though she initially thought it "too luxurious for a person of my plebian tastes and habits."[54] She took her first drive in the "new creature" with E.W. and his youngest son, Robert, writing, "I feel like calling it 'she.' There is so much life and beauty, and real 'womanliness' about 'her.'"[55] She also appreciated its utility, using it not only for road trips and shopping excursions but also to ferry around her friends and neighbors. In 1916 she told Virginia, "The auto did good service on election day, taking all sorts and kinds of people to the polls."[56] It carried parties of La Jolla women to the San Diego County Federation of Women's Clubs meetings, the Greek Theater in Point Loma, and lectures at the downtown YWCA, among other places. The car and its chauffeur, Higgins, also met friends and family members at the train station in Del Mar and transported them to South Molton Villa or Miramar.

Ellen thanked her brother profusely for the gift: "I can't tell you what it has meant to me, nor express my gratitude for the joy of its being. Of course, I am giving in time and work and money and heart service what I have and am in the world to work that has been laid upon us, but all this is so greatly magnified by this aid. It almost seems like a living creature that has come into the service with all the beauty and strength and power of dominion."[57]

Employees

Although she had a limousine and a chauffeur at her disposal, Ellen was reluctant to take on additional servants. For many years she and Virginia had tidied up after themselves, only hiring a housekeeper when it became absolutely necessary. Ellen's early diaries contained entries like "Busy 'cleaning up the house' till 2:30 p.m.," "Busy all morning cleaning up basement room, kitchen, etc.," "Cleaning kitchen and pantry, looking over fruit, etc., all morning," and "At work all the morning, cleaning house."[58]

Such a thing could take place only in America, according to one British visitor who commented on the situation in 1906: "Where in England could you find a lady sweeping her own rooms, cooking her dinner and washing her dishes, who would then sit down and write a cheque for ten thousand pounds for the nearest technical school, in which she took a most intelligent and practical interest?"[59]

Virginia's insistence led Ellen to hire a housekeeper, though it took her some time to find a woman who would work for less than $50 a month. Virginia wrote, "You do not like to keep house and neither do I, except in my own."[60] By 1910 Ellen had a full-time housekeeper, as well as a librarian, Ida Loring, who later managed Ellen's rental cottages. However, Ellen was reluctant to have an additional maid or cook, telling her sister, "I would rather not keep two 'regulars' in the house, because unless they are congenial and harmonious, I don't think it works well."[61]

Over the years Ellen's housekeepers both cooked and cleaned, as Virginia required regular and substantial meals. They also provided dinners to guests, though Ellen hesitated to ask them to do it very often. A meal for the Harpers, for example, consisted of "stewed chicken with dumplings, mashed potatoes, peas, spinach and carrots, cornbread, with blackberries, rhubarb and cake for dessert." Ellen told her sister, "I had got Miss Bebb pretty well down to the 'elementals' when I am alone, but that evening the 'spread' would have satisfied even you."[62]

E.W. tried to persuade Ellen to hire additional help, such as a "lady secretary" who could assist with her growing correspondence and keep track of requests for financial aid: "Your deafness and your general liability of having your good nature imposed upon, should be recognized by you and acted upon by you." He added, "I have urged on you, before, that there was no reason for your economizing."[63]

Ellen, however, resisted her brother's blandishments. She wrote, "You would have me live a life of ease and comfort—as the world thinks befits the octogenarian, you would have me surround myself with servants who should relieve me of all cares and petty duties. You cannot understand what an absolute bore such a life would be to me. There is nothing that I like better than the time when my housekeeper takes her 2 weeks annual vacation and I am left sole arbiter of my own domains. The presence of 'servants' is always an embarrassment to me (perhaps reversion to a plebian ancestry)."[64]

Concerned about his sister, E.W. persuaded attorney Harper to move to La Jolla, ostensibly to supervise the construction of her new house but in fact to look after her interests. Harper had served as general counsel for the Scripps newspapers from 1899 to 1915. In the summer of 1916 he and his wife, Edith, moved from Cincinnati, having purchased the W. C. Sheppard House at the corner of Prospect Street and Torrey Pines Road.[65]

A small, wiry, and bespectacled man in his fifties, Harper was a Roosevelt Republican with strong progressive sympathies. He had a good eye for detail and a habit of preserving records "of every minutiae of everything he ever had anything to do with."[66] He worked full time as Ellen's lawyer and financial agent from 1909, helping to manage her investments, philanthropic activities, and property transactions. "It is not as an attorney that I regard him especially," Ellen told her brother, "more as a confidential adviser; and as a medium for investigating matters that are submitted to me; and carrying on certain activities in which I am interested."[67]

Harper kept an office in the Scripps Building at Seventh Avenue and C Street before gradually migrating to the library at South Molton Villa, bringing a great quantity of files and papers with him. Ellen grumbled that her library had grown into "a general rendezvous for his numerous community clients in La Jolla."[68] She was particularly frustrated when he brought out the contents of his old office in Cincinnati. She complained to E.W., "He has had (I don't know how many tons of stuff) boxed up and sent out here." She spoke to him politely about moving his work to his own house but found that "it requires something more than diplomacy to dislodge a tenant who has grown to assume a sort of ownership or perpetuation of tenure."[69] Finally, she just asked him to leave.

Ellen was not often alone at South Molton Villa, despite her good intentions. Her house stood at the center of a complex of village institutions—St. James by-the-Sea, the La Jolla Woman's Club, the playground and community center, and The Bishop's School—making it a routine destination for neighbors, friends, and family. Anyone was welcome to walk in her garden, and interested visitors could view the library on request. She seemed to enjoy the attention, for she kept track of callers in a series of guest books that she annotated with short descriptions of friends.

Years later, Ellen's companion Hilda Gardner asked her about her interest in other people. Ellen explained, "It's more than that. It is my *belief* in other people. We are all human. So much depends on heredity, manner of life, and surroundings. We have got to study out why people are what they are. I do not believe that anyone is bad. These lines apply to adults just as much as to children."[70] She used her home, library, and gardens to draw people from all walks of life in the hopes that the beauty of the surroundings would provide both inspiration and serenity.

The Sinews of War

Between 1916 and 1918 Ellen Scripps engaged in several more philan-thropic ventures, the most important of which was the creation of the La Jolla Sanitarium, later known as the Scripps Memorial Hospital and Metabolic Clinic. This project came to her attention during World War I, a conflict that brought back memories of her own youthful participation in women's aid societies during the 1860s. Although the hospital served civilians rather than soldiers, it reflected the humanitarian interests of the La Jolla community during a time of war.

War news was on the front page of every American newspaper from the start of the conflict on July 28, 1914. La Jolla women found them-selves particularly moved by stories about the influx of Belgian refugees into France, the Netherlands, and Great Britain. The *San Diego Union* reported that thousands of people—mostly women, children, and old men—had been forced to abandon their homes as the German army advanced into Flanders. At Louvain, those unable to flee were "actually starving and living in ruins."[1]

In October 1914 Ellen worked with the La Jolla Woman's Club to collect clothing for the Belgian refugees. She told her sister, "The late war news is awakening people to a sense of their duties and privileges. Bales of clothing—good clothing, too—are going to England (the Pacific Coast Co. and the Canadian Railway Co. are taking everything free)."[2]

By the end of the month, she noted in her diary, "Great quantities of clothing coming in to Club House. Women busy receiving, sorting, and packing all day."[3] They also began knitting socks, cholera bells, balaclava helmets, and other items for soldiers in the field. In October 1914 she wrote her sister, "We are knitting for dear life. What is being done in Rushville? Anything?"[4]

Ellen knew a good deal about the progress of the war because of her brother's access to policy making in Washington, DC. As the owner of a large media company with a wire service, a syndication arm, and national papers, E.W. played a role in shaping the public's perception of President Woodrow Wilson, whom E.W. first met in July 1914. His newspapers also brought the war closer to home, particularly after the sinking of the RMS *Lusitania* in May 1915.[5] He warned Ellen, "Germany has awakened the sleeping military dogs of the United States and, in doing so, she has called into existence the greatest military power that the earth has ever known."[6]

The war exacerbated political divisions between those who condemned the conflict as a product of capitalism and those with more conservative views. E.W. anticipated "social revolution" due to the "great hoards of big business men who have gathered at Washington, and on whom the President was depending, or was supposed to be depending upon, too much for counsel in the present emergency."[7] Labor unions, socialists, and pacifist groups publicly opposed U.S. participation in the conflict; so did respected female activists like Helen Keller and Jane Addams. Others, while preferring neutrality, thought that America had an obligation to protect democratic governments from the imposition of German autocracy.[8]

Opinion in La Jolla was divided. Maud Foster Weston, for example, favored neutrality, reading "a paper of her own on Peace" at the woman's club celebration of Jane Addams Day.[9] At Christmas, she donated an olive tree to be planted on the grounds of the club "as an emblem of peace at a time of world warfare."[10] Others expressed anti-German sentiments, making life so difficult for German-born photographer Leopold Hugo that he moved to Pasadena rather than face continual harassment.

Ellen, for her part, hoped for peace but believed that war would inevitably continue. In 1916, when it appeared that Germany might be willing to accept overtures of peace from the Allies, she doubted the story's sincerity, writing, "Personally, I am inclined to side with *The London Mail* in its opinion of the German 'peace offer'—as 'an impudent, old peace trick which is becoming as hackneyed as the conjuring of rabbits out of a hat.'" She added, "But then I'm 'all English,' and may not look with an all-impartial eye on the matter."[11]

Until June 1917, when the Espionage Act effectively prohibited freedom of speech, pacifists and isolationists could express their views at La Jolla's community house. In 1916 Max Eastman, editor of the *Masses*, gave a speech entitled "The Only Way to End the War." Ellen described him as "a very genial, gentle gentleman" who argued that, owing to humans' natural "pugnacity and gregariousness (so-called patriotism) there must always be fighting except by agreed alliances of nations."[12] In July she listened to an evening lecture on Germany by journalist and labor organizer Albert Rhys Williams, who would witness firsthand the Russian Revolution of 1917. She noted, "Sharply socialistic and very effective."[13]

Other war-related events included a 1916 lecture series by Dr. Jerome Hall Raymond entitled The War—What For? The Underlying Causes of the War Madness in Europe.[14] Hendrika van der Flies of The Hague later spoke to "a full house" on the needs of Belgian children. Ellen noted in her diary: "In the afternoon a number of people call on her and buy some of the souvenirs they have made from the German bombs by Belgian soldiers in the trenches."[15]

The United States entered World War I, or the Great War, on April 6, 1917, following more than two years of neutrality. After U-boats began sinking American ships in the North Atlantic, President Woodrow Wilson asked Congress to "formally accept the status of belligerent which has thus been thrust upon it."[16]

Following the declaration of war, Ellen met with Eleanor Parkes of the La Jolla Woman's Club to start a local branch of the San Diego chapter of the American Red Cross. The group met in the community house and other venues, offering courses in first aid, elementary hygiene and care for the sick, and surgical dressings. Ellen learned to make ambulance pads, triangular bandages, and bed sheets. By August the La Jolla branch had shipped 6,687 items to its parent chapter, including operating gowns, gauze surgical dressings, bandages, clothing, and towels.[17]

La Jollans also began to limit their consumption of foodstuffs—wheat, meat, fat, and sugar—to comply with recommendations made by the U.S. Food Administration under Herbert Hoover. They planted vegetable gardens and turned the quadrangle of The Bishop's School into a potato patch. Mary Ritter gave an afternoon party in which "the refreshments were as Hooverian as possible," Ellen wrote. "The fruit cake was made of rice flour with raisins . . . the cookies of oatmeal, potato flour, nuts, and molasses."[18] Her niece Floy, meanwhile, began offering only two courses for dinner at her Altadena mansion and serving neither coffee nor tea.[19]

The conservation of food appealed to Ellen, who eliminated meat, pastries, puddings, and fried foods from her diet. She told her sister, "I never felt in more perfect condition of physical health." She added, "I really believe this Hooverian conservation scheme is going to do as much good in conserving the health of the people of the United States as in saving the Europeans from actual starvation."[20]

Realizing that Virginia could not subsist on a largely vegetarian diet, Ellen suggested that her sister take charge of the cooking when she returned to La Jolla from Rushville. "If you will do it scientifically and psychologically and patriotically—why you will be doing 'your bit' in the service of both country and the community," she wrote. "To me all days are meatless, at least 2 meals a day are wheatless and, practically *almost* every meal is both sweetless and fatless. But I know that other people can not do as I do; and I don't want them to."[21]

In the meantime, Ellen facetiously asked her sister whether the small dog belonging to Reverend Bedford-Jones, chaplain at St. James by-the-Sea, might be usefully "converted into sausages for the starving Belgians." She added, "Of course, I have never been in sympathy with any of the clergy who have officiated here; and I can't see that they have done any good—except to please a class who did not need them—who were not hungering and thirsting after righteousness."[22]

Ellen was proud of the sacrifices made by community members. She told her brother, "I do not see any of the semblance of apathy with which the nation is credited. Everyone seems to me . . . thoroughly alive to the seriousness of the situation; a recognition of the real purpose of the war, and a determination as to its ultimate outcome."[23]

Ellen also admired the fortitude of civilians in England. She noted that the town of Letchworth in Hertfordshire had taken in three thousand civilian refugees from Belgium. With most of their men at war, women had taken to "driving butcher's carts, dispensing drugs, working in the fields."[24] A female relative worked in a British munitions factory before returning home to care for her grandparents, the Gardners, who had lost a son on the battlefield.[25] Ellen told her brother, "The Americans are the better talkers, but the English are the doers and the givers of themselves the best of what they have and are—to the cause."[26]

At over eighty years of age, Ellen realized that she could contribute little but money to the war effort: "I can't give man (or woman) power in the field or hospital, or factory. So I have to fall back on the one remaining factor vouchsafed me—money."[27] She had bought more than $125,000 (about $2.3 million) worth of Liberty Bonds by 1919, noting that the success of this venture "seems to be of so transcendentally vital an issue of the war."[28] Still, by conserving food and living as economically as possible, she hoped to share some of the sacrifices being made by a younger generation. Harper told E.W., "She takes the war very seriously; is economizing, conserving, planning to make every dollar count. . . . She seems to want to feel that she can do things without anybody knowing about it."[29]

Camp Kearny

In May 1917 the U.S. Army selected the Linda Vista mesa in San Diego near Miramar as the site of a training facility for twenty-eight thousand soldiers on their way to fight in the trenches of Belgium and France. E.W. grumbled at the news: "With five thousand or more marines in Balboa Park, four or five thousand at Fort Rosecrans, two thousand aviators, and these twenty-five thousand other soldiers, I imagine that San Diego is destined to be little more than a big military camp and naval station."[30]

Miramar, once a remote ranch surrounded by sagebrush and chaparral, now became accessible to the outside world. It was no longer a "quiet and retired place" where E.W. could retreat from business concerns.[31] William E. Ritter, on viewing the preparations for the military camp, said that his first impression was that of "great depression, that the mesa would never again be what it had been to him in his drives and visits to Miramar."[32]

Camp Kearny opened in September as a "war suburb" of nearly twelve hundred buildings, including warehouses, mess halls, hospitals, a library, a theater, an auditorium, a post office, and a civic center with a restaurant, bowling alleys, billiard tables, and a shooting gallery. Service organizations such as the Red Cross and the YMCA also operated buildings, as did the Knights of Columbus, the Jewish Welfare Board, the Christian Science Church, and the American Library Association, among others.[33]

Ellen contributed to life at Camp Kearny by financing the construction of a YWCA "hostess house" to serve as the headquarters for visitors who came to visit the enlisted men. Architect Julia Morgan, who later built Hearst Castle in San Simeon, designed the wooden structure with a low-pitched roof, wide eaves, and a veranda that faced the sunset.[34] Alice Klauber, a local artist, planned the decorative scheme, adding Chinese "good luck" lanterns and softly shaded reading lamps, while Margaret Fanton donated her collection of Indian rugs. Kate Sessions, meanwhile, did the landscape design.[35]

At the opening of the hostess house, Ellen found herself received "as a sort of grand mogul."[36] The San Diego City Council designated November 30, 1917, as Ellen Scripps Day in recognition of her donation, while the YWCA held a large reception hosted by Brigadier General and Mrs. George H. Cameron, Mayor Louis J. Wilde, YWCA president Mrs. Philip Morse, and others. Ellen viewed the structure and described it as "a very homelike, attractive, and artistic building."[37]

Ellen used her automobile to bring friends and acquaintances to Camp Kearny. She told E.W., "It is a wonderful city 'over there.' One drives through its streets (?) dumbfounded at its immensity and its orderliness." Again, she thanked him for the car, describing it as a "great asset to my work of 'service,' and joy in my life. . . . I am going twice a week now to Camp Kearny, taking those whose interest and help in the cantonment is beyond words. I can't help hearing on every hand the words of appreciation and gratitude intended for myself, but which, if referred to the inception—and conception of what I have done belongs wholly to you."[38]

La Jolla women played a significant role in entertaining officers and enlisted men, providing teas, dinners, and beach parties. Virginia and her friends occasionally went to the barracks with flowers for the hospital, returning with a "soldier boy" whom they hosted at South Molton Villa.[39] Every Sunday evening, many clubwomen opened their homes to soldiers and gave them a homemade supper, "some people entertaining 15 or 20."[40] Ellen's sister-in-law Emma Scripps hosted a dozen soldiers every Sunday afternoon at her home, Braemar, in Pacific Beach, offering "boating and bathing and supper to their hearts' content."[41]

In November 1917 Ellen lunched at the club with a band of soldiers who had spent the morning in La Jolla soliciting pledge cards for food conservation. She told her sister, "It was a fine repast of 4 courses. . . . Menu (which I know you like to hear about) hot clam chowder with crackers; hot macaroni and cheese; with various kinds of appetizing sandwiches; and fig jam; fruit salad with wafers, ice cream and cake; coffee interspersed and finally a table full of baskets of oranges and apples which they took as souvenirs." Afterward, the soldiers gave a "splendid concert" on the veranda.[42]

On Wednesdays and Saturdays trucks from Camp Kearny brought several hundred men to La Jolla for dinner at the woman's club and community house, followed by band concerts and dances on the playground's tennis courts. Ellen described it as "a wonderful experience—like a dream in a past reincarnation." Some four or five hundred khaki-clad soldiers danced with women and girls, including teachers from The Bishop's

School, "while we spectators sat on the side seats knitting, with only the moonlit sky for a canopy."[43] On Christmas Day, 1917, an estimated three thousand soldiers and civilians enjoyed a celebration at the community house and playground that included field sports, a theatrical performance, the lighting of the giant Christmas tree, supper, and dancing.[44]

In 1918 an enlisted men's club was established in the Southern Trust and Commerce Bank Building at the corner of Girard and Wall Streets, with easy chairs, writing tables, a piano, and a pool table. Ellen loaned Frances Norris $150 (about $2,360) so she could establish a restaurant adjoining the club.[45] That summer the army erected tents in the Little Court south of the playground for convalescent soldiers.[46]

Many officers' wives also found a home in the village. Ellen noted in November 1917, "There are over 70 of them already established in La Jolla." They joined the woman's club as "transient members," filling the tearoom and auditorium with conversation.[47]

Patriotism

Ellen felt a strong sense of responsibility for the community of La Jolla, refusing to leave for Washington, DC, where E.W. had established a new home in 1917. He pleaded, "Come! Be an 'old sport'! and prove your old-time contention that notwithstanding you are a woman and notwithstanding that you are much older than me, you can outdo me in enterprise!" He added that his oldest son, James, could use her help in establishing control over the Scripps papers: "You were a tremendously important factor in the old days when the concern was young, and I believe that you would certainly be a very valuable factor now when it is old and when it is about to pass finally from old hands to new."[48]

Ellen declined, explaining to him, "In these crucial times which demand 'universal service,' I am pledged to give of what I am and have to the common cause and I am conscious that nowhere else can I render this service as I can right here." She expressed surprise that San Diegans set a high value on "my views and utterances" and wanted her to speak at public meetings. "Of course, I can't do those things," she wrote. "A natural timidity and reticence as well as a consciousness of mental disability—or rather inability—would prevent me from public posturing. . . . Nevertheless, I can't ignore the fact that I do possess and can exert a power and an influence in the community that imposes an obligation on me that I must accept."[49]

Ellen read several inspiring papers before the La Jolla Woman's Club, despite her general dislike of public speaking. In 1918 she offered a short "New Year's Greeting," in which she responded to political divisions within the club, saying, "Life is too short, and the world is too pregnant with a mighty creative force seeking deliverance, for us to fritter away our time and energies in factional or individual fault finding."[50]

On the anniversary of Abraham Lincoln's assassination, she compared the European conflict to the Civil War: "It behooves us to remember that America's great wars have been conceived and carried out not for greed of power, extension of territory, political ambition, but for the holy cause of Liberty." She reminded her audience that, once before, Americans had "seemed willing to sacrifice anything and everything for a meaningless peace." Lincoln, however, stood his ground, with the result that slavery finally had been abolished.[51] In another speech, she told members of the woman's club, "We are the women to whom the world looks; upon whom the world depends in these crucial times. Each and every one of us is part and parcel of the great whole." She echoed the sonnet written by the English war poet Rupert Brooke: "'Now God be thanked who has matched us with this hour!'"[52]

Finally, in early 1919 Ellen read a memorial tribute to those friends and relatives who had passed away in the last year, including a young musician named Clyde Collison, whom she had met at Camp Kearny. She described the boy as "so filled with the love of life and enthusiasm and inspiration that it will be always this living spirit which comes to us when we think of him or seem to hear again his wonderful music—the boy whose silver star of service has been changed to gold!"[53]

Caught up in the patriotic spirit, many La Jollans became increasingly hostile to moderation on the subject of Germany. In the summer of 1917 William E. Ritter initiated a series of open-forum meetings at the community house "as a means of informing the public on the underlying significance of war." He intended to consider aspects of autocracy and democracy, but, according to Ellen, "most of the audience didn't seem to be able to get any farther than the conflict between Germany and her antagonists. They didn't want to be 'educated,' they only wanted a confirmation of their own opinions of Germany, utter devilishness, and conversely our own glorification." Ritter's statements were "hissed, and he himself denounced from the floor—both by men and women—as a pro-German." She told E.W., "Outside of the biological colony, and a small coterie of sympathetic friends, I don't think Prof. Ritter is decidedly persona grata in the community."[54]

A month later, when Lieutenant Harry D. Trounce, a former La Jolla resident, spoke on his wartime experiences, residents kept him answering questions for more than an hour. Ellen asked Harper if any of the speakers had a pro-German attitude: "He laughed as he said that if there was any pro-German, or even pacifist, there, he wouldn't have dared to peep. He would have stood a chance of being mobbed so strong and so enthusiastic was the feeling of the audience."[55]

Socialist speakers also generated controversy. In April 1918 muckraking journalist Lincoln Steffens lectured at the First Unitarian Church on the recent Bolshevik Revolution and intended to give a second talk, "The Menace of Peace," the following night. His speech on Russia followed on the heels of San Diego's Liberty Day bond drive and parade, causing a number of people to complain about his remarks. Chief of Police S. P. McMullen showed up at the church, holding up a copy of the *San Diego Sun*, and demanded to know if the journalist had said that all governments, including the United States, were "rotten." Steffens replied, "I admit that I have criticized the United States government for 25 years." McMullen then stopped Steffens from speaking, according to the *San Diego Union*, saying, "No man who is publicly criticizing this government in times like this can speak here—not while I am chief of police."[56]

Ellen, who had helped Rev. Howard B. Bard and the Templeton Johnsons bring Steffens to San Diego, initially thought that the newspapers had brewed up a "tempest in a tea pot." However, after reading "the objections and threats" made by both Mayor Wilde and Councilman

Walter P. Moore and recalling "the latter's course at the time of the I.W.W. persecution and the San Diego 'vigilantes,'" she was grateful that Steffens got out of town on the night train "without being driven out in a coat of tar and feathers."[57]

Patriotism was encouraged by government propaganda and fed by newspapers, magazines, and other forms of media. When Ellen and her friends viewed the silent film *Hearts of the World* (1918), directed by D. W. Griffith, they found themselves so "wrapped in a spirit of intensity" that they rose to their feet with the rest of the audience when the orchestra started to play "La Marseillaise." "There was much silent weeping; but an intense 'stillness,'" she wrote.[58]

Scripps Memorial Hospital

Films and photographs depicting the wartime Red Cross inspired many people to consider the state of health care in San Diego. At the time, the city had relatively few hospitals, given the growing number of residents. The County Hospital, established in 1880, provided free care to those who otherwise would not be able to afford it. Originally located downtown, it moved to a large brick facility at the north end of Front Street in 1904. St. Joseph's Hospital and Sanitarium, founded by the Sisters of Mercy and opened in 1890, had a large building at University Avenue and Sixth Street. Other private hospitals included the Agnew Sanitarium and the Paradise Valley Sanitarium in National City.

Some residents traveled farther afield for medical care. Anna Bentham went to the Good Samaritan Hospital in Los Angeles with diabetes-related issues, while John P. Scripps had blood tests at Alder's Sanitarium in San Francisco due to symptoms of "dropsy," or edema. In 1914 the latter died of endocarditis at the age of twenty-seven.[59]

Ellen generally had little use for hospitals, taking the Christian Science approach to health. She told her sister in 1894, "I wouldn't waste my money on sanitariums. My theory is that nature will always take care of herself—if allowed to!"[60] She realized, however, that friends and family members benefited from extended care. Her diaries contain numerous references to La Jolla residents who suffered from rheumatism, heart disease, pneumonia, broken limbs, and other ailments. Her brother Will spent a considerable amount of time in Michigan's Battle Creek Sanitarium, while E.W. suffered from various maladies that required the attention of a doctor.

In 1916 E.W. was approached by Helena "Lena" Parker Kendall about establishing better hospital facilities in San Diego. The wife of surgeon Dr. Oscar J. Kendall and the daughter of Dr. and Mrs. P. J. Parker, she had founded the Talent Workers of San Diego for the purpose. Her organization received the support of the La Jolla Woman's Club in 1912.[61]

At the same time, the Sisters of Mercy planned an expansion of St. Joseph's and began fund-raising. They solicited money from E.W. and asked if he would permit his name to be used in their subscription efforts. He agreed, thinking he would try out the role of "ordinary everyday garden variety of philanthropist." He was not confident, however, that their accommodations would significantly improve even if they did receive the necessary funds.[62]

Inspired by the obvious need for medical services, E.W. founded the San Diego Diagnostic Group Clinic with funds provided by the John P. Scripps Memorial Foundation in February 1917. Modeled after the Mayo Clinic in Rochester, Minnesota, it was intended to be a place where workingmen and women could have their ailments diagnosed at a nominal cost. E.W. promised $250,000 (about $4.6 million in 2016 dollars) and offered to meet any deficit in maintenance up to $30,000 a year (about $555,000). If successful, he planned to open the John P. Scripps Memorial Hospital for Working Men and Women as "a memorial to my deceased son."[63]

The anticipated hospital was never built, however, due to the outbreak of war and the enlistment of many physicians and surgeons. E.W., moreover, lost interest in the scheme. He told Dr. Robert Pollock, "I like to start things going—to initiate something new," but admitted to a "constitutional aversion to long-sustained effort" and a dislike of "the grind of administering, supervising, or even observing closely a going institution."[64]

Instead, Ellen decided to contribute to a new hospital in La Jolla. In 1916 the neighboring Kline House had been converted into a six-bed sanitarium by Dr. Samuel Gillispie and his wife, Ada, who had recently arrived in La Jolla from Kansas. Before that, the building had housed students from The Bishop's School while another dormitory was under construction.[65] In December Ellen's librarian, Ida Loring, entered the hospital with bronchitis, giving her the opportunity to view the situation firsthand. She came to the conclusion that the house was "altogether unsuited for the work" and that another structure needed to be built.[66]

In March 1917 Ellen spoke with Ada Gillispie about buying lots in Block 17, close to the Kline House and across the street from South Molton Villa. She asked Harper to investigate.[67] In June she authorized her lawyer to purchase Lots 43, 44, and 45 for $5,800 (about $107,000). She told him, "I expect to assist financially to a substantial amount, in providing the site and building for the hospital."[68]

At first, Ellen planned to make an investment rather than a gift. Recognizing that Ada Gillispie intended to remain in control of both the construction and the operation of the new hospital, she instructed Harper to offer a lease and ask for 6 percent interest. Ada wrote, "I certainly do not feel that I am asking Miss Scripps to *give* the money for a hospital. I assuredly believe she will receive interest on every cent invested. And you surely know I hope to someday call it mine because I will have actually paid for it."[69]

Concerned to keep costs down, Ada hired architect William Sterling Hebbard rather than Irving J. Gill and his nephew Louis. Harper explained, "There is a widespread feeling in the village that the Gills do work in a very expensive way and Mrs. Gillispie had a vital interest in keeping down the cost; so I let her select the architect."[70] The problem remained construction costs. Harper was not convinced that they would be able to build the structure for under $25,000 (about $462,000). In fact, he told Ellen that, given the state of her finances, it would be better to delay the project until after the war.

Ellen, however, decided that the hospital needed to be built. She told her lawyer, "The needs for such an institution grow daily and will probably increase in the near future in something of a geometrical proportion; cost of material and wages will increase instead of diminish as time goes on. And in a few months the difficulty of getting either men or material may reach a crisis." She added, "I don't want to relieve Mrs. Gillispie of either responsibility or effort at economy, but I am inclined to think the building should go on—with perhaps certain restrictions." E.W. agreed, telling her that they should "spend freely . . . in the public service, even to the extent of burdening our estates with obligations."[71]

In a subsequent letter, Ellen elaborated on the need for a hospital with more than six beds. In March 1918 an automobile accident on Torrey Pines Road caused four operations scheduled at the La Jolla Sanitarium to be canceled. Most of the accident victims had to be transported to San Diego, while the body of a dead man had to be left on the sanitarium's porch overnight pending the arrival of the coroner and undertaker. She told Harper, "It is such happenings as these that show the rapidly increasing need of a larger and well-equipped institution; and which makes me feel that I have a personal obligation to see the need supplied."[72]

Ellen did not personally supervise the construction of the hospital but left it to Harper and Ada Gillispie. She considered the latter to be "a level-headed businesswoman" who could be trusted not to run up the bills.[73] Still, she was excited enough about the new venture to imagine her own life as a doctor or a nurse. She told her sister, "If I were only 50 years younger than I am I would throw up everything else, and go into this work, which seems to be the one for which women are particularly fitted. The only thing that troubles me is that there is no place for me in the world's work—and sacrifice. I was born out o'time!"[74]

The new hospital, opened in November 2, 1918, occupied a concrete building built along Prospect Street opposite The Bishop's School. With three stories, it contained eight patient rooms, a three-bed ward, an operating room, a diet kitchen, a hydrotherapy room, and a glass-enclosed porch and solarium.[75] The Frances E. Brown Room was endowed by the La Jolla Woman's Club in honor of their former president.[76]

Many of the early patients suffered from a virulent strain of influenza known as the Spanish flu, a pandemic that lasted from 1918 to 1920 and infected an estimated 500 million people across the world. Killing 3 to 6 percent of the global population, it remains one of the deadliest natural disasters in human history. The origins of the flu remain uncertain, but the disease almost certainly spread along military supply lines in the United States and Europe. The disease reached San Diego by October 1918, causing city officials to ban public gatherings and to close down public facilities such as schools, libraries, bathhouses, gymnasiums, churches, and theaters.[77] Quarantines surrounded military bases such as Fort Rosecrans and Camp Kearny. In October 1918 Ellen noted in her diary, "All public places, including Hostess House, are closed on account of danger of contagion of 'Spanish flu.'"[78] In early December she told her sister, "The new sanitarium in La Jolla has been compelled—against its intentions—to take Flu patients. They have seven from one family—in South La Jolla. But they have given up the entire lower floor to cases of the kind, so making it practically an isolated hospital. However, none of the cases in this part of the suburbs are of a serious nature; what would probably in ordinary times be called simply 'bad colds.'"[79]

Among the Scripps family members and friends who died of influenza was Edith McRae Scripps, the widow of E.W.'s son John. Her death was treated in "so matter of fact a way," Ellen wrote, that she wondered whether "the war and the pandemic of influenza have familiarized us with this 'episode' in life; or whether we have gained a truer sense of its significance."[80]

Ellen continued to support the hospital, describing it as "one of the few successful public ventures I have indulged in."[81] Over the course of the next decade, she financed the construction of a new fireproof hospital building at 464 Prospect Street designed by Louis Gill. It opened in September 1924 with fifty-seven beds, as well as medical, obstetrical, and surgical departments. The former La Jolla Sanitarium became the Scripps Metabolic Clinic—a research unit—while the new hospital was named Scripps Memorial Hospital in honor of the late Julia Anne "Annie" Scripps.[82] In 1930 Ellen anticipated that her house would become an important part of this medical complex.[83]

World War I ended with the signing of an armistice between the Allies and Germany on November 11, 1918. Front-page headlines in the *San Diego Union* read, "World War Ends," "Soldiers Revolt in Berlin," "Emperor Flees to Holland," "Germany Breaking Ties That Bound It to Past," and "German Revolution Is Raging Wildly Throughout Empire and People Oust Government Heads."[84]

The announcement of peace had been anticipated for more than a week, with the *San Diego Sun* announcing the end of warfare on November 7. Ellen wrote in her diary, "Put out the flag but feel like little demonstration and the new regime carries so heavy a burden."[85] She anticipated "the beginning of a bigger, all-inclusive war for construction instead of destruction," adding, "I think it will be the coming years that will try men's souls."[86]

La Jolla marked the end of the conflict with a celebration at the playground and community house, which Ellen had built. An evening parade of automobiles and pedestrians followed in the wake of a marching band from Camp Kearny. Afterward, ceremonies included religious and patriotic addresses, prayers led by Reverend Bedford-Jones, and the singing of hymns and national anthems from each of the Allied nations, ending with "The Star-Spangled Banner." As a finale, organizers burned the German kaiser in effigy.[87]

Ellen remained home with her friend Eliza Howard and had "an old fashioned 'confab'" while the rest of the village rejoiced: "Like me, she felt more like weeping than rejoicing." She wrote, "They called it a peace, but a peace built on vengeance and hatred is worse than war. I suppose I shall yet be damned as a pro-German—as many better and wiser people will be—probably including President Wilson."[88] Despite her doubts about the public celebration of the armistice, she contributed $5,000 (about $78,700) to the United War Work parade held later that week.[89]

Midterm elections in which the Republican Party gained control of both the U.S. House and the Senate revealed voters' increasing dissatisfaction with the situation at home. For his part, E.W. thought that "our government's actions of a most arbitrary kind—in the way of suppressing free speech and a free press and in its handling of the matter of the draft—have produced a tremendous amount of ill-feeling on the part of vast numbers of individuals." He told his sister, "To a large extent, the people of this country have been terrorized. Speakers and writers have not dared to express themselves freely in what they speak and write." People had been induced to buy Liberty Bonds by volunteer committees engaged in "a sort of blackmail." He was not surprised that voters expressed "a certain amount of resentment" with Wilson's administration, writing, "There has been a vastly greater amount of unpatriotism than has been evident on the surface."[90]

Ellen, too, recognized that social and political rifts were bound to become deeper now that the war had ended. She hoped, however, that the community spirit that had swept the country would last a little longer. The war years, however challenging, had been a special moment for those committed to progressive causes. In early 1919 she wrote, "Sometimes it seems to me that I have lived more—and grown more—in the past year, than in all the past decades, and I think most of us if we could analyze ourselves and make comparisons of the present with the past, would say the same." She asked her brother whether he, too, had noticed "the subtle changes that have taken place in people—not nations or parties, or policies; but the human individual—since he has been forced into a new atmosphere of thought and living."[91]

Convinced that the war had revealed a new American spirit, Ellen dedicated the next decade of her life to making people aware of their responsibilities in a global world. She supported national and international communities fighting for peace, suffrage, Prohibition, education, and other progressive causes. No longer bound by provincial interests or concerns, she believed that women throughout the country "are all finding our true selves as combatants in world struggle for righteousness; as workers for the good of all."[92]

CHAPTER 14

Still Roaring in the 1920s

On August 23, 1923, Ellen quietly celebrated the fiftieth anniversary of the founding of the *Detroit Evening News*, the newspaper that had founded the Scripps family fortune. She noted in her diary, "I and E.W. the only living persons who were present on the occasion of its birth."[1] Their three brothers—James, Will, and George—were dead, along with the first generation of newspapermen who had worked with them.

The newspaper became increasingly profitable as advertising expanded, consumer spending increased, and the nation experienced a period of vigorous economic growth. In 1924 the net profits of the *Detroit Evening News* were estimated at over $3,114,000 (about $43.2 million in 2016 dollars), up more than 300 percent since 1918. E.W. wrote, "It is my impression that, with the possible exception of The Chicago Tribune, The Detroit News is the most profitable paper in the United States."[2]

Ellen's wealth grew exponentially during the 1920s. Between December 1920 and May 1922, the increase in her stockholdings amounted to "over a million dollars."[3] By 1925 she was worth well over $30 million (about $416 million), a conservative estimate, making her the richest person in San Diego.[4] She topped the list of San Diego taxpayers, paying $135,000 (about $1.83 million) in 1924. The next richest people in the city were Amelia Timken Bridges, who paid $75,000 (about $1 million), and Josephine Scripps, who paid $22,000 (about $297,000). Ellen noted, "The taxes of the supposed big money men were a mere *bagatelle* mostly not going beyond the third figure."[5] The richest people in the city were all women.

Nearing the end of her life, Ellen considered what to do with her money. Younger members of the Scripps family already led lives of "ease and luxury" and did not need to become multimillionaires.[6] She viewed inherited wealth as fundamentally undemocratic, tending toward the creation of an American aristocracy or, in her words, an "autocracy of Wall St.—a plutocracy."[7] In fact, E.W. advised her not to leave any of her *Evening News* stock to his heirs but instead to give it to the city of San Diego: "It seemed to me fitting that you should give most to those whom you loved most. If, instead of an individual, you chose the whole community to be your beneficiary, that is a matter of your own sentiment, and it seemed fitting and proper."[8]

E.W.'s advice appealed to Ellen, and in the last decade of her life, she began the most expansive phase of her philanthropy. She contributed substantial amounts of money to local institutions and public spaces, including the Torrey Pines State Reserve, the Zoological Society, the Natural History Museum, the San Diego Museum Association, the La Jolla Library, the children's pool, the YWCA, and Associated Charities of San Diego. She also turned her attention to national and international educational organizations such as the Claremont Colleges, Cleveland College, the Egypt Exploration Society, the Woman's Christian College in the Orient, Constantinople Women's College, and Yenching University, among others.

A New City

San Diego expanded rapidly after 1920. With a population of approximately seventy-five thousand, the city was significantly smaller than its California neighbors, Los Angeles and San Francisco, "but there is no question of her 'growing'!" Ellen wrote.[9] The beauty of the region, showcased at the Panama-California Exposition of 1915–16, drew in tens of thousands of new residents in subsequent years. Real estate developers continued to develop "streetcar suburbs" such as Golden Hill, Kensington, Mission Beach, and University Heights, while paved roads took automobiles from downtown San Diego to Warner's Springs and Julian. In 1923 a transcontinental highway connected San Diego with Washington, DC, along a southern route. Traffic increased dramatically; the number of automobiles and trucks on the road grew from eighteen thousand in 1920 to thirty thousand in 1923.[10]

As E.W. had anticipated, San Diego turned into a "navy town." In 1919 the navy established a naval base, fuel depot, hospital, marine barracks, and other facilities under the command of Rear Admiral Roger Welles.[11] The Naval Hospital in Balboa Park was dedicated in 1922, followed by the Naval Training Station and the Marine Corps Base in the following year.[12]

La Jolla, meanwhile, developed into a suburb with electricity, paved roads, and automobiles. In a 1919 speech before the La Jolla Woman's Club, Ellen described the changes that had taken place since 1894, including "paved streets, fire protection, water in abundance, gas, electricity, telephone, automobile."[13] The first paved road was the Torrey Pines Grade, completed in 1915, followed by Prospect Street (1918), La Jolla Boulevard (1920), Girard Avenue (1922), and others.[14] Ellen remarked on the rapid change in the appearance of La Jolla: "Things go and grow so fast that we are being ushered into new worlds as with the suddenness of a new birth. Driving home in the evening from Del Mar; a city of electric lights springs out before one's eyes from the mesa of sage brush and greasewood."[15]

In 1924 a high-speed electric railway connected the village with Pacific Beach, Mission Beach, Ocean Beach, Point Loma, and San Diego.[16] The old railroad depot, one of the oldest structures in the village, was torn down to make way for a new terminal at the corner of Fay Avenue and Prospect Street.[17] Projected "improvements" included a country club, a high school, new churches and parsonages, and additional residences. By the end of the 1920s, the village had two new hotels, Casa de Mañana (1924) and La Valencia Hotel (1926); the La Jolla Beach and Yacht Club (1927); and its first apartment house on Prospect Street.

Books and Paintings

Ellen contributed to La Jolla's educational and cultural infrastructure by supporting the construction of the La Jolla Memorial Library in 1921. A longtime trustee of the La Jolla Library Association, she wanted the new building to serve as both a community center and a memorial to U.S. soldiers who had lost their lives in service of the country.[18] She provided more than half the cost of construction and contributed a substantial sum to its endowment. The structure, now known as the Athenaeum Music & Arts Library, was designed by architect William Templeton Johnson in the Spanish Revival style. It opened in 1921 at the corner of Wall Street and Girard Avenue. The old Reading Room was moved to Draper Avenue before making its way to the campus of The Bishop's School in 2005.

Ellen felt strongly about books, having created an extensive collection of her own. "'A good book is the next best thing in life to a true friend,'" she wrote, quoting Walter de la Mare. "It gives all it has to give, solely for the asking, and wants nothing in return, but just a thankful blessing on the man who wrote it.'"[19] She also copied a quote by Francis Bacon, "'Some books are to be tasted. Others are to be swallowed and some few are to be swallowed [chewed] and digested.'"[20]

In 1924 Ellen presented the library with a copy of William Leon Dawson's *Birds of California*, a four-volume illustrated work that she had financed from its inception. It contained detailed entries on the 580 species and subspecies of birds found in the state by one of the leading ornithologists of the early twentieth century. This edition also included original watercolor paintings by Allan Brooks. Other copies went to the San Diego Natural History Museum, Knox College, and the Claremont Colleges.[21]

The new library included an art gallery that displayed works by San Diego and La Jolla artists. Ellen agreed to add the room after being approached by librarian Nina Waddell and clubwoman Eleanor Parkes about a site for future exhibitions. She also invited a group of artists to tea on her birthday, October 18, 1918, to see Albert Valentien's final bound volume of California wildflowers.[22] This group would become the La Jolla Art Association. Emily "Nora" Landers, an early member, produced oils and watercolors in her south La Jolla bungalow, overgrown with roses and flower vines. One visitor recalled her as "very bright and intense. . . . She is unbalanced, beyond doubt, but interesting in her way."[23] Helen DeLange, who came to San Diego in 1907, produced landscape and flower paintings, while Alfred Mitchell became one of the leading American plein air painters of his day.[24] Other early members included Charles Fries, Alice Klauber, and Maurice Braun.[25]

Ellen donated several pieces of art to the library, including six drawings by Walter J. Fenn. She also commissioned the La Jolla artist to design a bookplate for the institution.[26] In 1922 she loaned her collection of wildflower paintings by Valentien to the library for an exhibition that attracted an estimated seven hundred people in its first month.[27]

San Diego's artistic climate shaped Ellen's taste in art. In Europe she had purchased a number of Pre-Raphaelite prints and copies of Old Masters. After 1900 she began to buy landscape paintings and photographs. In 1911 she bought an image of the Mission San Diego de Alcalá from Charles A. Fries, who became one of the best-known landscape painters in Southern California. Shortly thereafter, she commissioned him to paint two more scenes.[28] She also owned impressionist or plein air paintings by local artists. In her bedroom, she hung a painting of Torrey Pines and a desert scene.[29]

Ellen preferred the paintings of the California impressionist Maurice Braun to modern works by Childe Hassam, George Bellows, and Robert Henri. After viewing a 1921 exhibit of contemporary American painters, she wrote, "To tell the truth, I don't care for this kind of work. But Maurice Braun has a room all to himself—full of glow and color, 65 paintings in all. He takes them East where I hope he will find more appreciation than he does here. I suppose he puts his prices beyond people's consciences or purses and there is an aggressiveness of color which wouldn't fit in when the real thing is at hand. Nevertheless, it is a joy to look at them!"[30] She patronized the Los Angeles–based sculptor G. Salvatore Cartaino Scarpitta, commissioning him to create a bust of her in 1923. His other works included bas-reliefs for the facades of the Los Angeles Stock Exchange and the Los Angeles County General Hospital and portrait busts of Bishop Johnson, George W. Marston, Dr. Edgar L. Hewitt, Milton McRae, and David Starr Jordan, among others. He told J. C. Harper that his goal was to "portray the spirit of the individual," and he was particularly drawn to the idea of sculpting "the most distinguished woman in California."[31]

Although she appreciated the growing arts community in San Diego, Ellen did not become a major donor to the Fine Arts Gallery of San Diego, later the San Diego Museum of Art, which opened in 1926. She counted herself a supporter as early as 1916, however, when Alice Klauber and others began to circulate membership forms to the greater San Diego community. She approved the plan to "perpetuate some of the buildings at the Exposition as a nucleus for a great art collection" and became a "life member" at the cost of $100 (about $2,320).[32] She permitted the Art Guild of San Diego to meet at South Molton Villa to paint her garden and later supported Eugene de Vol's art school in Balboa Park, the San Diego Academy of Fine Arts.[33]

Egyptology

Ellen's projects for the educational advancement of San Diego included a collection of Egyptian antiquities and archaeological books that she received as a result of her membership in the London-based Egypt Exploration Society. She was not particularly interested in archaeology, or so she claimed, but she told a friend that she had "always been interested in the origins of things—how things began."[34]

The opening of the Suez Canal in 1869 brought waves of tourists to Egypt in the late nineteenth century, including members of the Scripps family. In December 1881, on her first visit to London, Ellen dined with her relation Edward Scripps Tudor and saw his "fine collection of Egyptian relics they had brought home from a trip up the Nile."[35] A year later, she and E.W. spent a month in Egypt. They toured Cairo, viewed the pyramids and the Great Sphinx at Giza, admired the ancient monuments of Thebes, and took a cruise up the Nile. She picked up some souvenirs, "simple antiquities," including a few scarab amulets that she had turned into earrings and a brooch at Tiffany's in Paris.[36] She lost many of these items when South Molton Villa burned down in 1915.

The Egypt Exploration Society, founded in 1882, promoted the exploration of the Nile Delta and launched an archaeological survey of Egypt. Swiss scholar Édouard Naville excavated Tell el-Maskhuta, Deir el-Bahari, and Thebes in an effort to find evidence for biblical stories about Egypt. British archaeologist W. M. Flinders Petrie, meanwhile, worked at various sites in the delta, including Tanis, Naucratis, and Tell Defenneh. Credited with founding the science of archaeology, Petrie preserved numerous sites from being plundered by treasure-hunters and poorly trained excavators looking only for museum pieces. He also trained a generation of Egyptologists, including Howard Carter, who discovered the tomb of Egyptian pharaoh Tutankhamun ("King Tut") in 1922.[37]

Ellen became a life member of the Egypt Exploration Society in 1911 after reading an appeal for money made by its first American staff member, Professor Thomas Whittemore of Tufts College.[38] She saw that subscribers would receive annual memoirs, illustrated reports, and a special seven-volume illustrated collection describing the operations in clearing and restoring the temple of Queen Hatshepsut at Deir el-Bahari.[39] Ellen must have thought it appropriate to learn more about Hatshepsut, Egypt's first female pharaoh, at a time when California voters were considering an amendment to the state constitution that would allow women to vote. She bought a $125 (about $2,570) life membership and began purchasing additional books published by the organization.[40]

At the time, the society sent artifacts to its major donors in return for yearly contributions. Ellen received her first package from Egypt in early 1912, containing "jacquard tapestries, representing in colored pieces certain dynasties; also head gear of Egyptian women, and bronze wolf with suckling twins—Romulus and Remus."[41] Having no wish to start a personal collection of Egyptian antiquities, Ellen deferred large donations until a local museum could be established. In 1916 she told Marie Buckman, secretary for the U.S. branch of the Egypt Exploration

Society, "An association for a comprehensive art museum in San Diego is now in its formative stage; and I shall be interested in obtaining such collections as may be of real value towards it."[42]

The San Diego Museum Association, established at the end of 1915, purchased many of the ethnology, archaeology, and anthropology exhibits that had been displayed at the Panama-California Exposition in Balboa Park. It established a permanent museum in the California Building and named Dr. Edgar L. Hewett as director in 1916. Ellen purchased a life membership in the organization and encouraged her sister to do so as well.[43]

In 1919 Ellen agreed to the Egypt Exploration Society's request to fund work that had been interrupted by World War I. She purchased the six-volume series *The Rock Tombs of El Amarna* with the view of transferring these and other items to the San Diego Museum. She accepted the title "Honorary Secretary for the State of California" but told the organization's national secretary, "You should understand that I am neither a curio, nor a scientific 'collector,' and that my interest in archaeology and kindred subjects is chiefly for its educational value for the people."[44]

Ellen became particularly interested in the excavations at Amarna, the capital city established by Pharaoh Akhenaten of the late Eighteenth Dynasty (ca. 1353 BCE). Akhenaten and his queen, Nefertiti, believed in a single deity, Aten, usually represented as a rayed solar disc, and dedicated several temples to this god. In the early twentieth century, scholars imagined Akhenaten as a pacifist and religious reformer who tried and failed to lead the Egyptian people away from polytheism. This appealed to Ellen, who encouraged her sister to visit Amarna on her world tour. Ellen wrote, "It is an ancient city 160 miles south of Cairo, on the eastern bank of the hill, built about 1,400 years before the Christian era, and is said to be the earliest landmark in the higher development of the human brain. It was founded by a young prince of the highest ideals. His name was Akhenaten—one of the pharaohs of Egypt. But he was a 'pacifist' and his young life (he died at 28) has a tragedy."[45]

The first shipment of antiquities from Amarna included red-and-blue-decorated pottery, a stone seat, some amulets, and jewelry. These went directly into the San Diego Museum's collection. Subsequent packages contained sculptured relief panels, tomb figurines (*ushabtis*), wooden objects, utensils, blocks inscribed with hieroglyphics, and fresco pavement panels.[46]

Ellen also received personal gifts, such as "a beautiful bit of pavement" that she mounted in silver and used as a paperweight. In 1920 she acknowledged the arrival of "mummy peas" drawn from seeds said to have been found at the excavation site. Planted in London, they had produced "a beautiful blue flower—the ancient Egyptian pea." She gave one seed to horticulturalist Kate Sessions and planted the other in her sun garden. The latter "grew and flourished," attracting much interest from her La Jolla neighbors. "The flower is small but of a peculiar color . . . a metallic blue, like the wings of a butterfly," she told Buckman.[47]

In 1925 Ellen turned over her large collection of books on Egypt to the scientific library at Balboa Park, having read many of them.[48] She impressed Professor Whittemore with her knowledge during an afternoon visit in La Jolla. He wrote, "I knew Miss Scripps was interested in Egyptology, but I was unprepared to find her so accurately versed in the history of the reign of Amenhotep III and so vivid in her conversation upon it."[49]

Ellen continued to support the Egypt Exploration Society by sending annual checks, though she warned, "My time is getting short, and you should be looking out for my successor. I am in my 92nd year, and the machinery of life can't go on forever."[50] Her bequest of $10,000 (about $135,000) allowed excavations at Amarna to continue through 1936. At this time, the museum gained some of its most valuable pieces, including a polished granite stela showing Akhenaten making an offering to Aten and a limestone column carved in relief with Nefertiti holding an ankh. Over four hundred objects from Amarna remain in the San Diego Museum of Man's collections.[51]

Natural History

Ellen also interested herself in preserving the natural history of California—its trees, plants, and fossils. In 1919 she told her sister about her meeting with archaeologist W. O. Bourne, "who says the whole of this coast is a rich deposit of antiquities, enough to equip the biggest and most interesting museum in the United States. He has recently unearthed a huge mastodon from the sand rocks between Bird Rock and Pacific Beach."[52]

In 1920 Ellen became the first major patron of the San Diego Society of Natural History. The organization, founded in 1874, had established its first museum in Balboa Park's Nevada Building. It displayed birds and mammals collected by naturalist Frank Stephens, as well as plants, shells, insects, minerals, and fossils. The space, however, proved inadequate for the donations and loans that began arriving in 1919, including the Baker-Kelsey shell collection and the Laurence Huey collection of bird skins and eggs.[53]

Dr. Fred Baker, a longtime trustee of the Scripps Institution, asked Ellen for help. As the newly elected president of the organization, he thought that the society needed to become involved in public education. For that reason, he recommended a move to larger quarters in the Foreign Arts Building, located on the Plaza de Panama. Scripps agreed to finance the move but asked the society to consider the construction of a permanent fireproof museum building. The old exposition buildings had not been built to last, and the cost of renovating them could be prohibitive. She promised $50,000 (about $695,000) paid in $2,000 monthly installments so long as the society began a public campaign to raise the funds necessary for a new building.[54] In the meantime, she funded the purchase of dinosaur, marine reptile, and mammal fossils from Charles H. Sternberg, a pioneer fossil hunter who moved to San Diego around 1920. She also paid for his 1921 trip to New Mexico.[55] Her sister purchased the Hornbeck collection of shells, minerals, and corals and donated it to the museum in April 1920.[56]

Ellen's acquaintance with naturalist and author John Burroughs (1837–1921) furthered her interest in natural history. A prolific essayist, Burroughs had a national reputation for his thoughtful observations on nature, conservation, religion, and philosophy. The octogenarian spent January 1920 in La Jolla as the guest of the Scripps sisters. He, his son

Julian, and their friends hosted a New Year's dinner at Wisteria Cottage, using poems as place cards. Ellen's read, "Serene, I fold my hands and wait / Nor care for wind, nor tide, nor sea."[57] Burroughs gave talks to the La Jolla Woman's Club, the community house, La Jolla High School, The Bishop's School, Francis W. Parker School, the University Club, and other local organizations. Virginia made sure that the Burroughs party took in the scenic beauty of California, taking them on auto tours of Balboa Park, Coronado, Tijuana, Paradise Valley, and Imperial Valley, among other places. Burroughs and his assistant, Dr. Clara Barras, returned to La Jolla in the winter of 1920–21.[58]

Interested in promoting children's access to nature, Ellen agreed to help the Zoological Society of San Diego create a zoo in Balboa Park. Founded in 1916 by Dr. Harry Wegeforth, Dr. Paul Wegeforth, Dr. Frank Baker, Commander J. C. Thompson, and Frank Stephens, the society took responsibility for the animals that had been brought to the Panama-California Exposition. In 1922 the society built a permanent zoo to provide sturdier enclosures for Kodiak bears like Caesar that frequently escaped from their cages. Ellen provided over $57,000 (about $806,000) for fencing, dams, and state-of-the-art living spaces for bears, lions, tigers, and other animals. She paid the director's annual salary of $5,000 (about $70,700) and funded the Scripps Aviary, which, at eighty-two feet high, was the tallest flight cage in the world at the time. She donated $50,000 (about $670,000) for a hospital and biological research institute, completed in 1927, and funded the purchase of the first gorillas, Mbongo and N'gagi.[59]

In December 1922 the Society of Natural History moved to the Canadian Building, now Casa de Balboa, which had 115,000 square feet of exhibit space. This permitted the society to develop what Joseph W. Sefton, Jr., called "pictorial demonstrations" detailing the life history of plants and animals.[60] Sefton, who served as president of the society from 1922 to 1965, worked with director Clinton Abbott to expand the operations of the society to include field trips, lectures, and a youth and school program.

Ellen offered $125,000 (about $1.69 million) to support the construction of a new fireproof museum after the Civic Auditorium in Balboa Park burned to the ground. She toured architect William Templeton Johnson's new Fine Arts Gallery in October 1925 and, according to her lawyer, "was greatly interested in the beautiful building, its artistic features, lighting schemes, natural and artificial."[61] She likely encouraged the architect to present plans for a similar building to the Society for Natural History. In the meantime, Johnson designed the San Diego Trust and Savings Bank (1927) and the Serra Museum (1928) before the stock market crash and the start of the Great Depression put construction on hold.

Finally, in 1932 work began on a new Natural History Museum. Johnson created an elegant Spanish Revival structure to house research collections and popular exhibits. Ellen did not live long enough to see the building completed, but she made sure that the society would remain solvent by providing an additional $50,000 (about $868,000) in her will. The museum opened on January 14, 1933, with 61,140 square feet for exhibits, workshops, a library, offices, laboratories, and storage rooms.[62]

Ellen's collection of California wildflower paintings by Albert Valentien came to the museum after her death, along with original Allan Brooks paintings of birds published in *Birds of California*. The museum also acquired approximately seventy of Ellen's books, including a fourteen-volume set of Romeyn B. Hough's *The American Woods* (1888–1913), containing 1,059 samples of wood; Richard Lydekker's *Library of Natural History* (1901); W. Leon Dawson's *Birds of Washington* (1909), along with many of his photographic prints; and John Gerard's *Herball, or Generall historie of plantes* (1630).[63]

Torrey Pines

Ellen believed that nature could be both educational and therapeutic, having derived great comfort from her frequent sightseeing trips through San Diego's backcountry. She particularly enjoyed driving between La Jolla and Del Mar. There, on the bluffs overlooking the sea, she occasionally saw some of the most "beautiful panoramas of color of sky and sea ever beheld in La Jolla."[64]

A grove of exceedingly rare *Pinus torreyana*, or Torrey pines, stood on the headlands north of La Jolla. Their twisted branches and irregular shapes attracted the attention of early naturalists, who lobbied the city to preserve the pines' habitat by creating a public park along the coast. By the turn of the century, the area had become a site for picnics and tally-ho parties.

By 1910 a coast road connected La Jolla and Del Mar, running from the Shores, up the Biological Grade, through the Torrey Pines, down the headlands, and across Los Peñasquitos Marsh. It was built under the auspices of the San Diego County Highway Commissioners—E. W. Scripps, John D. Spreckels, and Albert G. Spalding—who worked to make the region accessible to automobile traffic. E.W. was particularly enthusiastic about the project, writing, "I shall probably never abandon this campaign until San Diego and San Diego County have the best and most practicable roads there are in the country."[65]

In order to prevent development from spoiling the scenic beauty of the park, Ellen purchased a section of land that, for unknown reasons, had been sold by the city to private investors, despite the fact that it contained a large number of Torrey pines. She acquired two hundred acres consisting of Pueblo Lot 1338 for $15,050 (about $400,000) in 1908 and Lot 1339 for $4,000 (about $101,000) in 1911–12. Her brother had intended to buy this property himself but found himself short on money. "I had my sister buy the land for me," he later explained, though he considered the price to be exorbitant. Ellen and E.W. intended to sell or give the property back to the city when it was needed for the park.[66]

By 1915 the coastal road had replaced the Camino Real as the leading route into San Diego from the north. Thousands of visitors heading to the Panama-California Exposition made their way through the scenic Torrey Pines State Reserve and, after stopping for a picnic, left behind garbage: "bottles and cans, lunch boxes, orange peels and colored supplements." Local residents, meanwhile, gathered up branches, pinecones, and sometimes entire trees to use as Christmas decorations. In January 1916 naturalist Francis B. Sumner found "about half a dozen trees from which larger branches had been cut or torn." He wrote to Mayor E. M. Capps, sending a copy to Ellen, about the danger to the grove: "Let us not add the Torrey Pine to the long list of interesting plants and animals which have been sent to extinction in America."[67]

The San Diego Floral Association and the San Diego Society of Natural History spearheaded an effort to protect the park. They recruited members to clean up the trash, install garbage bins, and remove advertising signs posted along the road. In September 1916 the city enacted Ordinance 5380, forbidding visitors to build fires or cause damage to the trees. This followed a serious fire in June that had burned "the mass of pine needles and lichens like peat beds."[68]

In 1921 Ellen hired Guy L. Fleming, a naturalist, to serve as caretaker of the park.[69] He had written to her on behalf of the Floral Association, asking if she would be interested in developing "one of the most unique and picturesque parks in the West."[70] He imagined that it could become "a park at the very gates of the city where San Diego can welcome her guests with true old California hospitality."[71] In the summer of 1921, plans for a lodge to accommodate tourists were submitted to the city park board.

The following year, Ellen commissioned landscape architect Ralph D. Cornell to suggest improvements. The latter advised against a botanical garden and the introduction of new plants, even natives like the coast live oak. Instead, he recommended the construction of a system of trails that would divert pedestrian traffic from particularly sensitive areas while at the same time providing scenic views.[72]

Ellen financed the construction of Torrey Pines Lodge, built between 1922 and 1923 at a cost of $25,000 (about $338,000). Architects Richard S. Requa and Herbert Jackson designed the structure in the style of Hopi Indian houses of the Arizona desert. Mexican laborers made as many as six hundred adobe bricks a day, attracting the attention of passersby. One artist constructed a furnace and made tiles, ollas for chimney pots, and "minor articles of pottery resembling the ancient." Ellen told her brother, "This adobe construction has made so favorable an impression that the Santa Fe [Railroad] in the development of its ranch lands has engaged the same men who did the Torrey Pines work to construct the new buildings they are putting up" in Rancho Santa Fe.[73] When completed, the lodge included restrooms, indoor and outdoor dining pavilions, and a lunchroom. Visitors could purchase Mexican and Indian rugs, blankets, pottery, and other souvenirs.

Stimulated by this venture, Ellen agreed to finance a lodge at Asilomar, a YWCA camp located on California's Monterey Peninsula.[74] Founded as a young women's summer camp and conference facility, the structures at Asilomar were built by architect Julia Morgan between 1913 and 1928 with the support of Phoebe A. Hearst, among others.

Ellen believed in public access to nature, so much so that she was blind to the damage being done by increased automobile traffic in the Torrey Pines Reserve. In 1928 she and Harper opposed efforts to build a faster and safer coastal highway on the cliff face east of the park, closer to Sorrento Valley and the old Camino Real.[75] The old route, even though it was paved, had proved dangerous because of its steep grade and curves. But the new plan made it possible for automobiles to avoid Torrey Pines Park entirely, eliminating the picturesque gateway into San Diego. Ellen and her lawyer feared that tourists would be subjected to commercial billboards and "hotdog stands" if the road ran through Sorrento Valley to Rose Canyon. It would be no better than the approach to Los Angeles, lined with shantytowns.[76]

Harper and other La Jolla businessmen advocated a coastal route built along the west side of the Torrey Pines Park headlands so that automobile traffic did not bypass the village on its way to San Diego.[77] Ellen went along with the plan, even though many of her closest relations opposed it. Katharine Scripps, for example, let Harper know in no uncertain terms that she opposed the proposed "Cliff Road."[78] The route would destroy one of the loveliest canyons in the park and prevent visitors from walking from the lodge to the beach. Cornell agreed, explaining, "Any additional road, cut through Torrey Pines, would be a scar and blemish to the Preserve."[79]

Although Ellen did not want the Torrey Pines Park to become limited to "a select few" who came to botanize or picnic, she accepted the ultimate decision of the courts to prohibit a road through the park. The alternate route bypassed the Torrey Pines Grade and went south through Rose Canyon into downtown San Diego, with the result that the park remains one of the most scenic and unspoiled areas in the city.[80]

The Lath House

In 1924 Ellen offered another gift to La Jolla in the form of a lath house built on her estate by landscape architects Gardner & Slaymaker. Popular features in Southern California gardens, these structures offered shelter for a wide variety of shade-loving plants such as ferns and begonias. Ellen gave the architects permission to create something both artistic and utilitarian, but she insisted that it include a tearoom for visitors. Nathaniel Slaymaker later described it as a "pioneering job," one with "no precedents, no prototypes, no literature on the subject."[81]

Built of California redwood, the lath house consisted of a rotunda with flanking wings built on a foundation of natural weathered rock. Because of the natural contour of the site, the east wing stood on a slightly higher level than the rotunda, while the west wing was lower. Built at an angle to the street, the lath house did not block views of the coast and sea.

Water features—fountains and cascades—provided an exotic touch, given the arid climate of the region. A fountain representing a boy and a frog, the work of Edward H. Berge of San Francisco, stood at the center of the rotunda, surrounded by Oriental tea jars and handmade green tiles on the floor. Four other fountains were located in various corners of the lath house, including one displaying two dolphins emitting water into a huge conch shell. Retaining walls were faced with native lichen-covered rock from a nearby mountain. The lighting system used lead waterproof conduits concealed behind crossbeams. Newspaper articles remarked on the large lanterns of hammered copper with orange mica in the place of glass.

Plants included ferns, pink begonias, cyclamen, primulas, hyacinths, and other bulbs purchased from Kate Sessions. Ellen also acquired rare begonias from Alfred D. Robinson, president of the San Diego Floral Association, who propagated more than one hundred new varieties in his lath house at Rosecroft on Point Loma. Emma Scripps, an avid gardener, helped with both the architecture and the design of the garden.[82]

The lath house had a tearoom with large landscape windows overlooking the Pacific. Here, a long cascade of water flowed down rocks into pools filled with goldfish. Japanese wicker chairs and tables were combined with Mexican pottery. Tablecloths and napkins were embroidered by Mexican women working at San Diego's Neighborhood House. Both the lath house and the tearoom were open to the public daily. Newspapers estimated that six hundred visitors passed through the lath house on opening day, April 22, coming away with "a glimpse of fairyland." Ellen wrote in her diary, "A great occasion—hundreds of visitors. Lit up in the evening until 8 p.m."[83]

The Patron Saint of La Jolla

In 1920 Ellen's widespread philanthropy came to the attention of a civic group in New York that dubbed her "the patron saint of La Jolla." They wrote to her, asking for a biographical sketch of her life to be read before the club. Astonished, she refused their request, explaining, "Inasmuch as I am 'less than the least of all the saints' my record would be of no value to them." She wrote her sister about this extraordinary occurrence, reflecting, "But lots of things are 'funny' these days!"[84]

Ellen became a local celebrity in the 1920s, invited to gallery openings, bridge parties, theatricals, and other entertainments. She even had a standing offer to ride in "the biggest and best airplane at North Island—at any time I say so, and without money and without price."[85] She dealt with "almost daily calls from people demanding attention—both social and business." She wrote, "There seems not a day that I can call my own."[86] On one occasion, an unknown couple showed up at noon, armed with a letter of introduction, and asked if they could tour her library. Later, a group of professors arrived on a tour of La Jolla and the Biological Station. Sometimes she could not even get her supper of tea and toast without being interrupted by callers. She told her sister, "The only meal I can be sure of getting without interruption is breakfast, and that is because I take it at 5 in the morning before anyone else (except the milkman) is up!"[87] When her housekeeper Miss Smith went on vacation, Ellen happily made her own meals and showed visitors "all over the house."[88]

Although Ellen had engaged her time and money in a wide variety of philanthropic ventures by 1924, she felt that she could do more. She told her brother, "There are several things I am doing, but rather in a tentative and moderate way—the Rushville building, the Zoological Gardens in Balboa Park, and the Torrey Pines, but I might do something bigger without encumbering myself—or anyone else."[89] Her next project, Scripps College for Women, remains her most enduring legacy.

CHAPTER 15

Educating Women

One of Ellen's final and perhaps most important projects was the foundation of Scripps College in 1926. The culmination of her long-standing interest in women's education and progressive reform, the school was intended "to give opportunity to women to diverge from old lives and conventional study and style and attempt the new," in the words of her sister-in-law Katharine Scripps.[1] Encouraged by the confidence and success of young women graduating from The Bishop's School, Ellen wanted to help women achieve college degrees.

By 1920 women made up approximately 47 percent of American undergraduates, up from 21 percent in 1870.[2] Most attended coeducational colleges and universities that trained women to become teachers, nurses, social workers, and librarians, among the few professions open to women at that time. A smaller number of young women went to elite women's colleges like Vassar, Smith, and Bryn Mawr that offered a liberal arts curricula similar to that found at Ivy League institutions. They too anticipated doing some kind of professional or public service work before becoming wives and mothers.

Ellen thought that all women—even upper-middle-class ones—could benefit from vocational training. She often mused about the careers that she might have taken up if she had been born in a different generation. Despite working for years as a journalist and editor, she felt that she had "no special gift for writing" and that her work on the Scripps newspapers had been "merely auxiliary, to collect facts."[3] She would have liked to be a doctor or psychologist had those jobs been available to nineteenth-century women. According to a friend, "If one wanted to please her it was to tell her that she would have made a fine physician."[4] She also recognized that her sister Virginia would have been far better off with a career suited to her energy, intelligence, and ambition.

Ellen pinned her hopes on young college women like Mary B. Eyre, whom she had helped financially. In 1920 Eyre had received her B.A. and M.A. from Stanford University and prepared for graduate work in psychology. Ellen told Virginia that her young protégée planned to write a paper for the *Survey*, a leading journal of the social work profession and social reform, on the need for established nurses in women's prisons. "It is so good to find women 'doing things' instead of spending their time in cooking dainties and embroidering underwear," she wrote.[5]

Passages

Ellen retained a sense of purpose—and optimism about the future—even as close family members died and her own health declined. She wrote in 1925, "I am conscious in my own life of no loss or lack of mentality, or service in advancing years," but when it came to "real activity, personal or social," she felt that she lacked the necessary physical stamina.[6] She tried to lead a quiet, well-regulated life, paying methodical attention to business and working steadily on her many projects, though social activities often interfered.

The loss of her sister was the first of several hard blows. Virginia died from heart failure in April 1921 at the age of sixty-nine while traveling with Floy Kellogg, Carolyn Macadam, and a group of girls from The Bishop's School. Characteristically, she had ignored doctors' warnings that her heart had been weakened by a severe illness in the summer of 1917 and had set out on an around-the-world tour. She suffered a heart attack in India and, after a solo trip to Egypt, returned to London, where she died.

Ellen fell into a mild depression after Virginia's death.[7] After attending memorial services in La Jolla and Rushville, Illinois, Ellen returned home to sort out her sister's affairs. She ordered several copies of a photograph of Virginia in front of Wisteria Cottage, taken in 1919, for distribution among her sister's many friends and relatives and tried to come to terms with this absence from her life. She wrote to a relative, "Do you know it just seemed impossible that Virginia *could* die. She seemed such a power of real life."[8]

To commemorate her sister, Ellen turned over their family house and farm to the citizens of Rushville for use as a community center and public park. The University of Illinois and the National Playground Association lauded Scripps Memorial Park, which included a swimming pool, athletic fields, and a children's playground, as an example to other communities in the state.[9]

Meanwhile, Ellen's own health began to deteriorate. Phlebitis caused swelling in one leg, forcing her to wrap it in elastic bands, while a sore on her forehead refused to heal. Her eyesight became so poor that she was often unable to read at night. With her white hair, stooped shoulders, and wrinkled skin, she felt like "one of the oldest Essenes."[10]

In January 1922 she tripped while trying to make her bed and broke her hip. She complained to her brother about the indignities of hospitalization:

> I am no longer my own mistress. I can't go where I would, or do what I like. I have to submit to be mauled around by alien hands; to stay where I am put; to be treated as a machine of a hundred different parts to be kept in order; to be fed, washed, manicured, dressed and undressed, pulsed and temperatured and hypodermised, stethoscoped, pulled and pushed and rolled; bumped and padded and cushioned and sand-bagged; the whole performance being punctuated by my howls and screeches, and when one series is ended a second of the like kind begins, so it keeps me busied for about 16 hours out of the 24; and the rest I spend in wild and visionary dreams functioned by the sub-conscious mind—which are not disagreeable.[11]

Having never before endured a serious illness, Ellen found herself an impatient patient with doctors, friends, and relatives and eager to return to an active life. Gradually, she learned to endure and respect the "kindness" of others, adding, "I feel a sort of pity for them that I don't respond to their well meaning efforts as well as I would like to."[12]

When she returned home from the sanitarium, she was cared for by her relative Hilda M. Gardner (b. 1872), who remained at South Molton Villa for the next decade. The great-granddaughter of Ellen's uncle John Dixie Scripps, Hilda had been born and raised in England, where she studied at the Royal Academy of Music. She taught at the Bramley School for sixteen years before heading to Jerusalem as the organist for the Anglican Mission. In 1917 she returned home from a three-year stint in Quebec to care for her ailing parents. She arrived in La Jolla in 1922 to take up a position as organist and music teacher at The Bishop's School. A good-natured and highly organized woman, she became known in La Jolla as "Ellen's British cousin and VIGILANT companion."[13] Ellen deeply appreciated Hilda's "simple sincerity, unselfishness, and practical common sense."[14]

At the end of 1922 Ellen fell and sprained her ankle as she got out of the Pierce-Arrow. She had been getting around on crutches and taking frequent automobile rides when the accident occurred. Her niece reported, "She is so anxious to do everything for herself. She has been talking about moving upstairs and letting her nurse go in the near future."[15]

Knowing that she would be unwilling to spend the money, her nephew Robert P. Scripps and Harper conspired to get her a new car—a Rolls Royce—and to refit her old car as an ambulance. Furious at their interference, she wrote a letter of protest to E.W.: "Mr. Harper has done many things which have grievously annoyed me; but I have excused him on the ground of his lacking the sense of understanding individualities as well as being the possessor of good intentions (!). But this is the limit. . . . I consider his . . . course in the matter an underhanded piece of impertinence, as well as a betrayal of confidence."[16] It took her nearly a month to calm down and admit that a new car would prove useful. When the limousine finally arrived in June 1923, she found it "all too comfortable and too beautiful, and too luxurious!" She wrote, "I feel ashamed to ride in it; but I suppose I shall get used to it, and it was—like every thing else that people do for other people—so utterly unnecessary!"[17]

The Rolls Royce and its chauffeur, Higgins, offered Ellen a degree of mobility at the end of her life. She generally stayed close to home, taking only short journeys to Claremont, Palm Springs, Lake Arrowhead, and Big Bear. In 1927 she took her last long trip to Yosemite National Park with her brother Will's wife, Katharine, and Hilda Gardner. They spent a week in a four-room bungalow among pines that seemed to reach to the sky.[18]

In August 1927 Ellen suffered a heart attack that prevented further travel. Although she had been to Claremont many times, she would never see the first building constructed at Scripps College—Toll Hall—nor the development of the Mediterranean-style campus set against the backdrop of the San Gabriel Mountains. She regretted her infirmity at such a time, telling Mary Eyre, "I don't mind dying, but life is just beginning to be so interesting."[19]

Pomona College

Ellen's introduction to college life in Claremont began in November 1908, when she and Virginia accepted an invitation from President George Gates and his wife, Isabelle, to attend Dedication Day at Pomona College. She first met the couple when they vacationed in San Diego the previous year, possibly accompanied by George Marston, who served as a member of Pomona's board of trustees. Gates, known for his good humor and charm, offered Ellen "a pressing invitation to visit himself and wife at Pomona," which she took up the following year.[20]

Pomona College had been founded in 1887 by a group of Congregationalists who sought to re-create "a college of the New England type" on the West Coast. The real estate boom of the 1880s promised to draw thousands of new residents to Southern California, and new enterprises, including schools and academies, sprang up seemingly overnight. Pomona College survived the "bust" of the early 1890s and took advantage of cheap land prices to establish a coeducational college campus in Claremont, as well as a preparatory school. The town site originally had a railroad station, a hotel, a farmhouse, and two or three small houses surrounded by cactus and chaparral. By 1908 Claremont had grown along with the college, hosting spacious bungalows, tree-shaded streets, and orange and lemon orchards.[21]

Having never been to Claremont, Ellen followed Gates's instructions and arrived by train from Riverside. She wrote in her diary, "Mrs. [Isabelle] Gates met us with buggy, taking us directly home. Her husband, herself, youngest son, 14, and 1 grandmother constitute the homestead." They lived at the corner of College Avenue and Fourth Street in an Arts and Crafts style house that looked much like the first South Molton Villa. Ellen noted, "Large accommodations and convenient house."[22]

Dedication Day began with an evening lecture by astronomer George E. Hale, founder of the Mount Wilson Observatory, followed by an academic procession around the campus the next morning. Ellen attended the dedications of the first dormitory on campus, Smiley Hall, Brackett Observatory, and the new Carnegie Library. Afterward she heard a sermon by Bishop Johnson, a new member of Pomona's board of trustees, entitled, "A Look into the Future."[23]

Over the next few years, Bishop Johnson encouraged Ellen to support both The Bishop's School and Pomona College. In 1914 she pledged $25,000 (about $611,000 in 2016 dollars) for the foundation of the Joseph H. Johnson Lectureship, which supplemented the college curriculum with addresses and lectures from outside speakers such as Jane Addams, Professor William M. Sloane, and poet John Masefield, among others.[24]

Ellen also became good friends with Professor Charles C. Stearns and his wife, Sophie, who spent their summers in La Jolla. In 1909 the couple stayed at Wisteria Cottage with their son Charles, who had returned home from Harvard. Two years later, they purchased Nina Waddell's cottage, Golden Rod, and moved it to a lot on Draper Street.[25] A professor of biblical history and literature, Stearns had a whimsical or "mystic" quality that Ellen found "had a peculiar charm for me in his conversations."[26]

In 1909 E.W. put his fourteen-year-old son Robert in Pomona College's Preparatory School under the direction of Stearns. The boy lived with the professor and his wife in their home on Tenth Street and College Avenue with a pet tarantula that ate grasshoppers from their orchard. Stearns described him as "just the kind of a healthy happy chap one thoroughly enjoys being around."[27]

Ellen also became acquainted with James A. Blaisdell, the new president of Pomona College. He spent an evening with her in 1914 before attending a Christmas concert at The Bishop's School.[28] His successful million-dollar fund-raising campaign would soon produce Rembrandt Hall, the Mabel Shaw Bridges Hall of Music, the Greek Theater, and the Harwood Hall for Botany, as well as a marine science laboratory in Laguna Beach.

In 1919 Blaisdell asked Ellen if she would contribute toward the construction of new dormitories for women on the Pomona College campus. A coeducational institution, Pomona housed 80 female students in Sumner Hall, an old wooden "boom hotel" built in 1887. Another 220 girls boarded in private homes throughout Claremont. Blaisdell described the former hotel as "a constant fire peril" and an eyesore that stood in the middle of campus.[29] Sumner Hall needed to be moved so that work could begin on the large central quadrangle anticipated in architect Myron Hunt's 1908 plan.

The new women's campus would be located on four city blocks between First and Third Streets east of College Avenue if the president and trustees could raise $60,000 (about $709,000) to purchase the land and another $400,000 (about $4.73 million) to build new concrete dormitories. Blaisdell emphasized the novelty of the project, writing, "So far as I know, there is no other such 'Woman's Campus' in any college of Southern California."[30] He added that Ellen's fellow patron George Marston recently had given $100,000 (about $1.18 million) for the construction of a quadrangle. In a subsequent letter, Blaisdell suggested that the project be named "the Scripps Campus for Women."[31]

Ellen agreed immediately, offering up to $110,000 (about $1.3 million) for the purchase of the land and the construction of dormitories. The college had already raised $50,000 (about $591,000) from Judge C. E. Harwood for the construction of what would become known as

Harwood Court. Built around a landscaped courtyard, the dormitory opened in 1920 and housed 135 students.

Ellen, however, did not want any publicity attached to her gift, much less her name. "Publicity is distasteful to Miss Scripps," her lawyer told Blaisdell. "It is also burdensome to her. Knox College, some years ago, made public a gift which she made to that institution and it brought upon her an avalanche of other applications."[32]

On February 22, 1921, Ellen attended the tenth anniversary celebration of Blaisdell's presidency, which included the dedication of Harwood Court and the groundbreaking for the Memorial Training Quarters. While the quadrangle had yet to be built, the campus once referred to as "the Sage-brush" sported lawns, shrubbery, trees, and flowers. Enrollment had grown from 404 students in 1911–12 to more than 750; the teaching force, meanwhile, had nearly doubled. Ellen attended commemorative addresses by George Marston, chairman of the board of trustees, and David P. Barrows, president of the University of California, followed by remarks by Blaisdell. As promised, none of the speakers mentioned her contribution.

Ellen described the event in a letter to Virginia: "'Tis the end of a perfect day—glorious sunshine, beautiful views, high intellectual aspirations and inspirations. Rather a tiring day, too, ending with a banquet to which I was invited but did not accept. . . . There was a big time with all the highbrows at the Greek Theater (think of calling it a 'Greek' theater)," followed by "the dedication of the new girls' dormitory, and inspection of the same with lots of introductions and the passing back and forth of verbal bouquets." She wrote, "Everybody seemed very happy—Bishop Johnson among the number. Mr. Stearns said he (the bishop) gave them the best talk he had ever heard from anyone."[33] She spent the next day looking around Claremont, "visiting the different institutions, attending morning chapel exercises, driving around the campus, and getting information on all matters from different sources."[34]

Years later, Blaisdell expressed his deep appreciation to Ellen for making possible Harwood Court and the women's campus, telling her that she had "saved the day." He wrote, "This wonderful gift . . . assured to us a great future for women's education. A few months later this purchase would have been an impossibility." He continued, "You have made me believe that whatever it costs, you prize the cognizance of large undertakings and the things towards which men are striving."[35]

A Women's College

Around 1924 Pomona College's president and board of trustees imagined creating a consortium of colleges modeled after the University of Oxford. Bishop Johnson originally came up with the idea as a solution to the kind of administrative and financial problems faced by regional institutions like Occidental College, the University of Southern California, and the California Institute of Technology. According to his biographer, "The Bishop's knowledge of great educational institutions in other parts of the world led him to visualize an integration of all these schools under a kind of Oxford plan, by which none would lose its identity, but through which all would be enormously strengthened."[36]

In order to keep their options open, Pomona officials focused on acquiring more land before the residential development of Claremont made that impossible. In 1923 Blaisdell wrote, "Ever since I came here my effort has been for land-land-land. I feel that the loss of it is really the greatest danger that we face in thwarting the future of the institution." He told J. C. Harper that the college stood a good chance to rival Stanford University, "though I should hope that we could maintain more of the personal relationship, as in the English colleges."[37]

At the end of 1923, Blaisdell outlined his plans to Ellen: "My own very deep hope is that instead of one great, undifferentiated university, we might have a group of institutions divided into small colleges— somewhat on the Oxford type—around a library and other utilities which they would use in common. In this way I should hope to preserve the inestimable *personal* values of the small college while securing the *facilities* of a great university. Such a development would be a new and wonderful contribution to American education."[38]

Ellen supported the institution's efforts to extend its campus by purchasing 250 acres of land, including Indian Hill, the site of the future

Rancho Santa Ana Botanic Garden, in early 1924. She wrote, "I am deeply interested in what President Blaisdell is planning. It is a forward looking project that I think means much for education. I do not believe I can put a considerable portion of my estate to better use than to assist him in the realization of his plans."[39]

Ellen also made possible the purchase of the Marcus E. Jones Herbarium, at that time the largest privately owned herbarium in the country. Blaisdell later said, "The purchase of that collection put Pomona on the map in a botanical way—abreast with Stanford and U.C. At that time it was said there was no collection as large west of Washington University at St. Louis."[40] Ellen also recognized the significance of her gift, telling her brother that among all her philanthropic achievements, "perhaps the biggest thing that has been really accomplished by my assistance is putting Pomona College on a national—if not an international—basis."[41]

At the same time, Blaisdell approached Harper with the idea of a women's college to ease the growing gender gap at Pomona. During World War I, the college had admitted women in the place of men who had left to serve in the armed forces in order to keep up the college's enrollment numbers.[42] By the 1922–23 academic year, women outnumbered men by 432 to 346.[43] Blaisdell wrote, "In the back of my head I have a vision of the Scripps College for Women which I am eager to see a reality. We could open it any day with a full quota of women, if we had dormitories in which they could live. Perhaps some time this can come to pass."[44]

On reading her lawyer's letter, Ellen "wanted to know what 'Scripps College for Women' meant." Harper told her that he knew nothing more about it and suggested that she speak to Blaisdell personally.[45] Subsequent correspondence clarified the idea. The president had learned that the college's acquisition of land from the Ontario Water Company could produce significant revenue: "This being the case, I had thought it possible that it might be made available for the education of a certain number of those young women who are so anxious to come here and cannot now be received. I do not know how much the income would be, but if with it we could possibly make a beginning in some form of institution separated from but affiliated with the College, that would be a great step forward." Blaisdell continued,

> You know how much it would mean to me if this next unit or college for women could bear the special influence and ideals and name of Miss Scripps. You and I have talked enough about the dangers incident to modern education to know how much I feel the need of an institution that in its very initiation is committed to breadth and tolerance and freedom. I know Miss Scripps would give such a college that attitude, and such an institution would be of incalculable value as a leaven in the lump here.[46]

The idea of creating a women's college committed to "breadth and tolerance and freedom" must have been intriguing; shortly after receiving the letter, Ellen traveled to Pomona College to celebrate the start of a $3 million (about $41.6 million) fund-raising campaign in November 1924. Festivities included a church service, a tour of Claremont, and a dinner "with song, singing, speech making."[47] Not long afterward, she committed to the development of the Claremont Colleges, in particular, Scripps College for Women.

In April 1925 Ellen met with Blaisdell to discuss "his plans and visions for Claremont" and later received a "large picture of the proposed plan for Claremont Colleges."[48] Blaisdell later recalled, "Our conversations were always brief. She left me with the impression of a remarkable power of visualizing things that she had never seen."[49]

By the end of 1925 plans for Scripps College were well under way. Blaisdell and his wife traveled to Europe to visit other educational institutions, a trip financed in part by Ellen. In the meantime, Pomona's acting president (and future president of Scripps College), Dr. Ernest J. Jaqua, met with Ellen. Harper wrote, "She has since stated to me that she was very much pleased with him."[50] Together they solicited members of the board of trustees and drew up articles of incorporation in October 1925.

At first, Ellen did not want the college to bear her name. She argued that her name was not "euphonious and would therefore not be pleasantly received" and, further, that the institution ought to be named after an educator rather than a philanthropist.[51] Blaisdell and others, however, persuaded her that her name would provide the new college with both prestige and some much-needed publicity.

Ellen got more publicity than she had bargained for when *Time* magazine published her photo on the cover of the February 1926 edition, along with an article touting her endowment of Scripps College. She knew nothing about it until the magazine appeared on the newsstands. The article remarked on the fact that she was eighty-nine years old, "a woman who taught school when Lincoln was a country lawyer, who helped found a newspaper in the year 1873," and it described some of her eccentricities, which included sleeping on her porch.[52]

In keeping with her other philanthropic projects, Ellen gave money with no strings attached. Her lawyer told the board of trustees, "It has been her policy always to leave to those who manage the enterprise absolute liberty. . . . I think I may say that Miss Scripps' great ambition is that you shall be ready to try out new experiments, be pioneers in the work of entering new fields if there is need of that, and that Scripps College shall illustrate what we hear spoken of as 'Academic Freedom'; that there shall be no clamp put on the search for truth in whatever direction it may be found."[53]

At the same time, Harper was not about to let the institution dispose of his employer's resources without oversight. Over the course of the next decade, he played a major role in the development of Scripps College, implementing what he considered to be Ellen's ideas for the school. As chairman of the board of trustees, he involved himself in every major (and many minor) decisions made by the college. He helped to select the first members of the board of trustees; participated in the choice of an architect; advised the building committee on the appearance of the campus, including the location of trees, shrubs, and flowers; recommended that classes on government be included in the curriculum; and considered the school's relationship to Pomona and the Claremont Colleges.[54]

Ellen hoped that the college would enable both the personal and the intellectual development of young women. "Life, it seems to me," she said, "is about the most important thing there is. One may learn stenography or typewriting or bookkeeping or even teaching, but preparation for life is fundamental and must be the foundation."[55] To that end, she believed that students' health—mental and physical—should be a central concern. Good food, quiet and comfortable rooms, and a physical education program were among her recommendations. According to one report, "She regarded physical exercise and health not as ends in themselves but as phases of mental health, affecting the energy, the temper, the courage and the outlook of the person."[56]

Ellen considered the beauty and tranquility of the Scripps campus to be part of the educational mission. Architect Gordon B. Kaufman, one of the pioneers of the Mediterranean Revival style, was directed to give the dormitories the appearance and atmosphere of a comfortable home. The first residential structure, Eleanor Joy Toll Hall, was furnished with art and antique furniture so that students could cultivate "a sense of the beautiful." Ellen told trustee Margaret Fowler, "Don't sacrifice appropriateness to economy. Don't even sacrifice desirability to economy."[57] Living daily with models of good design, proportion, and color, students would learn more about design than they could in classrooms or visits to museums. After her death, another trustee reported that Ellen had said: "I am thinking of a college campus whose simplicity and beauty will unobtrusively seep into the student's consciousness and quietly develop a standard of taste and judgment."[58]

In 1927 the ninety-year-old Ellen was too frail to attend the inauguration of Dr. Jaqua as the first president of Scripps College or to receive her honorary degree from Pomona. She also missed the ceremonial dedication of Toll Hall. However, she recorded the event in her diary, writing, "Inauguration of Scripps and Claremont Colleges at Claremont. Katharine [Scripps] and the Rays the only members of the family able to go up." She congratulated Blaisdell by telegram and sent a thank-you note for the gift of a "beautiful basket of roses from 'Girls of Scripps College.'"[59]

Ellen continued to care deeply about what the Scripps women felt and thought about the new institution. Ava Blank, who worked at the college in 1928, wrote, "I remember the penetrating look she gave me when she said, 'You know, everybody tells me it is a fine college, but I want to know from you what the girls think about it.'"[60] In April 1928 she invited members of the first freshman class to La Jolla, where they toured many of the institutions that she had founded, walked through her gardens and library, and ended the day with ice cream and cake in the sunroom of South Molton Villa. She met each of her fifty-four guests individually, "making each one feel that she was genuinely welcomed." Caroline Bennett Anderson later wrote, "She talked about the campus as if she had been here." Years later, many students recalled "unexpected kindnesses" in the form of Christmas gifts and holiday cards.[61]

Ellen's pride in Scripps College led her to display a model of the campus "in a public window in La Jolla for all to see."[62] She saw the college as an extension of her progressive vision for La Jolla and hoped that local residents would send their daughters there. In 1933 Mrs. Florence Burnham provided a Scripps College scholarship to graduates from San Diego, Coronado, Point Loma, and Herbert Hoover High Schools, while Mr. and Mrs. J. C. Harper offered funds to support graduates of La Jolla High School.[63]

By the end of the 1920s, other patrons of the Claremont Colleges included mining engineers Seeley W. Mudd and William L. Honnold. The former left a bequest of $1 million (about $13.5 million) to the colleges for advancing the group plan, one of the largest gifts in the history of California higher education.[64] Blaisdell became president of the Claremont Colleges, while Charles K. Edmonds took over the presidency of Pomona.

In 1931 Ellen gave an additional gift of $75,000 (about $1.17 million) for the construction of Harper Hall at College Avenue and Tenth Street. The building served as administrative offices for the associated colleges and seminar rooms for the graduate school (later Claremont Graduate University), founded in 1925. She is said to have written the inscription carved on the west front: "This building is a symbol of a house not made by hands in which shall dwell the spirit of truth, justice, and comradeship."[65]

Other donations included the browsing room library in Ellen Browning Hall, a scholarship fund, landscaping costs, and countless emergency expenses. Ellen gave $2,000 (about $31,100) to botany professor Dr. P. A. Munz for his sabbatical expenses; she also made possible an educational exchange with Mexico and a student trip to China.[66] She contributed to the construction costs of a new house for Blaisdell after he stepped down as president of Pomona, as she thought that he should have "one of the outstanding houses in the community," given his leadership role in the Claremont Colleges.[67] Finally, she added to her previous gifts $100,000 (about $1.55 million) for the funding of the Nathaniel Wright Stephenson Chair of History and Biography at Scripps College.[68]

Ellen ensured that most of her books went to the Claremont Colleges after her death, an estimated 2,434 books and 20 large portfolios of art prints. The remainder of her collection was distributed among the San Diego Natural History Museum, the Fine Arts Association, the San Diego Library, The Bishop's School, the La Jolla Library, Scripps Cottage at San Diego State University, the Serra Museum, the San Diego Zoological Society, Scripps Hospital, and the Scripps Institution of Oceanography.[69]

Members of Ellen's family supported, and continue to support, Scripps College. A group of "honorary alumnae" that included Katharine Peirce Scripps, Nackey Scripps, Emma Jessop Scripps, Floy Scripps Kellogg, Ellen Scripps Ellis, and Grace Scripps Clark raised money for initiatives such as a loan fund to make it possible for scholarship girls to borrow money for additional college expenses.[70] In 1928 Grace Scripps Clark contributed a significant amount of money toward the construction of a residence hall in honor of her father, James E. Scripps. Other family members and friends who supported, and continue to support, the institution include Margaret Scripps Hawkins (née Culbertson), Ellen Browning Scripps Davis (class of 1934), Ellen Clark Revelle and her daughter Carolyn Revelle, J. C. Harper and his daughter Ruth Munger, and Scripps employees Harry L. Smithton and W. C. Crandall.

Ellen supported these efforts wholeheartedly and tried to get additional family members to pitch in. She wrote to her nephew Will Scripps, "I have endeavored to add to the family's 'record of usefulness and honor,' to use a phrase of your father's. I am deeply interested in Scripps College. I am sure that it will reflect credit on the family name, as through the years the facilities increase for preparing young women for lives of usefulness."[71]

The Death of E.W.

In 1929 Scripps College opened its third residence hall, Ellen Browning Hall, built in memory of E. W. Scripps. Ellen's beloved younger brother died in March 1926 while cruising off West Africa in his yacht. Deeply saddened, Ellen contributed a substantial portion of the funds needed to finish that building. "She said, rather decisively, that she desired to complete it as a memorial to her brother E.W.," wrote her lawyer, J. C. Harper.[72]

Having always considered E.W. to be a "great man," Ellen was surprised and disheartened to find that the younger generation did not appreciate his genius. Granted, E.W. had remained a deeply private person who was "known to fewer people than any other publisher of his day," according to an obituary in the *Cleveland Plain Dealer*.[73] But she thought that his public service to the nation, particularly his support of the Scripps Institution of Oceanography, the National Science Association, and the Foundation for Population Research at Ohio's Miami University, would have brought him more attention, particularly from the *Cleveland Press*. According to Harper, "She commented upon the contrast which was afforded by the *Plain Dealer* speaking in such warm appreciation of a rival's work and no mention made in the newspaper to which her brother had made very large contributions in its upbuilding and development."[74]

When the *Detroit Evening News* failed to publish a substantial obituary of E.W., Ellen considered it a "deliberate slight." She blamed George Booth, who she felt should have been more grateful for the opportunities given to him by both E.W. and George H. Scripps. Harper wrote, "It is evident that the omission has made a deep and painful impression upon her."[75]

Ellen also considered her brother James's legacy, particularly in light of her niece's contribution to Scripps College. James had been disappointed in his public and philanthropic work; he had spent a great deal of time and money on Trinity Episcopal Church, a reformed church, only to see it come under the control of the Protestant Episcopal Church. He had also helped to found the Detroit Art Museum, giving liberally but getting virtually no recognition. According to one contemporary, "He felt that he was a failure in trying to do for the public." As a result, he left most of his fortune to his children, who proceeded to live privileged, even opulent, lives. Ellen felt that if he had lived longer, he would have devoted more of his fortune to public works, rather than leaving it to future generations.[76]

E.W., on the other hand, provided for his family but did not make them extraordinarily rich. His wife, Nackie, received an annuity of $60,000 per annum (about $829,000), while his daughter, Nackey, got half that amount annually along with a $200,000 trust (about $2.76 million). The remainder was put into the E. W. Scripps Trust so that his only surviving son, Robert P. Scripps, could continue to invest in the Scripps-Howard newspapers. He explained this to Ellen: "I didn't want to make Bob a very rich man—I mean as rich a man as he would inevitably become if he were my sole residuary heir."[77] The trust came to an end in 2012 only after the last of Robert P.'s children passed away, a provision that led (ironically) to the creation of more than two dozen billionaires, all progeny of Robert.

E.W. did not leave money to the children of his sons, John and James, who died in 1914 and 1921, respectively. He had been angered by the fact that James's widow, Josephine, had gained control over several Scripps newspapers on the West Coast. Although he considered her to be a woman of "extraordinary business capacity," he felt that she had "plunged into a business situation such as I have not myself felt that I had the capacity to handle successfully."[78] He told his grandchildren that he had suffered not only "great financial loss but great personal mortification on account of what I considered an act of piracy in the case of their mother and her associates." He also resented the fact that Milton E. McRae had refused to allow him to care for or educate their grandson John Paul Scripps, son of John and Edith McRae Scripps. As a result, he made it clear that his newspaper enterprise "was a Scripps concern and it wasn't a McRae or Stedem or Holtsinger concern, and that only to a Scripps or to Scrippses should its possession go after my death."[79]

Ellen did not share her brother's hostility toward the younger generation. For example, she thought that Josephine was trying to protect her children's interests, adding, "I was a good deal impressed by her calm, judicial way of looking at things and methods of making conclusions." She even considered giving her some of her own stock, a move that E.W. opposed.[80]

Like her brother, however, Ellen disapproved of inherited wealth. She felt that the stock she had received from her brother George was "due compensation" for her work on the Scripps papers, not an inheritance. She added, "Of course I may have over-estimated the value of the compensation; but at least it was honest in my understanding and judgment."[81] She regretted the fact that people received great sums of money without having earned it, though she would go on to leave one quarter of her *News* stock to her niece Grace Scripps Clark and a considerable part of her estate to her brother Fred, among other bequests.

Ellen imagined the women of Scripps College as her true heirs, each working to achieve goals unimagined by an older generation. They would break free from rules and conventions, experiment with new ideas, and develop new ways of understanding the world. "Miss Scripps was very much interested in everything connected to women," a young friend wrote. "She said she thought women ought to be the equal of men; they should have their work, interest and place just as much as men should. This was really her idea and hope."[82] Scripps College became the place where this dream would come true.

Conclusion

As she aged, Ellen gradually retreated from La Jolla society, preferring the company of her magazines, papers, and books. She subscribed to sixty-two periodicals and received weekly shipments of books from New York. She collected poetry, drama, and fiction; histories of the Great War; books on international affairs and the new science of psychology; travel narratives; biographies; and natural histories of plants and animals, among other genres. In 1928 her lawyer wrote, "She spends substantially all the time on the lounge under the east window in her little office, reading, writing letters, etc."[1]

Work remained an important part of her identity. She started her 1928 diary with two inspirational quotes: "Count that day lost, whose low descending sun views from thy hand no worthy action done" and the first stanza of clergyman S. Hall Young's untitled poem:

> Let me die working.
> Still tackling plans unfinished, tasks undone!
> Clean to its end, swift may my race be run.
> No laggard steps, no faltering, no shirking;
> Let me die working![2]

Ellen continued to keep track of her financial affairs, keeping a daily accounting diary and managing three separate bank accounts. Harper noted, "Her eyesight was not so good but she was unwilling to give it up; said she did not want anyone to know what she was doing with these funds." He told her that she ought to use the services of her agent, W. C. Crandall, "but she continued to do as of old only when in the few instances she was utterly unable to accomplish it herself."[3]

Ellen's account books contain lists of donations to organizations such as the Neighborhood House, the Community Chest, St. Augustine High School, San Diego's Chinese Mission, the Children's Home, the Civic Opera, and the Girl Scouts. In 1930 she donated $1,000 (about $14,200 in 2016 dollars) toward the restoration of the Mission San Diego de Alcalá.[4] She gave money to the National Woman's Party "toward a campaign for putting women in Congress" and contributed to a scholarship fund established by the National Association of Colored Women's Clubs. She supported the ACLU, the League to Abolish Capital Punishment, the League for Industrial Democracy, the American Foundation for the Blind, the National Kindergarten Association, the National Child Labor Commission, the National Women's Trade Union League of America, the American Association of University Women, and Near East Relief.[5] She contributed to famine and flood relief in China, a home for tubercular children in Switzerland, and a Baptist mission in central Africa. In 1929 she sent $1,000 (about $13,800) to Jane Addams so that she could attend the Sixth Congress of the Women's International League of Peace and Freedom in Prague.[6] She also helped fund the Lafayette Escadrille Memorial outside Paris, dedicated to the memory of the American aviators who flew with the French military during World War I.[7]

In 1931 Ellen made her last contribution to La Jolla in the form of the children's pool, a bathing area protected by a sea wall. E. W. Scripps first came up with the idea in 1922, suggesting the creation of a southward-curving pier that would form "a little harbor for rowboats and launches" and "a safe bathing place for children and women." E.W. wrote, "It seems to me that a pier like this and a little harbor like this would be a perfect complement to your playground and to The Bishop's School, and even to your Club House and home."[8] Shortly afterward, Hiram Newton Savage conducted a preliminary survey and determined that the job could be done. It was not until 1931, however, that work was finally undertaken by Savage and architect William Templeton Johnson. Ellen was "delighted" with the result, telling Harper that "she had no idea that so much would be made of it" by the press and public.[9]

The disposition of her estate occupied Ellen's thoughts in the last years of her life. Her last will and testament, first written in 1922, contained twenty-three codicils and ran to 148 printed pages. She provided large endowments for many of the organizations that she had supported over the years and left relatively modest sums of money to family members and friends. Her brother Fred inherited the bulk of her real estate, while niece Grace received one-quarter of Ellen's *Detroit Evening News* stock. She left South Molton Villa in the hands of her trustee, Robert P. Scripps, to be used for the benefit of the community after her death.[10]

By 1931 Ellen's health was deteriorating rapidly. One visitor noted, "She was there in body but her spirit was far away."[11] On her last meeting with newspaper editor Robert Paine, she clung to his hand and said, "'Mr. Paine, everything is all right. I'm all right.'" He wrote, "To save my life, I couldn't help kissing her withered hand, later to worry lest she might take it as impudence. But, she told Miss Gardner that it pleased her much."[12] Her doctor noted, "She makes a great effort to remain cheerful when clear moments permit."[13]

Ellen accepted death as inevitable and laughed at the idea that heaven might await her. "Think of the millions and millions of people who have lived in this world," she said to Harper, "and the idea of their gathering around the throne and playing harps."[14] She asked to be cremated and buried at sea, adding that she did not want her ashes scattered on the surface of the water but put in a receptacle and dropped in, with no ceremony.[15]

Ellen died in the early hours of Wednesday, August 3, 1932, as a result of lung congestion. She was ninety-five years old. Dr. James W. Sherrill wrote that he saw no evidence of congestive heart failure or kidney disease in the months leading up to her death but instead suspected cancer in the colon or reproductive organs. She was attended by three nurses, Hilda Gardner, and her nephew Robert.[16]

Ellen's obituary appeared on the front pages of the *San Diego Union* and the *San Diego Sun* just hours after her death. The Associated Press carried the story across the country to Boston, New York, Chicago, and Washington, DC, and to regional papers in the Scripps-Howard chain. The *New York Times* described her as "one of the pioneers of modern American journalism" who saved the Scripps newspapers from disaster through "her business acumen and her implicit faith in the abilities of her younger brother."[17] A woman who had perfected "the art of living," as well as the art of giving, she revealed "all the graces of a mid-Victorian in the midst of an active, modern American existence."[18]

Ellen left behind only a few members of an older generation who remembered her unconventional approach to life. Most other people, including her nieces and nephews, recalled her gentle temperament and self-effacing manner. They saw her as a genteel white-haired old lady, the fairy godmother of La Jolla, and even "the most beloved woman in California."[19] This is how she continues to be characterized today.

Thanks to the efforts of her lawyer, J. C. Harper, her "wonderful" and "contradictory" character survives in letters, papers, and memoirs collected and preserved after her death. In the archives of Scripps College, we find the strong-minded businesswoman who felt no need to seek approval from others or to repress her individuality in any way.

One of Ellen's most intriguing characteristics was her ability to embrace modernity in an entirely American way. She shed the trappings of class and the boundaries of race, extending her philanthropy to institutions that promised to transform both culture and society. She believed that education could raise people out of squalor and poverty, producing better citizens and more enlightened individuals. She trusted in the future of science and in the creative power of the human mind. At the same time, she recognized the need to create and sustain community in an age of rapid urban growth and technological change.

Positive thinking, optimism about the future, direct action, and love of humanity are reflected in the following quote, paraphrased from Unitarian clergyman Edward Everett Hale. Ellen told her brother, "Look *up*ward, not *down*ward. Look *out*ward, not *in*ward. Look *for*ward, not *back*ward," and, finally, "lend a hand."[20]

NOTES

Preface

1. "Memoirs of Ellen Browning Scripps: Personal Reminiscences by Mary Bennett Ritter," Berkeley, CA, April 5, 1937, EBSC, drawer 1, folder 36.

Introduction

1. "In California."
2. Cowan, "Investments in Humanity," 110–11.
3. Ellen B. Scripps to E. W. Scripps, Rotterdam, July 19, 1888, EBSC, drawer 2, folder 33.
4. Ross and Catlin, *Landmarks of Detroit*, 428–29.
5. Ellen B. Scripps to E. W. Scripps, Detroit, December 19, 1890, EBSC, drawer 2, folder 33.
6. Lears, *No Place of Grace*, 4–5.
7. Ellen B. Scripps, speech, May 13, 1918, EBSC, drawer 22, folder 36.
8. "In California."
9. Ellen B. Scripps to E. W. Scripps, La Jolla, January 21, 1925 (copy), EBSC, drawer 3, folder 10.
10. "Miss Ellen Scripps Dies at Age of 95," *New York Times*, August 4, 1932; "A Modern Mid-Victorian," *New York Times*, August 5, 1932; Cowan, "Investments in Humanity," 111; "Rushville Woman Makes 'Investments in Humanity': Ellen Browning Scripps, Now of La Jolla, California, Invests Her Fortune to Help Others," *Peoria Sunday Morning Star*, August 3, 1924.
11. Louis Uchitelle, "The Richest of the Rich, Proud of a New Gilded Age," *New York Times*, July 15, 2007.

1. A Lapsed Victorian

1. Katharine P. Scripps to Ada Peirce McCormick, La Jolla, July 25, 1927, APMP, box 2666, folder 10.
2. Hilda Gardner, notes, June 7, 1956, EBSC, drawer 1, folder 41.
3. "Memoranda of Conference between J. C. Harper and Mary B. Eyre," EBSC, drawer 37, EBS biographical material C–H.
4. J. C. Harper, memorandum, September 17, 1928, EBSC, drawer 1, folder 10; J. C. Harper, memorandum, September 30, 1927, EBSC, drawer 26, folder 20; J. C. Harper to George G. Booth, February 10, 1921, EBSC, drawer 1, folder 10.
5. EBSC, drawer 37, EBS biographical material C–H.
6. EBSC, drawer 37, EBS biographical material I–R.
7. E. W. Scripps, autobiography, 9, OU MSS 117, series 4, box 11; Scripps, *Memorials of the Scripps Family*, 34–36, 65, 173–75; "John Scripps, 1865, Registry of Events. Items of Earliest Recollections," EBSC, drawer 27, folder 44; Haymond, *History of Harrison County*, 259–60, 272; E. W. Scripps to Charles Dwight Willard, January 2, 1913, OU MSS 117, series 4, box 2, vol. 4.
8. "Historical Notes on Bookbinding," *Publishers Weekly*, September 14, 1895.
9. "A Short Memoir of Ellen Mary Scripps," EBSC, drawer 27, folder 25; Tyson, "Lady Huntingdon's Reformation," 580–93.
10. Aunt Mary to Ellen B. Scripps [1840], EBSC, folder 1, drawer 65.
11. James Mogg Scripps to William Armiger Scripps, Rushville, December 7, 1844, EBSC, drawer 27, folder 43.
12. Annie Scripps to Ellen B. Scripps, Rushville, June 6, 1882, EBSC, drawer 3, folder 37. See also James Mogg Scripps to William Armiger Scripps, Rushville, February 20, 1847, April 28, 1848, EBSC, drawer 27, folder 43.
13. Elizabeth Mary Scripps Sharp, "Early Days of the James Mogg Family," PAS/SC, drawer 41, folder 72.
14. SC 37, EBS biographical material C–H.
15. E. W. Scripps, autobiography, 54, OU MSS 177, series 4, box 11.
16. Dyche, "John Locke Scripps, Lincoln's Biographer," 337.
17. James E. Scripps, partial autobiographical work (copy), 1905, PAS/SC, drawer 40, folder 37.
18. Dyche, "John Locke Scripps, Lincoln's Biographer," 337; E. W. Scripps, autobiography, 44, OU MSS 117, series 4, box 11.
19. E. W. Scripps, autobiography, 44, OU MSS 117, series 4, box 11.
20. J. C. Harper to George G. Booth, February 10, 1921, EBSC, drawer 1, folder 10; "Ellen Browning Scripps and Knox College," 13–14; James E. Scripps, partial autobiographical work (copy), 1905, PAS/SC, drawer 40, folder 37.
21. James E. Scripps to William Armiger Scripps, Rushville, January 18, 1850, EBSC, drawer 27, folder 38; Pooley, *The Settlement of Illinois*, 419. John Moggs remarked, "James appears to be desirous of getting a good education. He is in the first class of Algebra and is not well satisfied unless at the head of that. I think Ellen also will

learn well." James Mogg Scripps to William Armiger Scripps, Rushville, December 6, 1848, EBSC, drawer 27, folder 43.

22. Cyril Arthur Player, "The Story of James Edmund Scripps," xii, 1943, OU MSS 119, box 7, file 17.

23. E. W. Scripps, autobiography, 541, OU MSS 117, series 4, box 11.

24. J. C. Harper, memorandum, December 5, 1928, EBSC, drawer 26, folder 20.

25. Goodspeed, "The Founding," 257.

26. James E. Scripps, partial autobiographical work (copy), 1905, PAS/SC, drawer 40, folder 37.

27. James E. Scripps, diary (copy), February 6, 1958, PAS/SC, drawer 40, folder 34. Willis J. Beecher, a relative of the more famous sons and daughters of Lyman Beecher, taught elocution at Knox College.

28. Ellen B. Scripps to George H. Scripps, Galesburg, March 15, 1857, EBSC, drawer 3, folder 29.

29. Ellen B. Scripps to George H. Scripps (copy), Galesburg, April 12, 1857, EBSC, drawer 3, folder 29.

30. Jessica W. Bechtel to J. C. Harper, Ocean Springs, MI, June 26, 1931, EBSC, drawer 1, folder 33.

31. Dyson, "Frederick in 1859."

32. Ellen B. Scripps to George H. Scripps, Hamilton, IL, June 20, 1864, EBSC, drawer 3, folder 29.

33. Ellen B. Scripps, untitled speech before the La Jolla Woman's Club, April 8, 1918, EBSC, drawer 22, folder 35.

34. "Soldiers' Aid Society," *Citizen*, October 23, 1861; "The Ladies Forever!," *Schuyler Citizen*, February 26, 1862.

35. [Ellen B. Scripps], "To the Friends of Sick and Wounded Soldiers," *Schuyler Citizen*, December 16, 1863; "Fair for the Benefit of Soldiers," *Schuyler Citizen*, February 3, 1864; "More about the Fair," *Schuyler Citizen*, February 17, 1864; "The Sanitary Fair, Grand Success! Receipts, $2,000!," *Schuyler Citizen*, February 24, 1864.

36. Ellen B. Scripps, untitled, undated writing, EBSC, drawer 22, folder 36.

37. Faust, *This Republic of Suffering*, 156.

38. E. W. Scripps, autobiography, 44, OU MSS 117, series 4, box 11.

39. Ellen B. Scripps, untitled speech to the La Jolla Woman's Club, April 8, 1918, EBSC, drawer 22, folder 35.

2. The Evening News

1. Ellen B. Scripps, untitled, April 8, 1918, EBSC, drawer 22, folder 35.

2. Ellen B. Scripps, paper, May 13, 1918, EBSC, drawer 22, folder 23.

3. Farmer, *History of Detroit*, 802–35 passim.

4. Gavrilovich, *The Detroit Almanac*, 289.

5. Schneider, *Detroit and the Problem of Order*, 36–46.

6. Farmer, *History of Detroit*, 929–31.

7. Ross, *Landmarks of Detroit*, 485.

8. Farmer, *History of Detroit*, 475.

9. James E. Scripps, partial autobiographical work (copy), 1905, PAS/SC, drawer 40, folder 37.

10. Maverick, *Henry J. Raymond*, 36.

11. E. W. Scripps, autobiography, 106, OU MSS 117, series 4, box 11.

12. James E. Scripps, diary, January 15, 1866, JESP, box 1; James E. Scripps to unknown, [ca. 1865–66], EBSC, drawer 27, folder 38.

13. James E. Scripps, diary, January 19, 1866, JESP, box 1.

14. Ellen recalled that she began work on the *Detroit Tribune* in 1867 or 1868 "and worked there two or three years until her father was taken ill in 1870." J. C. Harper, memorandum, September 4, 1928, EBSC, drawer 26, folder 20.

15. Ellen B. Scripps, diary, January 3, 1871, EBSC, drawer 22, folder 37.

16. Ellen B. Scripps to [John] Bagby, Detroit, April 30, 1870, EBSC, drawer 1, folder 69.

17. E. W. Scripps, autobiography, 36, 68, OU MSS 117, series 4, box 11.

18. Julia "Annie" Scripps to George H. Scripps, Rushville, May 13, 1864, EBSC, drawer 27, folder 48.

19. E. W. Scripps, autobiography, 54, OU MSS 117, series 4, box 11.

20. E. W. Scripps, autobiography, 88, OU MSS 117, series 4, box 11.

21. E. W. Scripps, autobiography, 151–52, OU MSS 117, series 4, box 11.

22. Ellen B. Scripps to E. W. Scripps, Rushville, November 17, 1872, EBSC, drawer 2, folder 20.

23. Ellen B. Scripps to E. W. Scripps, Rushville, January 19, 1873, EBSC, drawer 2, folder 20. John J. Bleeker dated Virginia Scripps during his youth in Rushville, IL, but could not convince her to marry him. They remained close friends, and later, she and Ellen persuaded him to move to Pasadena, where he served as the Scripps family doctor. Charles R. Kellogg, "Ellen Scripps' Life," EBSC, drawer 1, folder 13.

24. E. W. Scripps, autobiography, 222, OU MSS 117, series 4, box 11.

25. E. W. Scripps, autobiography, 149–50, OU MSS 117, series 4, box 11.

26. Ellen B. Scripps to E. W. Scripps, Rushville, December 15, 1872, EBSC, drawer 2, folder 20.

27. Ellen B. Scripps to E. W. Scripps, Rushville, February 23, 1873, EBSC, drawer 2, folder 20.

28. Ellen B. Scripps to E. W. Scripps, Rushville, April 20, 1873, EBSC, drawer 2, folder 20.

29. Ellen B. Scripps to E. W. Scripps, Rushville, June 10, 1873, EBSC, drawer 2, folder 20.

30. Ellen B. Scripps to E. W. Scripps, Rushville, June 10, 1873, EBSC, drawer 2, folder 20.

31. James E. Scripps, ledger book, 1873–74, September 30, 1873, JESP, box 2.

32. James E. Scripps, diary, May 28, 1875, JESP, box 1.

33. E. W. Scripps, autobiography, 154, 169, OU MSS 117, series 4, box 11.

34. E. W. Scripps, autobiography, 177, OU MSS 117, series 4, box 11.

35. E. W. Scripps, autobiography, 145, OU MSS 117, series 4, box 11.

36. Preece, *Edward Willis*, 33.

37. Paine, "The Mother of Soul," 3.

38. E. W. Scripps, autobiography, 558, OU MSS 117, series 4, box 11; James E. Scripps, diary, January 16, 1877, JESP, box 1.

39. Cyril Arthur Player, "The Story of James Edmund Scripps," 150, 152, OU MSS 119, box 7, file 17; Trimble, *The Astonishing Mr. Scripps*, 28.

40. E. W. Scripps, autobiography, 117–18, OU MSS 117, series 4, box 11.

41. E. W. Scripps, autobiography, 155, 169, OU MSS 117, series 4, box 11.

42. E. W. Scripps to Ellen B. Scripps, St. Louis, May 28, 1880, EBSC, drawer 2, folder 21.

43. E. W. Scripps, autobiography, 136, OU MSS 117, series 4, box 11; Cyril Arthur Player, "The Story of James Edmund Scripps," 155, OU MSS 119, box 7, file 18.

44. James E. Scripps, diary, February 22, 1879, JSEP, box 1.

45. E. W. Scripps, autobiography, 154, 157, OU MSS 117, series 4, box 11.

46. E. W. Scripps, autobiography, 551, OU MSS 117, series 4, box 11; Ellen B. Scripps to E. W. Scripps, Detroit, February 17, 1881, EBSC, drawer 2, folder 22.

47. James E. Scripps, diary, October 18, 1880, JESP, box 1.

48. E. W. Scripps, autobiography, 281, OU MSS 117, series 4, box 11.

49. E. W. Scripps, autobiography, 240–41, 281, OU MSS 117, series 4, box 11.

50. E. W. Scripps to Ellen B. Scripps, St. Louis, August 18, 1880, EBSC, drawer 2, folder 21.

51. Ellen B. Scripps to E. W. Scripps, Detroit, August 12, 1880, August 19, 1880, EBSC, drawer 2, folder 21.

52. Ellen B. Scripps to E. W. Scripps, Detroit, August 13, 1880, EBSC, drawer 2, folder 21.

53. Ellen B. Scripps to E. W. Scripps, Detroit, August 19, 1880, EBSC, drawer 2, folder 21.

54. Ellen B. Scripps to E. W. Scripps, Hot Springs, April 11, 1880, EBSC, drawer 2, folder 21.

55. Ellen B. Scripps to E. W. Scripps, Detroit, June 30, 1880, EBSC, drawer 2, folder 21.

56. Trimble, *The Astonishing Mr. Scripps*, 81–82.

57. Ellen B. Scripps to E. W. Scripps, Detroit, April 13, 1881, EBSC, drawer 2, folder 22.

58. Ellen B. Scripps to E. W. Scripps, Detroit, August 3, 1881, EBSC, drawer 2, folder 23.

59. E. W. Scripps to Ellen B. Scripps, Cleveland, June 19, 1881, EBSC, drawer 2, folder 23.

60. Scripps, *Five Months Abroad*; "Notes Abroad: Mr. Scripps' European Letters to Be Republished in Book Form," *Detroit Evening News*, October 8, 1881.

61. Paine, "Ellen Browning Scripps," 11.

62. Annie Scripps to Ellen B. Scripps, Rushville, April 20, 1883, EBSC, drawer 3, folder 27.

63. E. W. Scripps, autobiography, 562–65, OU MSS 117, series 4, box 11.

64. E. W. Scripps to Ellen B. Scripps, St. Louis, January 31, 1884, EBSC, drawer 2, folder 25; E. W. Scripps to Ellen B. Scripps, West Chester, July 2, 1888, EBSC, drawer 2, folder 29.

65. E. W. Scripps, autobiography, 566, OU MSS 117, series 4, box 11.

66. Booth later became the publisher of the Evening News Association, the founder of the Booth Publishing Company, and an important patron of the arts in Detroit.

67. E. W. Scripps, autobiography, 234, 436–37, OU MSS 117, series 4, box 11.

68. Ellen B. Scripps to E. W. Scripps, Florence, January 31, 1888, EBSC, drawer 2, folder 28.

69. Ellen B. Scripps to E. W. Scripps, Paris, November 20, 1887, EBSC, drawer 2, folder 27.

70. Ellen B. Scripps to E. W. Scripps, Neuhausen, July 8, [1888], EBSC, drawer 2, folder 29.

71. Ellen B. Scripps to E. W. Scripps, Whitby, September 22, 1887, EBSC, drawer 2, folder 27.

72. Ellen B. Scripps to George H. Scripps, Menaggio, Italy, June 13, 1888, EBSC, drawer 3, folder 29.

73. E. W. Scripps to Ellen B. Scripps, Cleveland, May 17, 1889, EBSC, drawer 2, folder 30.

74. Ellen B. Scripps to E. W. Scripps, Rotterdam, July 19, 1888, EBSC, drawer 2, folder 29. Emphasis in original.

75. Cyril Arthur Player, "The Story of James Edmund Scripps," 506, OU MSS 119, box 7, file 21.

76. E. W. Scripps to Ellen B. Scripps, West Chester, December 16, 1889, EBSC, drawer 2, folder 31.

77. E. W. Scripps to James E. Scripps, West Chester, December 16, 1889, EBSC, drawer 2, folder 31.

78. E. W. Scripps to Ellen B. Scripps, West Chester, November 13, 1889, EBSC, drawer 2, folder 31;Ellen B. Scripps to E. W. Scripps, Rushville, November 18, 1889, EBSC, drawer 2, folder 31; [J. C. Harper], biographical material on E. W. Scripps, EBSC, drawer 26, folder 51.

79. Ellen B. Scripps to E. W. Scripps, Rushville, November 24, 1889, EBSC, drawer 2, folder 31.

80. The day-to-day operation of the businesses fell into the hands of Booth, E. Willis Osborn, and Milton McRae, all of whom E.W. had trained. E. W. Scripps to J. C. Harper, February 26, 1901, EBSC, drawer 27, folder 32; McCabe, *Damned Old Crank*, 190–91.

81. Ellen B. Scripps to E. W. Scripps, Lynton, August 29, 1889, EBSC, drawer 2, folder 30.

3. *The Realm of Queen Calafia*

1. Julia "Annie" Scripps to E. W. Scripps, Alameda, February 4, 1892; Ellen B. Scripps, diary, January 16, 17, 1890, EBSC, drawer 22, folder 40; Ellen B. Scripps to E. W. Scripps, Alameda, January 2, 1890, EBSC, drawer 2, folder 32; EBS, diary, January 5, 17, 1890, EBSC, drawer 22, folder 40.

2. Ellen B. Scripps to Eliza Virginia Scripps, Alameda, January 1, 1890, EBSC, drawer 3, folder 15.

3. Ellen B. Scripps to E. W. Scripps, Alameda, January 2, 1890, EBSC, drawer 2, folder 32; Ellen B. Scripps, diary, January 5, 17, 1890, EBSC, drawer 22, folder 40.

4. Ellen B. Scripps to Eliza Virginia Scripps, Alameda, January 1, 1890, EBSC, drawer 3, folder 15.

5. Ellen B. Scripps to E. W. Scripps, Los Angeles, March 14, 1890, EBSC, drawer 2, folder 32.

6. Ellen B. Scripps, diary, February 17, 1890, EBSC, drawer 22, folder 40.

7. [Ellen B. Scripps to E. W. Scripps], [January 1890], EBSC, drawer 2, folder 32.

8. Carpenter, "The Climate," 250–51.

9. Ellen B. Scripps to E. W. Scripps, Los Angeles, March 14, 1890, EBSC, drawer 2, folder 32.

10. Ellen B. Scripps, diary, March 8, 1890, EBSC, drawer 22, folder 40.

11. Ellen B. Scripps to E. W. Scripps, Chicago, April 9, 1890, EBSC, drawer 2, folder 32.

12. Ellen B. Scripps to E. W. Scripps, Alameda, January 2, 1890, EBSC, drawer 2, folder 32.

13. Bellamy, *Looking Backward*, 43, 53, 99, 153.

14. E. W. Scripps to Ellen B. Scripps, West Chester, March 20, 1890, EBSC, drawer 2, folder 32.

15. Ellen B. Scripps to E. W. Scripps, Alameda, January 2, 1890, EBSC, drawer 2, folder 32; Carnegie, "Wealth," 653–65.

16. E. W. Scripps to Ellen B. Scripps, San Diego, March 23, 1891, EBSC, 2, folder 34.

17. In 1890 and 1891 the Scrippses bought two tracts of 160 acres, the Douglas tract and another owned by Freeman & Gay, as well as an 80-acre tract belonging to Louise Vollmer. Half of the 160-acre Douglas tract was conveyed to the Scrippses by Klauber & Levi in 1892 and 1894. Miramar Ranch, 1903–12, EBSC, drawer 11, folder 16; "Map of Scripps Landholdings in Miramar Ranch, 1891," PAS/SC, drawer 42, folder 50.

18. In 1888 Ellen visited a site outside Barcelona called Miramar that commanded a "beautiful prospect of land and sea." Ellen B. Scripps, diary, December 24, 1888, EBSC, drawer 22, folder 39.

19. Ellen B. Scripps, accounting diaries, 1894–97, 88, EBSC, drawer 6, folder 26.

20. E. W. Scripps to Ellen B. Scripps, Miramar, June 26, 1896, EBSC, drawer 2, folder 44; E. W. Scripps to Ellen B. Scripps, Miramar, November 4, 1892, drawer 2, folder 39.

21. Ellen B. Scripps to E. W. Scripps, Detroit, September 13, 1891, EBSC, drawer 2, folder 36.

22. "Mr. Parsons' Trip to Miramar: What He Saw There to Particularly Please the Eye of a Professional Landscape Architect," *San Diego Sun*, January 6, 1903; Trimble, *The Astonishing Mr. Scripps*, 216.

23. Ellen B. Scripps to E. W. Scripps, Detroit, July 17, 1892, drawer 2, folder 37.

24. H. Ponting to "Doc," March 15, 1956, PAS/SC, drawer 39, folder 62.

25. E. W. Scripps, "History of the Scripps Concern," 188, OH MSS 117, series 4, box 7, folder 2.

26. E. W. Scripps to Ellen B. Scripps, Cincinnati, May 17, 1899, EBSC, drawer 2, folder 45.

27. Baldasty and Jordan, "Scripps' Competitive Strategy," 269.

28. E. W. Scripps, "History of the Scripps Concern," 483, OH MSS 117, series 4, box 7, folder 2.

29. E. W. Scripps, "History of the Scripps Concern," 318, OH MSS 117, series 4, box 7, folder 2.

30. E. W. Scripps to Ellen B. Scripps, Kansas City, October 4, 1898, EBSC, drawer 2, folder 45.

31. Paine, "Ellen Browning Scripps," 11. See also Baldasty, *E. W. Scripps*, 138–44.

32. Baldasty and Jordan, "Scripps' Competitive Strategy," 267; Trimble, *The Astonishing Mr. Scripps*, 181, 209–11; McCabe, *Damned Old Crank*, 203–4.

33. E. W. Scripps to Ellen B. Scripps, Mount Clemens, MI, September 8, 1899, EBSC, drawer 2, folder 45.

34. E. W. Scripps to Lemuel T. Atwood, Miramar, August 11, 1903, EBSC, drawer 7, folder 16.

35. E. W. Scripps to F. W. Kellogg, Miramar, August 3, 1905, OH 117, series 1.2, box 8, folder 3.

36. Ellen B. Scripps to E. W. Scripps, Chicago, July 11, 1894, EBSC, drawer 2, folder 43; Ellen B. Scripps to E. W. Scripps, Detroit, September 13, 1891, EBSC, drawer 2, drawer 2, folder 36.

37. E. W. Scripps to Ellen B. Scripps, Miramar, August 13, 1895, EBSC, drawer 2, folder 43.

38. "A Tented City by the Tide," 84–85.

39. Randolph, *La Jolla Year by Year*, 47, 55, 57.

40. Ellen B. Scripps to Virginia Scripps, Miramar, February 24, 1895, EBSC, drawer 3, folder 15.

4. *A Young Jewel*

1. Ellen B. Scripps, accounting diary, 1894–97, 134, EBSC, drawer 6, folder 24.

2. Ellen B. Scripps to E. W. Scripps, Chicago, July 11, 1895, EBSC, drawer 2, folder 43.

3. "Reminiscences," Ellen Mills, biographical subject file, LJHS.

4. Randolph, *La Jolla Year by Year*, 11.
5. "La Jolla by the Sea."
6. Ellen B. Scripps, accounting diary, 1894–97, EBSC, drawer 6, folder 24.
7. Ellen B. Scripps, diary, May 20, November 22, 29, 1896, December 1, 31, 1896, EBSC, drawer 22, folder 47. Anton Reif was a German-trained architect who had partnered with A. W. Delaine and Domenick P. Benson, successively, from 1887 to 1890. John B. Stannard (1852–1942) began working as an architect in San Diego in 1887 and is best known for the Louis Bank of Commerce Building. Stannard and Reif worked together on the Albert Morse Block (1896), located at 740–744 Market Street in downtown San Diego. Brandes, *San Diego Architects*, 146–47, 167–68; City of San Diego, "East Village Combined Historical Surveys 2005," table 4.
8. Ellen B. Scripps to E. W. Scripps, Chicago, June 18, 1896, EBSC, drawer 2, folder 44.
9. Will Scripps supervised the construction of South Molton Villa, as Ellen was in Europe from May to October 1897. Ellen B. Scripps, diary, March 31, 1898, EBSC, drawer 23, folder 2.
10. Ellen B. Scripps to Eliza Virginia Scripps, [Bar Harbor], August 29, 1895, EBSC, drawer 3, folder 15.
11. South Molton Villa guest books, 1897–1915, EBSC, drawer 25, folder 56.
12. EBSC, drawer 37, EBS biographical material C–H.
13. Ellen B. Scripps, diary, January 1, 8, May 25, 1898, EBSC, drawer 23, folder 2.
14. Eliza Virginia Scripps to E. W. Scripps, St. Joseph, MO, September 25, 1892, EBSC, drawer 26, folder 44.
15. Ellen B. Scripps to E. W. Scripps, Palomar, August 31, 1901, EBSC, drawer 2, folder 47.
16. Ellen B. Scripps, "La Jolla Then and Now," EBSC, drawer 22, folder 19.
17. Ellen B. Scripps to Eliza Virginia Scripps, La Jolla, June 7, 1916, EBSC, drawer 3, folder 17.
18. Schaelchlin, *La Jolla*, 77–79.
19. Anson P. Mills, diary, January 1, 1898, LJHS.
20. Anson P. Mills, diary, July 4, 1898, LJHS; Ellen B. Scripps, diary, July 4, 5, 1898, EBSC, drawer 23, folder 2; Olten and Kuhn, *Images of America*, 18.
21. Anson P. Mills, diary, August 1, 1898, March 22, 1902, LJHS.
22. Anson P. Mills, diary, July 8, 22, 1899, May 8, 1901, August 12, 1902, LJHS.
23. Anson P. Mills, diary, June 9, 1898, LJHS.
24. Ellen B. Scripps, diary, February 8, 1899, EBSC, drawer 23, folder 3.
25. Ellen B. Scripps, diary, February 3, 10, 17, 24, 1899, EBSC, drawer 23, folder 3.
26. Randolph, *San Diego Year by Year*, 28; Schaelchlin, *La Jolla*, 79.
27. Ellen B. Scripps, untitled, undated speech, EBSC, oversize: cabinet, box 5; "Clubs," *San Diego Union*, November 3, 1907; Myrtle G. Gordon, "The First Fifty-Five Years: A Brief History of the La Jolla Woman's Club, 1894-1949," October 9, 1993, 2, LJWC.

28. Ellen B. Scripps, diary, January 4, 1899, EBSC, drawer 23, folder 3.

29. Ellen B. Scripps, diary, October 4, 18, 25, 1899, EBSC, drawer 23, folder 3.

30. Sarah A. Taylor, "History of the La Jolla Woman's Club 1898–1917," 7, LJWC.

31. Ellen B. Scripps, diary, April 2, 1903, EBSC, drawer 23, folder 7; "Country Club Women Meet," *San Diego Union*, April 3, 1903.

32. "Thorpe, Rose Alnora (Hartwick)," in *The National Cyclopaedia of American Biography*, 10:252.

33. Ellen B. Scripps, diary, March 2, 1890, EBSC, drawer 22, folder 40.

34. Guinn, *A History of California*, 2:593–94; Olten and Kuhn, *Images of America*, 12.

35. Ellen B. Scripps to Virginia Scripps, Miramar, February 15, 1895, EBSC, drawer 3, folder 15; Hunter, "Harraden, Beatrice"; May and May, "Historical Nomination," 12.

36. Ellen B. Scripps to Eliza Virginia Scripps, Miramar, February 24, 1895, EBSC, drawer 3, folder 15.

37. Anson P. Mills, diary, September 7, 1898, LJHS.

38. University of California, *Graduates, 1864–1905*, 123; Edwards, "The Alumni—1905," 395; *Ninety-Seventh Annual Report of the Hawaiian Evangelical Association*, 10.

39. Ellen B. Scripps, diary, March 30, 1899, EBSC, drawer 23, folder 3.

40. Ellen B. Scripps, diary, February 26, 27, March 5, 1903, and memoranda at the end of the diary, EBSC, drawer 23, folder 7. See also accounts of real estate transactions in EBSC, drawer 12, folder 34.

41. Ellen B. Scripps, diary, March 13, 1897, EBSC, drawer 23, folder 1; Ellen B. Scripps, accounting diary, November 5, 1897, EBSC, drawer 6, folder 24.

42. Ellen B. Scripps, diary, January 8, 1898, EBSC, drawer 23, folder 2.

43. Ellen B. Scripps, diary, June 9, 1898, EBSC, drawer 23, folder 2.

44. Ellen B. Scripps, diary, March 14, 1898, EBSC, drawer 23, folder 2.

45. Ellen B. Scripps, diary, March 27, 1899, EBSC, drawer 23, folder 3; Ellen B. Scripps, diary, July 6, 1898, EBSC, drawer 23, folder 2.

46. Ellen B. Scripps, diary, March 29, 1898, EBSC, drawer 23, folder 2; Ellen B. Scripps, diary, July 7, 15, 26, 27, 1899, EBSC, drawer 23, folder 3; Ellen B. Scripps, diary, November 2, 1901, EBSC, drawer 23, folder 5; "At the Seaside: La Jolla Notes of Interest," *San Diego Union*, November 26, 1899. See also "Week at La Jolla," *San Diego Union*, November 12, 1899.

47. Anson P. Mills, diary, November 23, 1899, LJHS.

48. Ellen B. Scripps, diary, September 28, 1899, EBSC, drawer 23, folder 3; Ellen B. Scripps, diary, August 7, 1908, EBSC, drawer 23, folder 12.

49. Eleanor F. Bennett, diary, March 31, 1906, HM 64263.

50. Ellen B. Scripps, diary, June 23, 1899, EBSC, drawer 23, folder 3.

51. Ellen B. Scripps to Eliza Virginia Scripps, La Jolla, April 22, 1916, EBSC, drawer 3, folder 17; Ellen B. Scripps to Virginia Scripps, La Jolla, November 3, 1920, EBSC, drawer 3, folder 21. See also Ellen B. Scripps, diary, November 4, 1898, EBSC, drawer 23, folder 2.

52. Ellen B. Scripps, diary, February 22, 1895, EBSC, drawer 22, folder 46; Ellen B. Scripps to Eliza Virginia Scripps, Miramar, February 24, 1895, EBSC, drawer 3, folder 15.

53. Ellen B. Scripps, diary, February 2, 1889, EBSC, drawer 22, folder 39; Bicknell, *Flowering Plants and Ferns*.

54. Ellen B. Scripps, diary, July 14, September 3, September 30, October 29, 1908, EBSC, drawer 23, folder 12.

55. Ellen B. Scripps, diary, May 24, 1909, EBSC, drawer 23, folder 13.

56. Ellen B. Scripps, diary, October 12, December 8, 1909, EBSC, drawer 23, folder 13; Ellen B. Scripps, diary, January 18, August 10, October 4, November 4, 16, December 13, 1910, EBSC, drawer 23, folder 14; Ellen B. Scripps, diary, July 16, December 31, 1912, EBSC, drawer 23, folder 16.

57. Ellen B. Scripps, diary, July 6, August 19, September 27, October 15, 1899, EBSC, drawer 23, folder 3; "Week at La Jolla," *San Diego Union*, November 12, 19, 1899.

58. E. W. Scripps to Ellen B. Scripps, September 14, 1899, EBSC, drawer 2, folder 45.

59. Ellen B. Scripps, diary, October 15, 1899, EBSC, drawer 23, folder 3.

60. Ellen B. Scripps, diary, February 4, 1904, EBSC, drawer 23, folder 8.

61. Ellen B. Scripps, diary, December 17, 1904, EBSC, drawer 23, folder 8. Gill's E. Milton Barber Residence stood at 108 W. Robinson Avenue, San Diego, CA.

62. Ellen B. Scripps, diary, April 27, 1905, EBSC, drawer 23, folder 9.

63. Ellen B. Scripps, diary, March 27, April 10, 25, 1905, EBSC, drawer 23, folder 9; Ellen B. Scripps, diary, August 27, 1905, EBSC, drawer 23, folder 9.

64. Ellen B. Scripps, diary, September 21, 1905, EBSC, drawer 23, folder 9.

65. "Old La Jolla," March 4, 1936, La Jolla Conservation Society Dinner, Nathan Rannells, biographical subject file, LJHS.

66. Sibley Sellew, interviewed in 1964, Sibley Sellew biographical file, LJHS.

67. Randolph, *La Jolla Year by Year*, 50; Mrs. Netta Powell Allen and Mrs. Beatrice Blankenship, interviewed by LJHS, January 1969, Margaret Fleming Allen, biographical subject file, LJHS.

68. Nathan Rannells, "Old La Jolla," March 4, 1936, La Jolla Conservation Society Dinner, Nathan Rannells, biographical file, LJHS; Marian Brown Kenyon, biographical subject file, LJHS; Margaret M. Sellew, "La Jolla 1902: From the Letters of Emily Elnora Landers," Sibley Sellew, biographical subject file, LJHS.

69. Margaret M. Sellew, "La Jolla 1902: From the Letters of Emily Elnora Landers," Sibley Sellew, biographical subject file, LJHS.

70. Ellen B. Scripps, "La Jolla Then and Now," EBSC, drawer 22, folder 19.

71. Ellen B. Scripps, "La Jolla Then and Now," EBSC, drawer 22, folder 19.

5. A Cold Shower of Gold

1. Ellen B. Scripps, accounting diary, 1894–97, EBSC, drawer 6, folder 26.

2. He added, "It is my conviction that if George H. Scripps had lived, he would not have made any one-third of his estate to grow to anything like the proportions

to which Ellen has caused hers to grow. I rather believe that, as between the two, Ellen had a higher order of business talent." E. W. Scripps, autobiography, 573–74, OU MSS 117, series 4, box 11.

3. E. W. Scripps to Ellen B. Scripps, West Chester, June 22, 1894, EBSC, drawer 2, folder 42.

4. E. W. Scripps to Ellen B. Scripps, May 2, 1902, EBSC, drawer 2, folder 48.

5. E. W. Scripps to Ellen B. Scripps, memorandum, [Miramar, March 16, 1901], drawer 2, folder 47.

6. Ellen B. Scripps to George H. Scripps, Menaggio, Italy, June 13, 1888, EBSC, drawer 3, folder 29.

7. E. W. Scripps to Ellen B. Scripps, Cleveland, September 17, 1899, EBSC, drawer 2, folder 45.

8. E. W. Scripps to Ellen B. Scripps, Cleveland, May 9, 1895, EBSC, drawer 2, folder 43.

9. Cyril Arthur Player, "The Story of James Edmund Scripps," 559, OU MSS 119, box 7, file 21.

10. Cyril Arthur Player, "The Story of James Edmund Scripps," 559, OU MSS 119, box 7, file 21.

11. E.W. told Ellen, "It was never my intention to be one of George's heirs." E. W. Scripps to Ellen B. Scripps, memorandum, [Miramar, March 16, 1901], drawer 2, folder 47.

12. E. W. Scripps to Ellen B. Scripps, West Chester, December 27, 1889, EBSC, drawer 2, folder 31.

13. Ellen B. Scripps to E. W. Scripps, Rushville, July 12, 1891, EBSC, drawer 2, folder 36.

14. E. W. Scripps to Ellen B. Scripps, August 17, 1891, EBSC, drawer 2, folder 36.

15. PAS/SC, drawer 40, folder 72.

16. Ellen B. Scripps to J. C. Harper, La Jolla, November 17, 1902, EBSC, drawer 1, folder 87. See also Eliza Virginia Scripps to EBS, Los Angeles, July 25, 1900, EBSC, drawer 2, folder 46 (misfiled).

17. Ellen B. Scripps to J. C. Harper, La Jolla, November 17, 1902, EBSC, drawer 1, folder 87.

18. Ellen B. Scripps to E. W. Scripps, Detroit, July 17, 1892, EBSC, drawer 2, folder 37.

19. James E. Scripps to George H. Scripps (copy), August 29, 1892, PAS/SC, drawer 40, folder 60.

20. J. C. Harper, notes, EBSC, drawer 1, folder 39; E. W. Scripps to Ellen B. Scripps, June 22, 1895, EBSC, drawer 2, folder 43; Cyril Arthur Player, "The Story of James Edmund Scripps," 441, OU MSS 119, box 7, file 20; E. W. Scripps, autobiography, 461–63, OU MSS 117, series 4, box 11.

21. E. W. Scripps to Ellen B. Scripps, June 24, 1895, EBSC, drawer 2, folder 43.

22. Eliza Virginia Scripps to Ellen B. Scripps, Los Angeles, July 25, 1900, EBSC, drawer 2, folder 46 (misfiled). George's will was dated Miramar, February 1, 1894. The first codicil, 1895, acknowledged his partnership with Scripps-McRae. The

second codicil, 1897, enlarged on this and authorized executors to fully perform conditions of said partnership. Cyril Arthur Player, "The Story of James Edmund Scripps," 565, OU MSS 119, box 7, file 21. See also Ellen B. Scripps to E. W. Scripps, Detroit, June 2, 1900, EBSC, drawer 2, folder 46.

23. Cyril Arthur Player, "The Story of James Edmund Scripps," 265, OU MSS 119, box 7, file 19. See also Ellen B. Scripps to Harper, La Jolla, October 19, 1902, drawer 1, folder 87.

24. E. W. Scripps to Ellen B. Scripps, Cleveland, September 27, 1899, EBSC, drawer 2, folder 45; Ellen B. Scripps, diary, October 12, 1899, EBSC, drawer 23, folder 3.

25. E. W. Scripps to EBS, Cincinnati, October 29, 1899, EBSC, drawer 2, folder 45.

26. Ellen B. Scripps, diary, November 14, 1899, EBSC, drawer 23, folder 3.

27. Ellen B. Scripps, diary, January 7, 1900, EBSC, drawer 23, folder 4.

28. Ellen B. Scripps, diary, February 9, 1900, EBSC, drawer 23, folder 4.

29. Ellen B. Scripps, diary, April 12, 13, 1900, EBSC, drawer 23, folder 4.

30. Ellen B. Scripps, diary, April 14, 15, 1900, EBSC, drawer 23, folder 4.

31. E. W. Scripps to Ellen B. Scripps, St. Paul, June 6, 1902, EBSC, drawer 2, folder 48; Cyril Arthur Player, "The Story of James Edmund Scripps," 579, OU MSS 119, box 7, file 21.

32. Ellen B. Scripps, diary, May 14, 1900, EBSC, drawer 23, folder 4.

33. Ellen B. Scripps to E. W. Scripps, Detroit, May 15, 1900, EBSC, drawer 2, folder 46. See also Ellen B. Scripps to E. W. Scripps, Detroit, May 17, 1900, EBSC, drawer 2, folder 46.

34. E. W. Scripps to Katharine Peirce Scripps, November 14, 1902, EBSC, drawer 27, folder 35; Cyril Arthur Player, "The Story of James Edmund Scripps," 570, OU MSS 119, box 7, file 21. See also PAS/SC, drawer 40, folder 12; E. W. Scripps, autobiography, 479–98, OU MSS 117, series 4, box 11; George H. Scripps probate records, JESP, box 3.

35. "To Contest the Will of George H. Scripps," *San Diego Union,* May 27, 1900; E. W. Scripps to Ellen B. Scripps, Cleveland, May 26, 1900, EBSC, drawer 2, folder 46.

36. Ellen B. Scripps to E. W. Scripps, Detroit, June 3, 1900, EBSC, drawer 2, folder 46.

37. Cyril Arthur Player, "The Story of James Edmund Scripps," 576–78, OU MSS 119, box 7, file 21.

38. E. W. Scripps to Ellen B. Scripps, St. Louis, May 18, 1900, EBSC, drawer 2, folder 46.

39. Ellen B. Scripps to E. W. Scripps, Detroit, June 3, 1900, EBSC, drawer 2, folder 46.

40. Katharine Peirce Scripps to E. W. Scripps, Frankfort, ME, November 17, 1902, EBSC, drawer 27, folder 35.

41. Ellen B. Scripps to E. W. Scripps, La Jolla, January 27, 1901, EBSC, drawer 2, folder 47.

42. Ellen B. Scripps to E. W. Scripps, Miramar, May 30, 1901, EBSC, drawer 2, folder 47; E. W. Scripps to Ellen B. Scripps, May 5, 1902, EBSC, drawer 2, folder 48; Ellen B. Scripps to E. W. Scripps, La Jolla, May 28, 1902, EBSC, drawer 2, folder 48.

43. Ellen B. Scripps to E. W. Scripps, Miramar, July 1, 1902, EBSC, drawer 2, folder 48.

44. J. C. Harper, memorandum, EBSC, drawer 1, folder 39.

45. E. W. Scripps, autobiography, 490, 495, OU MSS 117, series 4, box 11.

46. E. W. Scripps to L. T. Atwood, February 12, 1901, EBSC, drawer 27, folder 32. See also E. W. Scripps to J. C. Harper, February 26, 1901, EBSC, drawer 27, folder 32; E. W. Scripps to J. C. Harper, January 15, 1901, EBSC, drawer 27, folder 32.

47. E. W. Scripps to J. C. Harper, February 12, 1901, EBSC, drawer 27, folder 32.

48. Ellen B. Scripps to E. W. Scripps, La Jolla, March 9, 1906, EBSC, drawer 2, folder 49.

49. Ellen B. Scripps to E. W. Scripps, Detroit, May 23, 1906, EBSC, drawer 2, folder 49.

50. Ellen B. Scripps to E. W. Scripps, Detroit, May 30, 1906, EBSC, drawer 2, folder 49; Sparrow-Simpson, *Lectures*, 192.

51. Cyril Arthur Player, "The Story of James Edmund Scripps," 650, OU MSS 119, box 7, file 21; Scripps v. Sweeney, 160 Mich. 148, 125 N.W. 72, *Northwest Reporter* 125 (1910): 72–85.

52. Ellen B. Scripps, memoranda, La Jolla, May 13, 1911, EBSC, drawer 27, folder 36.

53. Ellen B. Scripps to E. W. Scripps, Rushville, July 31, 1894, EBSC, drawer 2, folder 42.

54. "In Memoriam," EBSC, drawer 1, folder 32.

6. Down to the Sea

1. Ellen B. Scripps to E. W. Scripps, Rushville, July 31, 1894, EBSC, drawer 2, folder 42.

2. Rozwadowski, *Fathoming the Ocean*, 29.

3. Steinberg, *The Social Construction*, 122.

4. Rozwadowski, *Fathoming the Ocean*, 11–16.

5. Kingsley, *Glaucus*.

6. Ellen B. Scripps, diary, October 16, 1899, EBSC, drawer 23, folder 3; Ellen B. Scripps, diary, July 17, 1901, EBSC, drawer 23, folder 5.

7. Kisling, *Zoo and Aquarium History*, 41.

8. Ellen B. Scripps, Europe diary, September 25, 1882, EBSC, drawer 24, folder 23; Ellen B. Scripps, Europe diary, August 14–19, 1882, EBSC, drawer 24, folder 22; Ellen B. Scripps, Europe diary, December 2, 1881, EBSC, drawer 24, folder 22.

9. Ellen B. Scripps, diary, January 9, 1901, EBSC, drawer 23, folder 5; Marian Brown Kenyon, biographical subject file, LJHS.

10. Ellen B. Scripps, diary, January 21, 22, 1902, EBSC, drawer 23, folder 6.

11. Eliza Virginia Scripps, poem, November 3, 1897–August 25, 1898, guest book: South Molton Villa, EBSC, drawer 25, folder 26.

12. Her collection of mosses is preserved in the Scripps Institution of Oceanography.

13. Ellen B. Scripps to Eliza Virginia Scripps, Miramar, February 20, 1895, EBSC, drawer 3, folder 15; "Snyder, Edward," in Leonard, *Who's Who in America, 1901–1902*, 1059. For a list of algae collected by Mary S. Stoddard, see Orcutt, *American Plants: Volume 2*, 392–99.

14. Ellen B. Scripps, diary, January 17, 1898, EBSC, drawer 23, folder 2.

15. Ellen B. Scripps, diary, June 2, 1898, EBSC, drawer 23, folder 2; Anson P. Mills, diary, February 18, October 13, 15, 1898, November 26, 1901, LJHS.

16. Rozwadowski, *Fathoming the Ocean*, 166.

17. Dexter, "History of American Marine Biology."

18. Hlebica, "William E. Ritter," 6.

19. Raitt and Moulton, *Scripps Institution of Oceanography*, 4.

20. Hlebica, "William E. Ritter," 6.

21. Raitt and Moulton, *Scripps Institution of Oceanography*, 14.

22. Ellen B. Scripps, diary, March 3, 1893, EBSC, drawer 22, folder 43.

23. Ellen B. Scripps, diary, April 4, 1899, EBSC, drawer 23, folder 3.

24. Shor, "How the Scripps Institution," 165.

25. The Hotel del Coronado had a tradition of using science as a tourist attraction. Pauly, *Biologists*, 203.

26. Ellen B. Scripps, diary, March 30, 1903, EBSC, drawer 23, folder 7.

27. Lydekker, *The New Natural History*; Ellen B. Scripps, diary, April 4, 1903, EBSC, drawer 23, folder 7.

28. Ellen B. Scripps, diary, July 12, 18, 22, 1903, EBSC, drawer 23, folder 7. In 1904 Ellen noted that she and Virginia went to "the Coronado Biological Reception to see the 'beasties.'" Ellen B. Scripps, diary, July 16, 1904, EBSC, drawer 23, folder 8.

29. William E. Ritter, "Philosophy of E. W. Scripps" (1944), 13–14, William E. Ritter Papers, SIO, MC4, box 4, folder 11.

30. Ellen B. Scripps, diary, August 2, 1903, EBSC, drawer 23, folder 7; E. W. Scripps to Fred Baker, Miramar, August 12, 1903, biographical files, SIO, AC5, box 15, folder 486.

31. Ellen B. Scripps, diary, August 21, 1903, EBSC, drawer 23, folder 7.

32. Raitt and Moulton, *Scripps Institution of Oceanography*, 19.

33. William E. Ritter, "Report of the San Diego Marine Biological Association," ca. 1903, William E. Ritter Papers, SIO, MC4, box 3, folder 19.

34. Raitt and Moulton, *Scripps Institution of Oceanography*, 19.

35. Raitt and Moulton, *Scripps Institution of Oceanography*, 21.

36. Raitt and Moulton, *Scripps Institution of Oceanography*, 21–22, 25; Ellen B. Scripps, diary, January 5, 1904, EBSC, drawer 23, folder 8. Ellen resigned her position as vice president of the board of trustees in July 1904. She explained to Ritter that she was willing to serve on the board but that the office of vice president was "likely to be something more than a perfunctory one—as hitherto—owing to the president's permanent absences from the city. I like your suggestion of putting Dr. [Fred] Baker in that office and making Mr. Wood secretary." Ellen B. Scripps, diary, July 9, 1904, EBSC, drawer 23, folder 8; Ellen B. Scripps to William E. Ritter, July 10, 1904, biographical files, SIO, AC5, box 15, folder 491.

37. Ellen B. Scripps, diary, May 20, 1903, EBSC, drawer 23, folder 7.

38. Raitt, "Give Us Room," 3; Ritter, Short History of the Scripps Institution for

Biological Research [1910–15], William E. Ritter Papers, SIO, MC4, box 3, folder 21.

39. Raitt, "Give Us Room," 3; Raitt and Moulton, *Scripps Institution of Oceanography*, 30; Ellen B. Scripps, diary, March 1, April 8, 9, 1905, EBSC, drawer 23, folder 9.

40. Day, "Early History"; Ritter, "The Marine Biological Station," 159.

41. Ellen B. Scripps, diary, July 3, 10, 1905, EBSC, drawer 23, folder 9.

42. Ellen B. Scripps, diary, November 14, 1905, EBSC, drawer 23, folder 9.

43. Ellen B. Scripps, diary, July 21, 1906, EBSC, drawer 23, folder 10.

44. Ellen B. Scripps, diary, July 30–August 1, 1906, EBSC, drawer 23, folder 10.

45. "Celebration at the Biological Station. Special Attractions!" August 6, 1906, William E. Ritter Papers, SIO, MC4, box 3, folder 21.

46. Ellen B. Scripps, diary, December 29, 1905, EBSC, drawer 23, folder 9.

47. E. W. Scripps to Ellen B. Scripps, Cincinnati, June 20, 1906, EBSC, drawer 2, folder 49. In the first six months of 1906, Ellen received $43,397 from George's estate and another $20,000 from her own holdings. J. C. Harper to Ellen B. Scripps, July 10, 1906, EBSC, drawer 1, folder 87.

48. Ellen B. Scripps, diary, January 30, 1906, EBSC, drawer 23, folder 10.

49. Hlebica, "William E. Ritter," 5. See also Ritter, "Mechanical Ideas."

50. Hlebica, "William E. Ritter," 5.

51. Ritter, *Charles Darwin*, 83. See also Ritter, "As to the Causes of Evolution."

52. Ritter, "The Marine Biological Station," 229; Ritter to Dr. S. J. Meltzer, December 21, 1916, William E. Ritter Papers, SIO, MC4, box 2, folder 9.

53. Ritter, "The Marine Biological Station," 229.

54. Ellen B. Scripps to E. W. Scripps, La Jolla, August 18, 1924, EBSC, drawer 3, folder 9.

55. Ellen B. Scripps, diary, February 10, 1899, EBSC, drawer 23, folder 3.

56. Emerson, "Progress of Culture."

57. Ellen B. Scripps, diary, January 2, 1904, EBSC, drawer 23, folder 8.

58. William E. Ritter to Robert P. Scripps, Berkeley, January 21, 1931, William E. Ritter Papers, SIO, MC4, box 3, folder 16.

59. William E. Ritter to J. H. Sorrells, Berkeley, October 31, 1941, William E. Ritter Papers, SIO, MC4, box 3, folder 16.

60. William E. Ritter to J. H. Sorrells, Berkeley, October 31, 1941, William E. Ritter Papers, SIO, MC4, box 3, folder 16.

61. Day, "Scripps Benefactions." For more information on the relationship between Ritter and E. W. Scripps, see Pauly, *Biologists*, 201–14.

62. Ritter, *More Than Gold*, 309.

63. Ellen B. Scripps, diary, October 22, 1905, EBSC, drawer 23, folder 9; "Memoirs of Ellen Browning Scripps: Personal Reminiscences by Mary Bennett Ritter," EBSC, drawer 1, folder 36.

64. Ellen B. Scripps, diary, August 22, October 1, 1906, EBSC, drawer 23, folder 10.

65. Ellen B. Scripps to Charles A. Kofoid, Miramar, July 30, 1906, biographical files, SIO, AC 5, box 15, folder 491.

66. Ellen B. Scripps to William E. Ritter, La Jolla, May 1, 1907, biographical files, SIO, AC 5, box 15, folder 491.

67. Ritter, *The Marine Biological Station*, 14.

68. Ellen B. Scripps to Fred Baker, La Jolla, May 1, 1907, biographical files, SIO, AC 5, box 15, folder 491.

69. Raitt and Moulton, *Scripps Institution of Oceanography*, 48.

70. E. W. Scripps to William E. Ritter, Miramar, November 9, 1908, EBSC, drawer 13, folder 22.

71. Ellen B. Scripps, diary, January 4, 1907, EBSC, drawer 23, folder 11.

72. E. W. Scripps, "Biological Station Begins to Be a Disappointment," Miramar, June 2, 1909, OU MSS 117, series 4, box 1, 2:186–97.

73. William E. Ritter, "Philosophy of E. W. Scripps" (1944), 114, William E. Ritter Papers, SIO, MC4, box 4, folder 1.

74. E. W. Scripps to Captain Crandall, Miramar, April 3, 1915, biographical files, SIO, AC 5, box 15, folder 488.

75. Shor, Shor, and Spiess, "The George H. Scripps Memorial Marine Biological Laboratory," 13. A plaque, "George H. Scripps Laboratory," was installed at the east entrance during construction with the date 1909, since the building was supposed to have been completed at that time.

76. Ellen B. Scripps to William E. Ritter, La Jolla, April 22, 1909, biographical files, SIO, AC 5, box 15, folder 491.

77. J. C. Harper to William E. Ritter, San Diego, February 25, 1909, biographical files, SIO, AC 5, box 15, folder 491.

78. E. W. Scripps to William E. Ritter, Miramar, February 9, 1905, biographical files, SIO, AC 5, box 15, folder 486.

79. E. W. Scripps, "An Odd Place: A New Town Where High Thinking and Modest Living Is to Be the Rule," biographical files, SIO, AC 5, box 15, folder 485. See also Raitt and Moulton, *Scripps Institution of Oceanography*, 77–78. Ellentown Road near the University of California, San Diego, campus commemorates Scripps's plan for this area.

80. Raitt and Moulton, *Scripps Institution of Oceanography*, 64; E.W. wrote, "Personally, I would prefer to have both my sister's and my brother's names appear in that of the institution itself, and if my sister would consent to this, I should strongly urge it." E. W. Scripps to Albert Schoonover, Miramar, November 25, 1911, biographical files, SIO, AC 5, box 15, folder 488.

81. Day, "Aspects."

82. E. W. Scripps to Ellen B. Scripps and members of the governing committee of the Scripps Biological Institution, Miramar, March 23, 1914, EBSC, drawer 2, folder 49.

83. Raitt and Moulton, *Scripps Institution of Oceanography*, 154.

84. Brueggeman, "History"; Raitt and Moulton, *Scripps Institution of Oceanography*, 73.

85. Ellen B. Scripps to Eliza Virginia Scripps, [La Jolla], October 30, 1916, EBSC, drawer 3, folder 15.

86. Ellen B. Scripps to Eliza Virginia Scripps, La Jolla, November 18, 1916, EBSC, drawer 3, folder 17. See also William E. Ritter to Ellen B. Scripps, Berkeley, April 2, 1924, William E. Ritter Papers, SIO, MC4, box 3, folder 16; Shor, "Zarh H. Pritchard"; Moure, *The World of Zarh Pritchard*; and Moulton, "Painting under the Ocean."

87. EBSC, drawer 14, folder 2; Johnson and Snook, *Seashore Animals of the Pacific Coast.*

88. William E. Ritter to Dr. Vaughan, January 22, 1931, William E. Ritter Papers, SIO, MC 4, box 3, folder 16.

89. Ellen B. Scripps to E. W. Scripps, La Jolla, October 11, 1921, EBSC, drawer 3, folder 1.

90. William E. Ritter, "Philosophy of E. W. Scripps" (1944), 117–18, William E. Ritter Papers, SIO, MC4, box 4, folder 11.

91. E. W. Scripps to Ellen B. Scripps, Washington, DC, October 22, 1921, EBSC, drawer 3, folder 1.

92. Ellen B. Scripps, "Notes on course of lectures delivered by Mrs. John Vance Cheney on the new education" [1899], 50, EBSC, drawer 22, folder 21.

93. Ellen B. Scripps to Eliza Virginia Scripps, La Jolla, November 16, 1918, EBSC, drawer 3, folder 19.

7. *Old Age, New Age*

1. Altholz, "The Warfare."

2. Satter, *Each Mind a Kingdom*, 23, 39.

3. Ellen B. Scripps to Eliza Virginia Scripps, La Jolla, April 20, 1916, EBSC, drawer 3, folder 17.

4. Ellen B. Scripps to George H. Scripps, Menaggio, Italy, June 13, 1888, EBSC, drawer 3, folder 29.

5. E. W. Scripps, "Socialism—Individualism—Fatalism," 1917, EBSC, drawer 1, folder 3.

6. Katharine Peirce Scripps to Ada Peirce McCormick, June 15, 1927, APMP, box 2666, folder 10.

7. "Memoirs of Ellen Browning Scripps: Personal Reminiscences by Mary Bennett Ritter," Berkeley, CA, April 5, 1937, EBSC, drawer 1, folder 36.

8. "Memoirs of Ellen Browning Scripps: Personal Reminiscences by Mary Bennett Ritter," Berkeley, CA, April 5, 1937, EBSC, drawer 1, folder 36.

9. William E. Ritter to Charles A. Kofoid, La Jolla, June 12, 1908, William E. Ritter Papers, SIO, MC4, box 1, folder 13.

10. Satter, *Each Mind a Kingdom*, 15, 17, 22, 38.

11. Satter, *Each Mind a Kingdom*, 3–4.

12. "Memoranda of Conference between J. C. Harper and Mary B. Eyre," EBSC, drawer 37, EBS biographical material C–H.

13. Willard and Livermore, *A Woman of the Century*, 283.

14. Julia "Annie" Scripps to Ellen B. Scripps, Rushville, September 11, 1884, EBSC, drawer 3, folder 37.

15. Julia "Annie" Scripps to Ellen B. Scripps, Milwaukee, February 26, 1885, EBSC, drawer 3, folder 28.

16. Julia "Annie" Scripps to Ellen B. Scripps, Hannibal, MO, December 28, 1885, EBSC, drawer 3, folder 28.

17. Julia "Annie" Scripps to George H. Scripps (copy), Hannibal, MO, March 24, 1886, PAS/SC, drawer 40, folder 19.

18. "The Week at La Jolla," *San Diego Union*, September 24, 1899. Mrs. John Vance Cheney ran the School of Life and Expression in Chicago, dedicated to teaching both children and adults "to recognize their true being, and their individual power to do and to express, in accordance with that power" through the medium of music. She also gave public lectures entitled "The New Philosophy of Life, or, The New Education." Harley, "A New Educator," 433–35; Willard and Livermore, *A Woman of the Century*, 170–71.

19. Ellen B. Scripps, "Notes on a course of lectures delivered by Mrs. John Vance Cheney on the New Education" [1899], 13–14, EBSC, drawer 22, folder 21; Ellen B. Scripps, diary, September 9, 12, 15, 19, 22, 26, 27, October 3, 1899, EBSC, drawer 23, folder 3. The lectures were held at Miss Ada Smith's house in San Diego.

20. Ellen B. Scripps, "Notes on a course of lectures delivered by Mrs. John Vance Cheney on the New Education" [1899], 21, 55, EBSC, drawer 22, folder 21.

21. Ellen B. Scripps, "Notes on a course of lectures delivered by Mrs. John Vance Cheney on the New Education" [1899], 21, 55, EBSC, drawer 22, folder 21.

22. Ellen B. Scripps, "Notes on a course of lectures delivered by Mrs. John Vance Cheney on the New Education" [1899], 21, 55, EBSC, drawer 22, folder 21.

23. Kirkley, "'Equality,'" 276.

24. Ellen B. Scripps, diary, April 15, 1909, EBSC, drawer 23, folder 13.

25. Waterstone, "Domesticating Universal Brotherhood," 295.

26. Ellen B. Scripps, diary, March 22, 1901, EBSC, drawer 23, folder 5.

27. Ellen B. Scripps, diary, March 28, 1901, EBSC, drawer 23, folder 5.

28. Ellen B. Scripps, diary, August 3, 1901, EBSC, drawer 23, folder 5.

29. Ellen B. Scripps, diary, January 12, 1905, EBSC, drawer 23, folder 9. Other members of the Theosophical reading group were Mary L. Dailey, Miss Jaeger, Mrs. McKee, Mrs. Maxwell, and Mrs. Woodsey of Oceanside.

30. Ellen B. Scripps, diary, May 31, 1904, EBSC, drawer 23, folder 8. Mrs. Prince later gave a lecture on karma. Ellen B. Scripps, diary, June 9, 1904, EBSC, drawer 23, folder 8.

31. Ellen B. Scripps, diary, May 19, 1904, EBSC, drawer 23, folder 8; Ellen B. Scripps,

diary, January 1, 1905, EBSC, drawer 23, folder 9; Ellen B. Scripps, February 5, 1905, EBSC, drawer 23, folder 9; Ellen B. Scripps, diary, March 31, July 8, September 29, 1907, EBSC, drawer 23, folder 11.

32. Bevir, "Annie Besant's Quest for Truth."

33. Besant, *The Laws of Higher Life*, 43.

34. Ellen B. Scripps, diary, September 16, 1906, EBSC, drawer 23, folder 10.

35. Ellen B. Scripps, diary, January 15, 1904, EBSC, drawer 23, folder 8; Ellen B. Scripps diary, January 2, 5, 9, 10, 12, February 6, March 5, 1908, EBSC, drawer 23, folder 12.

36. "Memoirs of Ellen Browning Scripps: Personal Reminiscences by Mary Bennett Ritter," Berkeley, CA, April 5, 1937, EBSC, drawer 1, folder 36.

37. Ellen B. Scripps to Eliza Virginia Scripps, La Jolla, December 14, 1916, EBSC, drawer 3, folder 17.

38. Kirkley, "'Starved and Treated Like Convicts,'" 11, 15.

39. Charles and Ethel Calloway, biographical subject file, LJHS.

40. Ellen B. Scripps, diary, September 10, 1902, EBSC, drawer 23, folder 6; Ellen B. Scripps, diary, June 19, 1903, EBSC, drawer 23, folder 7.

41. Ellen B. Scripps, diary, August 18, 1903, EBSC, drawer 23, folder 7.

42. Ellen B. Scripps, diary, January 9, 1908, EBSC, drawer 23, folder 12.

43. Ellen B. Scripps, diary, May 15, 1906, EBSC, drawer 23, folder 10.

44. These items were given to Nackey Scripps Meanley after Ellen's death. H. L. Smithton to W. C. Crandall, Cincinnati, May 5, 1933, EBSC, drawer 17, folder 8.

45. Ellen B. Scripps to Eliza Virginia Scripps, La Jolla, February 19, 1921, EBSC, drawer 3, folder 22.

46. Ellen B. Scripps to E. W. Scripps, October 11, 1921, EBSC, drawer 3, folder 1.

47. "Memoranda of Conference between J. C. Harper and Mary B. Eyre," EBSC, drawer 37, EBS biographical material C–H.

48. Ellen B. Scripps, diary, March 20, 1908, EBSC, drawer 23, folder 12.

49. Ellen B. Scripps, diary, March 4, 1909, EBSC, drawer 23, folder 13.

50. Ellen B. Scripps to Eliza Virginia Scripps, La Jolla, February 19, 1919, EBSC, drawer 3, folder 20. She continued, "The lady 'presiding' (I can't remember her name) is Miss Parkes' old 'healer' when she was given up and left at death's door by the notable physicians she had consulted. There was a 'select' audience, in each of whom Mrs. —— demonstrated her psychic or spiritual gifts."

51. Ellen B. Scripps to E. W. Scripps, La Jolla, May 7, 1924, EBSC, drawer 3, folder 8.

52. Eddy, *Science and Health*, 412. See also Satter, *Each Mind a Kingdom*, 3–4.

53. Ellen B. Scripps to E. W. Scripps, Hamilton, IL, July 23, August 8, 1890, EBSC, drawer 2, folder 23.

54. Ellen B. Scripps to Eliza Virginia Scripps, June 27, 1918, EBSC, drawer 3, folder 19; Ellen B. Scripps to E. W. Scripps, La Jolla, April 12, 1924, EBSC, drawer 3,

folder 8; Ellen B. Scripps to E. W. Scripps, March 11, 1925, EBSC, drawer 3, folder 10. In 1924 E. W. told Ellen, "This Christian Science craze has been the cause of very much personal discomfort to me for many years past." Instead of giving his La Jolla property to the group, he explained that he would prefer to give a reward "to some fellow who would devote himself intelligently and capably to blowing up the whole Christian Science institution." E. W. Scripps to Ellen B. Scripps, April 30, 1924, EBSC, drawer 3, folder 8.

55. Ellen B. Scripps to E. W. Scripps, Detroit, May 30, 1906, EBSC, drawer 2, folder 49.

56. Ellen B. Scripps, diary, November 30, 1898, EBSC, drawer 23, folder 2.

57. Ellen B. Scripps, diary, April 26, 1898, EBSC, drawer 23, folder 2; "Prospectus."

58. Ellen B. Scripps, diary, September 18, 1908, EBSC, drawer 23, folder 12.

59. "Memoranda of Conference between J. C. Harper and Mary B. Eyre," EBSC, drawer 37, EBS biographical material C–H.

60. Jones, *Social Law*, 167–68.

61. "Memoranda of Conference between J. C. Harper and Mary B. Eyre," EBSC, drawer 37, EBS biographical material C–H.

62. "Memoranda of Conference between J. C. Harper and Mary B. Eyre," EBSC, drawer 37, EBS biographical material C–H.

63. Ellen B. Scripps to E. W. Scripps, La Jolla, June 7, 1914, EBSC, drawer 1, folder 45. In 1916 she wrote to Virginia, "The Convention seemed unable to carry out its mighty promises of progress—as to women delegates, women preachers, shortening of the Lord's Prayer; Ten Commandments, etc., etc., and the Liturgy will be as long and dreary and meaningless as ever. Something will have to 'break loose' somewhere!" Ellen B. Scripps to Eliza Virginia Scripps, La Jolla, October 25, 1916, EBSC, drawer 3, folder 17.

64. "Questionnaire reply regarding old age, 1921," EBSC, drawer 1, folder 3. A decade later, she voiced her opinion about the Virgin Birth, the nature of the Trinity, "and other things in Christian creeds that she regards as absurd." J. C. Harper, memorandum, May 15, 1931, EBSC, drawer 26, folder 20.

65. McKanan, *Prophetic Encounters*, 84.

66. Blavatsky, *The Key to Theosophy*, 39.

67. Braude, *Radical Spirits*, chap. 3.

68. Albanese, *A Republic*, 323–35.

69. Fuller, *Woman in the Nineteenth Century*, 37.

70. Albanese, *A Republic*, 319.

71. Ellen B. Scripps, paper, May 13, 1918, EBSC, drawer 22, folder 22.

72. Ellen B. Scripps, speech before the La Jolla Woman's Club, undated, EBSC, drawer 22, folder 36.

73. Ellen B. Scripps, speech before the La Jolla Woman's Club, undated, EBSC, drawer 22, folder 36.

8. *A Feminist Speaks Out*

1. Lears, *Rebirth of a Nation*, 79.

2. E. W. Scripps, "Class Antagonism," OU MSS 117, series 4, box 1, vol. 1, bk. 1.

3. Satter, *Each Mind a Kingdom*, chap. 1 passim; EBS, "Paper written for but not read before the Club," May 13, 1918, EBSC, drawer 22, folder 23.

4. Ellen B. Scripps to E. W. Scripps, La Jolla, June 7, 1914, SC 1/45.

5. Buhle, *Women and American Socialism*, chap. 2.

6. McKanan, *Prophetic Encounters*, 136.

7. Buhle, *Women and American Socialism*, 161.

8. Buhle, *Women and American Socialism*, 109.

9. Debs, "Jesus, the Supreme Leader."

10. Ellen B. Scripps, diary, September 9, 1908, EBSC, drawer 23, folder 12.

11. Ellen B. Scripps, diary, September 23, October 6, 8, 1908, EBSC, drawer 23, folder 12; "Hallowe'en Has Hold at La Jolla," *San Diego Union*, November 5, 1908.

12. Davis, "The Next Little Dollar," 33; Fletcher, *Memoirs of Ed Fletcher*, 207; Adams, *The Man John D. Spreckels*, 196, 294.

13. Bridges, *Municipal Reform*, 58. See also William E. Smythe, "Responsible Government for California," *Out West* 26, no. 5 (May 1907): 456–61.

14. Adams, *The Man John D. Spreckels*, 25, chap. 10 passim, 201.

15. Davis, "The Next Little Dollar," 28–29; Adams, *The Man John D. Spreckels*, chap. 10; Fletcher, *Memoirs of Ed Fletcher*, 205.

16. Lee, "William E. Smythe." Losing the race, Smythe went on to found the Little Landers Colony in San Ysidro; he also wrote a history of San Diego in which he characterized Spreckels as "a private monopolist" who remained "kindly, liberal, and reasonably responsible to popular demands." Lee, "The Little Landers Colony"; Smythe, *History of San Diego*, 2:522.

17. E. W. Scripps to J. C. Harper, Miramar, January 2, 1908, EBSC, drawer 26, folder 53; Fletcher, *Memoirs of Ed Fletcher*, 269; Smythe, *History of San Diego*, 2:477; Smythe, *San Diego and Imperial Counties*, 2:418–20; Bridges, *Municipal Reform*, 62.

18. E. W. Scripps, "Interview with 'Boss' Hardy," May 1908, June 9, 1908, OU MSS 117, series 4, box 1, vol. 1. Hardy owned and operated several markets; stockyards in San Diego and Tijuana; and the Cudahy Packing Company, a company that produced hides, tallow, poultry food, and fertilizer. *San Diego City and County Directory*, 1905, 200.

19. E. W. Scripps, "Interview with 'Boss' Hardy," May 1908, June 9, 1908, OU MSS 117, series 4, box 1, vol. 1. Scripps described Hardy as "a perfect type of local Boss" who managed to co-opt both Republicans and Democrats. Although nominally leader of the Republican organization, Hardy "also has such control of the local situation that he can, and does, dominate the local Democratic party, and is able to, and has, even, appointed the delegates."

20. E. W. Scripps, "Interview with 'Boss' Hardy," May 1908, June 9, 1908, OU MSS

117, series 4, box 1, vol. 1. According to E.W., Hardy said that "Marston was a good man and a strong man . . . whose work for the city had been of tremendous value to the community." "'However,' Hardy said, 'he is my rival.'"

21. Marston, *George White Marston*, 1:326.

22. Marston, *George White Marston*, 2:60.

23. E. W. Scripps to W. A. Sloane, Miramar, January 23, 1908, EBSC, drawer 27, folder 21; E. W. Scripps, "Disquisition: Interview with 'Boss' Hardy," OH 117, series 4, box 1, bk. 1, 175–98.

24. Adams, *The Man John D. Spreckels*, 305.

25. E. W. Scripps to W. A. Sloane, Miramar, January 23, 1908, EBSC, drawer 27, folder 21.

26. E. W. Scripps, disquisition, "A Visit from Heney," December 21, 1909, OU MSS 117, series 4, box 1, vol. 4. He described the struggle between Lincoln-Roosevelters and the Regulars as "a contest between two bands of aristocrats for the control of the state government." E. W. Scripps to Prof. George H. Boke, Miramar, April 20, 1909, EBSC, drawer 27, folder 17.

27. E. W. Scripps to William Ritter, Miramar, February 24, 1911, biographical files, SIO, AC5, box 15, folder 488.

28. Ellen B. Scripps, diary, February 7, 1905, EBSC, drawer 23, folder 9; Ellen B. Scripps, diary, January 16, 1907, EBSC, drawer 23, folder 11.

29. Ellen B. Scripps, untitled, [ca. 1912], EBSC, drawer 22, folder 36.

30. Ellen B. Scripps, untitled, [ca. 1912], EBSC, drawer 22, folder 36.

31. Kneeland, "The Modern Boston Tea Party"; Cooney, "California Women Suffrage Centennial"; Cott, *The Grounding of Modern Feminism*, 28.

32. Ellen B. Scripps, diary, October 12, 1911, EBSC, drawer 23, folder 15.

33. E. W. Scripps to Elliott H. Pendleton, Miramar, March 14, 1914, OH MS 117, series 1.2, box 20, folder 1.

34. Ellen B. Scripps, untitled, EBSC, drawer 22, folder 36.

35. At the end of 1909, E.W. noted that "Reactionaryism has taken the country, and the peoples' leaders are developing discretion . . . I am doing my level best and blowing hard to keep the spark of revolt alive." E. W. Scripps to W. H. Porterfield, Miramar, December 28, 1909, EBSC, drawer 27, folder 17.

36. Bartoli, "Adventurers"; Miller, "Just Another Day?," 169–77.

37. Baillie, *High Tension*, 14.

38. Gardner, *Lusty Scripps*, 178; Trimble, *The Astonishing Mr. Scripps*, 299–305; Knight, *I Protest*, 395–404.

39. E. W. Scripps to Ellen B. Scripps, Miramar, May 18, 1911, OU MSS 117, series 1.2, box 17, folder 10.

40. Ellen B. Scripps, untitled, undated writing, EBSC, drawer 22, folder 36.

41. Miller, "Just Another Day?," 180–97.

42. "Socialists Prepare to Fight New Street Law," *San Diego Sun*, January 9, 1912.

43. Rabban, "The IWW Free Speech Fights," 1082.

44. Pourade, *The History of San Diego*, chap. 8.

45. Schroeder, "The History of San Diego's Free Speech Fight," 122–23.

46. *Kornbluh, Rebel Voices, no. 4.*

47. "Street Speaking Will Be Stopped; Traffic Referendum a Failure," *San Diego Sun*, March 25, 1912.

48. "Police Brutality to Man Arouses One Sun Reader," Editorial Page, *San Diego Sun*, April 1, 1912.

49. "San Diego's Problem: Resume of Troubles," *San Francisco Call*, May 21, 1912. In the late 1870s Spreckels organized a group in San Francisco known as the Vigilantes in reaction to the violence inspired by labor leader Denis Kearney. Adams, *The Man John D. Spreckels*, 77.

50. "Stop 72 I.W.W.'s; Deport Many More," *San Diego Sun*, April 4, 1912.

51. "Editor Abducted in Auto; Names Are Known and Prosecution Is Promised," *San Diego Sun*, April 6, 1912; "Sauer's Paper Is 'Pied' by Invaders at Night," *San Diego Sun*, May 16, 1912.

52. Schroeder, "The History of San Diego's Free Speech Fight," 124, 144; Miller, "Just Another Day?," 192–93.

53. Schroeder, "The History of San Diego's Free Speech Fight," 160–61; Goldman, *Living My Life*, 1:494–501; "Emma Goldman In; Hooed by Crowd; Can't Get a Hall," *San Diego Sun*, Tuesday, May 14, 1912.

54. "Sauer's Paper Is 'Pied' by Invaders at Night," *San Diego Sun*, May 16, 1912.

55. Ellen wrote in her diary, "Serious trouble reported from San Diego. Emma Goldman departed and her manager Dr. Reitman tarred and feathered and sent out of town." Ellen B. Scripps, diary, May 15, 1912, EBSC, drawer 23, folder 16.

56. Ellen B. Scripps, untitled speech [May 15, 1912], EBSC, drawer 22, folder 36.

57. Trimble, *The Astonishing Mr. Scripps*, 318–19.

58. Ellen B. Scripps to Harper, La Jolla, May 10, 1914, EBSC, drawer 1, folder 89.

59. Ellen B. Scripps to E. W. Scripps, La Jolla, June 29, 1914, EBSC, drawer 1, folder 45.

60. E. W. Scripps to Gilson Gardner, Miramar, July 5, 1913, OU MSS 117, series 1.2, box 19, folder 6; E. W. Scripps to Ellen B. Scripps, Washington, DC, June 27, 1914, EBSC, drawer 2, folder 49. E.W. continued, "He went through the usual stunt of giving me the history of his life—left a poor orphan at thirteen; a newsboy; a laborer; a street car conductor; a real estate agent; an insurance agent; and finally a congressman. He confessed to being ignorant, and pled as an excuse that he never had time to learn anything. He said that Mr. Spreckels had made him Congressman for the purpose of beating Evans, the Progressive candidate."

61. Ellen B. Scripps to Clarence A. McGrew, February 20, 1913, OU MSS 117, series 1.2, box 19, folder 2.

62. Ellen B. Scripps to E. W. Scripps, La Jolla, September 13, 1917, EBSC, drawer 2, folder 50.

63. E. W. Scripps to Charles Dwight Willard, Disquisition "Attitude Toward Labor," April 29, 1911, OU MSS 117, series 4, box 2, vol. 3; Baldasty, *E. W. Scripps*, 21; E. W. Scripps to Joseph Fels, February 3, 1910, OU MSS 117, series 4, box 2, vol. 3.

64. Stoltzfus, *Freedom from Advertising*, 35–36, 58, 116–19. See Baldasty, *E. W. Scripps*, chap. 7.

65. Ellen B. Scripps, diary, February 11, 1914, EBSC, drawer 23, folder 18.

66. E. W. Scripps to Ellen B. Scripps, Chicago, May 21, 1914, EBSC, drawer 2, folder 49.

67. In 1924 Ellen identified herself as a progressive, writing that although she had voted for Woodrow Wilson in 1912, she had been strongly impressed by Robert M. La Follette. "Joins the Progressive Cause: Philanthropist Tells Why She Will Aid Progressive," *San Diego Sun*, October 16, 1924.

9. Sweet Virginia

1. Mabel Clark, biographical subject file, LJHS.

2. Judith Morgan, "The Miss Scripps Nobody Knows," *San Diego Union*, July 30, 1967, GI.

3. Mrs. Avery T. (Katie B.) Holmes, biographical subject file, LJHS.

4. E. W. Scripps to Ellen B. Scripps, *Ohio* at sea, June 1, 1923, EBSC, drawer 3, folder 6.

5. E. W. Scripps to Ellen B. Scripps, *Ohio* in Singapore, January 10, 1925, EBSC, drawer 3, folder 10.

6. Eliza Virginia Scripps to Ellen B. Scripps, Los Angeles, July 25, 1900, EBSC, drawer 2, folder 46.

7. Eliza Virginia Scripps to Ellen B. Scripps, Los Angeles, July 25, 1900, EBSC, drawer 2, folder 46.

8. Helen Hunter Getsinger, biographical subject file, LJHS; Mrs. Avery T. (Katie B.) Holmes, biographical subject file, LJHS.

9. Morgan, "The Miss Scripps Nobody Knows," GI.

10. Helen Getsinger, biographical subject file, LJHS.

11. "My Trip to La Jolla" (1910), Mabel Clark, biographical subject file, LJHS.

12. Morgan, "The Miss Scripps Nobody Knows," GI.

13. Morgan, "The Miss Scripps Nobody Knows," GI.

14. Ellen B. Scripps to Eliza Virginia Scripps, La Jolla, October 26, 1913, EBSC, drawer 3, folder 16.

15. Ellen B. Scripps to Eliza Virginia Scripps, La Jolla, November 2, 1913, EBSC, drawer 3, folder 16.

16. "My Trip to La Jolla," 1910, Mabel Clark, biographical subject file, LJHS.

17. Ellen B. Scripps, diary, December 17, 1905, EBSC, drawer 23, folder 9; Ellen B. Scripps, diary, February 25, 1906, EBSC, drawer 23, folder 10.

18. Waddy, *A Parish by the Sea*, 51.

19. In May 1907 Ellen went with Irving J. Gill to see the First Methodist Episcopal Church (1905–6) at Ninth Avenue and C Street in San Diego, which Gill had

designed. Ellen decided that she did not want a Gothic Revival structure and asked Gill to create an alternative design. Two months later, Ellen noted in her diary, "Saw Mr. Gill's plans for church, etc. Did not altogether approve. He is to draw new ones." Ellen B. Scripps, diary, May 2, July 14, 15, September 11, 12, 14, 26, 27, 1907, EBSC, drawer 23, folder 11.

20. Ellen B. Scripps, diary, March 8, 1908, EBSC, drawer 23, folder 12.

21. "Baptismal Font Children's Gift," *San Diego Union*, March 3, 1908, 5:3.

22. Beatrice Blankenship, interviewed by LJHS staff, January 1969, Netta Powell Allen and Margaret Flemming Allen, biographical subject file, LJHS.

23. E. W. Scripps, "Eliza Virginia Scripps," May 9, 1921, OU MSS 117, series 4.

24. Eliza Virginia Scripps to Ellen B. Scripps, Los Angeles, July 25, 1900, EBSC, drawer 2, folder 46.

25. Virginia chronicled her memories in a poem, "Our Trip to Spain" (1888), EBSC, drawer 26, folder 49.

26. Netta Powell Allen, interviewed by LJHS staff, 1969, biographical subject file, LJHS.

27. "News from La Jolla," *San Diego Union*, June 11, 1899; "The Week at La Jolla," *San Diego Union*, October 8, 1899.

28. "Local Brevities," *San Diego Union*, June 19, 1902, 6:2.

29. "Popular La Jolla," *San Diego Evening Tribune*, May 4, 1900.

30. Ellen B. Scripps to E. W. Scripps, Hilo, April 4, 13, 1902, EBSC, drawer 2, folder 48.

31. Ellen B. Scripps to Ellen Kellogg, La Jolla, May 2, 1906, FWKC.

32. Ellen B. Scripps to Eliza Virginia Scripps, La Jolla, October 17, 1913, EBSC, drawer 3, folder 16.

33. Ellen B. Scripps, diary, October 6–14, 1904, EBSC, drawer 23, folder 8. E.W. had asked Ellen to inquire about purchasing a statue of *Crouching Venus*.

34. Ellen B. Scripps, diary, January 1–2, 1915, EBSC, drawer 23, folder 19.

35. Ellen B. Scripps, diary, January 1, March 7, July 31, August 14, 1916, EBSC, drawer 23, folder 20.

36. Ellen B. Scripps to Eliza Virginia Scripps, La Jolla, November 11, 1916, EBSC, drawer 3, folder 17.

37. Ellen B. Scripps to Eliza Virginia Scripps, La Jolla, December 13, 1916, EBSC, drawer 3, folder 17.

38. Ellen B. Scripps to Eliza Virginia Scripps, Miramar, March 9, 1895, EBSC, drawer 3, folder 15.

39. Ellen B. Scripps to E. W. Scripps, La Jolla, July 27, 1917, EBSC, drawer 2, folder 50; "Woman Author Passing Summer at La Jolla," *San Diego Union*, July 28, 1907, 12:6.

40. Ellen B. Scripps, diary, July 3, 1912, EBSC, drawer 23, folder 16.

41. Ellen B. Scripps to Eliza Virginia Scripps, La Jolla, December 11, 1916, EBSC, drawer 3, folder 17.

42. Helen Gardner to Floy Kellogg, Detroit, August 30, 1904, FWKC.

43. Cartwright, "Robert Henri's San Diego," 221–22.

44. Marjorie Henri to Theresa Gatewood Lee, La Jolla, August 3, 1914, RHP.

45. Marjorie Henri to Theresa Gatewood Lee, La Jolla, August 3, 1914, RHP.

46. Marjorie Henri to Theresa Gatewood Lee, La Jolla, August 3, 1914, RHP.

47. Morgan, "The Miss Scripps Nobody Knows," G1.

48. J. C. Harper, memorandum, August 23, 1929, EBSC, drawer 26, folder 20.

49. Ellen B. Scripps to Eliza Virginia Scripps, La Jolla, October 29, 1914, EBSC, drawer 3, folder 16; Ellen B. Scripps to Eliza Virginia Scripps, La Jolla, November 27, 1916, EBSC, drawer 3, folder 17.

50. J. C. Harper, memorandum, December 5, 1928, EBSC, drawer 26, folder 20.

51. Ethel Calloway, 1964, biographical subject file, LJHS. Netta Allen wrote that Virginia Scripps "was really very kindhearted, but not the gentle person that Miss Ellen Scripps was." Netta Powell Allen, 1969, biographical subject file, LJHS.

52. Morgan, "The Miss Scripps Nobody Knows," G2.

53. Ellen B. Scripps to Eliza Virginia Scripps, La Jolla, May 31, 1916, EBSC, drawer 3, folder 17.

54. Ellen B. Scripps to Eliza Virginia Scripps, La Jolla, November 9, 1916, EBSC, drawer 3, folder 17.

55. Ellen B. Scripps to Eliza Virginia Scripps, La Jolla, [October 31], 1917, EBSC, drawer 3, folder 18.

56. Ellen B. Scripps to Eliza Virginia Scripps, La Jolla, September 30, 1917, EBSC, drawer 3, folder 18.

57. Ellen B. Scripps to Eliza Virginia Scripps, La Jolla, November 9, 1916, EBSC, drawer 3, folder 17.

10. Educating Girls

1. Ellen B. Scripps, "The Playground," n.d., EBSC, drawer 22, folder 26.

2. Solomon, *In the Company of Educated Women*, 58.

3. Stevens, *A Bishop Beloved*, 35–36.

4. Turney, *The History of a Parish*, chap. 4; "In Death Undivided: Hand in Hand into Shadows: Charles E. Bentham and Wife Are Dead Together," *Los Angeles Daily Times*, January 15, 1915.

5. Ellen B. Scripps, diary, September 14, 26, 27, 1907, EBSC, drawer 23, folder 11.

6. Ellen B. Scripps diary, January 21, 1908, EBSC, drawer 23, folder 12.

7. Ellen B. Scripps, diary, October 30, 1908, EBSC, drawer 23, folder 12.

8. Ellen B. Scripps to James A. Blaisdell, September 24, 1914, EBSC, drawer 1, folder 73; "Questionnaire reply regarding old age, 1921," biographical material, EBSC, drawer 1, folder 47; Waddy, *A Parish by the Sea*, 80, 107.

9. Ellen B. Scripps, diary, January 3, 10, 1909, EBSC, drawer 23, folder 13; Mitchell, *Reviewing the Vision*, 8–9.

10. The Bishop's Day School is now the Self-Realization Fellowship Church, 3068 First Avenue, San Diego, CA.

11. Ellen B. Scripps, diary, August 12, October 20, 1909, EBSC, drawer 23, folder 13.

12. Roorbach, "The Bishop's School for Girls," 654.

13. Hines, *Irving Gill*, 76.

14. Ellen B. Scripps to J. C. Harper, September 15, 1910, November 8, 1910, EBSC, drawer 1, folder 87.

15. Ellen B. Scripps to Eliza Virginia Scripps, October 5, 1917, EBSC, drawer 3, folder 18.

16. Caroline S. Cummins, biographical subject file, LJHS.

17. Caroline S. Cummins, biographical subject file, LJHS.

18. "Club Women Study California Law on Divorce," *San Diego Union*, October 31, 1910, 5:5.

19. Ellen B. Scripps, diary, May 8, 1912, EBSC, drawer 23, folder 16; Ellen B. Scripps, diary, January 24, 1913, EBSC, drawer 23, folder 17.

20. *La Leyenda* [yearbook], 1914, SDHS, Ephemera/Education: The Bishop's School; Ellen B. Scripps to Eliza Virginia Scripps, June 6, 1916, EBSC, drawer 3, folder 17.

21. Mitchell, *Reviewing the Vision*, 13; Ellen B. Scripps to Eliza Virginia Scripps, October 25, 1914, EBSC, drawer 3, folder 16.

22. Mitchell, *Reviewing the Vision*, 14–15. Among the members of the class of 1914 were several girls for whom admission to either Vassar or Stanford was their main ambition: Louise Fleming, Helen Logie, Jean Miller, and Erna Reed. *La Leyenda* [yearbook], 1914, SDHS, Ephemera/Education: The Bishop's School.

23. Ellen B. Scripps to Eliza Virginia Scripps, May 22, 1919, EBSC, drawer 3, folder 20.

24. Ellen B. Scripps to Eliza Virginia Scripps, October 25, 1914, EBSC, drawer 3, folder 16.

25. "In Death Undivided."

26. The San Diego Bishop's School, headed by Mrs. Alyda D. MacLain and Miss Isoline L. Lang, was a separate institution, independent of The Bishop's School in La Jolla. The San Diego Bishop's School, "Announcement for 1916–1917," SDHS, Ephemera/Education: The Bishop's School.

27. Ellen B. Scripps to Eliza Virginia Scripps, November 11, 1916, EBSC, drawer 3, folder 17. In 1915 Bentham Hall was named in memory of Dorothy Bentham, daughter of the late Reverend and Mrs. Charles E. Bentham.

28. Gilman, "Women Who Go to College," 717–18.

29. "$50,000 Donated to Build School Dormitory," *San Diego Union*, May 1, 1915.

30. Ellen B. Scripps to Eliza Virginia Scripps, May 12, 1916, EBSC, drawer 3, folder 17.

31. Ellen B. Scripps to Eliza Virginia Scripps, October 5, 1917, EBSC, drawer 3, folder 18. Gilman left Bishop's in 1918 and returned to Boston to take up a position as head of religious education at the Cathedral Church of St. Paul.

32. Mitchell, *Reviewing the Vision*, 17; Ellen B. Scripps to Eliza Virginia Scripps, October 6, 1917, EBSC, drawer 3, folder 18.

33. Ellen B. Scripps to Eliza Virginia Scripps, November 20, 1917, EBSC, drawer 3,

folder 18; Ellen B. Scripps to Eliza Virginia Scripps, March 5, 1921, EBSC, drawer 3, folder 22.

34. Mitchell, *Reviewing the Vision*, 17; Ellen B. Scripps to Eliza Virginia Scripps, May 7, 1916, EBSC, drawer 3, folder 17.

35. Hamilton, *A Vision for Girls*, 64; Cummins, "Random Reminiscences," *Bishop's School Alumnae News*, Summer 1970, SDHS, Ephemera/Education: The Bishop's School; Ellen B. Scripps to Eliza Virginia Scripps, September 16, 1917, EBSC, drawer 3, folder 18.

36. Ciani, "Revelations of a Reformer," 102–23.

37. Her married name was Katherine Haskell Read. New and Cochran, *Early Childhood Education*, 687–88.

38. "Southern California's Institutions of Learning Stand Unequaled in America Today," *Los Angeles Times*, August 16, 1919.

39. "Plans to Build Women's School: Big College May Be Erected in San Diego," *Los Angeles Times*, March 3, 1910; "Woman's College for San Diego Plan of Bishop Johnson," *San Diego Union*, March 2, 1910.

40. Ellen B. Scripps to Eliza Virginia Scripps, October 25, 1914, EBSC, drawer 3, folder 16.

41. Ellen B. Scripps to Eliza Virginia Scripps, February 15, 1921, EBSC, drawer 3, folder 22.

42. In 1916 Ellen wrote that her brother E.W. visited The Bishop's School "and went all over the building with her [Gilman], and gave his opinions and criticisms quite freely. He thinks the chapel should have had an entrance on the street. By the way, they are having stalls designed for it, instead of moveable seats." Ellen B. Scripps to Eliza Virginia Scripps, November 25, 1916, EBSC, drawer 3, folder 17.

43. Ellen B. Scripps to Eliza Virginia Scripps, May 29, 1916, EBSC, drawer 3, folder 17.

44. Ellen B. Scripps to Eliza Virginia Scripps, June 2, 1918, EBSC, drawer 3, folder 19.

45. Ellen B. Scripps to Eliza Virginia Scripps, June 7, 1916, EBSC, drawer 3, folder 17.

46. Ellen B. Scripps to Eliza Virginia Scripps, February 16, 1921, EBSC, drawer 3, folder 22.

47. Mitchell, *Reviewing the Vision*, 24–25; Ellen B. Scripps to Eliza Virginia Scripps, July 6, 1918, EBSC, drawer 3, folder 19.

48. Ellen B. Scripps to Eliza Virginia Scripps, January 18, 20, 1921, EBSC, drawer 3, folder 22.

49. Ellen B. Scripps to Eliza Virginia Scripps, February 14, 1921, EBSC, drawer 3, folder 22.

50. Mitchell, *Reviewing the Vision*, 29; Ellen B. Scripps to Eliza Virginia Scripps, March 9, 1921, EBSC, drawer 3, folder 22.

51. Edith Stevens Haney, "Fifty Year Memories," SDHS, subject file: The Bishop's School.

52. Mitchell, *Reviewing the Vision*, 31–32, 45, 47.

53. Ellen B. Scripps to Eliza Virginia Scripps, August 9, 1920, EBSC, drawer 3, folder 21.

54. Ellen B. Scripps to Eliza Virginia Scripps, December 14, 1920, EBSC, drawer 3, folder 21.

55. Ellen B. Scripps to Eliza Virginia Scripps, January 31, March 16, 1921, 1921, EBSC, drawer 3, folder 22. Cummins wrote, "When Scripps Hall was the only building and classes met in sections of the drawing room, Mrs. Bentham's office was the small room nearest the entrance from Cuvier Street and next to the Bishop's bedroom and bath." Cummins, "Random Reminiscences." The bishop stayed with Ellen in what he referred to as the "Prophet's Chamber." Ellen B. Scripps to Eliza Virginia Scripps, October 24, 1914, EBSC, drawer 3, folder 16.

56. J. C. Harper, "Memorandum: New Building for Bishop's School," July 22, 1924, EBSC, drawer 11, folder 43.

57. Address of Miss Mary B. Eyre at a Scripps College Convocation, October 18, 1935, EBSC, drawer 1, folder 1; letter read by Dr. James A. Blaisdell at a memorial service on October 18, 1932, "In Memoriam: Ellen Browning Scripps, 1836–1936, compiled by J. C. Harper," EBSC, drawer 1, folder 32.

11. The Playground and Community House

1. *San Diego City and County Directory*, 1913.

2. Ellen Mills, biographical subject file, LJHS; Randolph, *La Jolla Year by Year*, 24–25.

3. Carol Olten, "Gentleman Farmer Swain: A Maverick Who Grew and Delivered Berries," *La Jolla Village News*, November 5, 2009. See also Scott R. Varley, comp., "Jethro Mitchell Swain, 1843–1917: Transcribed from his personal diaries from 1910–1917 during the years he lived in La Jolla, Calif.," MS, LJHS.

4. Eleanor F. Bennett, diary, May 31, 1905, HM 64262.

5. Marian Brown Kenyon, biographical subject file, LJHS.

6. Descendants, *La Jolla, California Black Pioneers*, 1–3, 5, 17, 19; Randolph, *La Jolla Year by Year*, 95.

7. Ellen B. Scripps to Rev. Howard Bard, La Jolla, June 26, 1915, EBSC, drawer 12, folder 33.

8. Boyer, *Urban Masses*, 245.

9. Hindman, *Child Labor*, 31.

10. Addams, *The Spirit of Youth*, 5–6.

11. Recchiuti, *Civic Engagement*, 127. The Keating-Owen Child Labor Act (1916), a federal law designed to end child labor, was declared unconstitutional in 1918.

12. Lee, "Play as an Antidote," 111–12.

13. Goodman, *Choosing Sides*, chap. 4; Boyer, *Urban Masses*, 181, 242–44, 279–80; "Many Cities Adopt Playground Plan," *New York Times*, July 26, 1908.

14. Lee, *Constructive and Preventive Philanthropy*, 123.

15. Hanmer, "A Playground Meeting," 176.

16. Lee, *Constructive and Preventive Philanthropy*, 219.

17. Bemis, "A New Substitute," 370.

18. Addams, *The Spirit of Youth*, 20.

19. Kirby, "The Recreation Movement," 220–21.

20. King and King, *Pathfinder Social Survey*, 11–13.

21. King and King, *Pathfinder Social Survey*, 3, 6, 9, 13, 17–18, 25.

22. Lewis, "'Well-Directed Play,'" 183–202.

23. King and King, *Pathfinder Social Survey*, 21, 27, 32–33.

24. "Ninth Ward Hoodlumism Receives a Check," *San Diego Union*, January 18, 1902; "Boys Are Arrested," *San Diego Union*, March 8, 1913; "Boy Robs Chain of Lunch Wagons," *San Diego Union*, August 28, 1911.

25. "Urge Playground as Preventive of Crime; National Association Secretary Pleads for Public Recreation Places," *San Diego Union*, June 5, 1908.

26. Roger Showley, "The Nolen Plan," *San Diego Union*, January 9, 1983.

27. Nolen, *San Diego*, 52, 55.

28. "The Playgrounds Movement," editorial, *San Diego Union*, January 9, 1909.

29. "Playgrounds Are Open for Summer; Average Daily Attendance Is More Than Sixty Boys and Girls," *San Diego Union*, July 2, 1911.

30. King and King, *Pathfinder Social Survey*, 24–25.

31. The board, appointed by the mayor, consisted of Daniel Cleveland, president; Mrs. Sara Herron Chafee, secretary; and members Mrs. Grace B. German, Rev. Howard B. Bard, Sherwood Wheaton, and Louis J. Wilde. Frank Marsh, "Playgrounds Rank Third of Pacific Coast; Provision Made for Best Development of Children; Funds Apportioned Annually from Budget for Development and Maintenance," *San Diego Union*, January 1, 1915.

32. "Great Playground Work to Begin December 1; Tract of Fifty Acres in Balboa Park Set Adie and Plans Perfected," *San Diego Union*, November 15, 1913.

33. Ellen B. Scripps, diary, July 11, 1914, EBSC, drawer 23, folder 18; "Exercises to Open New Playground on Golden Hill," *San Diego Union*, July 11, 1914; "Two Thousand Boys and Girls Gambol and Sing to Dedicate New Golden Hill Playground; Hundreds Attend Exercises Celebrating Opening of Park for Children," *San Diego Union*, July 12, 1914.

34. "San Diego Club," *San Diego Union*, March 28, 1910; Smythe, *The History of San Diego*, 2:579–80.

35. Sarah A. Taylor, "History of the La Jolla Woman's Club 1898–1917," 8, LJWC; Ellen B. Scripps, diary, June 29, 1904, EBSC, drawer 23, folder 8.

36. Ellen B. Scripps to Rev. Howard Bard, La Jolla, June 26, 1915, EBSC, drawer 12, folder 33.

37. "La Jolla Kiddies to Have a Modern Playground," *San Diego Union*, June 23, 1914, 2:2.

38. Ellen B. Scripps, diary, September 20, 29, 1911, EBSC, drawer 23, folder 15; Ellen B. Scripps, diary, August 2, 1912, EBSC, drawer 23, folder 16. In 1903 Ellen

acquired the triangular-shaped Lot 19 in Block 33 from the Botsfords; in 1909 she bought Lot 18 from the recently married Charlotte Orr, who had lost her husband in a drowning accident. In 1911 she bought Lot 17 from Nina Waddell. Block 33, La Jolla Park, EBSC, drawer 12, folder 34; Ellen B. Scripps, diary, July 19, 21, September 30, 1909, EBSC, drawer 23, folder 13. She added a codicil to her will offering these lots to the city of San Diego after her death "to be used in perpetuity as a public park or playground."

39. Block 33, La Jolla Park, EBSC, drawer 12, folder 34. "Mrs. Waddell of her own accord sold me her property on Draper St. . . . These leave me in possession of the whole of Block 33, with the exception of Dr. Howard's places and the 50 feet on the other end of Miss Pugh's." After a lengthy legal process, she acquired the Howard and Pugh properties. Ellen B. Scripps to Mary Ritter, La Jolla, March 7, 1914, EBSC, drawer 2, folder 12; Ellen B. Scripps to J. C. Harper, June 20, July 19, August 14, 28, October 22, November 7, 1914, EBSC, drawer 1, folder 89.

40. Ellen B. Scripps, diary, April 3, 1914, EBSC, drawer 23, folder 18.

41. "La Jolla Playground to Be Opened July 3," *San Diego Union*, June 27, 1915, 2:3.

42. Ellen B. Scripps to J. C. Harper, La Jolla, May 10, 1914, EBSC, drawer 1, folder 89. In July she approved a petition to close Kline Street between Cuvier and Draper in order to enlarge the size of the grounds. Ellen B. Scripps, diary, July 1, 1914, EBSC, drawer 23, folder 18. Virginia Scripps, who owned Lots 3–15 in Block 19, planned to give them to The Bishop's School.

43. "La Jolla Playground to Be Opened July 3," *San Diego Union*, June 27, 1915.

44. Ellen B. Scripps, diary, May 19, 1914, EBSC, drawer 23, folder 18.

45. Ellen B. Scripps, diary, May 23, June 22, 1914, EBSC, drawer 23, folder 18.

46. The club was located on Lots 1, 2, 3, 4, 5, and 6 in Block 32 of La Jolla Park. Ellen offered the club the use of her home until the new clubhouse was completed. On October 1, 1913, she wrote in her diary, "Woman's Club opened. Meet in my basement room. Between 30 and 40 present. After the business meeting adjourn to the upper room and look over the plans for the new Club House." Ellen B. Scripps, diary, October 1, 1913, EBSC, drawer 23, folder 17.

47. "Talkative Houses," 448–55; Hines, *Irving Gill*, 173–74. According to Mary Ritter, she initially imagined "a simple, cottage-like building to cost about seven or eight thousand dollars." Architect Irving Gill, however, convinced her that the structure should be built of concrete in the same manner as The Bishop's School. Ritter, *More Than Gold*, 305, 308–9.

48. Ellen B. Scripps, diary, October 5, 1914, EBSC, drawer 23, folder 18; Ellen B. Scripps, speech before the La Jolla Woman's Club, [October 5, 1914], EBSC, drawer 22, folder 32. The formal opening of the club took place on January 4, 1915. Clubwomen and guests from all over San Diego brought the attendance to between seven and eight hundred people. Ellen presented the deed to the club during a program of music and speeches. A memorial tablet was placed to the left

of the entrance. Ellen B. Scripps, diary, January 4, 1915, EBSC, drawer 23, folder 19; Myrtle G. Gordon, "The First Fifty-Five Years: A Brief History of the La Jolla Woman's Club, 1894–1949," LJWC, 4.

49. Ellen B. Scripps to E. W. Scripps, La Jolla, June 13, 1914, EBSC, drawer 1, folder 45.

50. Ellen B. Scripps to E. W. Scripps, La Jolla, June 20, 1914, EBSC, drawer 1, folder 45.

51. "Unique Playground Plan for La Jolla; Miss Scripps Spending $50,000 for City," *San Diego Union*, September 7, 1914; Wallis, "San Diego's $200,000 Community House and Playground," 28. Heavy rainfall eventually led to the roofing of the locker rooms. Hines, *Irving Gill*, 174–78.

52. Wallis, "San Diego's $200,000 Community House and Playground," 27–28.

53. Wallis, "San Diego's $200,000 Community House and Playground," 27. The girls' section also accommodated boys under the age of ten. "La Jolla Playground to Be Opened July 3," *San Diego Union*, June 27, 1915.

54. "La Jolla Playground to Be Opened July 3," *San Diego Union*, June 27, 1915.

55. E. W. Scripps to Ellen B. Scripps, Miramar, May 29, 1915, EBSC, drawer 2, folder 49; copy of deed, PAS/SC, drawer 39, folder 67. The deed was filed July 6, 1915.

56. "'Playground Paradise' to Be Also a Temple of Free Speech Is Gift to All Children from Five to Fifty," *Rushville Press*, July 3, 1915, EBSC, drawer 12, folder 36.

57. J. C. Harper, "Notes on Life of Ellen Browning Scripps," EBSC, drawer 1, folder 10.

58. Copy of deed, PAS/SC, drawer 39, folder 67.

59. J. C. Harper to Ellen B. Scripps, Denver, August 19, 1914, EBSC, drawer 12, folder 33.

60. Ellen B. Scripps to J. C. Harper, La Jolla, May 7, 1915, EBSC, drawer 12, folder 33.

61. Ellen B. Scripps to J. C. Harper, La Jolla, August 28, 1914, EBSC, drawer 1, folder 89.

62. "Playground Given to City; La Jolla Fairyland for Tots Dedicated," *San Diego Union*, July 4, 1915.

63. Ellen B. Scripps, presentation of deed to the city of San Diego, [July 3, 1915], EBSC, drawer 12, folder 33. The *San Diego Union* reported her as saying: "'I have long contemplated presenting a gift to the children of San Diego. . . . I wanted to give them something that would help make them happy. At first I considered turning my residence into a home for motherless children. When I decided that it was too large and expensive for such an institution, I began beautifying the property where the playground is situated and turned it into a park that children might romp and play on the grass and enjoy God's outdoors as they have a right to do. Suddenly it occurred to me that a playground was needed in La Jolla, and I immediately planned to provide one. With the aid of these men on the platform with me, I have fulfilled my heart's desire, and it is with great pleasure that I turn over to the children of San Diego this beautiful playground. I sincerely hope that they will feel free to come and go, and look upon it as their own.'" Much of this language is drawn from a letter from Ellen to Rev. Howard Bard dated June 26, 1915. "Playground Given to City; La Jolla Fairyland for Tots Dedicated," *San

Diego Union, July 4, 1915; Ellen B. Scripps to Rev. Howard Bard, La Jolla, June 26, 1915, EBSC, drawer 12, folder 33.

64. "Given More Playgrounds We'll Need Fewer Reform Schools," *San Diego Sun*, July 7, 1915.

65. "Playground Given to City; La Jolla Fairyland for Tots Dedicated," *San Diego Union*, July 4, 1915.

66. Ellen B. Scripps, diary, July 3, 1915, EBSC, drawer 3, folder 19. Not long afterward, Reverend Bard came to her house with a "handsome book of photographs of Play Ground and . . . Community House." Ellen B. Scripps, diary, July 15, 1915, EBSC, drawer 3, folder 19.

67. Rev. Howard Bard to Harper, San Bernardino, July 18, 1915, EBSC, drawer 12, folder 4.

68. Ellen B. Scripps, diary, November 7, 1915, EBSC, drawer 3, folder 19. In 1914 Raymond had published an outline of his university extension lectures on the origins of the Great War. Raymond, *The War—What For?*

69. Ellen B. Scripps, diary, January 6, 7, 9, 1916, EBSC, drawer 23, folder 20.

70. Ellen B. Scripps to Eliza Virginia Scripps, La Jolla, October 4, 1916, EBSC, drawer 3, folder 17.

71. Ellen B. Scripps, diary, March 5, 6, 1917, EBSC, drawer 23, folder 21; Ellen B. Scripps, "The Playground" [March 5–6, 1917], EBSC, drawer 22, folder 26.

72. L. Inman Samuels to J. C. Harper, La Jolla, November 4, 1926, EBSC, drawer 11, folder 21; Fisher, "African Americans."

12. South Molton Villa

1. "Firebugs Burn Scripps' La Jolla Homes, Chapel," *San Diego Union*, August 8, 1915.

2. Ellen B. Scripps, diary, August 7, 1908, EBSC, drawer 23, folder 12. Ellen had spent the day in downtown San Diego with her neighbor Eliza Howard, wife of Dr. Howard.

3. "Real Estate Transfers," *San Diego Union*, August 10, 1905, 8:6. In 1903 Edith M. Seaman accompanied Ellen and Virginia on a trip to Palm Springs. Ellen B. Scripps, diary, May 24, 1903, EBSC, drawer 23, folder 7.

4. Ellen B. Scripps, diary, August 30, 1905, EBSC, drawer 23, folder 9.

5. Diane Kane, "Wisteria Cottage Description and Alterations," MS, December 5, 2011; Irving Gill, "Alterations in Residence of Miss Virginia Scripps," drawn up December 24–27, 1907, University of California, Santa Barbara.

6. Ellen B. Scripps, diary, November 29, 1907, EBSC, drawer 6, folder 26.

7. Ellen B. Scripps, diary, June 1, 2, 4, 5, 1908, EBSC, drawer 6, folder 26; Ellen B. Scripps, accounting diary, July–September 1908, EBSC, drawer 6, folder 26; Ellen B. Scripps, diary, April 4, 1911, EBSC, drawer 23, folder 15.

8. She bought the sun porch furniture in 1899 while in Asheville, North Carolina, with her brother George. She wrote in her diary, "Mr. Bailey (the rustic work

dealer) called with his nephew and I ordered from him $20 worth of rustic porch furniture for La Jolla." Ellen B. Scripps, diary, November 27, 1899, EBSC, drawer 23, folder 3.

9. Ellen B. Scripps, diary, August 1, 3, 1912, EBSC, drawer 23, folder 16; J. C. Harper, memo, "Miss Scripps' New House," September 18, 1928, EBSC, drawer 11, folder 24.

10. South Molton Villa was wired for electricity in 1906. Ellen B. Scripps, diary, September 16, October 4, 1906, EBSC, drawer 23, folder 10.

11. Ellen B. Scripps, diary, August 1, 1912, EBSC, drawer 23, folder 16.

12. Ellen B. Scripps, diary, January 25, 28, February 15, 18, 24, 28, April 2, 23, 27, 1908, EBSC, drawer 23, folder 12; Ellen B. Scripps, accounting diary, January–March 1908, EBSC, drawer 6, folder 26; J. C. Harper, memo, September 18, 1928, PAS/SC, drawer 39, folder 79. During the conversion of South Molton Villa into the Museum of Contemporary Art, Ellen Revelle moved the bungalow to its current location, 2491 Horizon Way in La Jolla.

13. Ellen B. Scripps, diary, March 18, 20, 1908, EBSC, drawer 6, folder 26.

14. Ellen B. Scripps to Eliza Virginia Scripps, La Jolla, April 20, 1916, EBSC, drawer 3, folder 17.

15. Ellen B. Scripps, diary, September 7, 1908, EBSC, drawer 23, folder 12.

16. Ellen B. Scripps, diary, October 10, December 4, 1908, EBSC, drawer 23, folder 12.

17. Ellen B. Scripps to Eliza Virginia Scripps, La Jolla, June 16, 1916, EBSC, drawer 3, folder 17.

18. Ellen B. Scripps to Eliza Virginia Scripps, La Jolla, June 21, 1916, EBSC, drawer 3, folder 17.

19. Ellen B. Scripps, diary, June 3, 1911, EBSC, drawer 23, folder 15; Ellen B. Scripps, diary, January 16, 17, March 17, 20, 1912, EBSC, drawer 23, folder 16.

20. Ellen B. Scripps, diary, January 16, 1912, EBSC, drawer 23, folder 16; Ellen B. Scripps, diary, September 1, 2, 1914, EBSC, drawer 23, folder 18; Ellen B. Scripps, accounting diary, April 5, 1916, EBSC, drawer 7, folder 1; Ellen B. Scripps, accounting diary, July 8, August 28, 1916, EBSC, drawer 7, folder 1.

21. Robert Mann Wood to Ellen B. Scripps, Fontana, WI, August 25, [1915], EBSC, drawer 25, folder 8.

22. Ellen B. Scripps, "To the People of La Jolla," *La Jolla Journal*, August 28, 1915, EBSC, drawer 25, folder 8; J. C. Harper, memorandum, "Civil Liberties," EBSC, drawer 1, folder 39.

23. Ellen B. Scripps, "To the People of La Jolla," *La Jolla Journal*, August 28, 1915, EBSC, drawer 25, folder 8.

24. "William Peck Tells Police He Burned 3 La Jolla Places," *San Diego Evening Tribune*, December 16, 1915; "Has Firebug Told All? Prosecution May Trap Others," *San Diego Union*, December 17, 1915; "Alleged Firebug's Defense Hinges on 'Third Degree,'" *San Diego Union*, February 4, 1916; "Peck to Serve 12 Years in Prison,"

San Diego Union, February 24, 1916; Ellen B. Scripps to Virginia Scripps, La Jolla, June 14, 1916, EBSC, drawer 3, folder 17.

25. Kate Bagby to Ellen B. Scripps, Rushville, IL, August 13, 1915, EBSC, drawer 25, folder 8.

26. Mary B. Atwater to Ellen B. Scripps, Helena, MT, August 18, 1915, EBSC, drawer 25, folder 8.

27. Hines, *Irving Gill*, 196.

28. Ellen B. Scripps, diary, October 2, 1915, EBSC, drawer 23, folder 19.

29. Ellen B. Scripps to J. C. Harper, La Jolla, August 28, 1914, EBSC, drawer 1, folder 89.

30. E. W. Scripps to J. C. Harper, Miramar, September 8, 1915, OU MSS 117, series 2, box 32, bk. 32.

31. E. W. Scripps to J. C. Harper, Miramar, "Personal and Confidential," September 8, 1915, OU MSS 117, series 2, box 32, bk. 32.

32. E. W. Scripps to Ellen B. Scripps, Miramar, August 19, 1915, OH MSS 117, series 1.2, box 21, folder 9.

33. By 1930 Ellen had realized that she "did not have the money to do as Henry Huntington had done, but that some modest program along the above line might be worked out." J. C. Harper to W. C. Crandall, La Jolla, January 15, 1930, EBSC, drawer 11, folder 13.

34. Ellen B. Scripps to Eliza Virginia Scripps, June 16, 1916, EBSC, drawer 3, folder 17.

35. Hines, *Irving Gill*, 179.

36. J. C. Harper, memorandum, August 6, 1935, EBSC, drawer 11, folder 24.

37. Katharine Peirce Scripps to Eliza Virginia Scripps, n.d., EBSC, drawer 26, folder 44.

38. Ellen B. Scripps to Grace Scripps Clark, La Jolla, December 30, 1927, EBSC, drawer 1, folder 76.

39. 700 Prospect Street, South Molton Villa, Second House, street file: Prospect Street, LJHS.

40. Inventory, April 12, 1933, EBSC, drawer 11, folder 24.

41. F. J. Higgins, interviewed by Barbara Dawson, 1965, LJHS; Ellen B. Scripps to Eliza Virginia Scripps, La Jolla, October 3, 1918, EBSC, drawer 3, folder 19.

42. Ellen B. Scripps, diary, July 20, 1916, EBSC, drawer 3, folder 17; South Molton Villa guest book, 1916–17, EBSC, drawer 25, folder 52.

43. South Molton Villa guest book, 1916–17, EBSC, drawer 25, folder 52.

44. E. W. Scripps to J. C. Harper, Miramar, February 18, 1916, OH MSS 117, series 2, box 32, bk. 32.

45. Ellen B. Scripps, diary, March 2, 1898, EBSC, drawer 23, folder 2.

46. Ellen B. Scripps to Eliza Virginia Scripps, La Jolla, October 18, 1914, EBSC, drawer 3, folder 16.

47. Ellen B. Scripps, diary, February 27, 1903, EBSC, drawer 23, folder 7.

48. Ellen B. Scripps, diary, May 23, 1907, EBSC, drawer 23, folder 11.

49. Ellen B. Scripps to Eliza Virginia Scripps, La Jolla, July 7, 1918, EBSC, drawer 3, folder 19.

50. J. C. Harper to E. W. Scripps, San Diego, August 11, 1916, EBSC, drawer 10, folder 44; J. C. Harper to C. F. Mosher, San Diego, September 18, 1916, EBSC, drawer 7, folder 22; J. C. Harper to W. P. Williams, San Diego, September 12, 1916, EBSC, drawer 10, folder 44. The car was a 6-48 B4 flat roof suburban Pierce-Arrow. William E. Bush, invoice, November 4, [1916], EBSC, drawer 10, folder 44.

51. Carol Olten, "Driving Miss Ellen: Fred Higgins at the Wheel in 1916," SDNews. com, http://www.sdnews.com/view/full_story/301722/article-Driving-Miss-Ellen—Fred-Higgins-at-the-wheel-in-1916.

52. F. J. Higgins, interviewed by Barbara Dawson, 1965, LJHS.

53. Ellen B. Scripps, diary, February 28, March 26, April 16, 1917, EBSC, drawer 23, folder 21.

54. Ellen B. Scripps to Eliza Virginia Scripps, La Jolla, November 4, 1916, EBSC, drawer 3, folder 17.

55. Ellen B. Scripps to Eliza Virginia Scripps, La Jolla, November 4, 1916, EBSC, drawer 3, folder 17.

56. Ellen B. Scripps to Eliza Virginia Scripps, La Jolla, November 9, 1916, EBSC, drawer 3, folder 17.

57. Ellen B. Scripps to E. W. Scripps, June 18, 1917, EBSC, drawer 2, folder 50.

58. Ellen B. Scripps, diary, March 29, May 4, 1901, EBSC, drawer 23, folder 5; Ellen B. Scripps, diary, June 23, 1902, EBSC, drawer 23, folder 6; Ellen B. Scripps, diary, October 22, 1906, EBSC, drawer 23, folder 10.

59. "Riches without Servants," letter to the editor, *Spectator*, February 17, 1906, EBSC, drawer 1, folder 40.

60. Eliza Virginia Scripps to Ellen B. Scripps, Los Angeles, July 25, 1900, EBSC, drawer 2, folder 46.

61. Ellen B. Scripps to Eliza Virginia Scripps, June 16, 1916, EBSC, drawer 3, folder 17.

62. Ellen B. Scripps to Eliza Virginia Scripps, La Jolla, April 25, 1916, EBSC, drawer 3, folder 17.

63. E. W. Scripps to Ellen B. Scripps, July 15, 1917, EBSC, drawer 2, folder 50.

64. Ellen B. Scripps to E. W. Scripps, La Jolla, September 16, 1918, EBSC, drawer 2, folder 51.

65. Ellen B. Scripps, diary, March 27, 1916, EBSC, drawer 23, folder 20; J. C. Harper, memorandum, "Miss Scripps' New House," September 18, 1928, EBSC, drawer 11, folder 24. The property, located at 1501 Torrey Pines Road, was built by real estate investor W. C. Sheppard in 1911. "Harper House / Sheppard House," in Schaelchlin, *La Jolla, a Historical Inventory*.

66. Ellen B. Scripps to E. W. Scripps, La Jolla, January 19, 1922, EBSC, drawer 3, folder 2.

67. Ellen B. Scripps to E. W. Scripps, La Jolla, October 11, 1922, EBSC, drawer 3, folder 4.

68. Ellen B. Scripps to E. W. Scripps, La Jolla, November 14, 1921, EBSC, drawer 3, folder 1.

69. Ellen B. Scripps to E. W. Scripps, La Jolla, January 19, 1922, EBSC, drawer 3, folder 2.

70. [Hilda M. Gardner], memo, n.d., EBSC, drawer 1, folder 43.

13. The Sinews of War

1. "Belgian Troops Forced Back as Siege of Antwerp Begins," *San Diego Union*, October 4, 1914; "Belgian Refugee Colonists," *San Diego Union*, October 24, 1914; "Hunger Will Drive Belgians to Attack Conquerors, Fears American Relief Commission," *San Diego Union*, November 29, 1914.

2. Ellen B. Scripps to Eliza Virginia Scripps, La Jolla, October 13, 1914, EBSC, drawer 3, folder 16.

3. Ellen B. Scripps, diary, October 31, 1914, EBSC, drawer 23, folder 18.

4. Ellen B. Scripps to Eliza Virginia Scripps, La Jolla, October 15, 1914, EBSC, drawer 3, folder 16.

5. E. W. Scripps to Ellen B. Scripps, Washington, DC, July 1, 1914, EBSC, drawer 2, folder 49.

6. E. W. Scripps to Ellen B. Scripps, Washington, DC, August 28, 1917, EBSC, drawer 2, folder 50.

7. E. W. Scripps to Ellen B. Scripps, Washington, DC, June 22, 1917, EBSC, drawer 2, folder 50.

8. Kennedy, *Over Here*, 20.

9. Ellen B. Scripps, diary, March 13, 1916, EBSC, drawer 23, folder 20.

10. Sarah A. Taylor, "History of the La Jolla Woman's Club 1898–1917," 43, LJWC.

11. Ellen B. Scripps to Eliza Virginia Scripps, La Jolla, December 11–13, 1916, EBSC, drawer 3, folder 17.

12. Ellen B. Scripps, diary, February 13, 1916, EBSC, drawer 23, folder 20; Eastman, *Understanding Germany*.

13. Ellen B. Scripps, diary, July 10, 1916, EBSC, drawer 23, folder 30.

14. Ellen B. Scripps, diary, January 23, February 12, 21, 1916, EBSC, drawer 23, folder 20; Raymond gave three series of lectures at the community house.

15. Ellen B. Scripps, diary, July 27, 1916, EBSC, drawer 23, folder 20.

16. Kennedy, *Over Here*, 13.

17. Ellen B. Scripps, diary, April 17, 1917, EBSC, drawer 23, folder 21; "Red Cross Shows Articles Made," *San Diego Union*, August 5, 1917.

18. Ellen B. Scripps to Eliza Virginia Scripps, La Jolla, October 22, 1917, EBSC, drawer 3, folder 18.

19. Ellen B. Scripps to Eliza Virginia Scripps, Altadena, November 7, 1917, EBSC, drawer 3, folder 18.

20. Ellen B. Scripps to Eliza Virginia Scripps, La Jolla, November 2, 1917, EBSC, drawer 3, folder 18.

21. Ellen B. Scripps to Eliza Virginia Scripps, La Jolla, November 16, 1917, EBSC, drawer 3, folder 18.

22. Ellen B. Scripps to Eliza Virginia Scripps, June 13, 1918, EBSC, drawer 3, folder 19.

23. Ellen B. Scripps to E. W. Scripps, La Jolla, June 18, 1917, EBSC, drawer 2, folder 50.

24. Ellen B. Scripps, diary, March 19, 1916, EBSC, drawer 23, folder 20.

25. Ellen B. Scripps to Eliza Virginia Scripps, La Jolla, November 1, 1916, EBSC, drawer 3, folder 17.

26. Ellen B. Scripps to E. W. Scripps, August 13, 1918, EBSC, drawer 2, folder 51.

27. Ellen B. Scripps to E. W. Scripps, August 13, 1918, EBSC, drawer 2, folder 51.

28. Ellen B. Scripps to E. W. Scripps, La Jolla, October 15, 1917, EBSC, drawer 2, folder 50; Ellen B. Scripps, accounting diary, May 9, 1918, EBSC, drawer 7, folder 3; Ellen B. Scripps, accounting diary, May 24, 1919, EBSC, drawer 7, folder 4.

29. J. C. Harper to E. W. Scripps, San Diego, September 8, 1917, EBSC, drawer 11, folder 47.

30. E. W. Scripps to Ellen B. Scripps, Washington, DC, May 26, 1917, EBSC, drawer 2, folder 50.

31. E. W. Scripps to Ellen B. Scripps, Washington, DC, May 26, 1917, EBSC, drawer 2, folder 50.

32. Ellen B. Scripps to Eliza Virginia Scripps, La Jolla, November 18, 1917, EBSC, drawer 3, folder 18.

33. Martin, "Patriotism and Profit"; "Camp Kearny Fast Assuming Form as Big Army of Workmen Labor on Mesa," *San Diego Union*, August 16, 1917.

34. Julia Morgan's Hostess House from Camp Fremont is located in Palo Alto, California, Historical Landmark 895.

35. Ellen provided $15,000 to the YWCA's War Work Council for this project. Ellen B. Scripps, diary, July 26, September 1, November 10, 16, 1916, EBSC, drawer 23, folder 20; Ellen B. Scripps, accounting diary, August 10, 1918, EBSC, drawer 7, folder 13; "Will Begin Work on 'Hostess Home,'" *San Diego Union*, October 9, 1917; "Camp Kearny Hostess House May Open Thanksgiving Day," *San Diego Union*, November 26, 1917.

36. Ellen B. Scripps to Virginia Scripps, La Jolla, November 25, 1917, EBSC, drawer 3, folder 18.

37. Ellen B. Scripps, diary, November 30, 1917, EBSC, drawer 23, folder 21.

38. Ellen B. Scripps to E. W. Scripps, La Jolla, January 6, 1918, EBSC, drawer 2, folder 51.

39. Ellen B. Scripps, diary, January 26, 1918, EBSC, drawer 23, folder 22.

40. Ellen B. Scripps to E. W. Scripps, September 13, 1917, EBSC, drawer 2, folder 50.

41. Ellen B. Scripps to Eliza Virginia Scripps, La Jolla, November 20, 1917, EBSC, drawer 3, folder 18.

42. Ellen B. Scripps to Eliza Virginia Scripps, La Jolla, November 2, 1917, EBSC, drawer 3, folder 18.

43. Ellen B. Scripps to Eliza Virginia Scripps, La Jolla, November 25, 1917, EBSC, drawer 3, folder 18.

44. Ellen B. Scripps to Eliza Virginia Scripps, La Jolla, November 27, 1917, EBSC, drawer 3, folder 18; "La Jolla Notes," *San Diego Union*, December 24, 1917; "La Jolla Notes," *San Diego Union*, December 31, 1917.

45. Ellen B. Scripps, diary, March 2, 7, April 16, 1918, EBSC, drawer 23, folder 22; "La Jolla Opens Club Room for Enlisted Men," *San Diego Union*, January 20, 1918; "La Jolla Room Opened for Soldiers on Leave," *San Diego Union*, February 26, 1918; *San Diego City and County Directory*, 1919, 1294.

46. Ellen B. Scripps, diary, May 22, October 24, 1918, EBSC, drawer 23, folder 22.

47. Ellen B. Scripps to Eliza Virginia Scripps, La Jolla, November 18, 1917, EBSC, drawer 3, folder 18.

48. E. W. Scripps to Ellen B. Scripps, Washington, DC, September 1, 1917, EBSC, drawer 2, folder 50.

49. Ellen B. Scripps to E. W. Scripps, La Jolla, November 11, 1917, EBSC, drawer 2, folder 50.

50. Ellen B. Scripps, diary, January 7, 1918, EBSC, drawer 23, folder 22; Ellen B. Scripps, "New Year's Greetings to Members of Woman's Club of La Jolla," EBSC, drawer 22, folder 20.

51. Ellen B. Scripps, untitled, April 8, 1918, EBSC, drawer 22, folder 35; Ellen B. Scripps, diary, April 8, 1918, EBSC, drawer 23, folder 22.

52. Ellen B. Scripps, paper, May 13, 1918, EBSC, drawer 22, folder 36.

53. Ellen B. Scripps, "Memorial Tribute Read before the Woman's Club, January 6, 1919," EBSC, drawer 22, folder 22.

54. Ellen B. Scripps, diary, July 2, 1917, EBSC, drawer 23, folder 21; Ellen B. Scripps to E. W. Scripps, La Jolla, August 28, 1917, EBSC, drawer 2, folder 50.

55. Ellen B. Scripps to Eliza Virginia Scripps, La Jolla, September 25, 1917, EBSC, drawer 3, folder 18.

56. "Steffens to Lecture on 'Menace of Peace,'" *San Diego Union*, April 26, 1918; "Muckrake Artist Is Stopped," *San Diego Union*, April 27, 1918.

57. Ellen B. Scripps, diary, March 8, April 27, 1918, EBSC, drawer 23, folder 22; Ellen B. Scripps to J. C. Harper, La Jolla, April 23, 1918, EBSC, drawer 1, folder 89.

58. Ellen B. Scripps to Eliza Virginia Scripps, La Jolla, May 21, 1918, EBSC, drawer 3, folder 19; Ellen B. Scripps, diary, May 20, 1918, EBSC, drawer 23, folder 22.

59. Ellen B. Scripps, diary, January 23, 1912, EBSC, drawer 23, folder 16; E. W. Scripps to Ellen B. Scripps, San Francisco, February 4, 1913, EBSC, drawer 2, folder 49.

60. Ellen B. Scripps to Eliza Virginia Scripps, Miramar, November 8, 1894, EBSC, drawer 3, folder 15.

61. E. W. Scripps to Mrs. Oscar J. Kendall, Miramar, May 13, 1916, OH MSS 117, series 1.2, box 22, folder 8; McGrew, *City of San Diego*, 2:390–91; Ellen B. Scripps, diary, March 6, 1912, EBSC, drawer 23, folder 16. In 1918 the Talent Workers opened a hospital for the families of servicemen. "News of the Hospital Field," 52; Ellen B. Scripps to Eliza Virginia Scripps, La Jolla, July 12, 1918, EBSC, drawer 3, folder 19.

62. E. W. Scripps to Milton A. McRae, Miramar, September 20, 1916, OH MSS 117, series 1.2, box 22, folder 11; E. W. Scripps to Dr. Robert Pollock, Miramar, November 15, 1916, OH MSS 117, series 1.2, box 22, folder 13.

63. E. W. Scripps to Milton A. McRae and J. C. Harper, Miramar, August 8, 1916, OH MSS 117, series 1.2, box 22, folder 10; E. W. Scripps to F. A. White, Miramar, January 27, 1917, OH MSS 117, series 1.2, box 23, folder 1; E. W. Scripps to Milton A. McRae, Miramar, February 14, 1917, OH MSS 117, series 1.2, box 23, folder 2; "The Diagnostic Hospital," 282; Pollock, "The San Diego Diagnostic Group Clinic," 104.

64. Ellen B. Scripps to J. C. Harper, La Jolla, February 26, 1918, EBSC, drawer 1, folder 89; E. W. Scripps to Dr. Robert Pollock, Miramar, November 15, 1916, OH MSS 117, series 1.2, box 22, folder 13. The clinic's space and medical equipment were turned over to the government for the duration of the war.

65. Eastman, *Good Company*, 45.

66. Ellen B. Scripps, diary, December 17, 1916, EBSC, drawer 23, folder 20; Ellen B. Scripps to J. C. Harper, La Jolla, June 14, 1917, EBSC, drawer 13, folder 25; Clarkson, *Ellen Browning Scripps*, 51–52.

67. Ellen B. Scripps, diary, March 9, 15, 1917, EBSC, drawer 23, folder 21.

68. Ellen B. Scripps to J. C. Harper, La Jolla, June 14, 1917, EBSC, drawer 13, folder 25.

69. Ada Gillispie to J. C. Harper, La Jolla, April 11, 1918, EBSC, drawer 13, folder 26.

70. J. C. Harper to Ellen B. Scripps, April 1, 1918, EBSC, drawer 1, folder 89.

71. Ellen B. Scripps to J. C. Harper, March 10, 1918, EBSC, drawer 1, folder 89.

72. Ellen B. Scripps to J. C. Harper, March 16, 1918, EBSC, drawer 1, folder 89.

73. Ellen B. Scripps to J. C. Harper, March 23, 1918, EBSC, drawer 1, folder 89.

74. Ellen B. Scripps to Eliza Virginia Scripps, July 12, 1918, EBSC, drawer 3, folder 19.

75. "Concrete Work Is Started on New Sanitarium," *San Diego Union*, June 20, 1918.

76. Ellen B. Scripps, diary, December 5, 1918, EBSC, drawer 23, folder 11.

77. "Influenza Seeks Victims in Vain; Everybody Out," *San Diego Union*, October 14, 1918.

78. Ellen B. Scripps, diary, October 2, 1918, EBSC, drawer 23, folder 22.

79. Ellen B. Scripps to Eliza Virginia Scripps, La Jolla, December 8–10, 1918, EBSC, drawer 3, folder 19.

80. Ellen B. Scripps to E. W. Scripps, January 31, 1919, EBSC, drawer 3, folder 1.

81. Ellen B. Scripps to E. W. Scripps, La Jolla, February 23, 1919, EBSC, drawer 3, folder 1.

82. Eastman, *Good Company*, 56.

83. Ellen B. Scripps to Emma Scripps, La Jolla, January 10, 1930, EBSC, drawer 3, folder 24.

84. *San Diego Union*, November 11, 1918.

85. Ellen B. Scripps, diary, November 7, 1918, EBSC, drawer 23, folder 11.

86. Ellen B. Scripps to Eliza Virginia Scripps, November 11, 1918, EBSC, drawer 3, folder 19.

87. Ellen B. Scripps to Eliza Virginia Scripps, November 11, 1918, EBSC, drawer 3, folder 19.

88. Ellen B. Scripps to Eliza Virginia Scripps, November 11, 1918, EBSC, drawer 3, folder 19.

89. "Friday Selected Parade Night for United War Work," *San Diego Union*, November 14, 1918.

90. E. W. Scripps to Ellen B. Scripps, *Kemah*, Jacksonville, FL, November 12, 1918, EBSC, drawer 2, folder 51.

91. Ellen B. Scripps to E. W. Scripps, La Jolla, February 23, 1919, EBSC, drawer 3, folder 1.

92. Ellen B. Scripps, "La Jolla Then and Now," EBSC, drawer 22, folder 19.

14. Still Roaring in the 1920s

1. Ellen B. Scripps, diary, August 23, 1923, EBSC, drawer 24, folder 3.

2. J. C. Harper to Ellen B. Scripps, Detroit, June 2, 1919, EBSC, drawer 1, folder 89; E. W. Scripps to Ellen B. Scripps, aboard *Ohio*, May 28, 1925, EBSC, drawer 3, folder 10.

3. Ellen B. Scripps to E. W. Scripps, La Jolla, July 18, 1922, EBSC, drawer 3, folder 3.

4. Ellen B. Scripps to E. W. Scripps, July 12, 1925, EBSC, drawer 3, folder 11; E. W. Scripps to Ellen B. Scripps, Ridgefield, CT, August 22, 1925, EBSC, drawer 3, folder 11.

5. Ellen B. Scripps to E. W. Scripps, La Jolla, September 5, 1925, EBSC, drawer 3, folder 11.

6. E. W. Scripps to Ellen B. Scripps, aboard *Ohio*, August 18, 1923, EBSC, drawer 3, folder 7.

7. Ellen B. Scripps to Eliza Virginia Scripps, La Jolla, November 4, 1920, EBSC, drawer 3, folder 21. She was unhappy to hear of "the rise of the Hearst chain and other similar ones like the Scripps-Howard which now numbers 25 dailies," considering these chains to be "fraught with evil, particularly when one considers it in connection with the steady trend towards consolidation or absorption of the weaker dailies by the strong. . . . [S]hould all the city dailies of the country be owned by 4 or 5 individuals or groups of owners the situation in this country would

become extremely serious." Ellen B. Scripps to E. W. Scripps, La Jolla, April 1, 1923, EBSC, drawer 3, folder 6.

8. E. W. Scripps to Ellen B. Scripps, aboard *Ohio*, August 18, 1923, EBSC, drawer 3, folder 7.

9. Ellen B. Scripps to Eliza Virginia Scripps, La Jolla, June 18, 1920, EBSC, drawer 3, folder 21.

10. Pourade, *The Rising Tide*, chap. 2.

11. Linder, "Rear Admiral Roger Welles," 53–70.

12. Shragge, "'I Like the Cut of Your Jib,'" 230–55.

13. Ellen B. Scripps, "La Jolla Then and Now," EBSC, drawer 22, folder 19.

14. Randolph, *La Jolla Year by Year*, 34, 76, 90, 102, 122.

15. Ellen B. Scripps to E. W. Scripps, La Jolla, July 27, 1917, EBSC, drawer 2, folder 50.

16. Ellen B. Scripps, diary, November 25, 1918, drawer 22, folder 23; Randolph, *La Jolla Year by Year*, 120, 135, 138; "La Jolla Asks Extension of New Fast Beach Line," *San Diego Union*, May 17, 1923; "La Jolla Building Plans Call for $1,500,000 Outlay," *San Diego Union*, October 5, 1924.

17. "Railway to Build La Jolla Station," *San Diego Union*, August 29, 1924.

18. J. C. Harper to William Templeton Johnson, September 10, 1920, EBSC, drawer 12, folder 32. Soldiers memorialized included John Mogg Scripps (1840–63), Basil Fielding Worsfold (1897–1915), Frank N. Bennett (1882–1918), and Ramon Frederick Moreno (1893–1920).

19. Ellen B. Scripps to Miss Smith, La Jolla, January 1, 1930, EBSC, drawer 12, folder 32.

20. Ellen B. Scripps, notecard, EBSC, drawer 20, folder 26.

21. Ellen B. Scripps, accounting diary, March 20, 1911, EBSC, drawer 6, folder 30; Ellen B. Scripps, diary, May 6, 1924, EBSC, drawer 24, folder 4; W. C. Crandall to Robert P. Scripps, March 34, 1939, EBSC, drawer 20, folder 26; Chambers, "Bibliographical Notes," 231–43.

22. Ellen B. Scripps, diary, October 18, 1918, EBSC, drawer 23, folder 22.

23. "My Trip to La Jolla, California," Mabel Clark, biographical subject file, LJHS.

24. In 1920 DeLange gave Ellen a book that she had written and decorated with her sister. Ellen B. Scripps, diary, October 9, 1920, EBSC, drawer 23, folder 24.

25. Self, "The History."

26. "Appreciation of Handsome New Library Attested by Rapidly Gaining Patronage," *San Diego Union*, December 7, 1921; Ellen B. Scripps, diary, February 11, 1921, EBSC, drawer 24, folder 1.

27. "Library Assured of Fine Exhibits," *San Diego Union*, April 5, 1922.

28. Ellen B. Scripps, diary, August 3, 13, 1911, EBSC, drawer 23, folder 15. She wrote in her diary, "Go again to see Mr. Fries' picture. Buy one of the San Diego Mission—$50."

29. She owned works by Theodore Earl Butler, William Alexander Griffith, Nora Landers, Warren E. Rollins, and Monona Van Cise, among others. Inventory,

South Molton Villa, April 12, 1933, EBSC, drawer 11, folder 24; Ellen B. Scripps, diary, September 18, 1900, EBSC, drawer 23, folder 4; Ellen B. Scripps, diary, January 26, 1905, EBSC, drawer 23, folder 9.

30. Ellen B. Scripps to Eliza Virginia Scripps, February 12, 1921, EBSC, drawer 3, folder 22; Ellen B. Scripps, diary, February 12, 1921, EBSC, drawer 24, folder 1; "Friends of Art Open Second Large Exhibit of Paintings," *San Diego Union*, January 30, 1921.

31. Ellen B. Scripps, diary, October 6, 24, November 5, 1923, EBSC, drawer 24, folder 3; Ellen B. Scripps, diary, March 31, April 1, 1923, EBSC, drawer 24, folder 4; Ellen B. Scripps, diary, June 12, 1926, EBSC, drawer 24, folder 5; J. C. Harper to E. W. Scripps, La Jolla, September 5, 1923, OH MSS 117, series 1.1, box 39, folder 1.

32. Ellen B. Scripps to Eliza Virginia Scripps, La Jolla, November 11, 1916, EBSC, drawer 3, folder 17.

33. Ellen B. Scripps to Eliza Virginia Scripps, La Jolla, June 14, 1916, EBSC, drawer 3, folder 17; Gertrude Gilbert to Ellen B. Scripps, San Diego, February 16, 1929, EBSC, drawer 13, folder 8.

34. "Memoranda of Conference between J. C. Harper and Mary B. Eyre," EBSC, drawer 37, EBS biographical material C–H. For more information, see Kamerling, "How Ellen Scripps Brought Ancient Egypt to San Diego."

35. Ellen B. Scripps, diary, December 4, 1881, EBSC, drawer 24, folder 22.

36. Ellen B. Scripps to Marie N. Buckman, La Jolla, October 27, 1919, EBSC, drawer 12, folder 10; receipt, Tiffany & Co., Paris, May 11, 1883, EBSC, drawer 24, folder 34.

37. Drower, "Petrie, Sir (William Matthew) Flinders (1853–1942)." The Egyptian Exploration Fund changed its name to the Egyptian Exploration Society in 1919.

38. "Reclaiming Egypt: The Exploration Fund Must Raise a Thousand Dollars," *New York Times*, February 12, 1911.

39. Ellen B. Scripps, accounting diary, March 18, 1911, EBSC, drawer 6, folder 30.

40. Ellen B. Scripps, accounting diary, June 17, 1911, EBSC, drawer 6, folder 30.

41. Ellen B. Scripps, diary, March 7, 1912, EBSC, drawer 23, folder 16.

42. Ellen B. Scripps to Marie N. Buckman, November 25, 1916, EBSC, drawer 12, folder 10.

43. Ellen B. Scripps to Eliza Virginia Scripps, La Jolla, November 11, 1916, EBSC, drawer 3, folder 17.

44. Ellen B. Scripps to Marie N. Buckman, La Jolla, October 27, 1919, EBSC, drawer 12, folder 10.

45. Ellen B. Scripps to Eliza Virginia Scripps, La Jolla, November 3, 1920, EBSC, drawer 3, folder 21. For more information on Akhenaten, see Hornung, *Akhenaten and the Religion of Life*; and Montserrat, *Akhenaten*.

46. Kamerling, "How Ellen Scripps Brought Ancient Egypt to San Diego," 79–80; San Diego Museum of Man, "The Ethnographic Collections."

47. Ellen B. Scripps, diary, November 1, 3, 1920, EBSC, drawer 23, folder 34; Ellen B. Scripps to Marie N. Buckman, La Jolla, November 10, 1920, November 16, 1921, June 20, 1923, EBSC, drawer 12, folder 10.

48. Ellen B. Scripps, diary, October 28, 29, 1925, EBSC, drawer 24, folder 5.

49. Ellen B. Scripps, diary, October 21, 1922, EBSC, drawer 24, folder 2; Thomas Whittemore to J. C. Harper, San Francisco, October 29, 1922, EBSC, drawer 12, folder 10.

50. Ellen B. Scripps to Marie N. Buckman, La Jolla, March 16, 1928, EBSC, drawer 12, folder 10.

51. Kamerling, "How Ellen Scripps Brought Ancient Egypt to San Diego," 85. Several artifacts from the Scripps / Egypt Exploration Society Collection toured with the exhibition *Pharaohs of the Sun*, organized by the Museum of Fine Arts, Boston, in 1999–2001.

52. Ellen B. Scripps to Eliza Virginia Scripps, La Jolla, October 17, 1919, EBSC, drawer 3, folder 20.

53. Engstrand and Bullard, *Inspired by Nature*, 63.

54. Ellen B. Scripps to Fred Baker, La Jolla, May 28, 1920, EBSC, drawer 12, folder 54.

55. Ellen B. Scripps, accounting diary, March 28, 1921, EBSC, drawer 7, folder 6; Ellen B. Scripps, diary, March 29, 1921, EBSC, drawer 24, folder 1.

56. Engstrand and Bullard, *Inspired by Nature*, 65. Ellen attended the opening of the museum and told her sister, "Your gift—the Hornbeck Collection—is another magnificent showing, with the framed and engrossed 'resolutions' with your picture in front evidence." Ellen B. Scripps to Eliza Virginia Scripps, La Jolla, December 18, 1920, drawer 3, folder 21.

57. Ellen B. Scripps, diary, December 5, 25, 1919, EBSC, drawer 23, folder 23; "Burroughs at La Jolla for Month," *San Diego Union*, January 8, 1920; Ellen B. Scripps, diary, January 1, 1920, EBSC, drawer 23, folder 24.

58. Ellen B. Scripps, diary, December 26, 1919, EBSC, drawer 23, folder 23; Ellen B. Scripps, diary, January 5, 7, 12, 16, 1920, EBSC, drawer 23, folder 24; Ellen B. Scripps, diary, December 3, 1920, EBSC, drawer 23, folder 24; Ellen B. Scripps to Eliza Virginia Scripps, La Jolla, November 11, 1920, December 5, 7, 9, 11, 14, EBSC, drawer 3, folder 21.

59. Shaw, "The San Diego Zoological Garden"; Ellen B. Scripps, accounting diary, January 16, 1922, EBSC, drawer 7, folder 7; Ellen B. Scripps to J. C. Harper, January 17, July 20, November 16, 1922, April 28, June 13, August 13, 1923, EBSC, drawer 13, folder 13; Ellen B. Scripps, diary, August 17, 1922, EBSC, drawer 24, folder 2; Ellen B. Scripps, accounting diary, April 26, 1923, EBSC, drawer 7, folder 8; Ellen B. Scripps, diary, September 8, 1923, EBSC, drawer 24, folder 3; "World's Greatest Flying Cage at Balboa Park Is Dedicated and Presented to San Diego Children," *San Diego Union*, September 9, 1923; Harry M. Wegeforth to Ellen B. Scripps, San Diego, July 15, 1925, EBSC, drawer 13, folder 13.

60. Joseph W. Sefton, Jr., to J. C. Harper, San Diego, May 3, 1922, EBSC, drawer 12, folder 54.

61. J. C. Harper, memorandum, October 27, 1925, EBSC, drawer 26, folder 20.

62. Engstrand and Bullard, *Inspired by Nature*, 100.

63. Library inventory, EBSC, drawer 20, folder 27.

64. Ellen B. Scripps, diary, November 16, 1916, EBSC, drawer 23, folder 20.

65. Ellen B. Scripps to H. W. Keller (copy), January 28, 1908, OH MSS 117, series 1.1, box 27, folder 18.

66. E. W. Scripps to George W. Marston, Miramar, May 3, 1908, OH MSS 117, series 1.2, box 14, folder 7; E. W. Scripps to George W. Marston, Miramar, June 15, 1908, EBSC, drawer 14, folder 12; Ellen B. Scripps, diary, June 30, 1908, EBSC, drawer 23, folder 12; Ellen B. Scripps, [June 11, 1911], EBSC, drawer 1, folder 87. In fact, E.W. considered the deal to be a "hold-up," or robbery. E. W. Scripps, disquisition, "An Easy Mark," April 8, 1909, OH MSS 117, series 4, box 1, vol. 2; George W. Marston to E. W. Scripps, San Diego, December 23, 1909, OH MSS 117, series 1.1, box 29, folder 1. In 1914 Ellen paid $5,000 for the paving of Torrey Pines Road. Ellen B. Scripps, expenses for 1914, EBSC, drawer 1, folder 89.

67. F. B. Sumner to E. M. Capps, January 14, 1916, EBSC, drawer 14, folder 12.

68. Walsh, "Preserving 'Nature's Artistry,'" 34; Ellen B. Scripps to Eliza Virginia Scripps, La Jolla, June 6, 1916, EBSC, drawer 3, folder 17.

69. Ellen B. Scripps to J. C. Harper, La Jolla, June 6, 1921, EBSC, drawer 14, folder 17; Guy Fleming to Ellen B. Scripps (copy), September 20, 1921, EBSC, drawer 14, folder 17.

70. Guy L. Fleming to Ellen B. Scripps, San Diego, September 22, 1916, EBSC, drawer 14, folder 17.

71. Guy L. Fleming, "Torrey Pines and Their Picturesque Setting Should Be Nucleus of Recreation Park at Gateway of City," *San Diego Union*, April 28, 1921.

72. J. C. Harper to E. W. Scripps, La Jolla, May 2, 1922, EBSC, drawer 14, folder 12; Ralph D. Cornell, "Report on Visit to Torrey Pines Park," April 3, 1922, EBSC, drawer 14, folder 12.

73. Ellen B. Scripps to E. W. Scripps, La Jolla, August 21, 1922, EBSC, drawer 3, folder 4; Ellen B. Scripps to E. W. Scripps, La Jolla, October 24, 1922, EBSC, drawer 3, folder 4.

74. Ellen B. Scripps, diary, October 10, 1925, EBSC, drawer 24, folder 5; Ellen B. Scripps, diary, June 26, 1926, EBSC, drawer 24, folder 6.

75. Ralph D. Cornell to W. C. Crandall, Los Angeles, March 12, 1928, EBSC, drawer 14, folder 26.

76. J. C. Harper, memorandum, December 11, 1929, EBSC, drawer 26, folder 20.

77. J. C. Harper to George W. Marston, La Jolla, June 29, 1929, EBSC, drawer 14, folder 26.

78. Katharine Scripps to J. C. Harper, December 2, 1929, EBSC, drawer 14, folder 26.

79. Ralph D. Cornell to J. C. Harper, Los Angeles, October 16, 1929, EBSC, drawer 14, folder 27.

80. J. C. Harper to Ralph D. Cornell, October 19, 1929, EBSC, drawer 14, folder 26; Walsh, "Preserving 'Nature's Artistry,'" 45.

81. Slaymaker, "El Descansadero," 12–14.

82. Ellen B. Scripps, accounting diary, January 3, February 16, 23, May 19, July 12, October 4, 1924, EBSC, drawer 7, folder 9; Ellen B. Scripps, diary, April 9, 1923, EBSC, drawer 24, folder 3.

83. Ellen B. Scripps, diary, April 22, 1923, EBSC, drawer 24, folder 3; unidentified newspaper article, 700 Prospect Street, street file: Prospect Street, LJHS; "Miss Ellen Scripps Formally Opens Her Lath House Flower Garden, Tea Room," *San Diego Union*, April 25, 1924; Ellen B. Scripps, diary, April 22, 1924, EBSC, drawer 24, folder 4.

84. Ellen B. Scripps to Eliza Virginia Scripps, La Jolla, November 3, 1920, EBSC, drawer 3, folder 21.

85. Ellen B. Scripps to Eliza Virginia Scripps, La Jolla, July 5, 1920, EBSC, drawer 3, folder 21.

86. Ellen B. Scripps to Eliza Virginia Scripps, La Jolla, August 4, 1920, EBSC, drawer 3, folder 21.

87. Ellen B. Scripps to Eliza Virginia Scripps, La Jolla, August 9, 1920, EBSC, drawer 3, folder 21.

88. Ellen B. Scripps to Eliza Virginia Scripps, La Jolla, July 15, 1920, EBSC, drawer 3, folder 21.

89. Ellen B. Scripps to E. W. Scripps, La Jolla, April 5, 1922, EBSC, drawer 3, folder 2.

15. Educating Women

1. Katharine Peirce Scripps to Ada Peirce McCormick, Fresno, June 15, 1927, APMP, box 2666, folder 10.

2. Solomon, *In the Company of Educated Women*, 58, 62–63; Newcomer, *A Century of Higher Education*, 46.

3. Mary B. Eyre, "A Few Memories of Miss Scripps' Views of Education for Women," October 18, 1935, EBSC, drawer 1, folder 1.

4. "Memoranda of Conference between J. C. Harper and Mary B. Eyre," EBSC, drawer 37, EBS biographical material C–H.

5. Ellen B. Scripps to Virginia Scripps, July 26, 1920, EBSC, drawer 3, folder 21.

6. Ellen B. Scripps to E. W. Scripps, La Jolla, August 11, 1925, EBSC, drawer 3, folder 11.

7. J. C. Harper to E. W. Scripps, La Jolla, December 2, 1921, OH MSS 117, series 1.1, box 38, folder 11.

8. Ellen B. Scripps, diary, August 3, 1921, EBSC, drawer 24, folder 1; Ellen B. Scripps to Frances Louisa Scripps, La Jolla, April 19, 1921, EBSC, drawer 3, folder 26.

9. J. C. Harper to Ellen B. Scripps, November 26, 1929, EBSC, drawer 26, folder 20; J. C. Harper to William E. Scripps, La Jolla, September 27, 1929, EBSC, drawer 26, folder 20.

10. Ellen B. Scripps to Eliza Virginia Scripps, La Jolla, October 23, 1920, EBSC, drawer 3, folder 21.

11. Ellen B. Scripps to E. W. Scripps, La Jolla, January 24, 1922, EBSC, drawer 3, folder 2.

12. Ellen B. Scripps to E. W. Scripps, La Jolla, June 12, 1922, EBSC, drawer 3, folder 3.

13. "Izetta Says: H.G. Insists She's Just 'An Old Timer'!," *La Jolla Light*, October 14, 1960; Hilda Gardner, biographical subject file, LJHS.

14. Ellen B. Scripps to Mrs. Weston, July 5, 1915, LJHS drawer 3, folder 59.

15. Nackey Scripps to E. W. Scripps, La Jolla, September 10, 1922, OH MSS 117, series 1.1, box 38, folder 16.

16. Ellen B. Scripps to E. W. Scripps, La Jolla, November 7, 1922, EBSC, drawer 3, folder 5.

17. Ellen B. Scripps to E. W. Scripps, La Jolla, June 13, 1923, EBSC, drawer 3, folder 6.

18. Katharine Peirce Scripps to Ada Peirce McCormick, Fresno, June 15, 1927, APMP, box 2666, folder 10.

19. "Memoranda of Conference between J. C. Harper and Mary B. Eyre," EBSC, drawer 37, EBS biographical material C–H.

20. Ellen B. Scripps, diary, August 20, September 13, 1907, EBSC, drawer 23, folder 11; Ellen B. Scripps, diary, November 11, 1908, EBSC, drawer 23, folder 12.

21. Sumner, *The Story of Pomona College*, 10, 119.

22. Ellen B. Scripps, diary, November 19, 20, 1908, EBSC, drawer 23, folder 12; George A. Gates to Ellen B. Scripps, Claremont, November 19, 1908, EBSC, drawer 29, folder 18. See also Wright, *Claremont Women*, 87–108.

23. Sumner, *The Story of Pomona College*, 335; Ellen B. Scripps, diary, November 21, 1908, EBSC, drawer 23, folder 12.

24. "Joseph Horsfall Johnson Lectureship," *Pomona College Quarterly Magazine* 3, no. 1 (October 1914): 22–24; "The Johnson Foundation," *Pomona College Quarterly Magazine* 7, no. 3 (March 1919): 89–91, 128–30; Ellen B. Scripps, accounting diary, memoranda, EBSC, drawer 6, folder 34; Ellen B. Scripps, diary, April 29, 1915, EBSC, drawer 23, folder 19.

25. Ellen B. Scripps, diary, May 17, August 21, 1909, EBSC, drawer 23, folder 13; Ellen B. Scripps, diary, September 20, 25, 29, 30, 1911, EBSC, drawer 23, folder 15.

26. "Women Playing Important Part in Life of La Jolla," *San Diego Evening Tribune*, July 4, 1908, 5; Ellen B. Scripps to E. W. Scripps, La Jolla, September 29, 1924, EBSC, drawer 3, folder 9.

27. Sumner, *The Story of Pomona College*, 328; Chandler and Lee, *The History of New Ipswich*, 635; Charles C. Stearns to E. W. Scripps, Claremont, September 25, [1909], OH MSS 117, series 1.1, box 29, folder 4.

28. Ellen B. Scripps, diary, December 13, 1914, EBSC, drawer 23, folder 18.

29. James A. Blaisdell to Ellen B. Scripps, Claremont, October 29, 1919, EBSC, drawer 30, folder 32.

30. James A. Blaisdell to Ellen B. Scripps, Claremont, October 29, 1919, EBSC, drawer 30, folder 32.

31. James A. Blaisdell to Ellen B. Scripps, Claremont, January 2, 1920, EBSC, drawer 30, folder 32.

32. J. C. Harper to James A. Blaisdell, Cleveland, September 27, 1920, EBSC, drawer 30, folder 32.

33. Ellen B. Scripps to Eliza Virginia Scripps, February 22, 1921, EBSC, drawer 3, folder 22.

34. Ellen B. Scripps, diary, February 21–23, 1921, EBSC, drawer 24, folder 1; Sumner, *The Story of Pomona College,* 120; "The Development of the Past Ten Years," 84, 87–88, 105–21.

35. James A. Blaisdell to Ellen B. Scripps (excerpt), October 3, 1923, EBSC, drawer 29, folder 18.

36. Stevens, *A Bishop Beloved,* 41.

37. James A. Blaisdell to J. C. Harper, Claremont, May 3, 1923, EBSC, drawer 30, folder 32.

38. J. C. Harper, memorandum, "Purchase of Additional Land," March 31, 1934, EBSC, drawer 29, folder 18.

39. J. C. Harper, memorandum, "Purchase of Additional Land," March 31, 1934, EBSC, drawer 29, folder 18.

40. J. C. Harper, conference with Dr. Blaisdell, March 6, 1934, EBSC, drawer 29, folder 18.

41. Ellen B. Scripps to E. W. Scripps, January 21, 1925 (copy), EBSC, drawer 3, folder 10.

42. "The Development of the Past Ten Years," 94.

43. Fitts, "Registration 1922–1923," 12.

44. James A. Blaisdell to J. C. Harper, November 6, 1924 (copy), EBSC, drawer 29, folder 18.

45. J. C. Harper to James A. Blaisdell, November 8, 1924 (copy), EBSC, drawer 29, folder 18.

46. James A. Blaisdell to J. C. Harper, November 15, 1924 (copy), EBSC, drawer 29, folder 18 and EBSC, drawer 32, folder 22.

47. Ellen B. Scripps, diary, November 18–20, 1924, EBSC, drawer 24, folder 4.

48. Ellen B. Scripps, diary, April 27, June 23, July 25, 1925, EBSC, drawer 26, folder 20.

49. J. C. Harper, conference with Dr. Blaisdell, March 6, 1934, EBSC, drawer 29, folder 18.

50. Ellen B. Scripps, diary, October 22, 1925, EBSC, drawer 24, folder 5; J. C. Harper, memorandum, October 21, 1925, EBSC, drawer 26, folder 20.

51. Memo to the trustees of Scripps College, 1932, EBSC, drawer 29, folder 18.

52. J. C. Harper to Mrs. Seline Rossell, La Jolla, March 22, 1926, EBSC, drawer 13, folder 17; "In California."

53. J. C. Harper, excerpt from meeting of board of trustees, May 24, 1926, EBSC, drawer 29, folder 18.

54. Scripps College, 1924–46, EBSC, drawer 30, folders 34–45; Scripps College, 1924–46, EBSC, drawer 3, folders 1–34; Scripps College, 1924–46, EBSC, drawer 32, folders 1–41; Scripps College, 1924–46, EBSC, drawer 33, folders 1–6.

55. J. C. Harper, memo, EBSC, 29/18.

56. Memo to the trustees of Scripps College, 1932, EBSC, drawer 29, folder 18.

57. Ellen B. Scripps to Margaret Fowler, La Jolla, March 14, 1927, EBSC, drawer 13, folder 18.

58. Memo to the trustees of Scripps College, 1932, EBSC, drawer 29, folder 18; Mary Patterson Routt, "Facts, Folks, and Fancies," *Beverly Hills Citizen,* August 11, 1932.

59. Ellen B. Scripps, diary, October 14, 1927, EBSC, drawer 24, folder 7.

60. Ava B. Blank to J. C. Harper, Los Angeles, February 20, 1936, EBSC, drawer 29, folder 18.

61. Memo to the trustees of Scripps College, 1932, EBSC, drawer 29, folder 18; Ellen B. Scripps, diary, April 23, 1928, EBSC, drawer 24, folder 8; Anderson, "Miss Scripps and Her College," 22; "North Shore Notes," *San Diego Union,* April 30, 1928.

62. Ellen B. Scripps, diary, November 3, 1927, EBSC, drawer 24, folder 7.

63. "Scholarship Gift for Girls from Mrs. Burnham," *San Diego Union,* January 31, 1933; "Scripps College Scholarship Is Offer for Girls," *San Diego Union,* February 12, 1933.

64. Lyon, *The History of Pomona College,* 247.

65. Lyon, *The History of Pomona College,* 281; Britt, "Ellen Browning Scripps: Far Sighted Humanitarian," 30.

66. Ellen B. Scripps to Robert P. Scripps and J. C. Harper, La Jolla, May 7, 1930, EBSC, drawer 13, folder 18; Ellen B. Scripps to J. C. Harper, La Jolla, June 8, 1931, EBSC, drawer 13, folder 18.

67. J. C. Harper, memorandum, La Jolla, February 25, 1928, EBSC, drawer 26, folder 20.

68. Memo to the trustees of Scripps College, 1932, EBSC, drawer 29, folder 18.

69. W. C. Crandall to Robert P. Scripps, March 24, 1939, EBSC, drawer 20, folder 26.

70. Minutes of the meeting of the Honorary Alumnae Association of Scripps College, Los Angeles, October 17, 1931, EBSC, drawer 29, folder 18.

71. Ellen B. Scripps to Thomas Scripps, La Jolla, May 4, 1928, EBSC, drawer 1, folder 45; Ellen B. Scripps to William A. Scripps, La Jolla, September 23, 1928 (draft), EBSC, drawer 1, folder 45.

72. J. C. Harper, memorandum, December 10, 1928, EBSC, drawer 26, folder 20.

73. "Scripps Will Be Buried at Sea," *Cleveland Plain Dealer,* March 14, 1926.

74. J. C. Harper, memorandum, March 22, 1926, EBSC, drawer 26, folder 20.

75. J. C. Harper, memorandum, April 12, 1926, EBSC, drawer 26, folder 20.

76. J. C. Harper, memorandum, September 27, October 29, 1928, EBSC, drawer 26, folder 20.

77. "Scripps Will Made Public," *Riverside Daily Press*, March 31, 1926, 1; E. W. Scripps to Ellen B. Scripps, *Kemah*, Annapolis, September 23, 1922, EBSC, drawer 3, folder 4.

78. E. W. Scripps, "Considering the interest of Jim's estate," January 20, 1921, OU MSS 117, series 4, box 5, vol. 9; E. W. Scripps to Ellen B. Scripps, *Ohio* en route to Miami, November 25, 1922, EBSC, drawer 3, folder 5. Ellen wrote that E. W. admired Josephine's "qualities of mind. He says he has never met another woman who has the grasp and understanding of intricate and involved business and ethical matters." Ellen B. Scripps to Eliza Virginia Scripps, La Jolla, March 27, 1921, EBSC, drawer 3, folder 22.

79. E. W. Scripps to Ellen B. Scripps, *Ohio* en route to Honolulu, March 12, 1923, EBSC, drawer 3, folder 6. In 1926 Josephine filed an unsuccessful lawsuit to recover approximately $10 million, claiming that her deceased husband had an unwritten "partnership" agreement with his father. Trimble, *The Astonishing Mr. Scripps*, 511; Ellen B. Scripps, diary, August 10, 1926, EBSC, drawer 24, folder 6.

80. Ellen B. Scripps to E. W. Scripps, La Jolla, October 23, 1921, EBSC, drawer 3, folder 1.

81. Ellen B. Scripps to E. W. Scripps, La Jolla, September 5, 1925, EBSC, drawer 3, folder 11.

82. "Memoranda of Conference between J. C. Harper and Mary B. Eyre," EBSC, drawer 37, EBS biographical material C–H.

Conclusion

1. Hilda Gardner, notes, June 7, 1956, EBSC, drawer 1, folder 41; Katharine Peirce Scripps to Ada Peirce McCormick, Fresno, June 15, 1927, APMP, box 2666, folder 10; "Memoranda of Conference between J. C. Harper and Mary B. Eyre," EBSC, drawer 37, EBS biographical material C–H; "The Accession List of Miss Scripps' Private Library," EBSC, drawer 20, folder 27.

2. Ellen B. Scripps, diary, inside front cover, 1928, EBSC, drawer 24, folder 8; J. C. Harper, memorandum, November 6, 1928, EBSC, drawer 26, folder 20.

3. J. C. Harper, biographical notes, September 1, 1928, EBSC, drawer 1, folder 13.

4. "$1,000 Is Added to Mission Fund by Miss Scripps," *San Diego Union*, February 13, 1930.

5. Ellen B. Scripps, accounting diary, April 3, October 19, 1924, EBSC, drawer 7, folder 9.

6. Ellen B. Scripps, accounting diary, March 11, June 18, September 11, 1929, EBSC, drawer 7, folder 14.

7. Ellen B. Scripps, accounting diary, June 13, 1925, EBSC, drawer 7, folder 10.

8. E. W. Scripps to Ellen B. Scripps, *Kemah* on James River, April 22, 1922, EBSC,

drawer 3, folder 2; E. W. Scripps to Ellen B. Scripps, *Kemah* off Annapolis, May 12, 1922, EBSC, folder 3, drawer 3.

9. J. C. Harper, memorandum, June 1, 1931, EBSC, drawer 26, folder 20; Hollins, "'Until Kingdom Come,'" 123–38.

10. J. C. Harper, memorandum, March 7, 1929, EBSC, drawer 26, folder 20. Ellen declined to provide an endowment for the upkeep of her house and gardens, although she was sad to think that they might be neglected after her death. J. C. Harper, memorandum, November 12, 1929, EBSC, drawer 26, folder 20.

11. Isabel F. Smith to J. C. Harper, New York, February 1, 1936, EBSC, drawer 29, folder 18.

12. Robert F. Paine to J. C. Harper, San Francisco, June 6, 1933, EBSC, drawer 1, folder 10.

13. Dr. James W. Sherrill to Robert P. Scripps, June 6, 1932, EBSC, drawer 1, folder 45.

14. Ellen B. Scripps to E. W. Scripps, La Jolla, November 21, 1925, EBSC, drawer 3, folder 12; J. C. Harper, memorandum, March 12, 1929, EBSC, drawer 26, folder 20.

15. J. C. Harper, memorandum, May 30, 1931, EBSC, drawer 26, folder 20.

16. Dr. James W. Sherrill to J. C. Harper, La Jolla, March 4, 1932, EBSC, drawer 1, folder 45; "Ellen Scripps Passes Away in La Jolla," *San Diego Union*, August 3, 1932; Hilda Gardner, notes, June 7, 1956, EBSC, drawer 1, folder 41.

17. "Miss Ellen Scripps Dies at Age of 95," *New York Times*, August 4, 1932.

18. "A Modern Mid-Victorian," *New York Times*, August 5, 1932.

19. "Ellen Scripps Passes Away in La Jolla," *San Diego Union*, August 3, 1932.

20. Ellen B. Scripps to E. W. Scripps, La Jolla, October 6, 1925, EBSC, drawer 3, folder 12. Unitarian clergyman Edward Everett Hale, at eighty-six years old, said, "Look up and not down, / Look forward and not back, / Look out and not in, / And lend a hand." Cited in Chaffin, "Old Age."

BIBLIOGRAPHY

Archives and Manuscript Materials

APMP	Ada Peirce McCormick Papers, 1850–1998, Special Collections, Raymond H. Fogler Library, University of Maine, Orono ME.
EBSC	Ellen Browning Scripps Collection, Ella Strong Denison Library, Scripps College, Claremont CA.
FWKC	F. W. Kellogg Collection, Altadena Historical Society, Altadena CA.
HM	Manuscripts Collection, Huntington Library, San Marino CA.
IJGP	Irving John Gill Papers, Architecture and Design Collection, Art, Design & Architecture Museum, University of California, Santa Barbara.
JESP	James E. Scripps Papers, 1858–1940, Bentley Historical Library, University of Michigan, Ann Arbor MI.
LJHS	La Jolla Historical Society, La Jolla CA.
LJWC	La Jolla Woman's Club, La Jolla CA.
OU MSS 117	E. W. Scripps Collection, 1868–1926, Robert E. and Jean R. Mahn Center for Archives & Special Collections, Ohio University Libraries, Athens OH.
OU MSS 119	Vance H. Trimble Papers on E. W. Scripps Biography, Robert E. and Jean R. Mahn Center for Archives & Special Collections, Ohio University Libraries, Athens OH.
PAS/SC	Patricia A. Schaelchlin / Scripps Family Research Collection, Ella Strong Denison Library, Scripps College, Claremont CA.
RHP	Robert Henri Papers, 1857–1958, American Literature Collection, Beinecke Rare Book and Manuscript Library, Yale University, New Haven CT.
SDHC	San Diego History Center, Research Library, San Diego CA.
SIO	Scripps Institution of Oceanography Archives, the Library, University of California, San Diego CA.

Published Works

Adams, Edward E. "Collusion and Price Fixing in the American Newspaper Industry: Market Preservation Trends, 1890–1910." *J&MC Quarterly* 79, no. 2 (Summer 2002): 416–26.

———. "How Corporate Ownership Facilitated a Split in the Scripps Newspaper Empire." *Journalism History* 27, no. 2 (Summer 2001): 56–63.

———. "Josephine Scripps: An Early Corporate Newspaper Pioneer." *Southwestern Mass Communication Journal* 14, no. 2 (Winter 1999): 81–92.

———. "The Newspaper Business and Anti-competitive Practices during the Gilded Age: A National Trend." *Southwestern Mass Communication Journal* 11, no. 2 (Spring 1996): 30–42.

———. "Secret Combinations and Collusive Agreements: The Scripps Newspaper Empire and the Early Roots of Joint Operating Agreements." *J&MC Quarterly* 73, no. 1 (Spring 1996): 195–205.

Adams, Edward E., and Gerald J. Baldasty. "Syndicated Service Dependence and a Lack of Commitment to Localism: Scripps Newspapers and Market Subordination." *J&MC Quarterly* 78, no. 3 (Autumn 2001): 519–32.

Adams, H. Austin. *The Man John D. Spreckels.* San Diego: Frye & Smith, 1924.

Addams, Jane. *The Spirit of Youth and the City Streets.* New York: Macmillan, 1921.

Albanese, Catherine L. *A Republic of Mind and Spirit: A Cultural History of American Metaphysical Religion.* New Haven: Yale University Press, 2006.

Allswang, John M. *The Initiative and Referendum in California, 1898–1998.* Palo Alto: Stanford University Press, 2000.

Alonso, Harriet Hyman. *Peace as a Women's Issue: A History of the U.S. Movement for World Peace and Women's Rights.* Syracuse: Syracuse University Press, 1993.

Altholz, Josef L. "The Warfare of Conscience with Theology." The Victorian Web. http://www.victorianweb.org/religion/altholz/a2.html.

Anderson, Caroline Bennett. "Miss Scripps and Her College." In *The Humanities at Scripps College: Views and Reviews,* 16–23. Los Angeles: Ward Ritchie, 1952.

Ashcraft, William Michael. "'The Dawn of the New Cycle': Point Loma Theosophists and American Culture, 1896–1929." PhD dissertation, University of Virginia, 1995.

Attie, Jeanie. *Patriotic Toil: Northern Women and the American Civil War.* Ithaca: Cornell University Press, 1998.

Baillie, Hugh. *High Tension: The Recollections of Hugh Baillie.* Freeport NY: Books for Libraries Press, 1970.

Baldasty, Gerald J. "Centralizing Control in Newspaper Chains." *American Journalism* 18, no. 2 (2001): 13–38.

———. *The Commercialization of News in the Nineteenth Century.* Madison: University of Wisconsin Press, 1992.

———. "The Economics of Working-Class Journalism: The E. W. Scripps Newspaper Chain." *Journalism History* 25, no. 1 (Spring 1999): 3–12.

————. *E. W. Scripps and the Business of Newspapers*. Champaign: University of Illinois Press, 1999.

————. "E. W. Scripps Papers Provide an Important Journalistic Window for Scholars." *American Journalism* 16, no. 1 (1999): 133–41.

Baldasty, Gerald J., and Myron K. Jordan. "Scripps' Competitive Strategy: The Art of Non-competition." *Journalism Quarterly* 70, no. 2 (Summer 1993): 265–75.

Bartoli, James. "Adventurers, Bandits, Soldiers of Fortune, Spies and Revolutionaries: Recalling the Baja California Insurrection of 1911 One Hundred Years Later." *Journal of San Diego History* 58, nos. 1–2 (Winter/Spring 2012): 71–102.

Beasley, Maurine Hoffman. *The First Women Washington Correspondents*. Washington DC: George Washington University, 1976.

Beatty, Jack. *Colossus: How the Corporation Changed America*. New York: Broadway Books, 2001.

Bednarowski, Mary F. *New Religions and the Theological Imagination in America*. Bloomington: Indiana University Press, 1989.

————. "Outside the Mainstream: Women's Religion and Women Religious Leaders in Nineteenth Century America." *Journal of the American Academy of Religion* 48 (1980): 207–31.

Bellamy, Edward. *Looking Backward, 2000–1887*. New York: New American Library / Signet, 1960.

Bemis, Fred P. "A New Substitute for Saloons." *Playground* 5, no. 11 (February 1912): 370–72.

Bennion, Sherilyn Cox. *Equal to the Occasion: Women Editors of the Nineteenth-Century West*. Reno: University of Las Vegas Press, 1990.

Bernard, Robert J. *Ellen Browning Scripps, Woman of Vision*. Claremont CA: Scripps College, 1959.

Besant, Annie. *The Laws of Higher Life*. Adyar: Theosophical Publishing House, 1903.

Bevir, Mark. "Annie Besant's Quest for Truth: Christianity, Secularism, and New Age Thought." Alpheus. http://www.alpheus.org/html/articles/theosophy/bevir 3.html.

Bicknell, C[larence]. *Flowering Plants and Ferns of the Riviera and Neighbouring Mountains*. London: Trübner & Co., 1885.

Black, Samuel F. *San Diego and Imperial Counties, California*. Vol. 1. Chicago: S. J. Clarke, 1913.

Blair, Karen J. *The Clubwoman as Feminist: True Womanhood Redefined, 1868–1914*. New York: Holmes & Meier, 1980.

————. *The Torchbearers: Women and Their Amateur Arts Associations in America, 1890–1930*. Bloomington: Indiana University Press, 1994.

Blavatsky, Helena Petrova. *The Key to Theosophy*. London: Theosophical Publishing, 1889.

Boyer, M. Christine. *Dreaming the Rational City: The Myth of American City Planning*. Cambridge MA: MIT Press, 1983.

Boyer, Paul. *Urban Masses and Moral Order in America, 1820–1920*. Cambridge MA: Harvard University Press, 1978.

Brandes, Raymond S. *San Diego Architects, 1868–1939*. San Diego: University of San Diego, 1991.

Braude, Ann. *Radical Spirits: Spiritualism and Women's Rights in Nineteenth-Century America*. Boston: Beacon Press, 1989.

Bridges, Amy. *Municipal Reform in the Southwest*. Princeton: Princeton University Press, 1997.

Britt, Albert. "Ellen Browning Scripps: Far Sighted Humanitarian." In *The Humanities at Scripps College*, 24–34. Los Angeles: W. Ritchie, 1952.

———. *Ellen Browning Scripps: Journalist and Idealist*. Oxford: Printed for Scripps College at the University Press, 1960.

Brueggeman, Peter. "History of the Scripps Institution of Oceanography Library." September 2000. http://scilib.ucsd.edu/sio/hist/library_history_brueggeman.pdf.

Buhle, Mari Jo. *Women and American Socialism, 1870–1920*. Urbana: University of Illinois Press, 1981.

Burlingame, Michael. *Abraham Lincoln: A Life*. Vol. 1. Baltimore: Johns Hopkins University Press, 2008.

Calhoun, Charles W., ed. *The Gilded Age: Perspectives on the Origins of Modern America*. Lanham MD: Rowman & Littlefield, 2007.

Campbell, Bruce F. *Ancient Wisdom Revived: A History of the Theosophical Movement*. Berkeley: University of California Press, 1980.

Campbell, W. Joseph. *Yellow Journalism: Puncturing the Myths, Defining the Legacies*. Westport CT: Praeger, 2001.

Carnegie, Andrew. "Wealth." *North American Review* 148, no. 391 (June 1889): 653–65.

Carpenter, Ford A. "The Climate of the Open Door." *Overland Monthly* 59, no. 3 (March 1912): 249–51.

Carter, Nancy Carol. "When Dr. Fairchild Visited Miss Sessions: San Diego 1919." *Journal of San Diego History* 50, no. 3 (Summer/Fall 2004): 75–89.

Cartwright, Derrick R. "Robert Henri's San Diego." In *Behold, America! Art of the United States from Three San Diego Museums*, edited by Amy Galpin, 224–43. San Diego: San Diego Museum of Art and D.A.P., New York, 2012.

Casserly, Jack. *Scripps: The Divided Dynasty*. New York: Donald I. Fine, 1993.

Chaffin, W. L. "Old Age." *Christian Register* 89, no. 47 (November 24, 1910): 1247.

Chambers, W. Lee. "Bibliographical Notes on Dawson's Birds of California." *Condor* 41, no. 6 (November 1939): 231–43.

Chandler, Charles Henry, and Sarah Fiske Lee. *The History of New Ipswich, New Hampshire, 1735–1914*. Fitchburg MA: Sentinel Printing, 1914.

Chandler, Robert J. "In the Van: Spiritualists as Catalysts for the California Women's Suffrage Movement." *California History* 73, no. 3 (Fall 1994): 188–201.

Chapman, Mary. *Making Noise, Making News: Suffrage Print and Culture and U.S. Modernism.* New York: Oxford University Press, 2014.

Ciani, Kyle E. "The Power of Maternal Love: Negotiating a Child's Care in Progressive-Era San Diego." *Journal of the West* 41, no. 4 (Fall 2002): 71–79.

———. "Revelations of a Reformer: Helen D. Marston Beardsley and Progressive Social Activism." *Journal of San Diego History* 50, nos. 3 and 4 (2004): 102–23.

City of San Diego and Marie Burke Lia & Associates. "Revised Draft: East Village Combined Historical Surveys 2005" (January 2005). https://www.sandiego.gov /sites/default/files/legacy/planning/programs/historical/pdf/surveydocs/eastvillage survey.pdf.

Clift, Elayne, ed. *Women, Philanthropy, and Social Change: Visions for a Just Society.* Medford MA: Tufts University Press, 2005.

Colgan, Chuck. *80 Years: Scripps Institution of Oceanography. A Historical Overview, 1903–1983.* La Jolla CA: Scripps Institution of Oceanography of the University of California, 1983. https://web.archive.org/web/20130620051746/http://scilib .ucsd.edu/sio/hist/80yearssio.pdf.

Cooney, Robert P. J., Jr. "California Women Suffrage Centennial: A Brief Summary of the 1911 Campaign." California Secretary of State. http://www.sos.ca.gov /elections/celebrating-womens-suffrage/california-women-suffrage-centennial/.

Cott, Nancy F. *The Grounding of Modern Feminism.* New Haven: Yale University Press, 1987.

Cowan, John F. "Investments in Humanity: How Miss Scripps Is Giving Away $30,000,000." *Success Magazine,* July 1924, 47, 110–11.

Croly, Jane Cunningham. *The History of the Woman's Club Movement in America.* New York: Henry G. Allen, 1898.

Davis, Mike. "The Next Little Dollar." In *Under the Perfect Sun: The San Diego Tourists Never See,* edited by Mike Davis, Kelly Mayhew, and Jim Miller, 17–144. New York: New Press, 2005.

Dawson, William Leon. *The Birds of California: A Complete, Scientific and Popular Account of the 580 Species and Sub-species of Birds Found in the State.* 4 vols. Los Angeles: Birds of California Publishing Co., 1921.

Day, Deborah. "Aspects of the Relationship of the Scripps Institution of Oceanography and the State of California." La Jolla CA: UCSD Libraries, 2001. https://web.archive .org/web/20130620041650/http://scilib.ucsd.edu/sio/hist/Day_Scripps_and_State .pdf.

———. "Early History of Collections at Scripps Institution of Oceanography." La Jolla CA: UCSD Libraries, 2004. https://web.archive.org/web/20130620034456/http:// scilib.ucsd.edu/sio/hist/Day_Early_History_of_Collections.pdf.

———. "Scripps Benefactions: The Role of the Scripps Family in the Founding of the Scripps Institution of Oceanography." La Jolla CA: UCSD Libraries, 2002.

https://web.archive.org/web/20130620072553/http://scilib.ucsd.edu/sio/hist/day
_scripps_benefactions.pdf.

"A Day's Possibilities in 'The San Diego Bay Region.'" *Sunset Magazine* 5, no. 4 (August 1900): 163–66.

Debs, Eugene V. "Jesus, the Supreme Leader." In *Labor and Freedom: The Voice and Pen of Eugene V. Debs*, edited by Will Jonson, 22–29. St. Louis: Phil Wagner, 1916.

Delbanco, Andrew. *The Abolitionist Imagination*. Cambridge MA: Harvard University Press, 2012.

Descendants of La Jolla's Black Pioneers. *La Jolla, California Black Pioneers and Pioneer Descendants, 1880–1974*. San Diego: Privately printed, 2010.

"The Development of the Past Ten Years." *Pomona College Quarterly Magazine* 9, no. 3 (March 1921): 84, 87–88, 105–21.

Dexter, Ralph W. "History of American Marine Biology and Marine Biological Institutions Introduction: Origins of American Marine Biology." *American Zoologist* 28, no. 1 (1988): 3–6.

"The Diagnostic Hospital." *Trained Nurse and Hospital Review* 58, no. 5 (May 1917): 282.

Diehl, Robert Warren. "To Speak or Not to Speak: San Diego 1912." MA thesis, University of San Diego, 1976.

Dillon, Michael. "'Satanic Journalism and Its Fate': The Scripps Chain Strikes Out in Buffalo." *American Journalism* 20, no. 2 (2003): 57–82.

Directory of San Diego City and County for 1893–94. San Diego: John Thorn, 1893.

Drowner, Margaret S. "Petrie, Sir (William Matthew) Flinders (1853–1942)." In *Oxford Dictionary of National Biography*, edited by H. C. G. Matthew and Brian Harrison. New York: Oxford University Press, 2004. http://0-wwwdnb.com.sally.sandiego.edu/view/article/35496.

Dyche, Grace Locke Scripps. "John Locke Scripps, Lincoln's Biographer." *Journal of the Illinois State Historical Society* 17, no. 3 (October 1924): 333–51.

Dyson, Howard F. "Frederick in 1859." http://schuyler.illinoisgenweb.org/OldTimesInSchuyler/otisfrederickin1859.html.

Eastman, Max. *Understanding Germany, The Only Way to End War, and Other Essays*. New York: M. Kennerley, 1916.

Eastman, Sarita. *Good Company: The Story of Scripps Health and Its People*. San Diego: Scripps Health, 2012.

Eddy, Mary Baker. *Science and Health with Key to the Scriptures*. Boston: First Church of Christ, Scientist, 1917.

"The Education of Women." *Harper's New Monthly Magazine* 15, no. 90 (November 1857): 776–83.

Edwards, Gurden, ed. "The Alumni—1905." *University of California Chronicle* 9, no. 4 (October 1907): 386–405.

Edwards, Rebecca. *New Spirits: Americans in the Gilded Age, 1865–1905*. New York: Oxford University Press, 2006.

Edwards, William A., and Beatrice Harraden. *Two Health Seekers in Southern California.* Philadelphia: L. B. Lippincott Co., 1897.

"Ellen Browning Scripps and Knox College." *Knox Alumnus,* Summer 1959, 13–14.

Ellwood, Robert, and Catherine Wessinger. "The Feminism of 'Universal Brotherhood': Women in the Theosophical Movement." In *Women's Leadership in Marginal Religions: Explorations outside the Mainstream,* edited by Catherine Wessinger, 68–87. Urbana: University of Illinois Press, 1993.

Emerson, Ralph Waldo. "Progress of Culture." Address read before the Phi Beta Kappa Society at Cambridge, July 18, 1867. http://rwe.org/progress-of-culture/.

Engstrand, Iris, and Anne Bullard. *Inspired by Nature: The San Diego Natural History Museum after 125 Years.* San Diego: San Diego Natural History Museum, 1999.

Farmer, Silas. *History of Detroit and Wayne County and Early Michigan.* 3rd ed. New York: Silas Farmer, 1890.

Faust, Drew Gilpin. *This Republic of Suffering: Death and the American Civil War.* New York: Alfred A. Knopf, 2008.

Ferguson, C. E. "San Diego's Progressive Spirit." *Overland Monthly,* 2nd ser., 54, no. 3 (March 1912): 261.

Fisher, Colin. "African Americans, Outdoor Recreation, and the 1919 Chicago Race Riot." In *"To Love the Wind and the Rain": African Americans and Environmental History,* edited by Dianne D. Glave and Mark Stoll, 63–76. Pittsburgh: University of Pittsburg Press, 2006.

———. *Urban Green: Nature, Recreation, and the Working Class in Industrial Chicago.* Chapel Hill: University of North Carolina Press, 2015.

Fitts, Charles T. "Registration 1922–1923." *Pomona College Quarterly Magazine* 11, no. 1 (October 1922): 12–14.

Flanigan, Sylvia Kathleen. "William Sterling Hebbard, Consummate California Architect, 1888–1930." MA thesis, University of San Diego, 1985.

Fletcher, Colonel Ed. *Memoirs of Ed Fletcher.* San Diego: Privately printed, 1952.

Foust, James C. "E. W. Scripps and the Science Service." *Journalism History* 21, no. 2 (Summer 1995): 58–65.

Fuller, Margaret. *Woman in the Nineteenth Century.* Boston: Brown, Taggard and Chase, 1860.

Gagen, Elizabeth A. "Making America Flesh: Physicality and Nationhood in Early Twentieth-Century Physical Education Reform." *Cultural Geographies* 11 (2004): 417–42.

Gardner, Gilson. *Lusty Scripps: The Life of E. W. Scripps.* New York: Vanguard Press, 1932.

Gaudiani, Claire, and Graham Burnett. *Daughters of the Declaration: How Women Social Entrepreneurs Built the American Dream.* New York: Public Affairs, 2011.

Gavrilovich, Peter, and Bill McGraw. *The Detroit Almanac: 300 Years of Life in the Motor City.* Detroit: Detroit Free Press, 2000.

Giesberg, Judith Ann. *Civil War Sisterhood: The U.S. Sanitary Commission and Women's Politics in Transition.* Boston: Northeastern University Press, 2000.

Gilman, Arthur. "Women Who Go to College." *Century Magazine* 36 (1888): 717–18.

Ginzberg, Lori D. *Women and the Work of Benevolence: Morality, Politics, and Class in the Nineteenth-Century United States.* New Haven: Yale University Press, 1990.

Goldman, Emma. *Living My Life.* 2 vols. New York: Cosimo Inc., 2008.

Goodman, Cary. *Choosing Sides: Playground and Street Life on the Lower East Side.* New York: Schocken Books, 1979.

Goodspeed, Thomas W. "The Founding of the First University of Chicago." *University Record* 6, no. 4 (October 1920): 239–58.

Grayzel, Susan R. *Women and the First World War.* New York: Longman/Pearson, 2002.

Guinn, J. M. *A History of California and an Extended History of Its Southern Coast Counties.* Los Angeles: Historic Record, 1907.

Gullett, Gayle. *Becoming Citizens: The Emergence and Development of the California Women's Movement, 1880–1911.* Champaign: University of Illinois Press, 2000.

Haber, Samuel. "The Nightmare and the Dream: Edward Bellamy and the Travails of Socialist Thought." *Journal of American Studies* 36, no. 3 (December 2002): 417–40.

Hacker, Jacob S., and Paul Pierson. *Winner-Take-All Politics: How Washington Made the Rich Richer—and Turned Its Back on the Middle Class.* New York: Simon & Schuster, 2010.

Hall, Jerome Raymond. *The War—What For? The Underlying Causes of the War Madness in Europe.* Berkeley: University of California Press, 1914.

Hamilton, Andrea. *A Vision for Girls: Gender, Education, and the Bryn Mawr School.* Baltimore: Johns Hopkins University Press, 2004.

Hamilton, Mildred Nicholas. "'Continually Doing Good': The Philanthropy of Phoebe Apperson Hearst, 1862–1919." In *California Women and Politics: From the Gold Rush to the Great Depression,* edited by Robert W. Cherny, Mary Ann Irwin, and Ann Marie Wilson, 77–96. Lincoln: University of Nebraska Press, 2011.

Haney, David. "John Scripps: Circuit Rider and Newspaperman." *Western Illinois Regional Studies* 9, no. 2 (Fall 1986): 7–35.

Hanmer, Lee F. "A Playground Meeting with Real Play on the Program." *Playground* 5, no. 5 (August 1911): 176–79.

Harley, Fanny M. "A New Educator." *Washington News Letter* 7, no. 7 (1902): 433–35.

Haymond, Henry. *History of Harrison County, West Virginia.* Morgantown WV: Acme, 1910.

Heffron, Jeanne Marie. "Edward Willis Scripps and Scripps Ranch." MA thesis, University of San Diego, 1990.

Heilmann, Ann. *Feminist Forerunners: New Womanism and Feminism in the Early Twentieth Century.* London: Pandora, 2003.

Hepner, Frances K. *Ellen Browning Scripps: Her Life and Times.* San Diego: San Diego State College, 1966.

Hindman, Hugh D. *Child Labor: An American History.* Armonk NY: M. E. Sharpe, 2002.

Hines, Thomas S. *Irving Gill and the Architecture of Reform.* New York: Monacelli Press, 2000.

Hlebica, Joe. "The Biological Colony: Scripps Institution of Oceanography, 1916–1924." *Explorations* 10, no. 1 (2003): 20–27.

———. "Scripps Family, First Generation of Commitment." *Explorations* 10, no. 1 (2003): 12–19.

———. "William E. Ritter, Scripps Visionary Builds Foundation for Century of Oceanography." *Explorations* 10, no. 1 (2003): 4–11.

Hollins, Jeremy. "'Until Kingdom Come': The Design and Construction of the La Jolla Children's Pool." *Journal of San Diego History* 51, nos. 3–4 (Summer/Fall 2005): 123–38.

Hornung, Erik. *Akhenaten and the Religion of Life*. Translated by David Lorton. Ithaca: Cornell University Press, 1999.

Horowitz, Helen Lefkowitz. *Alma Mater: Design and Experience in the Women's Colleges from Their Nineteenth-Century Beginnings to the 1930s*. New York: Alfred A. Knopf, 1964.

———. "Designing for Genders: Curricula and Architecture at Scripps College and the California Institute of Technology." *Pacific Historical Review* 54, no. 4 (November 1985): 439–61.

Hunter, Fred. "Harraden, Beatrice (1864–1936)." In *Oxford Dictionary of National Biography*, edited by H. C. G. Matthew and Brian Harrison. New York: Oxford University Press, 2004. http://0-www.oxforddnb.sally.sandiego.edu/view/article/33720.

"In California: Miss Ellen Scripps . . . Another Oxford Rises." *Time*, February 22, 1926, 20–22.

Johnson, Myrtle Elizabeth, and Harry James Snook. *Seashore Animals of the Pacific Coast*. New York: Macmillan, 1927.

"The Johnson Foundation." *Pomona College Quarterly Magazine* 7, no. 3 (March 1919): 89–91, 128–30.

Jones, Barbara Schillreff, ed. *The Complete Writings of Kate Sessions in "California Garden,"* *1909–1939*. San Diego: San Diego Floral Association, 1998.

Jones, Rufus. *Social Law in the Spiritual World: Studies in Human and Divine Inter-relationship*. Philadelphia: John C. Winston, 1904.

Jordy, William H. *Progressive and Academic Ideals at the Turn of the Twentieth Century*. New York: Oxford University Press, 1972.

"Joseph Horsfall Johnson Lectureship." *Pomona College Quarterly Magazine* 3, no. 1 (October 1914): 22–24.

Kamerling, Bruce. "Anna and Albert Valentien: The Arts and Crafts Movement in San Diego." *Journal of San Diego History* 24, no. 3 (Summer 1978): 343–66.

———. "Hebbard & Gill, Architects." *Journal of San Diego History* 36, nos. 2–3 (1990): 106–29.

———. "How Ellen Scripps Brought Ancient Egypt to San Diego." *Journal of San Diego History* 38, no. 2 (Spring 1992): 73–92.

———. *Irving J. Gill, Architect*. San Diego: San Diego Historical Society, 1993.

Kaplan, Richard L. "The Economics of Popular Journalism in the Gilded Age." *Journalism History* 21, no. 2 (Summer 1995): 65–79.

———. "Press, Paper, and the Public Sphere." *Media History* 21, no. 2 (2015): 42–54.

Kennedy, David M. *Over Here: The First World War and American Society.* New York: Oxford University Press, 1980.

Kessler, Carol Farley. *Daring to Dream: Utopian Fiction by United States Women before 1950.* Syracuse: Syracuse University Press, 1995.

King, Edith Shatto, and Frederick A. King. *Pathfinder Social Survey of San Diego.* San Diego: Labor Temple Press, 1914.

King, Tim. "The Edward W. Scripps Trust Ends." October 19, 2012. http://www.scripps.com/press-releases/821-the-edward-w-scripps-trust-ends.

Kingsley, Charles. *Glaucus: or The Wonders of the Shore.* London: Macmillan, 1855. http://www.gutenberg.org/files/695/695-0.txt.

Kirby, Gustavus T. "The Recreation Movement: Its Possibilities and Limitations." *Playground* 5, no. 7 (October 1911): 217–24.

Kirkley, Evelyn A. "'Equality of the Sexes, but . . .': Women in Point Loma Theosophy, 1899–1942." *Nova Religion: The Journal of Alternative and Emergent Religions* 1, no. 2 (April 1998): 272–88.

———. "'Starved and Treated like Convicts': Images of Women in Point Loma Theosophy." *Journal of San Diego History* 43, no. 1 (Winter 1997): 1–27.

Kisling, Vernon N., Jr., ed. *Zoo and Aquarium History: Ancient Animal Collections to Zoological Gardens.* New York: CRC Press, 2011.

Kneeland, Marilyn. "The Modern Boston Tea Party: The San Diego Suffrage Campaign of 1911." *Journal of San Diego History* 34, no. 4 (Fall 1977): 35–42.

Knight, Oliver, ed. *I Protest: Selected Disquisitions of E. W. Scripps.* Madison: University of Wisconsin Press, 1966.

Kornbluh, Joyce L., ed. *Rebel Voices: An IWW Anthology.* Chicago: C. H. Kerr, 2011.

"La Jolla by the Sea." *Land of Sunshine* 11, no. 7 (July 1899).

Leake, Paul. *History of Detroit.* 2 vols. Chicago: Lewis, 1912.

Lears, T. J. Jackson. *No Place of Grace: Antimodernism and the Transformation of American Culture, 1880–1920.* Chicago: University of Chicago Press, 1981.

———. *Rebirth of a Nation: The Making of Modern America, 1877–1920.* New York: HarperCollins, 2009.

Leasher, Evelyn, ed. *Letter from Washington, 1863–1865.* Detroit: Wayne State University Press, 1999.

Lee, Joseph. *Constructive and Preventive Philanthropy.* New York: Macmillan, 1913.

———. "Play as an Antidote to Civilization." *Playground* 5, no. 4 (July 1911): 110–26.

Lee, Lawrence B. "The Little Landers Colony of San Ysidro." *Journal of San Diego History* 21, no. 1 (Winter 1975): 26–51.

———. "William E. Smythe and San Diego, 1901–1908." *Journal of San Diego History* 19, no. 1 (Winter 1973): 10–24.

Leonard, John W., ed. *Who's Who in America, 1901–1902*. Chicago: A. N. Marquis, 1901.

Lewis, Robert. "'Well-Directed Play': Urban Recreation and Progressive Reform." In *Impressions of a Gilded Age: The American Fin de Siècle*, edited by Marc Chenetier and Rob Kroes, 183–202. Amsterdam: Amerika Instituut of University of Amsterdam, 1983.

Lightman, Bernard V. *Victorian Popularizers of Science: Designing Nature for New Audiences*. Chicago: University of Chicago Press, 2007.

Linder, Bruce. "Rear Admiral Roger Welles—San Diego's First 'Navy Mayor.'" *Journal of San Diego History* 49, no. 2 (Spring 2003): 53–70.

Lydekker, Richard. *The New Natural History*. New York: Merrill & Baker, 1890.

Lyon, E. Wilson. *The History of Pomona College, 1887–1969*. Claremont: Pomona College, 1977.

MacPhail, Elizabeth C. *Kate Sessions: Pioneer Horticulturist*. San Diego: San Diego Historical Society, 1976.

Marston, Mary Gilman. *George White Marston: A Family Chronicle*. 2 vols. Los Angeles: Ward Ritchie, 1956.

Martin, John. "Patriotism and Profit: San Diego's Camp Kearny." *Journal of San Diego History* 58, no. 4 (Fall 2012): 247–72.

Marzolf, Marion. *Up from the Footnote: A History of American Journalists*. New York: Hastings, 1977.

Matthews, Jean V. *The Rise of the New Woman: The Women's Movement in America, 1875–1930*. Chicago: Ivan R. Dee, 2003.

Maverick, Augustus. *Henry J. Raymond and the New York Press*. Hartford CT: A. S. Hale, 1870.

May, Ronald V., and Dale Ballou May. "Historical Nomination of Windemere, The John & Agnes Kendall / Joseph Falkenhan & Irving Gill Beach Cottage." State of California, Resources Agency, Department of Parks and Recreation, February 2010.

McCabe, Charles, ed. *Damned Old Crank: A Self-Portrait of E. W. Scripps Drawn from His Unpublished Writings*. New York: Harper & Brothers, 1951.

McCarthy, Kathleen D. *American Creed: Philanthropy and the Rise of Civil Society, 1700–1865*. Chicago: University of Chicago Press, 2005.

———. *Lady Bountiful Revisited: Women, Philanthropy, and Power*. New Brunswick: Rutgers University Press, 1990.

———. *Women, Philanthropy, and Civil Society*. Bloomington: Indiana University Press, 2001.

———. *Women's Culture: American Philanthropy and Art, 1830–1930*. Chicago: University of Chicago Press, 1991.

McClain, Molly. "The Bishop's School, 1909–2009." *Journal of San Diego History* 53, no. 4 (2008): 235–67.

———. "The La Jolla of Ellen Browning Scripps." *Journal of San Diego History* 57, no. 4 (Fall 2011): 273–92.

———. "The Scripps Family's San Diego Experiment." *Journal of San Diego History* 56, nos. 1–2 (2010): 1–30.

McCoy, Esther. *Five California Architects.* New York: Reinhold, 1960.

McGrew, Clarence Alan. *City of San Diego and San Diego County.* Vol. 2. Chicago: American Historical Society, 1922.

McKanan, Dan. *Prophetic Encounters: Religion and the American Radical Tradition.* Boston: Beacon Press, 2011.

McRae, Milton A. *Forty Years in Newspaperdom: The Autobiography of a Newspaper Man.* New York: Brentano, 1924.

McWilliams, Carey. *Southern California: An Island on the Land.* Salt Lake City: Peregrine Smith, 1973.

Meade, Rebecca J. *How the Vote Was Won: Woman Suffrage in the Western United States, 1868–1914.* New York: New York University Press, 2004.

Middlebrook, R. P. "The High Iron to La Jolla: The Story of a Railroad." *Journal of San Diego History* 7, no. 1 (January 1961), https://www.sandiegohistory.org /journal/61january/iron.htm.

Miller, Grace Louise. "The San Diego Progressive Movement, 1900–1920." MA thesis, UC Santa Barbara, 1976.

Miller, Jim. "Just Another Day in Paradise? An Episodic History of Rebellion and Repression in America's Finest City." In *Under the Perfect Sun: The San Diego Tourists Never See,* edited by Mike Davis, Kelly Mayhew, and Jim Miller, 169–77. New York: New Press, 2005.

Mills, Eric L. *The Scripps Institution: Origin of a Habitat for Ocean Science,* edited by Elizabeth N. Shor. San Diego: Scripps Institution of Oceanography, 1993.

Mills, Kay. *A Place in the News: From the Women's Pages to the Front Page.* New York: Dodd, Mead, 1988.

Mitchell, Thomas W. "The Republican Experiment and The Bishop's School." *Journal of San Diego History* 30, no. 2 (Spring 1984): 105–23.

———. *Reviewing the Vision: A Story of The Bishop's Schools.* San Diego: Privately printed, 1979.

Montserrat, Dominic. *Akhenaten: History, Fantasy and Ancient Egypt.* New York: Rout-ledge, 2000.

Moore, Dorothea. "The Work of the Women's Clubs in California." *Annals of the American Academy of Political and Social Science* 28 (September 1906): 59–62.

Morris, William. *News from Nowhere,* edited by Krishan Kumar. New York: Cambridge University Press, 1995.

Moulton, Robert H. "Painting under the Ocean." *Technical World Magazine* 19, no. 1 (March 1913): 49–51, 130, 132.

Moure, Nancy Dustin Wall. *The World of Zarh Pritchard.* Carmel CA: William A. Karges Fine Art, 1999.

Nasaw, David. *The Chief: The Life of William Randolph Hearst.* Boston: Houghton Mifflin, 2000.

Negley, Glenn Robert, and J. Max Patrick. *The Quest for Utopia.* New York: Schumann, 1952.

New, Rebecca S., and Moncrieff Cochran, eds. *Early Childhood Education: An International Encyclopedia.* Westport CT: Greenwood, 2007.

Newcomer, Mabel. *A Century of Higher Education for American Women.* New York: Harper, 1959.

"News of the Hospital Field." *Modern Hospital—Advertisements* 10, no. 1 (January 1918): 42–55.

Ninety-Seventh Annual Report of the Hawaiian Evangelical Association. Honolulu: Honolulu Star-Bulletin, 1919.

Nolen, John. *San Diego: A Comprehensive Plan for Its Improvement.* Boston: Geo. H. Ellis, 1908.

Northwest Reporter. St. Paul MN: West, 1910.

Olten, Carol, and Heather Kuhn. *Images of America: La Jolla.* Charleston SC: Arcadia, 2008.

O'Neill, Kate. "Schoolmarm in the City Room." *Michigan Quarterly Review* 3, no. 1 (Winter 1964): 18–22.

Onslow, Barbara. *Women of the Press in Nineteenth-Century Britain.* New York: St. Martin's, 2000.

Orcutt, Charles Russell, ed. *American Plants: Volume 2, Botany of Southern California.* San Diego: Privately printed, 1909.

Paine, Robert F. "Ellen Browning Scripps." In *The Story of Scripps-Howard: A Study in Personality, Policy and Achievement in Journalism.* Cincinnati OH: Scripps Howard, 1929.

———. "The Mother of Soul." *Scripps Howard News* 1, no. 2 (January 1927): 3–4.

Pauly, Philip J. *Biologists and the Promise of American Life: From Meriwether Lewis to Alfred Kinsey.* Princeton NJ: Princeton University Press, 2000.

Pennewell, Almer M. "John Scripps, Methodist Circuit Rider Extraordinary." *Journal of the Illinois State Historical Society* 53, no. 5 (Autumn 1965): 265–78.

Pollock, Robert. "The San Diego Diagnostic Group Clinic." *California State Journal of Medicine* 15, no. 4 (1917): 104.

Ponder, Stephen. "Partisan Reporting and Presidential Campaigning: Gilson Gardner and E. W. Scripps in the Election of 1912." *Journalism History* 17, nos. 1–2 (Spring/Summer 1990): 3–13.

Pooley, William V. *The Settlement of Illinois from 1830 to 1850.* Madison: University of Wisconsin, 1908.

Pourade, Richard F. *The History of San Diego.* 7 vols. San Diego: Union-Tribune, 1960–77.

Preece, Charles. *E. W. and Ellen Browning Scripps: An Unmatched Pair.* Chelsea MI: BookCrafters, 1990.

"Prospectus." *Metaphysical Magazine* 1, no. 1 (January 1895): i.

Rabban, David M. *Free Speech in Its Forgotten Years, 1870–1920.* New York: Cambridge University Press, 1999.

———. "The IWW Free Speech Fights and Popular Conceptions of Free Expression before World War I." *Virginia Law Review* 80, no. 5 (August 1994): 1055–158.

Raitt, Helen. "Give Us Room: First Installment of History of Scripps Institution of Oceanography." Radio KGB, December 17, 1961, 3, http://scilib.ucsd.edu/sio /hist/raitt_give_us_room.pdf.

Raitt, Helen, and Beatrice Moulton. *Scripps Institution of Oceanography.* Los Angeles: W. Ritchie, 1967.

Rakow, Lana F., and Cheris Kramarae, eds. *The Revolution in Words, Righting Women, 1868–1871.* New York: Routledge, 1990.

Randolph, Howard S. F. *La Jolla Year by Year.* La Jolla: Library Association of La Jolla, 1955.

Rannells, Nathan L. "La Jolla No. 1." *Journal of San Diego History* 4, no. 4 (October 1958). http://www.sandiegohistory.org/journal/58october/lajolla.htm.

Raymond, Jerome Hall. *European Capitals and Their Social Significance.* Berkeley: Lederer, Street & Zeus, 1914.

———. *The War—What For? The Underlying Causes of the War in Europe.* Berkeley: University of California Press, 1914.

Recchiuti, John Louis. *Civic Engagement: Social Science and Progressive-Era Reform in New York City.* Philadelphia: University of Pennsylvania Press, 2007.

Ritter, Mary Bennett. *More Than Gold in California, 1849–1933.* Berkeley: Professional Press, 1933.

Ritter, William E. "As to the Causes of Evolution." *Science,* n.s. 57, no. 1,481 (May 18, 1923): 583–85.

———. *Charles Darwin and the Golden Rule.* Washington DC: Science Service, 1954.

———. *The Marine Biological Station of San Diego.* San Diego: Frye and Smith, 1910.

———. "The Marine Biological Station of San Diego." *University of California Publications in Zoology* 9, no. 4 (1912): 137–48.

———. "Mechanical Ideas in the Last Hundred Years of Biology." *American Naturalist* 72, no. 741 (July–August 1938): 315–23.

Robens, Alma Kathryn. "Charlotte Baker: First Woman Physician and Community Leader in Turn of Nineteenth-Century San Diego." MA thesis, San Diego State University, 1992.

Robinson, Alfred D. "San Diego—the City Beautiful." *Overland Monthly,* 2nd ser., 54, no. 3 (March 1912): 259–60.

Rogers, Millard F., Jr. *Rich in Good Works: Mary M. Emery of Cincinnati.* Akron OH: University of Akron Press, 2000.

Roorbach, Eloise. "The Bishop's School for Girls: A Progressive Departure from Traditional Architecture." *Craftsman* 26, no. 6 (September 1914): 653–56.

Ross, Robert B., and George B. Catlin. *Landmarks of Detroit: A History of the City.* Rev. ed. Detroit: Evening News Association, 1898.

Rozwadowski, Helen M. *Fathoming the Ocean: The Discovery and Exploration of the Deep Sea.* Cambridge MA: Harvard University Press, 2008.

Russo, Ann, and Cheris Kramarae, eds. *The Radical Women's Press of the 1850s.* New York: Routledge, 1991.

Rynbrandt, Linda J. *Caroline Bartlett Crane and Progressive Reform: Social Housekeeping as Sociology.* New York: Garland, 1999.

Sanders, Kathleen Waters. *Mary Elizabeth Garrett: Society and Philanthropy in the Gilded Age.* Baltimore: Johns Hopkins University Press, 2008.

San Diego City and County Directory. San Diego CA: Fisher, Ward and Pomeroy, 1899.

San Diego City and County Directory. San Diego CA: Olmstead Company, 1895–97.

San Diego City and County Directory. San Diego CA: San Diego Directory Co., 1901–25.

San Diego Museum of Man. "The Ethnographic Collections." http://www.museum ofman.org/ethnographic-collections.

Santucci, James. "Women in the Theosophical Movement." *Explorations: Journal for Adventurous Thought* 9 (Fall 1990): 71–94.

Satter, Beryl. *Each Mind a Kingdom: American Women, Sexual Purity, and the New Thought Movement, 1875–1920.* Berkeley: University of California Press, 1999.

Schaelchlin, Patricia A. "Anson Peaslee Mills in His Cultural Context: An Interpretation of His Diaries, 1898–1932." MA thesis, San Diego State University, 1979.

———. *La Jolla, a Historical Inventory.* San Diego, 1977.

———. *La Jolla: The Story of a Community, 1887–1987.* San Diego: Friends of the La Jolla Library, 1988.

———. *The Newspaper Barons: A Biography of the Scripps Family.* San Diego: San Diego Historical Society, 2003.

Schaffer, Sarah J. "A Significant Sentence upon the Earth: Irving J. Gill, Progressive Architect: Part I: New York to California." *Journal of San Diego History* 43, no. 4 (1997): 218–39.

———. "A Significant Sentence upon the Earth: Irving J. Gill, Progressive Architect: Part II: Creating a Sense of Place." *Journal of San Diego History* 44, no. 1 (1998): 24–47.

Schilpp, Madelon Golden, and Sharon M. Murphy. *Great Women of the Press.* Carbondale: Southern Illinois University Press, 1983.

Schneider, John C. *Detroit and the Problem of Order, 1830–1880: A Geography of Crime, Riot, and Policing.* Lincoln: University of Nebraska Press, 1980.

Schroeder, Theodore. "The History of San Diego's Free Speech Fight." In *Free Speech for Radicals,* edited by Theodore Schroeder, 116–90. Riverside CT: Hillacre, 1916. https://archive.org/details/cu31924030461630.

Scott, Anne Firor. *Natural Allies: Women's Associations in American History.* Urbana: University of Illinois Press, 1991.

Scripps, Ellen Browning. *A Sampling from Travel Letters, 1881–1883*. Claremont CA: Scripps College, [1973].

Scripps, Emma. "She Said It with Flowers." Kate Sessions issue, *California Garden* 44, no. 3 (Autumn 1953): 7.

Scripps, James E. *Five Months Abroad, or, The Observations and Experiences of an Editor in Europe*. Detroit: F. B. Dickerson, 1882.

———. *Memorials of the Scripps Family: A Centennial Tribute*. Detroit: Privately printed, 1891.

Scripps, John Locke. *The First Published Life of Abraham Lincoln*. Detroit: Cranbrook Press, 1900.

Scripps, Paul K. *Heritage: The Scripps Family Story*. Cincinnati OH: Scripps Howard, 1988.

Self, Susan. "The History of the La Jolla Art Association." La Jolla Art Association, 2002. http://www.lajollaart.org/about_ljaa/historyljaa.pdf.

Shanks, Rosalie. "The I.W.W. Free Speech Movement: San Diego, 1912." *Journal of San Diego History* 19, no. 1 (Winter 1973): 25–33.

Sheehy, Michael. "Capitalism as a Necessary Evil: How E. W. Scripps Charted a Cautious Course toward the Left." *American Journalism* 28, no. 2 (Spring 2011): 7–21.

Shor, Elizabeth N. "How the Scripps Institution Came to San Diego." *Journal of San Diego History* 27, no. 3 (Summer 1981): 161–73.

———. "Zarh H. Pritchard" (2010). http://scilib.ucsd.edu/sio/hist/Shor-Pritchard.pdf.

Shor, George G., Elizabeth N. Shor, and Fred N. Spiess. "The George H. Scripps Memorial Marine Biological Laboratory of the Scripps Institution of Oceanography, University of California, San Diego." Historic Structure Report to the California Office of Historic Preservation, October 1979. http://scilib.ucsd.edu/sio/hist/caljsiol_sio1sc817n79-26.pdf.

Shragge, Abraham J. "'I Like the Cut of Your Jib': Cultures of Accommodation between the U.S. Navy and Citizens of San Diego, California." *Journal of San Diego History* 48, no. 3 (2002): 230–55.

Simpson, Edgar. "'Predatory Interests' and 'The Common Man': Scripps, Pinchot, and the Nascent Environmental Movement, 1908 to 1910." *Journalism History* 39, no. 3 (Fall 2013): 145–55.

Simpson, Lee M. A. *Selling the City: Gender, Class, and the California Growth Machine, 1880–1940*. Palo Alto: Stanford University Press, 2004.

Sklar, Kathryn Kish, and James Brewer Stewart, eds. *Women's Rights and Transatlantic Anti-slavery in the Era of Emancipation*. New Haven: Yale University Press, 2007.

Slaymaker, Nathaniel E. "El Descansadero, a Garden under Lath, La Jolla." *California Southland* 8, no. 76 (April 1926): 12–14, 29. https://archive.org/details/calsouthl78unse.

Smythe, Ted Curtis. *The Gilded Age Press, 1865–1900*. Westport CT: Praeger, 2003.

Smythe, William Ellsworth. *History of San Diego, 1542–1908*. 2 vols. San Diego: History Company, 1908.

———. *San Diego and Imperial Counties, California: A Record of Settlement, Organization, Progress and Achievement.* Chicago: S. J. Clarke, 1913.

Solomon, Barbara Miller. *In the Company of Educated Women: A History of Women and Higher Education in America.* New Haven: Yale University Press, 1985.

Solomons, Selina. *How We Won the Vote in California: A True Story of the Campaign of 1911.* San Francisco: New Woman, 1912.

Sparrow-Simpson, W. J. *Lectures on S[aint] Bernard of Clairvaux.* London: J. Masters, 1895.

Steinberg, Philip E. *The Social Construction of the Ocean.* New York: Cambridge University Press, 2001.

Stevens, George E. "Scripps' Cincinnati *Post:* Liberalism at Home." *Journalism Quarterly* 48, no. 2 (Summer 1971): 231–34.

Stevens, W. Bertrand. *A Bishop Beloved: Joseph Horsfall Johnson, 1847–1928.* New York: Morehouse, 1936.

Stoltzfus, Duane C. S. *Freedom from Advertising: E. W. Scripps's Chicago Experiment.* Champaign: University of Illinois Press, 2007.

Summers, Mark Wahlgren. *The Gilded Age or, The Hazard of New Functions.* Upper Saddle River NJ: Prentice Hall, 1997.

Sumner, Charles Burt. *The Story of Pomona College.* Boston: Pilgrim Press, 1914.

Sweeney, Michael S., Paul Jacoway, and Young Joon Lim. "Weighing the Costs: The Scripps-McRae League Reports the War in Cuba." *American Journalism* 31, no. 2 (2014): 213–35.

"Talkative Houses: The Story of a New Architecture in the West, Told by the Women's Club Building at La Jolla." *Craftsman* 28, no. 5 (August 1915): 448–55.

"A Tented City by the Tide." *Land of Sunshine: A Magazine of California and the Southwest* 5, no. 2 (July 1896): 84–85.

"Thorpe, Rose Alnora (Hartwick)." In *The National Cyclopaedia of American Biography,* 10:252. New York: James T. White, 1900.

Tiffin, Susan. *In Whose Best Interest? Child Welfare Reform in the Progressive Era.* Westport CT: Greenwood Press, 1982.

Trimble, Vance H. *The Astonishing Mr. Scripps: The Turbulent Life of America's Penny Press Lord.* Ames: Iowa State University Press, 1993.

Turney, Catherine. *The History of a Parish.* Sierra Madre CA: Privately printed, 1985.

Tyson, John R. "Lady Huntingdon's Reformation." *Church History* 64, no. 4 (December 1995): 580–93.

University of California. *Graduates, 1864–1905.* Berkeley: University of California, 1905.

Venet, Wendy Hamand. "The Emergence of a Suffragist: Mary Livermore, Civil War Activism, and the Moral Power of Women." *Civil War History* 48, no. 2 (2002): 143–64.

Waddy, Lawrence H. *A Parish by the Sea: A History of Saint James-by-the-Sea Episcopal Church, La Jolla, California.* La Jolla CA: St. James Bookshelf, 1988.

Wallach, Janet. *The Richest Woman in America: Hetty Green in the Gilded Age.* New York: Nan A. Talese / Doubleday, 2012.

Wallis, Chester Geppert. "San Diego's $200,000 Community House and Playground." *American City* 22, no. 1 (January 1920): 27–29.

Walsh, Victor A. "Preserving 'Nature's Artistry': Torrey Pines during Its Formative Years as a City and State Park." *California History* 85, no. 2 (2008): 24–49.

Walton, Andrea, ed. *Women and Philanthropy in Education.* Bloomington: Indiana University Press, 2005.

Ware, Alan. *The American Direct Primary: Party Institutionalization and Transformation in the North.* New York: Cambridge University Press, 2004.

Waterstone, Penny Brown. "Domesticating Universal Brotherhood: Feminine Values and the Construction of Utopia, Point Loma Homestead, 1897–1920." PhD dissertation, University of Arizona, 1995.

Webster, Martha Farnham. *Seventy-Five Significant Years: The Story of Knox College, 1837–1912.* Galesburg IL: Wagoner, 1912.

Weigle, Clifford F. "The Young Scripps Editor: Keystone of E.W.'s 'System.'" *Journalism Quarterly* 41 (Summer 1964): 360–66.

Wells, Jonathan Daniel. *Women Writers and Journalists in the Nineteenth-Century South.* New York: Cambridge University Press, 2011.

White, Lee A. *The Detroit News: 1873–1917.* Detroit: Evening News Association, 1918.

Willard, Frances E., and Mary A. Livermore, eds. *A Woman of the Century: Fourteen Hundred-Seventy Biographical Sketches Accompanied by Portraits of Leading American Women.* Buffalo: Charles Wells Moulton, 1893.

Wilson, William H. *The City Beautiful Movement.* Baltimore: Johns Hopkins University Press, 1989.

Wright, Judy. *Claremont Women, 1887–1950: They Created a Culture.* Claremont CA: Claremont Historical Resources, 2007.

Zacher, Dale E. *The Scripps Newspapers Go to War, 1914–18.* Champaign: University of Illinois Press, 2008.

Zunz, Olivier. *Philanthropy in America: A History.* Princeton: Princeton University Press, 2012.

INDEX

Barrows, David P., 204
Bartholow, E. D., 152–53
Bartlett, Jean, 113
Barton, Marguerite, 130–31
Bechtel, Jessica W., 9
Bedford-Jones, Reverend, 165, 177
Beecher, Charles, 9
Beecher, Edward, 8
Beecher, Willis J., 221n27
Bellamy, Edward, xxi, 33
Bennett, Eleanor, 134
Bentham, Anna Frances O'Hare, 122–23, 125–26, 172
Bentham, Charles Edward, 122–23, 126
Berge, Edward H., 194
Besant, Annie, 85–86
Bicknell, Clarence, 49
Billemeyer, Mary, 59
Birchby, H. Gough, 144
Birds of California (Dawson), 182, 190
The Bishop's School: athletics at, F21, 127; Bentham Hall, 126, 246n27; campus expansion, 126; class of 1914 members, 246n22; college preparatory courses of, 125–28, 131–32; community service focus, 127–28; EBS's support of, xvi, 121, 123–24, 132, 202, 211; founding of, xxvi, 121, 122–24; headmistresses of, 125–27, 130–32; images of, F21, F22; and the La Jolla community, 129–30; Reading Room moved to, 182
Blades, Fanny Bagby (cousin), 24, 31, 47
Blaisdell, James A., 203–11
Blanchard, Jonathan, 9
Blank, Ava, 209–10
Blavatsky, Helena Petrovna, 84, 85
Bleeker, John J., 222n23
Booker, George M., 134
Booth, George Gough, 26, 55, 112, 212, 224n66, 224n80

Booth, John Wilkes, 11
Boss, William, 7
Botsford, Frank, 42
Bourne, W. O., 188
Bowen, Horace, 30–31, 83
Bowles, Samuel, 15
Braun, Maurice, 85, 183
Bridges, Amelia Timken, 179–80
Brighton Aquarium, 64
Britt-Scripps House (San Diego), 36
Brooke, Rupert, 170
Brooks, Allan, 182, 190
Browning, J. H., 3
Bryn Mawr School, 122
Buckman, Marie, 185–86
Bungalow (South Molton Villa), 150
Burnham, Florence, 210
Burroughs, John, 131, 188–89

Cabral, Manuel, 67
Calloway, Ethel, 119
Canfield, B. H., 38
Capps, Edwin M., F23, 144–45, 191
Carey, Hettie, 139
Carnegie, Andrew, xvi, 34
Carruth, William Herbert, 73
Carter, Howard, 185
Challenger expedition, 65–66
chapel (The Bishop's School), 129
Chartism (labor movement), 2
Chase and Ludington's (general store), 51
Cheney, Abigail Perkins, 83–84, 237n18
Chicago Day Book (adless newspaper), 109
Chicago Tribune (newspaper), 7
child labor, 134–35, 137–38, 248n11
children's pool (La Jolla), 180, 216–17
Christianity: and alternative religions, 80–81; EBS's views on, 2, 72–73, 90–91, 239n63–64; ideals for women in, 81, 82
Christian Science, 89–90, 239n54

Christian socialism, 96

Cincinnati Post (newspaper): in family disputes, 28; in George H.'s will, 58; stock held by EBS, 52; stock held by E.W., 56; stock held by George H., 53; stock held by Virginia, 112; successes of, 37, 55

Civil War, xix, 7, 10–12, 13, 170

Claremont Colleges: EBS's support of, xvi, 207, 210–11; founding of, 205, 207; inauguration of, 209; patrons of, 210, 211; Pomona College, 201–7; Scripps College for Women, F31, F32, 197, 201, 206–12, 214

Clark, Grace Messinger Scripps (niece), 21, 116, 155, 211, 214, 217

Clark, Mabel, 112–13

Cleary, Harriet, 47

Cleveland Plain Dealer (newspaper), 212

Cleveland Press (newspaper): covering E.W.'s death, 212; EBS's travel writing for, 25; E.W.'s role at, 22–23, 54–55, 56; family disputes over, 28–29; in George H.'s will, 58; libel suits against, 24; stock held by EBS, 52; stock held by George H., 53; success of, 37, 55

Cochran, Negley D., 109

Collison, Clyde, 170

The Communist Manifesto (Marx and Engels), 95

Cornell, Ralph D., 192, 193

Crandall, W. C., 216

Cummins, Caroline S., 131–32, 248n55

"Curfew Must Not Ring Tonight" (poem), 46

Darrow, Clarence, 102

Darwin, Charles, 72

Davis, Ellen Browning Scripps, 211

Dawson, William Leon, 182, 190

Dearborn, Charles, 51, 157

Debose, Thomas, 134

Debs, Eugene V., 96

Dee, Michael J., 20

de la Mare, Walter, 182

DeLange, Helen, 183, 261n24

Democratic Free Press (newspaper), 7

Detroit (MI), 13–14

Detroit Evening News (newspaper): EBS's role at, xvii–xviii, 20–21, 22, 25–26, 37; E.W.'s obituary in, 212; E.W.'s work at, xvii, 24, 26, 28; in family disputes, 28, 55, 58, 60; founding of, 19; in George H.'s will, 58, 60; George H.'s work at, xvii, 55; incorporation of, 22, 52; under James E., xvii–xviii, 21, 22; stock held by EBS, xix, 20–21, 52; stock held by George H., 22, 52, 53; stock held by James E., 22, 52; success of, xix, 19–21, 179; Will's work at, xvii

"The Diver" (poem), 61–62

"Each in His Own Tongue" (poem), 73

Eastman, Max, 164

Eddy, Mary Baker, 83, 89

Edmonds, Charles K., 210

education: of EBS, xvii, 6–10, 220n21; impact of child labor on, 137–38; impact of World War I on, 206; opportunities for women in, xvii, 121–22, 197–98, 208–9

Egypt Exploration Society, 184, 185–87, 262n37, 263n51

Ellentown (proposed community), 76–77

Engels, Friedrich, 95

enlisted men's club (La Jolla), 169

Episcopal Church: and The Bishop's School, 121; EBS's views on, 81, 91, 165, 239n63; St. James by-the-Sea, 91, 114, 148–49; Virginia's involvement in, 91, 113–14

philanthropy (EBS) (*continued*)
School, 121, 123–24, 132, 202; and
the Egypt Exploration Society, 184–
87; and the La Jolla library, 182–83,
211; and the La Jolla playground,
134, 139–47, 250n38–39, 251n63;
and the La Jolla Woman's Club,
139–40, 141, 162–63, 250n46–48;
and the Marine Biological Association, 61, 63, 67–71, 73–78; and the
Museum of Natural History, 188–90;
organizations supported by, xvi, 141,
180, 216, 218; and Pomona College,
201–7; reasons for, xx, xxii–xxiii,
61–62, 121, 218; recognition of, xxii,
195, 204, 207–8, 235n80; and the
San Diego Zoo, xvi, 189, 211; and
Scripps College, 197; and Scripps
Memorial Hospital, 162, 174–76;
supporting churches, 91, 114; and
Torrey Pines State Reserve, xvi, 180,
190–94, 264n66; and the YWCA
Hostess House, 167–68
"The Phoenix of La Jolla" (poem), 156
Physical Geography of the Sea (Maury), 63
piers, 77, 78
playground (La Jolla), F22, 139–47, 177,
250n38–39, 251n63
Playground Association of America,
135–36
playground movement, 134–37, 138–39,
249n31
PLM (Partido Liberal Mexicano), 102
politics: divisions during World War I,
163–64; EBS's views on, xx, 8–9, 100–
101, 103, 106–8, 109, 143, 177–78,
243n67; E.W.'s views on, 98–99, 102–
3, 107–9, 177–78; following World
War I, 177–78; and the free speech
fight, 102–7; impact of the Civil War
on, 11, 13; in San Diego, 96–99

Pollock, Robert, 173
Pomona College, 201–7
pool (La Jolla), 180, 216–17
Poole, Horace, 45
Porterfield, William H., 98
Portland News (newspaper), 37
Post Publishing Company, 26
Prince (EBS's horse), 157
Pritchard, Zarh Howlison, 78
progressive reforms: and alternative
religions, 91–93; EBS's support of,
94, 95–96; impact of Civil War on,
13; impact of World War I on, 178;
women's education, 122, 197–98
"The Progress of Culture" (Emerson),
73
prohibition movement, 8, 100, 118, 152
psychology, 90
Pulitzer, Joseph, 23, 42

quadripartite agreement, 54, 60, 61

railroads, 150–51, 181
Rannells, Nathan, 50, 133
Raymond, Jerome Hall, 146, 164,
252n66, 256n14
Read, Katherine Haskell, 128, 247n37
Red Cross, 164–65
Reif, Anton, 42, 227n7
Reitman, Ben, 106, 242n55
religion: alternative forms of, 80–81;
Christian Science, 89–90, 239n54;
EBS's views on, 2, 72–73, 80–
81, 239n63–64; New Thought
movement, 80–81, 82–84, 91–92;
Spiritualism, 88–89, 91–92; Theoso-
phy, 31, 80–81, 84–88, 91–92
Remedial Institute and School of Philos-
ophy (Alameda), 30–31
Requa, Richard S., 192
Restarick, Henry B., 115

Seaman, Edith M., 252n3

Seashore Animals of the Pacific Coast (Johnson and Snook), 78

Seattle Star (newspaper), 37

The Secret Doctrine (Blavatsky), 84

Sefton, Joseph W., Jr., 189

Sessions, Katherine: relationship with EBS, 36, 48, 187; work at The Bishop's School, 124; work at Camp Kearny, 167; work at South Molton Villa, 48–49, 50, 151, 194

Sharp, Elizabeth Mary Scripps (sister): birth of, 3; childhood of, 5; and George H.'s estate, 59–60; health of, 11, 74; image of, F12

Sherrill, James W., 217

Ships That Pass in the Night (Harraden), 47

Sinnett, Alfred Percy, 86

Sisters of Mercy, 173

Slater, John, 88–89

Slaymaker, Nathaniel, 194

Sloane, William A., 99

Smythe, William E., 97, 240n16

Snook, Harry James, 78

Snyder, Mary, 36, 65, 70, 85

Socialist Party, 95–96

social reforms: and alternative religions, 91–93; EBS's views on, 8–9, 11, 13; impact of the Civil War on, 10–11, 13; and political divisions, 95–96; and the suffrage movement, 100–101; and women's education, 122

Soldiers' Aid Society, 10

South Molton Villa: construction of, 40, 41–42, 227n9; conversion into Museum of Contemporary Art, 253n12; in EBS's estate distribution, 270n10; electricity at, 253n10; elevator in, 155; employees of, 159–60; fire at, 148–49, 151–53; furniture in, 155–56, 252n8; garage of, 157–58; gardens of, 47–49, 151, 194–95; images of, F10, F25; lath house and tearoom of, 194–95; library of, F16, 50, 150; naming of, 42–43; openness of, 161, 195; renovations to, 49–50, 149–51, 153–56

Spalding, Albert G., 85, 191

Spanish flu, 176

Spencer, Herbert, 72

Spiritualism, 88–89, 91–92

Spokane Press (newspaper), 37

Spreckels, John D., F17, 96–99, 103, 105, 191, 240n16, 242n49

Springfield Republican (newspaper), 15

Stannard, John, 42, 227n7

Stanton, Elizabeth Cady, 95

Stearns, Charles C., 202–3, 204

Stearns, Sophie, 202

Steffens, Lincoln, 102, 171

Stephens, Frank, 188, 189

Sternberg, Charles H., 188

Stevenson, Elliot G., 60

St. James by-the-Sea Episcopal Church, 91, 114, 148–49

St. Joseph's Hospital, 172, 173

St. Louis Chronicle (newspaper): under E.W., 23, 24, 56; founding of, 23; in George H.'s will, 58; in the Scripps-McRae League, 37; stock held by EBS, 52; stock held by George H., 53; successes of, 55

St. Louis Post-Dispatch (newspaper), 23

St. Mary's Chapel, 129

Stone, Lucy, 16

strikes, 37–38, 94

Success (magazine), xxii

suffrage movement, 100–101

Sumner, Francis B., 191

Swain, Alice, 133–34

163–64; Spanish flu, 176; U.S. entrance into, 164

Yaw, Ellen Beach, 116
YMCA (Young Men's Christian Association), 136

Yosemite National Park, F30, 201
Young, S. Hall, 215
YWCA (Young Women's Christian Association), 136, 167, 193

zoo (San Diego), xvi, 189, 211

CPSIA information can be obtained
at www.ICGtesting.com
Printed in the USA
LVOW03*0722300617

539846LV00002B/6/P